Guide to Rural England

THE SOUTH OF ENGLAND

Bedfordshire, Berkshire, Buckinghamshire, Gloucestershire, Hampshire, Hertfordshire, Isle of Wight, Oxfordshire and Wiltshire

By Peter Long

Published by:
Travel Publishing Ltd
Airport Business Centre, 10 Thornbury Road,
Estover, Plymouth PL6 7PP

ISBN13 9781904434979

First Published: 2001 *Second Edition: 2004*
Third Edition: 2006 *Fourth Edition: 2008*
Fifth Edition 2010

COUNTRY LIVING GUIDES:

East Anglia	Scotland
Heart of England	The South of England
Ireland	The South East of England
The North East of England	The West Country
The North West of England	Wales

PLEASE NOTE:

All advertisements in this publication have been accepted in good faith by Travel Publishing and they have not necessarily been endorsed by *Country Living* Magazine.

All information is included by the publishers in good faith and is believed to be correct at the time of going to press. No responsibility can be accepted for errors.

Editor: Peter Long

Printing by: Latimer Trend, Plymouth

Location Maps: © Maps in Minutes ™ (2010) © Collins Bartholomews 2010 All rights reserved.

Cover Photo: Images clockwise from top left:
Stourhead Gardens, Stourton, Wiltshire © Britain on View Photo Library
Beach Huts at Calshot, Hampshire © Alamy
Blenheim Palace, Woodstock, Oxfordshire © Alamy
Hailes Abbey, Winchcombe, Gloucestershire © Alamy

Text Photos: see page 351

Foreword

From a bracing walk across the hills and tarns of The Lake District to a relaxing weekend spent discovering the unspoilt hamlets of East Anglia, nothing quite matches getting off the beaten track and exploring Britain's areas of outstanding beauty.

Each month, *Country Living Magazine* celebrates the richness and diversity of our countryside with features on rural Britain and the traditions that have their roots there. So it is with great pleasure that I introduce you to the *Country Living Magazine Guide to Rural England* series. Packed with information about unusual and unique aspects of our countryside, the guides will point both fair-weather and intrepid travellers in the right direction.

Each chapter provides a fascinating tour of the South of England area, with insights into local heritage and history and easy-to-read facts on a wealth of places to visit, stay, eat, drink and shop.

I hope that this guide will help make your visit a rewarding and stimulating experience and that you will return inspired, refreshed and ready to head off on your next countryside adventure.

Susy Smith

Susy Smith
Editor, Country Living magazine

PS To subscribe to *Country Living Magazine* each month, call 01858 438844

Foreword

Introduction

This is the fifth edition of *The Country Living Guide to Rural England - The South* which has a new eye-catching cover and redesigned preliminary pages. Peter Long, a very experienced travel writer has, of course, completely updated the contents of the guide and ensured that it is packed with vivid descriptions, historical stories, amusing anecdotes and interesting facts on hundreds of places in Bedfordshire, Berkshire, Buckinghamshire, Gloucestershire, Hampshire, Hertfordshire, The Isle of Wight, Oxfordshire and Wiltshire. In this respect we would like to thank all the Tourist Information Centres who helped us to provide you with up-to-date information. The advertising panels within each chapter provide further information on places to see, stay, eat, drink, shop and even exercise!

The guide however is not simply an "armchair tour". Its prime aim is to encourage the reader to visit the places described and discover much more about the wonderful towns and villages as well as the beauty and charm of the varied rural landscapes and coastlines of the South of England. Whether you decide to explore this region by wheeled transport or on foot we are sure you will find it a very uplifting experience.

We are always interested in receiving comments on places covered (or not covered) in our guides so please do not hesitate to use the reader reaction forms provided at the rear of this guide to give us your considered comments. This will help us refine the content of the next edition. We also welcome any general comments which will help improve the overall presentation of the guides themselves.

For more information on other titles in the *Country Living Rural Guide* series and the full range of travel guides published by Travel Publishing please refer to the order form at the rear of this guide or log on to our website (see below).

Travel Publishing

Did you know that you can also search our website for details of thousands of places to see, stay, eat or drink throughout Britain and Ireland? Our site has become increasingly popular and now receives hundreds of thousands of visits. Try it!

website: www.findsomewhere.co.uk

Contents

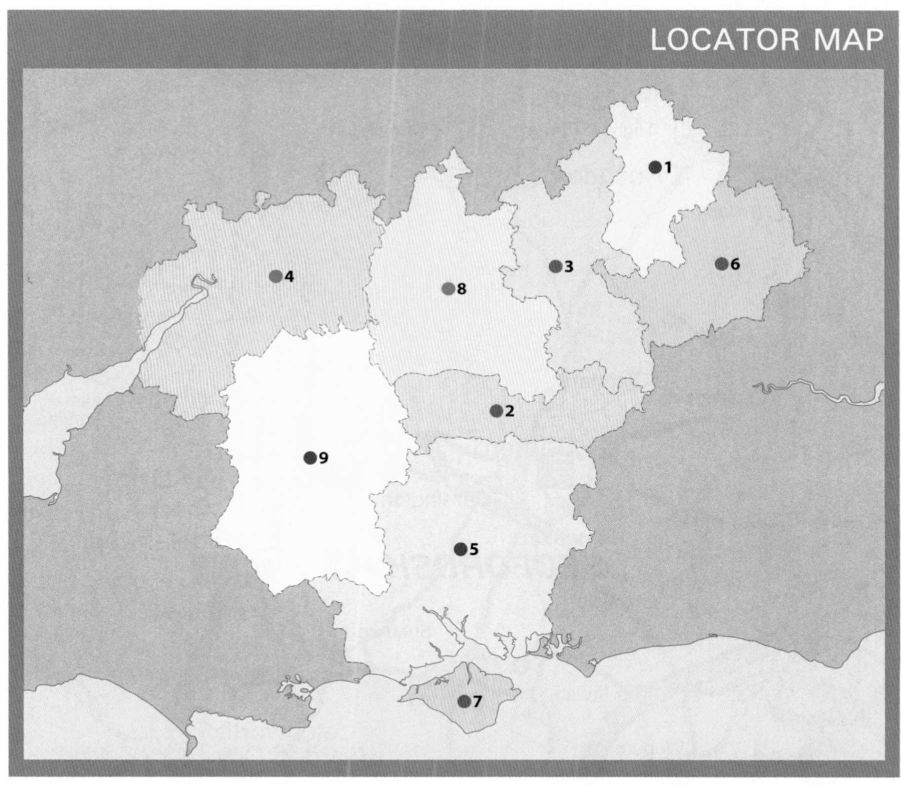

LOCATOR MAP

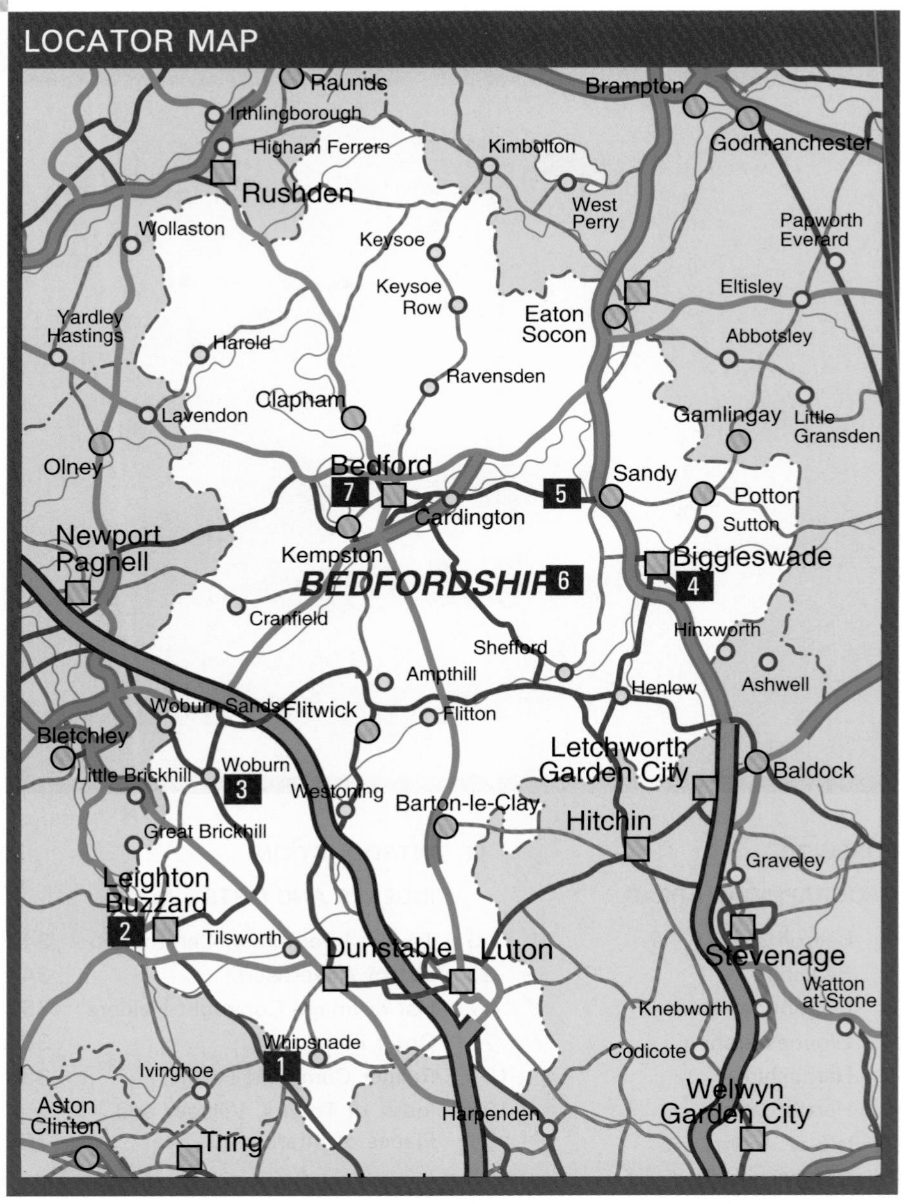
Raunds
Brampton
Irthlingborough
Higham Ferrers
Kimbolton
Godmanchester
Rushden
West Perry
Wollaston
Keysoe
Papworth Everard
Keysoe Row
Eltisley
Yardley Hastings
Eaton Socon
Harold
Abbotsley
Ravensden
Clapham
Lavendon
Gamlingay
Little Gransden
Olney
Bedford
Sandy
Potton
Cardington
Sutton
Newport Pagnell
Kempston
Biggleswade
BEDFORDSHIRE
Cranfield
Hinxworth
Shefford
Ampthill
Ashwell
Henlow
Woburn Sands
Flitwick
Flitton
Bletchley
Letchworth Garden City
Little Brickhill
Woburn
Baldock
Westoning
Barton-le-Clay
Hitchin
Great Brickhill
Graveley
Leighton Buzzard
Tilsworth
Dunstable
Luton
Stevenage
Watton at-Stone
Knebworth
Whipsnade
Codicote
Ivinghoe
Welwyn Garden City
Aston Clinton
Harpenden
Tring
1
2
3
4
5
6
7

1 | Bedfordshire

It may be the third smallest county in England, after Rutland and the Isle of Wight, but Bedfordshire offers multifarious delights. It's a county of picturesque villages and historic houses, mills and farms, woodland and nature reserves, great views from the Chilterns escarpment and with well-established walking and cycle routes. In the Bedfordshire heartlands are to be found two of England's leading animal attractions, Woburn Safari Park and Whipsnade Wildlife Park.

The Great Ouse and the Grand Union Canal, once commercial arteries, are finding a new role as leisure attractions, with miles of scenic walks or leisurely cruises to be enjoyed. The south of the county is dominated by the towns of Luton and Dunstable, while the central region of Bedfordshire is an area of ancient settlements and a rich diversity of places to see. Here is perhaps the most impressive dovecote in the country, with nests for 1500 birds, while just outside Sandy is the headquarters of the Royal Society for the Protection of Birds. At nearby Cardington, the skyline is dominated by the huge hangars where the R100 and R101 airships were built. Houghton House at Houghton Conquest is widely believed to have been the inspiration for the House Beautiful in John Bunyan's *The Pilgrim's Progress*. Bunyan was born in the village of Elstow, a little way south of Bedford, and many of the places most closely associated with the writer can be visited, in both the town and the village. Bedford, the county capital, offers a blend of history and modern amenity, all set against the backdrop of the River Great Ouse, which passes through the town and many pleasant villages on its journey across the county.

ADVERTISERS AND PLACES OF INTEREST

Luton

Luton Hoo | Luton Museum and Art Gallery

Stockwood Craft Museum | Someries Castle

The largest town in Bedfordshire and perhaps best known for Luton Airport, Vauxhall cars – and, for those with long memories of radio days, the Luton Girls Choir. This large choir, with girls aged between 12 and 23, was for many years one of the most popular in the country, with frequent live and radio performances. The choir was disbanded in 1976, but the recordings are still in demand. Although the town has expanded rapidly from a market town in the early 19th century to a major industrial centre by the mid 20th century, it still boasts more than 100 listed buildings and three Conservation Areas. Luton first began to prosper in the 17th century on the strength of its straw plaiting and straw hat-making industries. These activities are amongst those featured at the **Luton Museum and Art Gallery**, housed within a delightful Victorian mansion in Wardown Park, a traditional town park with tennis and bowls. The park was opened to the public in the early years of the reign of Edward VII, but not the house, which was first a restaurant and then, during the First World War, a military hospital. It was not until 1931 that the town's museum and art gallery, originally housed in the library, moved here. As well as featuring a re-creation of a Victorian shop and pub, the museum is also home to a range of collections covering the hat trade (including the Women's Hat Industry Collection of more than 600 hats – viewing by appointment), costume, jewellery, straw-plaiting, fine arts, local history, archaeology and childhood. As lace-making was one of the two main cottage industries in Bedfordshire, visitors will not be surprised to learn that the museum also has the largest collection of lace anywhere in the country outside London.

Visitors can also take a step back in time by seeking out **Stockwood Craft Museum and Gardens**. Occupying a Georgian stable block, the museum has a collection of Bedfordshire craft and rural items enhanced by frequent craft demonstrations. The walled garden is equally impressive and the Period Garden includes knot, medieval, Victorian, cottage, Dutch and Italian sections. The Hamilton Finlay Sculpture Garden showcases six pieces of sculpture by the internationally renowned artist Ian Hamilton Finlay in a lovely natural setting. The Mossman Collection of over 60 horse-drawn vehicles, the largest of its kind on public display in Britain, is also housed here. The story of transport comes into the 20th century in the Transport Gallery, whose exhibits include bicycles, vintage cars and a model of the Luton tram system. Replicas of some of the vehicles on display have happened in, including *Ben Hur* and *Out of Africa*.

Luton Hoo

Just to the south of the town is the magnificent house **Luton Hoo**, originally designed by Robert Adams and set in 1500 acres of parkland landscaped by Capability Brown. Construction of the house began in 1767, though it was extensively remodelled in 1827 and again in 1903, when the interior was given a French style for Sir Julius Wernher, who installed his fabulous art collection in the house. Luton Hoo is a private hotel and is no longer open to the public.

Just southeast of Luton is **Someries Castle**, the remains of a fortified medieval manor house dating from the middle to late 15th century. The earliest surviving brick building in the county, both the gatehouse and chapel have survived and are still a very impressive sight. The original castle on this site belonged first to the de Someries family and then to the Wenlocks, and the house, of which only a romantic ruin remains, may have been built for the Lord Wenlock who died at the Battle of Tewkesbury in 1471, when the Yorkist victory ended the Wars of the Roses.

Around Luton

SLIP END

1 mile S of Luton on the B4540

Woodside Animal Farm

Woodside Animal Farm is home to more than 200 different breeds and there are hundreds of animals and birds to see and feed. The farm's many attractions include a walk-through monkey house, red squirrel enclosure, alpaca family, fabulous flamingos and hand-reared racoons. There are indoor and outdoor picnic and play areas, crazy golf, pony and tractor rides, a bouncy castle, farm shop, craft shop and coffee shop.

WHIPSNADE

5 miles SW of Luton off B489

Whipsnade Tree Cathedral   Wild Animal Park

This small village with a charming, simple church is surrounded by common land on which stands **Whipsnade Tree Cathedral** (see panel below). After the First World War, a

Whipsnade Tree Cathedral

Whipsnade Tree Cathedral Trustees, c/o Chapel Farm, Whipsnade, Dunstable, Bedfordshire LU6 2LL
Tel: 01582 872406
website: www.nationaltrust.org.uk

Situated on the edge of Whipsnade Village Green the **Tree Cathedral** combines a range of different varieties of trees and shrubs laid out to the plan of a cathedral. There is a nave, transepts, chancel, cloisters and four chapels and an outer cloister walk enclosing a wide area with a dew pond as its focal point

Owned by the National Trust the Tree Cathedral is managed by trustees and cared for and maintained by volunteers. The planting continues in order to maintain the principle features for future generations.

There is an annual inter-denominational service held each year in June. There is a small car park signposted from the B4540 in Whipsnade.

local landowner, Edmund Kell Blyth, planted a variety of trees that have grown into the shape of a medieval cathedral, with a nave, transepts, cloisters and chapels, and trees for the walls. Designed 'in a spirit of faith, hope and reconciliation' as a memorial to friends of Blyth killed in the war, it's a curiously moving place. The tree Cathedral was acquired by the National Trust in 1960.

To the south of the village can be seen the white silhouette of a lion cut into the green hillside, which is reminiscent of the much older White Horse at Uffington. A magnificent landmark, the lion also advertises the whereabouts of **Whipsnade Wild Animal Park**, the country home of the Zoological Society of London. Whipsnade first opened its doors in 1931, attracting over 26,000 visitors on the first Monday, and in the years since, it has grown and developed and continues to provide fun and education for thousands of visitors each year. There are 2500 animals on show in the park's 600 acres, and behind the scenes Whipsnade is at the forefront of wild animal welfare and conservation, specialising in the breeding of endangered species such as cheetahs, rhinos and the scimitar-horned oryx. There are daily demonstrations – penguin feeding, sea lions, free-flying birds – and other attractions include a railway safari, Discovery Centre, Children's Farm and Adventure Playground. Feeding time for the animals is always a popular occasion, while humans who feel peckish can make tracks for the Café on the Lake or (in summer) the Lookout Café, or graze on ice cream and snacks from the many refreshment kiosks in the park.

DUNSTABLE

2 miles W of Luton on the A505

Church of St Peter · Dunstable Downs

Dunstable is a bustling town that grew up at the junction of two ancient roads, Icknield Way and Watling Street, and was an important centre in Roman Britain, when it was known as Durocobrivae. The town's finest building is undoubtedly the **Priory Church of St Peter**, all that remains of a Priory founded by Henry I in 1131; only the nave actually dates from that time. It was at the Priory that Archbishop Cranmer's court sat in 1533 to annul the marriage of Henry VIII and Katherine of Aragon.

On the B4541 Dunstable-Whipsnade road, **Dunstable Downs** commands some of the finest views over the Vale of Aylesbury and along the Chiltern Ridge. Designated a Site of Special Scientific Interest and a Scheduled Ancient Monument, it has much to attract the visitor, including the Chilterns Gateway Centre with interpretive displays and gifts, circular walks and a picnic area; it's a popular spot with hang-gliders and kite-flyers, and a refreshment kiosk is open all year round. South of Dunstable Downs, at the junction of the B4541 and B4540, Whipsnade Heath is a small area of woodland containing fungi and some unusual plants.

Dunstable Downs

TOTTERNHOE

6 miles W of Luton off the A505

Totternhoe Knolls

This attractive village is situated below **Totternhoe Knolls**, a steeply sloped spur of chalk that is now a nature reserve known nationally for its orchids and its butterflies. On the top of the spur are the remains of a motte and bailey castle dating from Norman times, with commanding views of the surrounding countryside.

BILLINGTON

8 miles W of Luton on the A4146

Mead Open Farm

Mead Open Farm is home to a variety of traditional and rare farm animals and offers a particularly wide range of attractions for children, including an indoor play barn, activity house, sandpit, indoor pets corner and ride-on toys. There's also a tearoom and shop, and a number of daily activities and weekly events. Farm Attraction of the Year 2009.

LEIGHTON BUZZARD

9 miles W of Luton on A505

All Saints Church

Greensand Ridge Walk

The town's interesting name tells a lot about its history: Leighton is Old English and refers to a centre for market gardening, whilst the Buzzard is a reference not to the bird of prey, but to a local clergyman, Theobald de Busar, the town's first Prebendary. The town's past prosperity as a market centre is reflected in the grandeur of its fine Market Cross, a 15th-century pentagonal structure with an open base and statues under vaulted openings all topped off by pinnacles. The market is still held here every Tuesday and Saturday.

The spire of **All Saints Church** is over 190 feet high and is a local landmark. This big ironstone church dates from 1277 and contains a number of endearing features in the form of graffiti left by the medieval stonemasons: one shows a man and a woman quarrelling over whether to boil or bake a simnel cake. Seriously damaged by fire in 1985, the church has been carefully restored to its medieval glory; the painstaking work included re-gilding the roof, which is particularly fine, with carved figures of angels. One of its chief treasures is a 13th-century oak eagle lectern.

Leighton Buzzard and its neighbour Linslade are on the Grand Union Canal and visitors can take leisurely boat trips along this once busy commercial waterway on the *Leighton Lady*.

Historic forms of transport seem to be the town's speciality, as visitors can also take a steam train journey on the **Leighton Buzzard**

Leighton Buzzard Railway

Leighton Buzzard Railway

Page's Park Station, Billington Road, Leighton Buzzard, Bedfordshire LU7 4TN
Tel: 01525 373888 Fax: 01525 377814
website: www.buzzrail.co.uk

One of England's premier narrow gauge heritage railways, **Leighton Buzzard Railway** was established in 1919 to carry sand from the quarries, which had opened up to supply the demand for sand during the First World War, in the north of the town through to the town's railway sidings and canal wharf. Built using war surplus materials and equipment, the line, since 1968, has carried a passenger service, mostly steam hauled, from Page's Park to Stonehenge Works in the countryside near the village of Heath and Reach.

Operated by volunteers of the Leighton Buzzard Narrow Gauge Railway Society, the trains pass through a modern housing estate before emerging into rolling countryside with views of the Chiltern Hills in the distance. The railway is now the home of the largest collection of narrow gauge locomotives in Britain and, of the 50 here, some 12 are steam driven. The oldest engine dates from 1877 whilst the newest is a diesel locomotive built especially for the line in 1999. The return journey takes just over an hour and the railway operates on Sundays and Bank Holiday weekends between March and October.

Railway (see panel above), one of England's premier narrow gauge operations. It was established in 1919 to move sand from the quarries opened up to supply sand during the First World War. From the late 1960s the quarries used road transport, but the railway was saved as a heritage line. It has the largest collection of narrow gauge locomotives in Britain. The 70-minute journey takes in bends, gradients and level crossings – something to delight at every turn. Call 01525 373888 for timetable details. The town lies at one end of the **Greensand Ridge Walk**, which extends across Bedfordshire to finish some 40 miles away at Gamlingay, Cambridgeshire. The name Greensand comes from the geology of the area, a belt of greensand that stretches from Leighton Buzzard up to Sandy and beyond. The walk passes many attractions, including the Grand Union Canal, Stockgrove Country Park, Woburn Abbey, Ampthill Park and Houghton House.

Ampthill

Ampthill Park · Alameda

This historic town, situated on a rise and with fine views over the surrounding countryside, was a great favourite with Henry VIII. It was here that Katherine of Aragon stayed during the divorce proceedings conducted by Henry's court at Dunstable. At that time there was also a castle here, built by Sir John Cornwall for his bride, the sister of Henry IV. On the site now stands Katherine's Cross, erected in 1773, which bears the arms of Castile and Aragon. On land given to his family by Charles II, the 1st Lord Ashburnham built the castle's replacement, **Ampthill Park**, in 1694. The house was enlarged a century later and the 300-acre park was landscaped by the ubiquitous Capability Brown. Ampthill Park is famous for its old oak trees, and visitors can also enjoy the views from the Greensand Ridge Walk, which runs through the grounds. An attractive feature of the town is the **Alameda** (Spanish for a public walk), an avenue of lime trees 700 yards long, presented to the town in 1827 by Lord and Lady Holland. Ampthill also boasts some fine Georgian and early 19th-century buildings, especially in Church Street, Tudor almshouses and the large Church of St Andrew, which has a noble west tower. Inside can be found some 15th century brasses and a 17th-century monument to Colonel Richard Nicholls that includes the cannon ball that killed him during the Battle of Sole Bay in 1672. Nicholls, who was born and lived most of his life in Ampthill, served the Stuart Kings and was commander of the force that defeated the Dutch at New Amsterdam. He re-named it New York in honour of the Duke of York, later James II.

Ampthill Park House

Around Ampthill

FLITTON

2 miles SE of Ampthill off the A507

de Grey Mausoleum

Next to the 15th-century church is the cruciform **de Grey Mausoleum**, a series of rooms containing a remarkable collection of sculpted tombs and monuments to the de Grey family of Wrest Park from 1615 to 1899. This is one of the largest sepulchral chapels attached to an English church.

SILSOE

3 miles SE of Ampthill off A6

Wrest Park

Although the manor of Wrest has been held by the de Grey family since the late 13th century, the house standing today dates from the 1830s. Built for the 1st Earl de Grey from the designs of a French architect, it follows faithfully the style of a French chateau of the previous century. The real glory of **Wrest Park** is the gardens, which extend over 90 acres. They are a living history of English gardening from 1700 to 1850 and are the work of Charles Bridgeman, with later adaptations by Capability Brown. The layout remains basically formal, with a full range of garden appointments in the grand manner – a Chinese bridge, an orangery, an artificial lake, a classical temple, and a rustic ruin.

Two buildings of particular interest are the Baroque Banqueting House, designed by Thomas Archer, which forms a focus of the view from the house across the lake, and the Bowling Green House, dating from about 1740 and said to have been designed by Batty

Langley, who was best known as a writer of architectural books for country builders, but built little himself. Immediately beside the house is an intricate French-style garden, with an orangery by the French architect Cléphane, flowerbeds, statues and fountains. The village of Silsoe itself boasts more than 130 listed buildings.

TODDINGTON

5 miles S of Ampthill on A5120

Toddington Manor

Situated on a hill above the River Flitt, this village is often overlooked, particularly by those travelling the nearby M1 who think only of the service station of the same name. However, the village is an attractive place, with cottages and elegant houses grouped around the village green. Unfortunately, all that remains of **Toddington Manor** is a small oblong building with a hipped roof, which is believed to be the Elizabethan kitchen of the large quadrangular house that was built here around 1570. Toddington is a place that makes much of its folklore and is host to Morris dancers in the summer, and mummers who tour the village providing traditional entertainment at Christmas. Local legend has it that a witch lives under Conger Hill – which is actually a motte that would, at one time, have had a castle on top.

RIDGMONT

4 miles W of Ampthill on the A507

Part of the Woburn Estate, this is a typical estate village where the owners of the land (in this case the Bedford family) provided the houses and other buildings. Here the workers lived in gabled, red brick houses. The church, designed by George Gilbert Scott, was also built at the expense of the estate.

WOBURN

6 miles W of Ampthill on the A4012

Woburn Abbey Wild Animal Kingdom

Aspley Woods

First recorded as a Saxon hamlet in the 10th century, and again mentioned in the Domesday Book, Woburn grew into a small market town after the founding of the Cistercian Abbey here in 1145. All but destroyed by fire in 1720, this pretty village has retained many of the pleasant Georgian houses that were built subsequently, and the attractive shop fronts give the place a cheerful air. Situated at a major crossroads, between London and the north, and Cambridge and Oxford, Woburn also saw prosperity during the stagecoach era and by 1851 had 32 inns.

Woburn Abbey (see panel opposite), ancestral home of the Dukes of Bedford, is renowned for its art treasures, its Humphry Repton deer park and its antiques centre. The estate was given to the 1st Earl of Bedford in the will of Henry VIII, but the original building was partially destroyed by fire, and the present stately home dates mainly from the 1700s. Its extraordinary stock of treasures includes paintings by Van Dyck, Gainsborough, Reynolds and the famous Armada portrait of Elizabeth I by George Gower. The Venetian Room showcases 21 views of Venice by Canaletto, while other rooms display outstanding collections of English and French furniture, porcelain and antique statuary. Another attraction on site is the Woburn Abbey Antiques Centre with more than 50 dealers housed in a reconstruction of city streets of bygone days that includes genuine 18th-century shop facades rescued from demolition.

Woburn Abbey

Woburn, Bedfordshire MK17 9WA
Tel: 01525 290666 Fax: 01525 290271
e-mail: enquiries@woburnabbey.co.uk
website: www.woburnabbey.co.uk

Built on the site of a Cistercian monastery founded in 1145 by Hugh de Bolebec, **Woburn Abbey** was given to the 1st Earl of Bedford in the will of Henry VIII and has been the home of the Dukes of Bedford for over 400 years. The original building was partially destroyed by fire and the present stately home dates mainly from the 18th century. Woburn Abbey houses one of the most impressive and important private art and furniture collections on view to the public.

Over 70 dealers are housed under one roof in a reconstruction of city streets in bygone days, with genuine 18th century shop façades that were rescued from demolition many years ago. Another attraction within the estate boundaries is the deer park, which, like the private gardens, was landscaped by Humphry Repton for the 6th Duke. Visitors to this marvellous place will also find gift shops, a pottery and a coffee shop.

A short distance north of the abbey is the **Wild Animal Kingdom and Leisure Park**, home to a vast range of animals including eland, zebra, hippos, rhinos, lions, tigers, elephants and sea lions. Visitors can combine the thrill of the Safari Drive with the fun of the Wide World Leisure Area, meet the animals in Animal Encounters, Australian Walkabout and Rainbow Landing, and attend the many demonstrations, keeper talks and feeding times. Children can let off steam in the indoor and outdoor playgrounds, travel on the Swan Boats and take a ride on the railway train. All the attractions are included in the entrance price.

There are fine views of Woburn Abbey and of Milton Keynes from **Aspley Woods**, one of the largest areas of woodland in Bedfordshire, set between Woburn and Woburn Sands. The woods offer peace, tranquillity and miles of tracks for walking.

MARSTON MORETAINE

3 miles NW of Ampthill off the A421.

Forest Centre

The Marston Vale Forest Centre and Country Park offers a splendid day out in the countryside for all the family. The 600 acres of wetland and woodland are home to a wide variety of wildlife, and the park provides excellent walking and cycling; bikes can be hired from the Forest Centre, which also has an interactive Discover the Forest exhibition, café bar, art gallery, gift shop, free parking and children's play area.

Biggleswade

Set on the banks of the River Ivel, which was once navigable through to the sea, Biggleswade was an important stop on the Great North Road stagecoach routes and several old inns have survived from that period. The town also has another link with transport, it was the home of Dan Albone (1860–1906), the inventor of the modern bicycle. He produced a number of variants, including a tandem and a ladies cycle with a low crossbar and a skirt guard, but is best known for his racing cycle, which in 1888 set speed and endurance records with the intrepid CP Mills in the saddle. Dan Albone's inventiveness was not confined to bicycles, he also developed the Ivel Agricultural Tractor, the forerunner of the modern tractor.

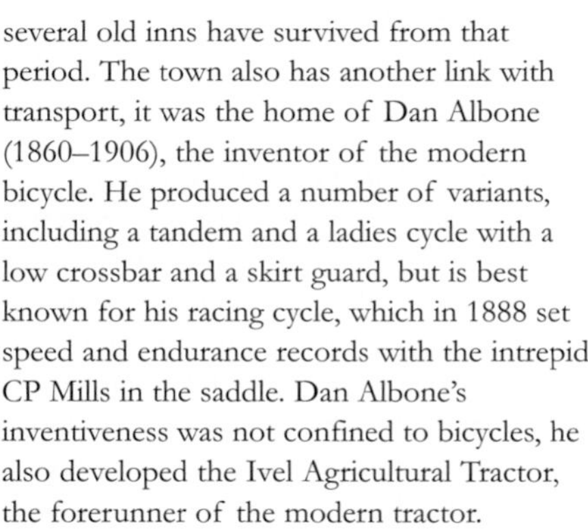

Around Biggleswade

SHEFFORD

5 miles SW of Biggleswade on the A507

The small town of Shefford grew up, as the name suggests, around a sheep ford across the Rivers Hitt and Flitt and enjoyed a brief status as an inland port on the Ivel Navigation. This waterway was built primarily to bring coal from Kings Lynn by way of the River Ouse. In North Bridge Street a wall plaque marks the house of the pastoral poet Robert Bloomfield, a poor farm labourer and shoemaker who found fame when he published *The Farmer's Boy* in 1800. The poet, who died, as he had lived, in extreme poverty, is buried in the churchyard at nearby Campton, Shefford's mother church. Shefford is also the starting point of the 21-mile-long cycle route, the Jubilee Way, a circular route that passes through undulating landscape and picturesque villages.

LOWER STONDON

6 miles S of Biggleswade off the A600

Transport Museum

Lower Stondon attracts visitors from near and far to its renowned **Transport Museum and**

Garden Centre. The museum, on the A600 next to Mount Pleasant golf course, contains a marvellous collection of several hundred exhibits covering all forms of transport – from motorcycles to cars, fire engines, buses, a Flying Flea and a Saro Skeeter helicopter – and covers the period from the early 1900s to the recent past. The centrepiece of the collection is a full size replica of Captain Cook's barque, *Endeavour*, in which he undertook one of his most important journeys in 1768. The replica was built using the original plans. Guided tours of the museum are available and there's a café selling light refreshments.

Sandy Lodge

SANDY

3 miles N of Biggleswade on A1

Sandy Lodge | The Roman Sandy Story

The sandy soil that gave the town its name helped it rise to fame as a market gardening centre in the 16th century. The 14th-century Church of St Swithun contains an interesting statue of Captain Sir William Peel, third son of Sir Robert Peel, famous Prime Minister and founder of the Police Force, who was one of the first recipients of the Victoria Cross for heroic action in the Crimean War. The **Roman Sandy Story**, housed in the Town Council offices, tells the story of the Romans in the area, based largely on excavations carried out in the 1980s and 1990s. Call 01767 681491 for opening times.

A little way southeast of the town, at **Sandy Lodge**, is the national headquarters of the Royal Society for the Protection of Birds and a nature reserve set in over 350 acres of open heath and woodland. As well as offering a great deal to those interested in birds, the formal gardens surrounding the mansion house are a delight. They were first created in the 1870s and restored in the 1930s by Sir Malcolm Stewart and are well worth visiting in their own right. Also on the site is a wildlife garden.

COCKAYNE HATLEY

5 miles NW of Biggleswade off the B1040/ B1042

Church of St John

The interior of the **Church of St John** is filled with an amazing array of medieval woodwork, carvings and stained glass. In the churchyard is the tomb of the Henley family, including the one-legged poet William Henley. He was a friend of Robert Louis Stevenson and was reputedly the inspiration for the character of Long John Silver in *Treasure Island*. He was also a friend of JM Barrie and it is said that Henley's daughter Margaret was the inspiration for his Wendy in *Peter Pan*.

BLUNHAM

5 miles N of Biggleswade off the A1

This quiet rural village was the home of the poet John Donne while he was rector here from 1622 until his death in 1632, a post he held while also Dean of St Paul's in London. While he was convalescing here after a serious illness in 1623, he wrote *Devotions*, which contains the immortal lines, "No man is an island, entire of itself ... And therefore never send to know for whom the bell tolls; it tolls for thee". Donne divided his time between London and Blunham, where he stayed in the house opposite the parish church. Inside can be seen some fine Norman work, interesting bosses and the chalice Donne presented to the church in 1626.

Another building of interest is the Old Vicarage, constructed of startling yellow and orange bricks in 1874.

MOGGERHANGER

3 miles NW of Biggleswade off the A603

Moggerhanger Park

Grade I-listed **Moggerhanger Park** was designed by Sir John Soane, architect of the Bank of England, and is set amidst 33 acres of gardens and parkland originally landscaped by Humphry Repton. Guided tours of this fine Georgian house are available daily during the summer months; the restaurant and tearooms are open all year round.

OLD WARDEN

3 miles W of Biggleswade off B658

Shuttleworth Collection | Swiss Garden

Bird of Prey Conservation Centre

This charming village of thatched cottages along a single street has developed its unique character as a result of the influence of two local families. In the early 18th century, Sir Samuel Ongley, a London merchant, ship-owner, and former director of the South Sea Company, bought this country seat for himself and his family, who stayed here for more than 200 years. In 1776, Robert Henley Ongley was awarded an Irish peerage for his services to Parliament, and it was his grandson, also called Robert, who created Old

Warden as it is seen today. Taking the original estate cottages, and building new ones, Sir Robert developed this rustic village and embellished the 12th-century church with some interesting Belgian woodwork. The church also contains some magnificent memorials to the Ongley family.

However, Sir Robert's most famous piece of work is the **Swiss Garden** (see panel below), laid out in the early 19th century. Within its 10 acres are ornate bridges, winding ponds, a breathtaking fernery and a number of tiny follies. In season, the early bulbs, primroses, rhododendrons and the old-fashioned roses make wonderful displays.

In 1872, his fortune depleted by the extensive building and remodelling programme, Sir Robert sold the estate to Joseph Shuttleworth. A partner in a firm of iron founders, it was Joseph who led the way to the development of the steam traction engine, and also built the Jacobean-style mansion house that can still be seen today. Another attraction on the estate is the **Bird of Prey Conservation Centre** where 300 birds of various species are on public display. In addition to training and flying birds of prey from around the world, the centre is firmly committed to conservation and education, working with schools to create displays and informative workshops; it laso has an Adopt a Bird Sceme. Regular flying demonstration times are 11.30am for the Owl Experience, 1.30pm for Birds of the World and 3pm for Out of Africa, featuring vultures, secretary birds, eagles, owls and falcons. The centre also includes a children's adventure playground, a picnic site, a restaurant and a gift shop.

Swiss Cottage, Old Warden

Also at Old Warden is the famous **Shuttleworth Collection** of historic aircraft. In 1923, the 23-year-old Richard Ormonde Shuttleworth, who had inherited the estate,

The Swiss Garden

Old Warden Park, Biggleswade, Bedfordshire SG18 9ER
Tel: 01767 627666
website: www.theswissgarden.co.uk

The **Swiss Garden** is set in 10 acres where visitors can wander among splendid shrubs and rare trees, at the centre of which is the Swiss Cottage. It brings together tiny follies, ornate bridges and winding ponds. Visitors can discover the breathtaking fernery and grotto, or lose themselves on the serpentine walks. In season the early bulbs and primroses, the rhododendrons and the old-fashioned roses make wonderful displays. Old Warden is a place of many other attractions, notably the Shuttleworth Collection. The Swiss Garden is licensed to hold civil wedding ceremonies. The Garden is open from 10am to 6pm on Sundays and from 1pm to 6pm every other day from March to September. Also open Sundays (and New Years Day) in January, February and October from 10am to 4pm.

bought his first aircraft, a de Havilland Moth. Over the years he added further planes to his collection. At the outbreak of the Second World War he naturally joined the RAF, but was sadly killed in a flying accident in 1940. After the war his mother put his collection on display and over the years other aircraft have been added. Housed in eight hangars, the collection now comprises some 40 airworthy craft, dating from 1909 (a Blériot) to 1955. Throughout the year there are a number of flying days when these grand old planes take to the skies. Many of them have been featured in films including *Reach for the Sky*, *The Battle of Britain* and *Pearl Harbour*. The planes are complemented by a number of vintage cars, motorcycles and bicycles.

A short drive north of Old Warden are two delightful villages, Ickwell and Northill. The former, which has a Maypole standing permanently on the green, is the birthplace of the great clockmaker Thomas Tompion. The 14th-century Church of St Mary, which dominates the village of Northill, is noted for some fine 17th-century glass and a one-handed clock built, it is thought, by Tompion's father. Some of the clocks could run for a year without rewinding; the Tompions also made barometers and sundials, including pieces for King William III.

STEWARTBY

10 miles W of Biggleswade off the A421

Stewartby takes its name from Sir Malcolm Stewart, founder of the London Brick Company. He had the village built in 1926 to house employees at the nearby brickworks, which were thought to be the largest in the world and at their peak turned out 650 million bricks a year. The kiln took over a year to reheat after it was closed during the Second World War.

Houghton House

HOUGHTON CONQUEST

9 miles W of Biggleswade off the B530

Houghton House

That this village is home to Bedfordshire's largest parish church seems fitting, as Houghton Conquest also has links with the county's most famous son, John Bunyan. On a hilltop a little way south of the village stands **Houghton House**, reputedly the inspiration for the House Beautiful in *The Pilgrim's Progress*. Built in 1615 for Mary, Countess of Pembroke, the house was visited by Bunyan in his days as an itinerant tinker. The property later came into the hands of the Dukes of Bedford, one of whom had it partially demolished, and the ruins are now in the care of English Heritage.

Bedford

Church of St Peter de Merton · Castle Mound

Church of St Paul · RCA Gallery

Bunyan Museum · Bedford Museum

Priory Country Park · Cecil Higgins Gallery

Bunyan Meeting Free Church · Glenn Miller

This lively cosmopolitan town owes its origins and development to the River Great Ouse, which remains one of the most important and attractive features of the town. Bedford was already a thriving market place before the Norman Conquest, and a market is still held on Wednesday and Saturday each week. There's also a farmer's market once a month and, in the summer months, a gourmet and speciality food market on Thursdays, and a flower and garden market on Fridays.

The town's oldest visible structure is **Castle Mound**, all that remains of a fortress built here shortly after the Battle of Hastings but destroyed in 1224. A timber-framed building has been constructed on top of the mound, which commands a spectacular view over the River Great Ouse.

The **Church of St Peter de Merton**, Saxon in origin, boasts a fine Norman south doorway that was not actually intended for this building but was brought here from the Church of St Peter in Dunstable. St Peter's is not Bedford's main church: that is **St Paul's Church** in the centre of St Paul's Square, a mainly 14th and 15th-century building, with some interesting monuments and brasses, and a stone pulpit from which John Wesley preached in 1758. Outside the church is a statue of one of the best-known sons of Bedford, John Howard, an 18th-century nonconformist landowner who denounced the appalling conditions in jails and prison ships. His name lives on in the Howard League for Penal Reform.

Bedford's most famous son, John Bunyan, was born just south of the town, in Elstow, but lived – and was twice imprisoned – in Bedford in the 1660s and 1670s. The son of a tinsmith, Bunyan followed the same trade as his father and so was able to travel the countryside more than most people of that time. In the 1650s, Bunyan met John Gifford, the then pastor of the Independent Congregation, which held its meetings at St John's Church. It was their lengthy discussions that led to Bunyan's conversion and he was baptised shortly afterwards by Gifford in a backwater that leads off the Great Ouse. In 1660, Bunyan was arrested for preaching without a licence. He was to spend 12 years in jail, time he put to good use by writing *Grace Abounding*, his spiritual autobiography. But it was during a second imprisonment, in 1676, that he began writing his most famous work, *The Pilgrim's Progress*. This inspired allegory of the way to salvation still entrances even non-believers with the beauty and simplicity of its language. Following his release from prison in 1672, Bunyan was elected pastor of the Independent Congregation.

The **Bunyan Meeting Free Church** was constructed in 1849 on the site of the converted barn where Bunyan used to preach. The magnificent bronze doors, with illustrations from *The Pilgrim's Progress*, were given to the church by the Duke of Bedford in 1676. Adjacent to the church is the **Bunyan Museum**, which graphically tells the story of the man as well as the times through which he lived. Among the many displays are the jug in which his daughter Mary brought him soup while in prison, his chair, his tinker's anvil, and the violin and flute that he made in prison. Call: 01767 627666.

Another tribute to Bunyan is **Bunyan's Statue**, which was presented to the town in 1874 by the Duke of Bedford. Made of bronze, the statue is the work of Sir JE Boehm; around the pedestal of the nine-foot figure, which weighs more than three tons, are three bronze panels depicting scenes from *The Pilgrim's Progress*.

Beside the river and running through the heart of the town are the Bedford

Priory Country Park, Bedford

Embankment Gardens, which provide a year-round display of plants. Close by is the **Priory Country Park**, an area of 206 acres with a diverse habitat, which represents the flood meadows, reed beds and woodland that once surrounded the town. In Park Road North, Hill Rise Wildlife Area is a site for nature conservation specialising in butterflies, amphibians and small mammals.

For an insight into the history of the town and surrounding area, the **Bedford Museum** is well worth a visit. Among the many interesting displays is a piece of wall that shows the construction of the wattle walls that were an essential building technique in the 14th century.

Housed within the unlikely combination of a Victorian mansion and an adjoining modern gallery, the **Cecil Higgins Art Gallery** (see panel below) was started in 1949 by a wealthy Bedford brewery family. Its treasures include an internationally renowned collection of watercolours, prints, and drawings, as well as some fine glass, ceramics and furniture. The permanent display includes works by Turner, Gainsborough, Picasso and Matisse, and a needle panel entitled Bunyan's Dream. This was designed by Edward Bawden in 1977 to commemorate the tercentenary of the publication of *The Pilgrim's Progress*, the 350th anniversary of John Bunyan's birth and the Queen's Silver Jubilee. The gallery contains a major archive of Bawden, notably his linocuts

Cecil Higgins Art Gallery

Castle Lane, Bedford,
Bedfordshire MK40 3RP
Tel: 01234 211222 Fax: 01234 327149
website: www.cecilhigginsartgallery.org

The Cecil Higgins Art Gallery is situated in pleasant gardens leading down to the river embankment and is a recreation of an 1880s home, with superb examples of 19th century decorative arts. Room settings include items from the Handley-Read collection and the famous Gothic bedroom containing works by William Burges.

In an adjoining gallery are housed renowned collections of watercolours, prints and drawings (exhibitions changed regularly – ring for details), and there are also ceramics, glass and the Thomas Lester Lace Collection.

A self-service coffee bar is on hand for refreshments and the gallery shop sells a range of souvenirs. Tours can be arranged for groups if booked in advance and there is a programme of lunchtime lectures & demonstrations (call for details).

and lithographs. Other contemporary work can be seen at the **RCA Gallery**, which showcases the visual arts, including film, photography and animation.

A building with more modern connections is the Corn Exchange in St Paul's Square, from where Colonel **Glenn Miller** frequently broadcast during the Second World War. A bust of the bandleader who gave the world *In the Mood* and *Moonlight Serenade* stands outside the Exchange, and in 1994 a plaque was unveiled on the 50th anniversary of his mysterious disappearance over the English Channel, after setting off in foggy weather in a single-engined Noorduyn 'Norseman' C-64 aircraft. East of Bedford, Clapham Twinwood Control Tower is the last place where Miller was seen alive. A small museum is open at weekends and Bank Holidays in the summer, and the Glenn Miller Festival of swing, jazz and jive is held annually on August Bank Holiday.

Around Bedford

ELSTOW

1 mile S of Bedford off the A6

Abbey Church Moot Hall

John Bunyan connections are everywhere in the picturesque village of Elstow. The cottage where he was born in 1628 no longer stands, but its site is marked by a stone erected in Festival of Britain Year, 1951. The **Abbey Church of St Helena and St Mary** has two renowned stained glass windows, one depicting scenes from *The Pilgrim's Progress*, the other scenes from the Holy War. Here, too, are the font where Bunyan was christened in 1628 and the Communion Table used when he attended service. Bunyan's mother, father and sister are buried in the churchyard. The church also tells the story of the ill-fated R101 airship (see under Cardington), and there's a handsome memorial in the churchyard.

Elstow's notable buildings include a charming row of Tudor cottages and **Moot Hall**, which was built in the 15th century. It served as a place for hearing disputes and as a store for equipment for the village fair. Restored by Bedfordshire County Council, it is now a museum depicting life in 17th-century England with particular reference to Bunyan.

CARDINGTON

1 mile E of Bedford off the A603

Hangars

The Whitbread brewing family is closely connected with Cardington. The first Samuel Whitbread was born in the village in 1720, and it was another Whitbread, also Samuel, who restored the church and endowed the red-brick almshouses of 1787 overlooking the green. Samuel and his son, also Samuel, are buried in the churchyard in a large table tome designed by Albert Richardson.

Cardington is best known for the two giant **Hangars** that dominate the skyline. Built in 1917 and 1927 to construct and house the airships that were once thought to be the future of flying, they are best known as the birthplace of the R100 and the R101. The R101 first took

St Mary's Church, Cardington

off from Cardington in October 1929 with 54 people on board for a five-hour flight over the southeast. The passengers enjoyed a four-course lunch in the luxurious dining saloon and were amazed at the airship's quietness – they could hear the sounds of traffic and trains below. In July 1930, the R101 started her maiden flight across the Atlantic and tied up in Montreal after an uneventful flight of 77 hours. In October of that year the world's biggest airship left the hangars at Cardington for her first trip to India. Disaster struck not long into the journey when the R101 crashed into a hillside near Beauvais in France. Forty-four people, including the Air Secretary Lord Thomson of Cardington, died in the crash, which was believed to have been caused at least in part by lashing rain that made the ship dip suddenly. The Church of St Mary contains memorials to both Samuel Whitbreads, and in the churchyard extension is the tomb of all those who perished in the R101 disaster, and the ragged flag recovered from the flames of the R101 airship.

WILDEN

4 miles NE of Bedford off the A421

Wild Britain

Wild Britain has quickly become one of the county's leading family attractions. It stands in 10 acres of land untouched by modern farming practices and specially selected by its founder Andrew Green. Some 60 varieties of wildflowers flourish here, an irresistible attraction for 60 species of butterfly. It is also home to terrapins and tortoises, rabbits, rodents, cockroaches and tarantulas. The Wondrous World exhibit displays the variety of life found in rain forests. Other attractions include an adventure playground, tearoom and gift shop, along with Moley Mine, where kids can don a hard hat and scramble, clamber and crawl through a tunnel to track down Moley the Mole.

STEVINGTON

4 miles NW of Bedford off A428

Post Mill

This is a typical English village with a church that was here at the time of the Domesday survey, a village cross decorated with capitals and a large finial, and a Holy Well that attracted visitors in the Middle Ages. It is claimed that it never freezes or dries up.

However, the most important building in the village is the **Post Mill**, the only one of the county's 12 remaining windmills that still retains its sails. Dating from the 1770s, the mill continued to operate commercially until 1936, having been rebuilt in 1921. Extensively restored in the 1950s, it is in full working order today. Though milling was an important part of village life here for many years, lace-making, too, was a thriving industry and mat makers also settled here, taking advantage of the rushes growing on the banks of the nearby River Ouse.

BROMHAM

2 miles W of Bedford off A428

Bromham Mill

This quiet residential village has a splendid

Bromham Church

ancient bridge with no fewer than 26 arches. Close to the river is a watermill that dates back to the 17th century. Now fully restored and in working order, **Bromham Mill** is also home to displays of natural history, a gallery with regularly changing exhibitions of contemporary craftwork and fine art, and a tearoom overlooking the river where, if you're lucky, you can watch kingfishers diving from the bank.

HARROLD

7 miles NW of Bedford off the A428

Harrold-Odell Country Park

A typical country village with an old bridge and causeway, an octagonal market house and an old circular lock-up that was last used in the 19th century. Close by is the **Harrold-Odell Country Park**, which covers 144 acres of landscaped lakes, river banks and water meadows that are home to a wealth of plant, animal and bird life (more than 160 species of birds have been spotted). The park was created as a result of excavating aggregates for the building of Milton Keynes.

Harrold-Odell Country Park

HINWICK

10 miles NW of Bedford off the A6

Built between 1709 and 1714, Hinwick House is a charming Queen Anne building that is still home to the descendants of the Orlebar family for whom it was constructed. Occasionally open to visitors, this delightful brownstone house, with details picked out in lighter coloured stone, has a particularly pleasing entrance hall and an interesting collection of furniture and paintings. Its 37 acres of grounds are a popular location for weddings, parties, events and location shots. Call 01933 356686.

Close by, on the Bedfordshire/ Northamptonshire border, is Santa Pod raceway, established in 1966 on a disused Second World War USAF base as Europe's first permanent drag racing venue. Call 01234 782828 for meeting details.

YIELDEN

10 miles N of Bedford off the A6

A village on the River Til, guarded by the earthworks of a long ruined castle. Mentioned in the Domesday Book, only an oblong motte, two large baileys and stone foundations remain of Yielden Castle, which is reputed to have been built on the site of the battle between the Romans and the Iceni in which the warrior queen Boadicea (Boudicca) was killed. One Christmas Day John Bunyan came to the village to preach in the church, as a result of which the incumbent vicar, William Bell, was removed from his post for allowing Bunyan this freedom.

LOCATOR MAP

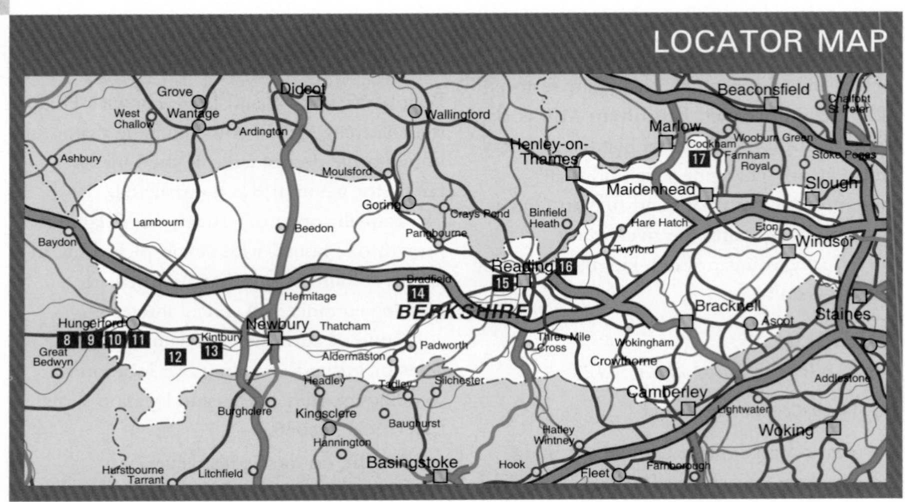

ADVERTISERS AND PLACES OF INTEREST

2 Berkshire

Dun Mill Lock, Kennet & Avon Canal

The Royal County of Berkshire receives its honorific title because one of the Queen's three official residences, Windsor Castle, lies within its boundaries. The most important landmark in the east of the county, the 900-year-old castle is the county's major tourist attraction.

Berkshire extends over some 485 square miles in the valley of the middle Thames and is divided into six main districts. The western area of the county is important for racing and the training of racehorses, with a top-class course at Newbury, and the training centres of Lambourn and East Ilsley.

Another feature of West Berkshire is the number of communication routes that flow across the region linking London with the West Country, dominated today by the M4 motorway. The ancient Ridgeway Path, England's oldest road, follows the county border with Oxfordshire, and the Kennet and Avon Canal, completed in 1810, crosses southern England from Bristol to join the River Thames at Reading. Entering the county at Hungerford, this major waterway passes through a charming rural landscape as it winds through villages and market towns. The canal prospered until the arrival of the Great Western Railway in 1841, after which it inevitably declined; by the 1950s it was largely unnavigable. After a full clearing and restoration programme, the canal can now once again be travelled its full length, providing a wide variety of leisure activities for thousands of visitors each year.

The central region of Berkshire is dominated by Reading, a thriving commuter town with excellent links to both London and the West Country. Though seeming to be very much a product of the past two centuries, it has a long and interesting history.

The Thames, forming the northern county border with Oxfordshire, has, especially along its southern banks, many delightful villages, which became fashionable thanks to the Victorian and Edwardian passion for boating, and they remain fashionable to this day.

Across Windsor Great Park, the remains of a royal hunting forest, lies Ascot racecourse, founded in 1711 by Queen Anne. Five days in June see the worlds of fashion and horseracing meet at the highest level at the Royal Ascot meeting.

Lambourn

Church of St Michael Seven Barrows

Lambourn Trainers' Association

Lying up on the Berkshire Downs, in the extreme west of the county, this village, which has the feel of a small town, is best known as a major centre for the training of racehorses. More than 1200 horses are trained here and there are more than 100 miles of gallops. The **Lambourn Trainers' Association** brings together racehorse trainers and individuals and organisations involved in the training of racehorses in the Lambourn area. It organises guided tours of the stables and trips to the gallops to view the horses going through their paces. Lambourn has been home to some of the greatest trainers in the history of the racing game, including Fred Winter and Fulke Walwyn over the jumps, Peter Walwyn on the flat and current incumbents Barry Hills, Clive Coc, Marcus Tregoning and Nicky Henderson.

St Michael's Church - Lambourn

Lambourn's medieval **Church of St Michael** is one of the finest parish churches in Berkshire. Originally Norman and constructed on the cruciform plan, it has been greatly altered and extended, though the west end still has its Norman doorway, complete with zigzag ornamentation. The lychgate was dedicated to the memory of William Jousiffe, who brought horses from Newmarket to Lambourn in the 1870s and thus established a still-flourishing industry.

To the north of the village are **Lambourn Seven Barrows**, one of the most impressive Bronze Age burial sites in the country and actually comprising no fewer than 32 barrows.

Around Lambourn

EAST ILSLEY

10 miles E of Lambourn off the A34

This attractive downland village has managed to retain several interesting features, in particular the winding mechanism of the now long disused village well by the pond. It was because of sheep that the village chiefly prospered – from the early 1600s East Ilsley held fortnightly sheep fairs that were second only in size to Smithfield, London. At their peak in the 19th century, permanent pens were erected in the main street to contain the animals and, on one day, it was recorded that 80,000 sheep were penned. During the 19th century the station in the nearby village of **Compton** became an important centre for the passage of sheep to and from the great East Ilsley sheep market, but the decline in the sheep trade resulted in the closure of the station.

About a mile south of Compton lie the

remains of an Iron Age fort, Perborough Castle, while to the northeast, just above the Ridgeway, is Lowbury Hill, where traces of a Roman temple and a Roman military outpost can be seen.

Today, along with its neighbour West Ilsley, the village is associated with racehorses, which use the gallops on the downs as their training grounds.

Newbury

Church of St Nicholas · Kennet & Avon Canal
West Berkshire Museum · Racecourse

This crossroads town has, for many years, dominated the rural area of West Berkshire. Prospering during the Middle Ages, and afterwards on the importance of the woollen industry, the town became famous as the Cloth Town. Among the various characters who made their money out of the weaving of the wool the best known is John Smallwood, always known as Jack of Newbury and the "richest clothier England ever beheld". Asked to raise two horsemen and two footmen for Henry VIII's campaign against the Scots, Jack raised 50 of each and led them himself. However, they only got as far as Stony Stratford in Buckinghamshire before news of the victory of Flodden reached them and they turned for home.

Evidence of the town's wealth can be seen in the splendid 'wool' **Church of St Nicholas**, which was constructed between 1500 and 1532. Built on the site of a Norman church, no expense was spared – Jack of Newbury gave the money for the magnificent five-bayed nave. The church has seen much restoration work, particularly during the Victorian age, but the fine pulpit and elaborately decorated nave roof have survived.

Kennet & Avon Canal, Newbury

After the Civil War, the town's clothing industry declined. However, the 18th century saw the construction of turnpike roads and Newbury became a busy coaching stop on the road from London to Bath. The town further opened up to travellers and the needs of carriers with the completion of the **Kennet and Avon Canal** in 1810. Newbury Lock, built in 1796, was the first lock to be built along the canal and it is also the only one to have lever-operated ground paddles (the sluices that let in the water), which are known as Jack Cloughs.

Back in the centre of the town, in the Market Square, is the **West Berkshire Museum**, housed in two of the town's most historic buildings, the 17th-century cloth hall and the adjacent 18th-century granary, a store once used by traders travelling the canal. The history of the canal is explained, and other exhibits include crafts and industries, the two Battles of Newbury (1643 and 1644) during the Civil War, the story of Greenham Common and local archaeology.

Those arriving in Newbury from the south will pass the Falkland Memorial, which has nothing to do with the 1980s conflict in the South Atlantic. It is in fact a memorial to Lord

Falkland, who was killed at the first battle of Newbury. To the east of the town lies **Newbury Racecourse**, which stages top-quality flat and National Hunt racing throughout the year.

Donnington Castle

Around Newbury

HAMPSTEAD NORREYS

6 miles NE of Newbury on the B4009

The Living Rainforest

Just to the north of the village lies **The Living Rainforest**, an education and conservation charity devoted to the raising of awareness about the world's rainforests. Here, in a tract of tropical rainforest inside a giant glasshouse, the temperature never falls below 70°F. Visitors can walk through the humid and shadowy jungles of the lowland tropical forests, the cool, orchid-festooned and ferny cloud forests, and the Amazon with its amazing flowers and wonderful bromeliads. There is also a unique collection of spectacular and rare plants, tranquil pools, the sounds of the tropics, and rainforest animals, including a pair of Goeldi's monkeys, marmosets, tree frogs, iguanas and Courtney the dwarf crocodile. Also on site are a shop selling plants and gifts, and a teashop. Signed from the A34/M4 J13 intersection.

DONNINGTON

1 mile N of Newbury on the B4494

Castle

Despite being so close to the town of Newbury, Donnington has managed to retain its village identity and atmosphere. To the west of the village, and visible from the road, is Donnington Grove House. Built in 1759, and designed by the architect John Chute, this was the home, in the late 18th century, of the Brummell family; Beau Brummell, the instigator of the Bath Society, lived here as a child.

However, most visitors to the village come to see **Donnington Castle** (English Heritage), a late-14th century defence that was built by Sir Richard Abberbury. Once a magnificent structure, only the twin-towered gatehouse survives amidst the impressive earthworks. The castle had its most eventful period during the Civil War when it was the scene of one of the longest sieges of the conflict. Charles I's troops were held here for 20 months and it was during this period that most of the castle was destroyed.

WINTERBOURNE

3 miles N of Newbury off the B4494

Snelsmore Common Country Park

Just south of the village lies **Snelsmore Common Country Park**, a heathland site surrounded by woodland. The common comprises several different habitats, including woodland, heathland and bog, and it supports a correspondingly wide variety of plant and animal life. It is a particularly important area for ground-nesting birds such as the nightjar and woodlark. The site has many footpaths and tracks and an area set aside for picnics.

WICKHAM

6 miles NW of Newbury on the B4000

Church of St Swithin

This ancient village with its typical Berkshire mix of brick and flint, thatch and tile is most notable for its **Church of St Swithin** that stands atop a hill with grand views across the Kennet valley. It has a Saxon tower – unique in the county – but it is the interior that is truly remarkable because of the elephants in the north aisle. Made of papier-mâché and gilded, they were purchased at the Paris Exhibition of 1862 and intended for the rectory. They were too large, however, so they now appear to support the spectacular wooden roof of the church.

HUNGERFORD

9 miles W of Newbury on the A4

Bear Hotel Tutti Day

Although not mentioned in the Domesday Book, by the Middle Ages this old market town was well established. The manor of Hungerford had some distinguished lords, including Simon de Montfort and John of Gaunt. Hungerford's heyday came in the 18th century when the turnpike road from London to Bath was built, passing through the town. By 1840, the town had eight coaching inns serving the needs of travellers and its prosperity continued with the opening of the Kennet and Avon Canal. The building of the railway took much of that trade away and the town reverted to its early, gentle lifestyle. However, several of the old coaching inns have survived, notably **The Bear Hotel** (see below). Although it has

THE BEAR HOTEL

Charnham Street, Hungerford, Berkshire RG17 OEL
Tel: 01488 682512 Fax: 01488 684357
website: www.thebearhotelhungerford.co.uk

Located in the thriving market town of Hungerford, **The Bear Hotel** is one of England's oldest coaching inns and has been the focus of hospitality since 1464.

The hotel has been sympathetically restored and refurbished and has thirty-nine individually designed bedrooms, an award-winning restaurant and bar, conference and wedding facilities with private entrance, and gardens set on the banks of the River Dunn.

Situated just over an hour by direct train from London, The Bear Hotel is ideally situated for short breaks, visiting friends or relatives or business. The hotel has a fascinating royal history full of romance and character. Henry VIII owned the manor of Chilton Foliat in which The Bear Hotel lay; Charles 1 used The Bear as a headquarters during the English Civil War in 1644. Later, Prince William of Orange, soon to be William III, was offered the crown of England at The Bear Hotel.

In the bedroom department there is a choice of compact doubles through to spacious suites with king-size beds. Some bedrooms have balconies and river views while others overlook the rooftops of Hungerford. The Bear is ideally suited for weddings and private events and the hotel is licensed for civil ceremonies. Ring for details.

BOW HOUSE

3-4 Faulkner Square, Charnham Street,
Hungerford, Berkshire RG17 0EP
Tel: 01488-680826
e-mail: bowhouseantiques@aol.com
website: www.bowhouselifestyle.com

Bow House has built up a large and loyal following from those who have been lucky enough to discover its unique charms. These include locals who use its house and room design services, and visitors who come a long way to browse its eclectic range of both modern and antique furniture and houseware. Owners Jo and Jess Preston travel throughout Europe to find the best of everything that catches their eye, which they think would look good in someone's home. Rather than shop across Europe, customers just have to make their way to the Berkshire market town of Hungerford.

It's hard to say what you'll find at Bow House as the stock changes constantly, which is why customers keep returning. What catches Jess and Jo's eye doesn't stay on display for long. From towels to tables, from cute coat hangers to dazzling dinner plates, you'll find them all at Bow House. There are chunky sofas and exquisite delicate jewellery, scarves and sunglasses, lovely children's toys, prints and perfumes too. Anything that enhances your home or your lifestyle can be found at Bow House – and if they don't have exactly what you want they'll help you to track it down.

THE EMPORIUM

112 High Street, Hungerford, Berkshire RG17 0NB
Tel: 01488 686959
e-mail: the-emporium@btconnect.com
website: www.emporium-hungerford.co.uk

The grandly named **The Emporium** is an established antiques centre occupying a stunning 17th Century building in the heart of the historic town of Hungerford. It offers a wide variety of items from around 50 specialist dealers who aim to provide a fine selection of quality antiques and gifts at affordable prices. The elegant layout of the shop perfectly compliments The Emporium's brilliant combination of contemporary and antique ranges; it has become a well established addition to Hungerford's renowned quality antique and modern independent shops.

Due to the amazing number and variety in the dealers who make up the Emporium, the products and colours in the shop are ever changing, making every visit a unique experience. Dealers include specialists in silver, jewellery, ceramics and fine art, plus glassware, scientific instruments and art nouveau period pieces, as well as gorgeous antique furniture, antique garden tools and painted pine, and oriental carpets and upholstery fabrics. Such a range can be overwhelming, were it not for the owners Barbara and Richard Mills, together with manager David Keig, who are always on hand to offer help and advice. Opening hours are 9.30 to 5pm Monday to Saturday, 10am to 4pm Sundays and Bank Holidays.

an impressive Georgian frontage, the building actually dates back to 1494, making it one of the oldest buildings in the town.

An event of great historical importance occurred in December 1688 when William of Orange arrived to stay at The Bear to negotiate with the Commissioners of King James II concerning the future of the monarchy. The result was the Glorious Revolution of 1689, generally accepted as the beginning of true Parliamentary democracy as William and his wife Mary were invited to take the throne by a Protestant Parliament.

Trip Barge, Hungerford

As well as still holding a weekly market, the town also continues the ancient tradition known as the Hocktide Festival or **Tutti Day** (tutti meaning a bunch of flowers). Held every year on the second Tuesday after Easter, the festival was originally used as a means of collecting an early form of council tax. During the colourful event, two men carrying a six-foot pole decorated with ribbons and flowers go around each household collecting the tax. To ease the burden of their visit, the men share a drink with the man of the house, give him an orange, and kiss his wife before collecting their

THE TUTTI POLE

3 High Street, Hungerford, Berkshire RG17 0DN
Tel: 01488 682515

A delightful traditional tea shop and restaurant on Hungerford's High Street. The same family has owned and run the business from the start in 1981 and the head chef has been with them for 28 years.

Home-made food is their speciality and they are particularly known for their toasted tea cakes and meringues, however a full three course lunch can also be enjoyed here, booking is recommended, particularly on Sundays. Food is served throughout the day from 9.00 a.m. to 5.30 p.m. Monday to Friday and 9.00 a.m. to 6.00 p.m. Saturday and Sunday.

The oldest parts of the bow window fronted building date from the 15th century, and there's plenty of room here and in the more modern extension, as well as seats for 50 outside. Situated near the canal it is perfect for a stroll after your visit.

Owners and staff are warm and friendly, and a visit here is always a pleasure. The unique name of The Tutti Pole refers to the annual ceremony of Hocktide, celebrated on the second Tuesday after Easter. Tutti Poles are still carried by the Tithingmen around the town on this day. Tutti means nosegay, the flowers which in this case are adorning a pole.

THE CROWN & GARTER

Inkpen Common, Inkpen, Hungerford, Berkshire RG17 9QR
Tel: 01488 668325
website: www.crownandgarter.com

In days gone by **The Crown & Garter** is reputed to have been a resting place for James II on his way to visit one of his mistresses. Today, this fine old traditional country inn, set in stunning countryside, offers outstanding food, purpose-built accommodation and a truly welcoming atmosphere.

The inn's ancient and unique charm can best be seen in the bar area, the oldest part of the building which boasts a huge inglenook fireplace and wooden beams. The bar stocks a fine selection of local and guest real ales, malt whiskies and fine wines as well as free broadband access.

In the restaurant you'll find a delicious and interesting variety of dishes all freshly prepared on the premises using mainly local produce. Meals can be enjoyed in either the cosy wood-panelled restaurant , the bar areas, outside on the new patio or in the enclosed beer garden beneath ancient English oak.

The accommodation comprises 8 purpose built bedrooms which surround a private, very pretty cottage garden complete with pond. The spacious bedrooms are tastefully decorated and equipped with comfortable beds, en suite facilities with power showers, flat screen TV, Freeview, radio, hospitality tray and hairdryer.

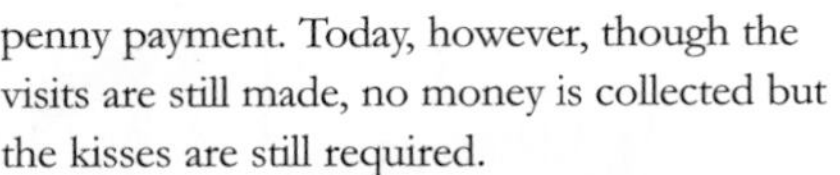

penny payment. Today, however, though the visits are still made, no money is collected but the kisses are still required.

Hungerford lies at the centre of the North Wessex Area of Outstanding Natural Beauty, designated as such in 1972. It stretches from the River Thames in the east to Devizes in the west, Wantage in the north and Andover in the south.

COMBE

7 miles SW of Newbury off the A338

Walbury Hill

The isolated hamlet of Combe is overlooked by **Walbury Hill**, which at 974 feet is the highest point in Berkshire and the highest chalk hill in England. A popular place for walking and hang-gliding, the hill offers terrific views and the bonus of an Iron Age fort on its summit. Close

THE FORBURY

Crossways, Kintbury, Hungerford, Berkshire RG17 9SU
Tel: 01488 658377

Overlooking its own 5 acres of unspoilt woodland and a stream, **The Forbury** has been offering quality bed & breakfast accommodation since 1972. The extended 17th century cottage was originally a thatched bakery with a double bread oven and inglenook fireplace. Today, there are 4 guest bedrooms, one of which is a family room with a connecting room for children. Guests are assured of a warm welcome at The Forbury and also, its speciality, a great full English breakfast! The attractive village of Kintbury is just a mile away and there are several local pubs serving excellent food.

THE QUEEN'S HEAD

Southend Road, Bradfield, Berkshire RG7 6EY
Tel: 01189 744332
e-mail: info@queens-bradfield.co.uk
website: www.queens-bradfield.co.uk

Occupying a sturdy Victorian building dating back to the 1850s, **The Queen's Head** at Bradfield has a warm down-to-earth charm, and customers receive a warm welcome from owners Andrew Loupekine and Laura Maton, both of them local people. The restaurant at The Queen's Head, with its duck egg blue walls, mix 'n' match wooden chairs, eclectic bric a brac and open fireplace, is a major attraction for discerning diners.

Andrew is the chef and his traditional British menu is a hit with the locals and visitors alike. You'll find Devilled Lamb's Kidneys, and Wood Pigeon with bacon and black pudding amongst the starters. The delicious main courses include favourite dishes Whole Roast Sea Bream with Fennel Salad and new potatoes, and Fillet of Beef with seared foie gras and sauté potatoes. In good weather, you can enjoy this fine fare in the neat and peaceful garden where there's also a children's play area. To accompany your meal, the bar offers great choice in drinks that includes Fuller's real ales and a lovely selection of wines, available by the glass. The Queen's Head is open all day every day; the kitchen is closed between 2.30pm and 6pm but you can still enjoy afternoon tea and cakes.

to the hill stands Combe Gibbet, one of the last public hanging places in the country. This gibbet was first used in 1676 to hang a pair of adulterous murderers, George Broomham and Dorothy Newman, and has a crossbar with a 'his' side and a 'hers' side.

GREENHAM

1½ miles SE of Newbury off the A34

Greenham Common and Crookham Common

Greenham Common and the adjacent **Crookham Common** make up the largest area of lowland heathland in Berkshire. In 1941 the common land was taken over by the Air Ministry and became an important military base, first for British squadrons and then for the US Air Force. In 1981 nuclear-armed Cruise missiles arrived at Greenham and the site became notorious for anti-nuclear demonstrations. The airbase is gradually being returned to nature and the site is once again open to the public. Designated a Site of Special Scientific Interest (SSSI), it is home to many rare and endangered plants and animals.

THATCHAM

3 miles E of Newbury on the A4

Thatcham Moor

Thatcham Nature Discovery Centre

Believed to be the oldest village in Britain, it is hard to imagine that this now large suburb of Newbury was once a small place. **Thatcham Moor** is one of the largest areas of inland freshwater reed beds in the country. As well as the reeds, which can grow up to six feet in height, the area supports numerous species of marshland and aquatic plants. Birds also abound here and it is an important breeding ground for reed and sedge warblers.

Thatcham Nature Discovery Centre,

situated close to the Thatcham Moors Local Nature Reserve, is a multi-activity based centre where visitors are encouraged to look, listen, touch and learn through an exciting range of interactive exhibits. In Discovery Hall they can find out what lives beneath the lake, get a bird's-eye view of the world, learn about local and global environmental issues or watch the wildlife from the comfort of the lakeside observation area. Open 10am to 5pm April to October. Closed Mondays except Bank Holidays and School Holidays.

Reading

Abbey · Gaol · Museum

Museum of English Rural Life

This thriving commuter town, which took its name from the Saxon chief Reada, is a delightful combination of more than 1000 years of history and a vibrant and modern city. There are Victorian brick buildings nestling beside beautiful medieval churches, famous coaching inns opposite high tech offices, and some of the best shopping in the area. Reading began as a Saxon settlement between the Rivers Thames and Kennet and, as a defensible site, was used by the Danes as a base for their attack on Wessex in the 9th century. The town grew up around its **Abbey**, which was founded in 1121 by Henry I, the youngest son of William the Conqueror, and it was consecrated by Thomas à Becket in 1164. The abbey went on to become one of the most important religious houses – its relics included a piece of Jesus' sandal, the tooth of St Luke, and a slice of Moses' rod. Henry, its great benefactor, was buried in front of the High Altar in 1136.

The atmospheric abbey ruins stand in Forbury Gardens on the banks of the River Kennet; these gardens are also home to the Maiwand Lion, a magnificent statue of a lion that commemorates the men of the Berkshire Regiment who died in the Afghan War of 1879.

Reading boasts several other pieces of distinguished public art, including the Robed Figure by Dame Elizabeth Frink and the Soane Obelisk designed by Sir John Soane, architect of the Bank of England. Adjacent to the abbey ruins is another of Reading's famous buildings – **Reading Gaol** where Oscar Wilde was imprisoned and where he wrote *De Profundis*. His confinement here also inspired the writer to compose the epic *Ballad of Reading Gaol* whilst staying in Paris in 1898.

Though the town developed during the Middle Ages as a result of a flourishing woollen industry, it was during the 18th century with the coming of both the turnpike roads and the opening of the Kennet and Avon Canal that the town boomed. By the 19th century, Reading was known for its three Bs: beer, bulbs and biscuits. As the trade of the canal and River Thames increased, the movement of corn and malt explains the growth of the brewing trade, and the leaders in the bulb trade were Sutton Seeds, founded here in 1806 but no longer in the town. The world renowned biscuit-making firm of Huntley & Palmer began life here in 1826, when Joseph Huntley founded the firm, to be joined, in 1841, by George Palmer, inventor of the stamping machine.

The Story of Reading, a permanent exhibition at the **Museum of Reading** in the Town Hall, is the ideal place to gain a full understanding of the history of the town, from the earliest times to the present day. Here, too, can be seen the world's only full-size replica of the Bayeux Tapestry, made in the 19th century and featuring Edward the Confessor, once Lord of the Royal Manor in Reading, as a central figure. As a contrast to the museum's displays depicting the life of the town in the 20th century, the Silchester Gallery is devoted to describing the day-to-day life at Calleva Atrebatum, the Roman town of Silchester, using Roman artefacts unearthed there during early excavations. This museum, one of the most go-ahead in the country, has special events and changing exhibitions throughout the year, so every visit will reveal something new and exciting to see.

In 1925 Reading Extension College became a university in its own right. Lying to the south of the town centre in Redlands Road, the **Museum of English Rural Life** (see panel below) houses the most comprehensive national collection of objects, books, photographs and archives relating to the history of food, farming and the countryside. Call 0118 378 8660.

Around Reading

SONNING

3 miles NE of Reading off the A4

This pretty little village leading down to the Thames is a popular spot to visit, especially on summer weekends. In 1399, after he had been deposed, Richard II brought his young bride Isabella here to be looked after in the palace of the Bishops of Salisbury. Her ghost is said to appear on the paths beside the river. On Grove Street stands Turpin's, a house that belonged to the aunt of Dick Turpin and which provided occasional refuge

Museum of English Rural Life

University of Reading, Whiteknights, PO Box 229,
Reading, Berkshire RG6 6AG
Tel: 0118 931 8660 Fax: 0118 975 1264
e-mail: rhc@reading.ac.uk
website: www.ruralhistory.org

The **Museum of English Rural Life** at the University of Reading is the English national centre for the history of food, farming and the countryside. With artefact, library and archive collections of international importance, the Centre tells the story of farming and the countryside in England over the past three hundred years. Discover an amazing range of country crafts, find out about Victorian farmhouse kitchens and explore England's largest collection of vintage ploughs, wagons and machinery, including a steam-powered threshing machine. There are captivating displays for visitors of all ages, as well as quizzes and trails for children and families plus an interactive computer area.

The Object Collections is one of the country's finest collections of objects related to daily life and work in the countryside. The Library has over 50,000 books and periodicals. The Archive includes the business records of major agricultural engineering firms, archives of national countryside organisations and a large collection of individual farm records. The Archive of Photographs and Illustrations has over 750,000 images of farming and rural life. Visitors wishing to consult the reference collection are asked to make an appointment in advance.

for the notorious highwayman. Behind the wall of the old bishop's palace is Deanery Gardens, a house built in 1901 to the design of Sir Edwin Lutyens.

WOODLEY

3 miles E of Reading off the A329

Museum of Berkshire Aviation

At Woodley Airfield the **Museum of Berkshire Aviation** (see panel below) celebrates the contribution the county has made to the history of aviation. The exhibits include Fairey, Handley-Page and Miles aircraft, which are shown along with fascinating pictorial records and archives. Call 0118 944 8089.

HURST

4½ miles E of Reading off the A321

Dinton Pastures Country Park

This attractive, scattered village is home to a Norman church, well endowed with monuments, and a row of fine 17th-century almshouses. The village bowling green is said to have been made for Charles II.

Just to the south lies **Dinton Pastures Country Park**, a large area of lakes, rivers, hedgerows and meadows rich in wildlife. Until the 1970s, this area was excavated for sand and gravel, but the former pits are now attractive lakes and ponds; one of them has been stocked for coarse fishing and the largest is set aside for canoeing and windsurfing.

WOKINGHAM

6 miles SE of Reading on the A329

This largely residential town has, at its centre, an old triangular market place with a matching triangular Town Hall built in 1860. In the mainly Victorian town centre is a sprinkling of attractive Georgian houses and shops, and the medieval parish church of All Saints. The most attractive building, however, is Lucas Hospital, built of mellow red brick and rather like a miniature Chelsea Hospital. It was originally built in 1666 as almshouses and a chapel, by Henry Lucas, a mathematician and MP for Cambridge University. Today, the hospital still cares for the elderly though now in the style of a retirement home. It can be visited by appointment with the resident matron.

Museum of Berkshire Aviation

Mohawk Way (off The Bader Way), Woodley, nr Reading, Berkshire RG5 4UE
Tel: 0118 944 8089
e-mail: MuseumBerksAv@gmail.com
website: www.museumofberkshireaviation.co.uk

Berkshire's dynamic contribution to aviation history is graphically re-captured at the museum. Run as a charitable trust, the museum is at the historic site of Woodley Airfield - once the centre of a thriving aircraft industry. Miles and Handley Page aircraft built at Woodley are being re-constructed and exhibited along with fascinating pictorial records and priceless archives. The museum welcomes group visits and runs an active educational programme for schools, linked to National Curriculum requirements, demonstrating the development of aviation techniques.

ARBORFIELD

4 miles S of Reading on the A327

California Country Park

Arborfield Garrison is the home base of REME, the Royal Electrical and Mechanical Engineers, and the site of their museum. To the south is **California Country Park**, a wooded beauty spot where the woods support 34 different species of tree, and the bogland provides a range of habitats for the many animals, birds and plants that are found here.

SWALLOWFIELD

5 miles S of Reading off the A33

Swallowfield Park

The manor house here, **Swallowfield Park**, has been associated with both royalty and other notables. The present house (unfortunately now a shell) was built in 1678 by Wren's assistant William Talman for the 2nd Earl of Clarendon who acquired the estate upon marrying the heiress. In 1719, the park was purchased by Thomas Pitt, a former Governor of Madras, who used the proceeds of the sale of a large diamond he bought while in India. The diamond can now be seen in the Louvre Museum, Paris. The story of Pitt and his diamond provided the inspiration for the novel, *The Moonstone*, by Wilkie Collins, who visited the house in 1860. The Italian Doorway, by Talman, is probably the house's most outstanding remaining feature and it marks the entrance to the walled garden. Here can be found a dog's graveyard where lies one of Charles Dickens' dogs. The novelist had bequeathed the pet to his friend and owner of the house, Sir Charles Russell.

Swallowfield Park

FINCHAMPSTEAD

8 miles S of Reading off the A327

Finchampstead Ridges

To the east of the village are **Finchampstead Ridges**, a popular spot for walkers that offers wonderful views across the Blackwater Valley. Simon's Wood has a varied mixture of conifers and broad-leaved trees, and in the wood and on the heath are siskin and flycatchers, dragonflies, damselflies and a wide range of invertebrates and lichens.

ALDERMASTON

9 miles SW of Reading on the A340

St Mary's Church   Aldermaston Wharf

Kennet & Avon Canal Visitor Centre

It was in this tranquil village, in 1840, that the William pear was first propagated by John Staid, the then village schoolmaster. First known as the Aldermaston pear, a cutting of the plant is believed to have been taken to Australia where it is now called the Bartlett pear.

Still retaining much of its original 12th-century structure, and with a splendid Norman door, the lovely **St Mary's Church** provides the setting for the York Mystery Cycle, nativity plays dating from the 14th century, which are performed here each year. Using beautiful period costumes and contemporary music, including a piece written by William Byrd, the cycle lasts a week and the plays attract visitors from far and wide.

Another old custom still continued in the village is the auctioning of the grazing rights of Church Acres every three years. Using the ancient method of a candle auction, a pin – in this case a horseshoe nail – is inserted into the tallow of a candle one inch from the wick. The candle is lit while bidding takes place and the grazing rights go to the highest bidder as the pin drops out of the candle.

Outside, under a yew tree in the churchyard, lies the grave of Maria Hale, formerly known as the Aldermaston witch. She was said to turn herself into a large brown hare and although the hare was never caught or killed, at one time a local keeper wounded it in the leg, and from then on it was observed that Maria Hale had become lame.

Aldermaston Wharf

Close to the village is a delightful walk along the Kennet and Avon Canal to **Aldermaston Wharf**. A Grade II-listed structure of beautifully restored 18th-century scalloped brickwork, the wharf houses a **Visitor Centre**, where the canalman's cottage tells the story of the creation, restoration and re-opening of the waterway link between the Thames and Bristol.

WOOLHAMPTON

9 miles W of Reading on the A4

This tranquil village on the banks of the Kennet and Avon Canal had a watermill at the time of the Domesday Survey of 1086 and was mentioned again in 1351, when the manor and mill were owned by the Knights Hospitallers. The present mill, built in 1820 and extended in 1875, was powered by a brook that runs into the Kennet. It was last used in 1930 and has since been turned into offices.

BEENHAM

9 miles W of Reading off the A4

UK Wolf Conservation Trust

Set in 6000 acres of beautiful woodlands, the **UK Wolf Conservation Trust** proves that wolves are not the big, bad, dangerous animals of nursery rhymes and legend. There are wolves here you can actually stroke and which are taken to schools, shows and seminars. The European wolves are the first to be successfully bred in England for 500 years, and the Trust also cares for packs of North American wolves. The site is open all year round, by appointment. Call 0118 971 3330.

PANGBOURNE

6 miles NW of Reading on the A417

Church Cottag Whitchurch Lock

Situated at the confluence of the River Pang and the River Thames, the town grew up in the late 19th and early 20th centuries as a fashionable place to live. As a result there are several attractive Victorian and Edwardian villas to be seen, including a row of ornate Victorian houses known as the Seven Deadly Sins. It was here that the author Kenneth Grahame retired, living at **Church Cottage** opposite the church. Grahame married late in life and it was while living here that he wrote *The Wind in the Willows* for his son.

Visitors to the town who cross the elegant iron bridge to neighbouring **Whitchurch** must still pay a toll, though now very small. The right to exact the toll has existed since 1792 and it is one of the very few surviving privately-owned toll bridges. It was at **Whitchurch Lock** that the characters in Jerome K Jerome's *Three Men in a Boat* abandoned their craft, after a series of mishaps, and returned to London.

BASILDON

8 miles NW of Reading on the A417

Basildon Park · Beale Park

This small village is the last resting place of the inventor and agricultural engineer, Jethro Tull, whose grave can be seen in the churchyard. The inventor of the seed drill and the horse-drawn hoe also wrote several books on farming and plant nutrition, including *The New Horse Hoeing Husbandry* and *An Essay on the Principles of Tillage & Vegetation.* Outside the churchyard is a classic pavilion built in memory of his parents by the late Mr Childe-Beale, which is, today, the focal point of **Beale Park**. Covering some 300 acres of ancient water meadow, the park is home to a wide range of birds and animals. There are small herds of unusual farm animals, including rare breeds of sheep and goats, Highland cattle, deer, and South American llama, more than 120 species of birds living in their natural habitat, and a pets' corner for smaller children. The park's work is not confined to the keeping of animals. A Community Woodland has been planted and an ancient reed bed restored. The park's other main attraction, housed in the pavilion, is the Model Boat Collection, which is one of the finest of its kind.

Basildon House

However, the village's main feature is **Basildon Park** (National Trust), an elegant, classical house designed in the 18th century by Carr of York and undoubtedly Berkshire's foremost mansion. Built between 1776 and 1783 for Francis Sykes, an official of the East India Company, the house has the unusual addition of an Anglo-Indian room. The interior, finished by JB Papworth and restored to its original splendour after World War Two, is rich in fine plasterwork, pictures and furniture, and the rooms open to the public include the Octagon Room and a decorative Shell Room. If the name Basildon seems familiar, it is probably as a result of the notepaper: the head of the papermaking firm of Dickinson visited the house and decided to use the name for the high quality paper his firm produced.

ALDWORTH

11 miles NW of Reading on the B4009

Aldworth Giants

The parish Church of St Mary is famous for housing the **Aldworth Giants** – the larger than life effigies of the de la Beche family, which date back to the 14th century. The head of the family, Sir Philip, who lies here with eight other members of his family, was the Sheriff of Berkshire and valet to Edward II. Though now somewhat defaced, the effigies were so legendary that the church was visited by Elizabeth I. Outside, in the churchyard, are the remains of a once magnificent 1000-year-old yew tree that was damaged in a storm.

Nearby, at **Little Aldworth**, is the grave of the poet Laurence Binyon who wrote the famous lines: "At the going down of the sun and in the morning, we shall remember them." Opposite the Bell Inn is one of the deepest wells in the country. Topped by great beams, heavy cogs and wheels, it is some 327 feet deep.

Windsor

Castle · Guildhall · St George's Chapel

Frogmore House · Savill Garden

Racecourse · Smith's Lawn · Legoland

Windsor Great Park · Long Walk

The Royal Windsor Wheel

Changing of the Guard · Savill Building

This old town grew up beneath the walls of the castle in a compact group of streets leading from the main entrance. Charming and full of character, this is a place of delightful timber-framed and Georgian houses and shop fronts, with riverside walks beside the Thames, and a wonderful racecourse. The elegant **Guildhall**, partly built by Wren in the 17th century, has an open ground floor for market stalls, while the council chambers are on the first floor. Concerned that they might fall through the floor on to the stalls below, the council members requested that Wren put in supporting pillars in the middle of the market hall. As his reassurances that the building was sound fell on deaf ears, Wren complied with their wishes but the pillars he built did not quite meet the ceiling – thereby proving his point!

Windsor Castle

A regular and magnificent spectacle that takes place at 11am Monday to Saturday in the summer months, weather permitting, is the **Changing of the Guard**. The correct term for the ceremony is actually Guard Mounting, when the new guard exchanges duty with the old guard. The Guard is provided by the resident regiment of Foot Guards in their full-dress uniform of red tunics and bearskins. They march up to and from the Castle accompanied by the Guards Band playing traditional military marches as well as popular songs.

The greatest attraction here is, of course, **Windsor Castle**, one of three official residences of the Queen (the others are Buckingham Palace and Holyrood House in Edinburgh). The largest castle in the country, and a royal residence for over 900 years, it was begun in the late 11th century by William the Conqueror as one in a chain of such defences that stood on the approaches to London. Over the years its role changed from a fortification to a royal palace; various monarchs added to the original typical Norman castle, the most notable additions being made by Henry VIII, Charles II and George IV. Various parts of the castle are open to the public, in particular the state apartments with their remarkable collection of furniture, porcelain and armour. Carvings by Grinling Gibbons are to be seen everywhere, and the walls are adorned with a plethora of masterpieces, including paintings by Van Dyck and Rembrandt. The Gallery shows changing displays from the Royal Library, including works by Leonardo, Michelangelo and Holbein. On a somewhat smaller scale, but nonetheless impressive, is Queen Mary's Dolls' House. Designed by Sir Edwin Lutyens for Queen Mary, this is a perfect miniature palace, complete with working lifts and lights and running water. Built on a 1-to-12 scale, it took three years to complete, and 1500 craftsmen were employed to ensure that every last detail was correct; the house was presented to the Queen in 1924.

In November 1992, a massive fire swept through the northeast corner of the castle and no-one in the country at the time will forget the incredible pictures of the great tower alight. Following five years of restoration, the damaged areas were re-opened to the public.

Within the castle walls is the magnificent **St George's Chapel**. Started by Edward IV in 1478, and taking some 50 years to finish, the chapel is not only one of the country's greatest religious buildings, but also a wonderful example of the Perpendicular Gothic style. It is the last resting place of 10 monarchs, from Edward IV himself to Henry VIII with his favourite wife Jane Seymour, Charles I, George V with Queen Mary, and George VI, beside whom the ashes of his beloved daughter Princess Margaret were laid in February 2002 and the body of his wife, the Queen Mother, in April 2002. It is also the Chapel of the Most Noble Order of the Garter, Britain's highest order of chivalry.

Frogmore House, a modest early 18th-century manor house in Home Park, has over the years acted as a second, more relaxed royal residence than the nearby castle. It was bought in 1792 for Queen Charlotte, consort of George III, and later became a favourite retreat of Queen Victoria, who remarked that

Frogmore House, Windsor

"all is peace and quiet and you only hear the hum of the bees, the singing of the birds". She and Prince Albert built a mausoleum in the grounds to house the remains of the Queen's mother, the Duchess of Kent, and their own – both Victoria and Albert are at rest here. The former library now contains furniture and paintings from the Royal Yacht *Britannia*. The house is surrounded by 30 acres of picturesque gardens containing masses of spring bulbs and some fine specimen trees.

To the south of the town stretches the 4800-acre **Windsor Great Park**, a remnant of the once extensive Royal Hunting Forest, and a unique area of open parkland, woodland, and impressive views. Within the park, at Englefield Green, is the **Savill Garden**, created by Sir Eric Savill when he was Deputy Ranger, and one of the finest woodland gardens to be seen anywhere. A garden for all seasons, its attractions include colourful flowerbeds, secret glades, alpine meadows and a unique temperate house. The gateway to the garden is the iconic **Savill Building**. Inspired by the shape of a leaf, the building's roof has a gold award-winning grid shell design and was created from sustainable resources from the forests within Windsor Great Park. The building contains a visitor centre, shopping, a boutique plant centre and a terraced restaurant.

The **Long Walk** stretches from the Castle to Snow Hill, some three miles away, on top of which stands a huge bronze of George III on horseback, erected there in 1831. The three-mile ride to nearby Ascot racecourse was created by Queen Anne in the early 1700s. On the park's southern side lies **Smith's Lawn**, where polo matches are played most summer weekends. Windsor Great Park is also the setting for the Cartier International competition, polo's highlight event held every July, and the National Carriage Driving Championships.

To the southwest, set in 150 acres of parkland, is **Legoland Windsor**, where a whole range of amazing Lego models is on display, made from over 20 million bricks. Designed for children aged 3 to 12 – and their families – the site also offers more than 50 rides, shows and attractions including a 3-D cinema and – new in 2010 – a Pirate Training Camp.

In a pleasant setting close to the River Thames, **Royal Windsor Racecourse** is one of the most attractive in the country. Though less grand than neighbouring Ascot, its Monday evening meetings always bring a good crowd, but many regret the decision to give up the jumping fixtures.

From May to the end of August, the town is graced with the **Royal Windsor Wheel**, a smaller brother of the London Eye. Weighing 365 tonnes and 50 metres high, the Wheel provides a spectacular 360 degree view of the surrounding area. There are 40 capsules seating up to six adults and two children, and the ride lasts approximately 12 minutes.

Around Windsor

ASCOT

6 miles SW of Windsor on the A329

Racecourse · Englemere Pond

A small village until 1711 when Queen Anne moved the Windsor race meeting to here and founded the world famous **Ascot Racecourse**. Its future was secured when the Duke of Cumberland established a stud at Windsor in the 1750s and, by the end of the century, the meetings were being attended by royalty on a regular basis. Today, Royal Ascot, held every June, is an international occasion of fashion and style with pageantry and tradition, and the very best flat-racing spread over five days.

To the west of the town is **Englemere Pond**, a Site of Special Scientific Interest and also a local nature reserve. Once part of the royal hunting ground, which surrounded Windsor Castle and is still owned by the Crown Estate, the main feature is the shallow acidic lake, which offers a wide range of habitats from open water to marsh, for the many species of plants, birds, animals and insects found here.

Ascot Racecourse

BRACKNELL

7 miles SW of Windsor on the A329

Windsor Forest Look Out Discovery Centre

Designated a new town in 1948, Bracknell has developed quickly from a small village in poor sandy heathland, with some 3000 inhabitants, into a large modern town of around 60,000 residents. It boasts one of the first purpose-built shopping centres in the country – opened in the 1960s. The centrally located Bill Hill is a very prominent landmark, seen from many parts of the town. At the top of the hill., a circular mound of earth is visible, hollowed out at the centre, which is all that remains of a Bronze Age round barrow. Used throughout that period, these burial mounds, which may cover either individuals or groups, are the most common prehistoric monuments in the country.

What remains of the great royal hunting ground, **Windsor Forest** (also called Bracknell Forest) lies to the south of the town and has more than 30 parks and nature reserves and some 45 miles of footpaths and bridleways. Of particular interest in the area is the **Look Out Discovery Centre**, an interactive science centre that brings to life the mysteries of both science and nature. In the surrounding 1600 hectares of Crown Estate woodland there are nature trails and walks to points of interest, as well as the inappropriately named Caesar's Camp. Not a Roman fort, this camp is an Iron Age hill fort built more than 2000 years ago although, close by, runs the Roman link road between London and Silchester. Known locally as the Devil's Highway, it is said to have acquired the name because the local inhabitants thought that only the Devil could have undertaken such a prodigious feat of engineering.

TWYFORD

10 miles W of Windsor on the A4

At Twyford, the River Loddon divides into two separate streams from which the town takes its name – double ford. With its watery location, it's not surprising that there have been several mills here. A miller is mentioned in a document of 1163, although the first mill is dated 1363. There was a silk mill here until 1845, and a flour mill until 1976 when it was destroyed by fire. The replacement modern mill lacks the traditional appeal, but it does continue the milling tradition in the town.

BINFIELD

8 miles SW of Windsor on the B3034

Pope's Wood

Binfield is famous as the boyhood home of the poet Alexander Pope. The family moved here after his father had amassed a fortune as a linen draper, and the boy Pope sang in the local choir and gained a local following for his poems about the Windsor Forest and the River Loddon. To the south of the village is **Pope's Wood**, where the poet is said to have sought inspiration. Other connections include the artist John Constable, who sketched the parish church while here on his honeymoon, and Norah Wilmot, who was one of the first lady racehorse trainers to be allowed to hold a licence in her own name, having been forced to train for years in the name of her head lad. The Jockey Club abandoned this archaic ruling as recently as 1966.

WARGRAVE

10 miles W of Windsor on the A321

Hannen Mausoleum Druids' Temple

This charming village developed as a settlement in the 10th century at the confluence of the Rivers Thames and Loddon on an area of flat land in a wooded valley. The peace that generally prevails here was disturbed in 1914 when suffragettes burnt down the church in protest at the vicar's refusal to remove the word obey from the marriage service. In the churchyard, undisturbed by the riot or anything since, stands the **Hannen Mausoleum**, a splendid monument that was designed for the Hannen family by Sir Edwin Lutyens in 1906.

Another interesting sight can be found on the outskirts of the village, at Park Place. In 1788 the estate was owned by General Henry Conway, Governor of Jersey. In recognition of his services, the people of the island gave the general a complete **Druids' Temple**. The massive stones were transported from St Helier to the estate and erected in a 25-foot circle in the gardens of his mansion. In 1870, Park Place was destroyed by fire and the estate broken up, but today the temple stands in the garden of Temple Combe, close to a house designed by the famed American architect, Frank Lloyd Wright. The only house of his in this country, it was built in 1958 to an elaborate U-shaped design; its many unusual features include suede-panelled interior walls.

SANDHURST

11 miles SW of Windsor on the A3095

Royal Military Academy Staff College Museum

Trilakes

The town is famous as being the home of the **Royal Military Academy**, the training place for army officers since it was established in 1907. The academy's **Staff College Museum** tells the history of officer training from its inception to the present day. Close by is **Trilakes**, a picturesque country park set in 18 acres with, of course, some lakes. This is a wonderful place to visit with children as there are a wide assortment of pets and farm animals that they can get to know, including miniature horses, pygmy goats, donkeys, aviary birds, pot-bellied pigs and Soay sheep.

DORNEY

2 miles NW of Windsor off the A308

Dorney Court Church of St Mary Magdalene

One of the finest Tudor manor houses in England, **Dorney Court**, just a short walk from the River Thames, has been the home of the Palmer family since 1530. Built in about 1440, it is an enchanting building, which also houses some real treasures, including early 15th and 16th-century oak furniture, beautiful 17th-century lacquer furniture, and 400 years of family portraits. It is here in 1665 that the first pineapple in England was grown.

On **Dorney Common** is the village of **Boveney**, which served as a wharf in the 13th century when timber was being transported from Windsor Forest. The flint and clapboard church of **St Mary Magdalene**, down by the riverside, was the setting for several scenes in Kevin Costner's film *Robin Hood, Prince of Thieves.*

BRAY

5 miles NW of Windsor on the B4447

Vicar of Bray

A pleasant riverside town, Bray has a good mix of attractive houses and period cottages from various centuries surrounding the Church of St Michael. The **Vicar of Bray**, celebrated in Goldsmith's famous poem, was a real person, the Rev.d Simon Alwyn. As the church fluctuated between dogmatic Protestantism and doctrinaire Catholicism, the Reverend's flexible principles allowed him to keep his post through the reigns of Henry VIII, Edward VI,

Maidenhead Clock Tower

Mary and Elizabeth I. He is buried in the churchyard here and a plaque in the Hinds Head Hotel tells the full story. In recent years, Bray has established itself as a gourmet's seventh heaven. It now boasts two of Heston Blumenthal's restaurants, The Fat Duck and The Hinds Head, as well as the famous French restaurant, The Waterside Inn.

MAIDENHEAD

7 miles NW of Windsor on the A4130

Brunel's Rail Bridge · Boulter's Lock · Maidenhead Commons and Cock Marsh

Transport has played a major role down the years in the history of Maidenhead, first with Thames traffic, then as a stop on the London-Bath coaching route, and finally with the coming of the railway, which helped to turn the town into a fashionable Victorian resort. The Maidenhead **Rail Bridge** was built by Isambard Kingdom Brunel in 1839 to carry his Great Western Railway over the Thames. The bridge, which comprises the widest, flattest brick arches in the world, was hailed at the time as the pinnacle of engineering achievement and has been immortalised in Turner's incredibly exciting and atmospheric painting *Rain, Steam and Speed.*

Boulter's Lock, one of the biggest on the Thames, takes its name from an old word for a miller. A flour mill has stood on Boulter's Island since Roman times. The island was also the home of Richard Dimbleby, the eminent broadcaster and father of the famous broadcasters David and Jonathan. To the north and west of the town, **Maidenhead Commons** and **Cock Marsh** contain a variety of habitats, including woodland, scrub thickets, grassland, ponds and riverside. Both are popular with walkers and nature-lovers: Cock Marsh is an important site for breeding waders, and both sites are rich in flora and invertebrate fauna.

COOKHAM

9 miles NW of Windsor on the A4094

Cookham Woods · Stanley Spencer Gallery

This pretty, small town, on the banks of the River Thames, has been fortunate in being protected by **Cookham Woods** (National Trust) from becoming a suburb of Maidenhead and still has a distinctive character of its own. The town was made famous by the artist Sir Stanley Spencer, who used Cookham as the setting for many of his paintings. He was born here in 1891 and was buried here on his death in 1959. The town's tribute to its most renowned resident is the **Stanley Spencer Gallery** (see panel on page 44), a permanent exhibition of his work, which is housed in the converted Victorian chapel Stanley visited as a child. His painting, *Resurrection,* which depicts recognisable locals

The Stanley Spencer Gallery

The Kings Hall, High Street, Cookham, Berkshire SL6 9SJ
Tel: 01628-471885
e-mail: info@stanleyspencer.org.uk
website: www.stanleyspencer.org.uk

The Stanley Spencer Gallery is unique as the only gallery in Britain devoted exclusively to an artist in the village where he was born and spent much of his life. To Spencer (1891-1959), Cookham and its surrounding area was the scene of heavenly visitations. Set in the heart of the village he immortalised, the gallery occupies the former Victorian Methodist Chapel where Spencer was taken to worship as a child. It contains a permanent collection of his work, together with letters, documents, memorabilia, and the pram in which Spencer wheeled his equipment when painting landscapes. It also displays important works on long-term loan, and mounts a winter and summer exhibition each year. Over a thousand works have been shown since the gallery opened in 1962.

Fern Lea the artist's birthplace is in Cookham High Street. The village remained a source of inspiration throughout his life and formed the setting for numerous biblical and figure paintings, as well as landscapes. The parish church, the High Street, Cookham Moor and the river are all recognisable from his pictures. Documents include the Chute Letters, written by Spencer to Desmond Chute during the First World War.

emerging from the graves in Cookham churchyard, caused some residents to protest when it was first exhibited in the 1930s. The Gallery is open seven days a week in the summer, Thursday to Sunday in winter. Call 01628 471 885.

BISHAM

11 miles NW of Windsor off the A404

"Breathing the very spirit of sweet peace", Bisham Abbey occupies a superb position with its churchyard sloping down to the Thames. The major attractions inside are the three sumptuous tombs of the Hoby family dating back to the late 16th and early 17th centuries. The most impressive is dedicated to Elizabeth, Lady Hoby, and shows her gorgeously attired in widow's weeds attended by her equally splendidly-dressed six children. At her feet lies the recumbent figure of a small boy. An enduring story claims that Lady Elizabeth beat the child to death for smudging his copy book.

Despite its name, Bisham was never inhabited by monks, but was built for the Knights Templar in 1338.

ETON

1 mile N of Windsor on the A355

Eton College

Just across the River Thames from Windsor, this town has grown up around **Eton College**, the famous public school that was founded in 1440 by Henry VI. Originally intended for 70 poor and worthy scholars, and to educate students for the newly created King's College., at Cambridge University, the college has been added to greatly over the years. Of the original school buildings, only the College Hall and the kitchen have survived; the great gatehouse and Lupton's Tower were added in the 16th century, and the

Alexandra Gardens, Eton

Upper School dates from around 1690. Guided tours of the college are available.

The school has kept many ancient traditions over the years, including the black tail mourning coats that were originally worn on the death of George III in 1820 and which are still worn today. For centuries the college has educated the great and the good, among them William Pitt the Elder, Harold Macmillan, Thomas Gray (author of *Elegy Written in a Country Churchyard*), Henry Fielding, Shelley, George Orwell, Ian Fleming and the Princes William and Harry. Eton has also been famous in the past for its strict discipline, personified in 1832 by a master who told the pupils when they rebelled: "Boys, you must be pure of heart, for if not, I will thrash you until you are."

SLOUGH

3 miles N of Windsor on the A355

Church of St Mary Museum

A small settlement until the creation of a trading estate in 1920, Slough then grew rapidly from around 7000 to 100,000. The area does have a long history, however, and a visit to **Slough Museum** makes for an interesting hour or two delving into the past. Slough has a lovely surprise in the shape of one of the most splendid churches in the county. The **Church of St Mary** is a real gem, notable particularly for the private family pew of the Kedermisters, totally screened from the main part of the church, and a library filled with painted panels.

In the Church of St Laurence at Upton, on the outskirts of Slough, is the grave of the astronomer Sir William Herschel (1738–1822) and a stained-glass window in his honour.

DATCHET

2 miles E of Windsor on the B470

Just across the river from Windsor Castle's Home Park, Datchet has a spacious green and some attractive riverside houses. The town featured in Shakespeare's *Merry Wives of Windsor* when Falstaff, concealed in a laundry basket, is brought here for his "Datchet mead" – ie a ducking in the river.

RUNNYMEDE

3 miles SE of Windsor off the A308

It was here in 1215, in a peaceful riverside meadow, that King John reluctantly placed his seal on Magna Carta, thereby establishing the principle of constitutional monarchy and the individual's right to liberty and justice. Despite the charter's importance, no memorial was placed here until the American Bar Association erected one in 1957.

Nearby, on an acre of ground given to the United States by the Queen, stands a memorial erected in 1965 in memory of President John F Kennedy. Officially opened by the Queen in the presence of JFK's widow and children, it includes an extract from the President's inaugural address. Higher up the hill is another memorial, erected in 1953 as a tribute to the 20,455 members of the Air Forces of the British Commonwealth who have no known grave. From this tranquil spot there are magnificent views across the Thames Valley.

LOCATOR MAP

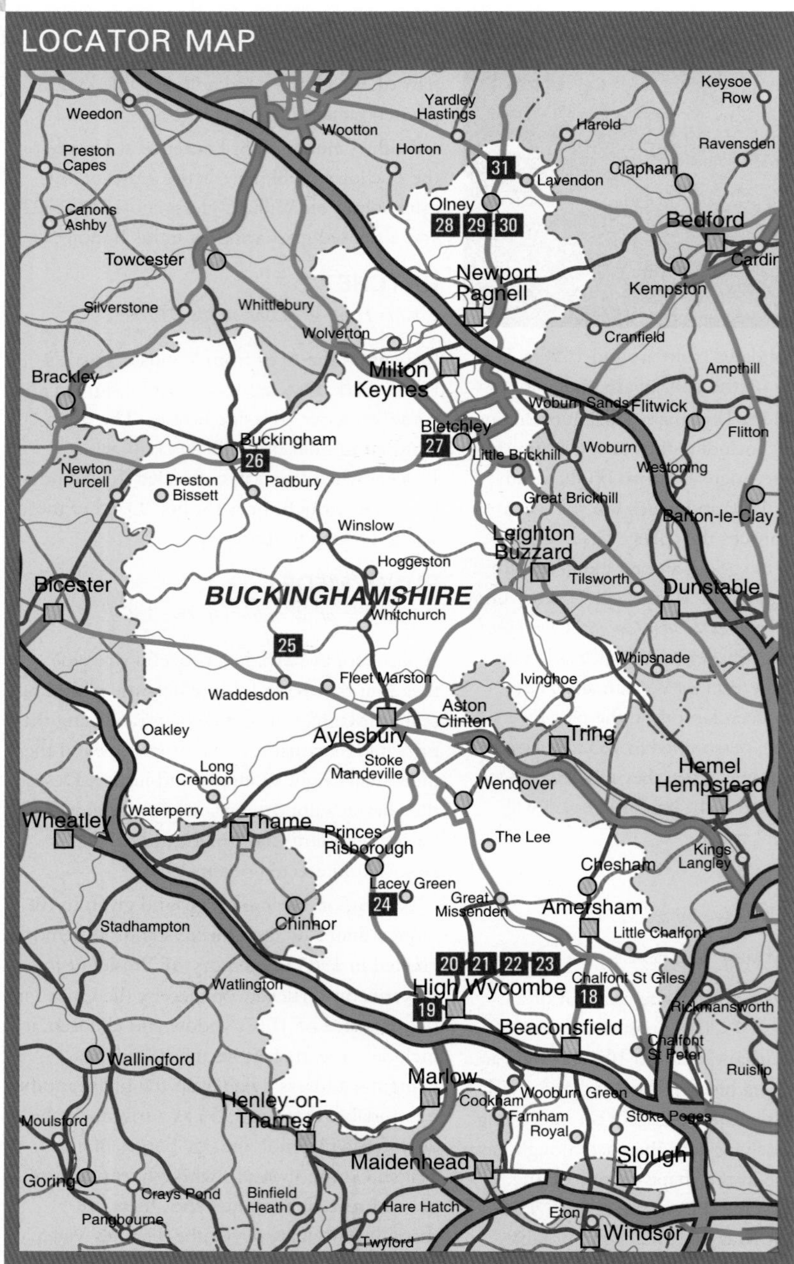

historic building · museum and heritage · historic site · scenic attraction · flora and fauna

3 | Buckinghamshire

Devotees of the ITV drama series *Midsomer Murders* will already have a good idea of what Buckinghamshire looks like – all the major outdoor locations lie within the county with the impossibly picturesque villages of Quainton, Waddesdon and Long Crendon featuring frequently.

The south of the county, with the River Thames as its southern boundary, lies almost entirely within the chalk range of the Chiltern Hills, most of which is classed as an Area of Outstanding Natural Beauty. The county town since the 18th century has been Aylesbury, the market centre for the attractive Vale of Aylesbury, which runs from the Chilterns in the south to Buckingham in the north. Here, the visitor will discover a rural patchwork of secluded countryside, woodland and valleys, waterways, charming villages and busy market towns. A thousand miles of footpaths include the ancient Ridgeway, and the quiet country lanes and gentle undulations make cycling a real pleasure; the Vale is at the heart of the new National Cycle Network. The area around the former county town of Buckingham is perhaps the least discovered part of Buckinghamshire, still chiefly rural, with a wealth of attractive villages and a number of fine houses, including Ascott House, a former Rothschild residence; Claydon House, where Florence Nightingale was a frequent visitor; Winslow Hall, designed by Wren; and Stowe, with its marvellous deer park. In this area are also two outstanding churches, the Saxon Church of All Saints at Wing and St Michael's Church at Stewkley, one of the finest Norman churches in the whole country. The northern region of the county is dominated by the new town of Milton Keynes, developed in the 1960s but incorporating several much older villages.

ADVERTISERS AND PLACES OF INTEREST

Chalfont St Giles

Chiltern Open Air Museum   Milton's Cottage

Among the various ancient buildings of interest in this archetypal English village there is an Elizabethan mansion, The Vache, which was the home of friends of Captain Cook. In the grounds is a monument to the famous seafarer. However, by far the most famous building in Chalfont St Giles is **Milton's Cottage**. John Milton moved to this 16th-century cottage, found for him by his former pupil Thomas Ellwood, in 1665 to escape the plague in London. Though Milton moved back to London in 1666, he wrote *Paradise Lost* and began work on its sequel, *Paradise Regained*, while taking refuge in the village. The only house lived in by the poet to have survived, the cottage and its garden have been preserved as they were at the time Milton was resident. The building is now home to a museum that includes collections of important first editions of Milton's works and a portrait of the poet by Sir Godfrey Kneller.

Another fascinating and unusual place to visit in the village is the **Chiltern Open Air Museum** (see panel opposite), which rescues buildings of historic or architectural importance due to be demolished from across the Chilterns region and re-erects them on its 45-acre site. The 30-odd buildings rescued by the museum are used to house and display artefacts and implements that are appropriate to the building's original use and history. Also on the museum site is a series of fields farmed using medieval methods where, among the historic crops, organic woad is grown, from which indigo dye is extracted for use in dyeing demonstrations.

Madame Tussaud, famous for her exhibitions in London, started her waxworks here in the village, and another well-known resident was Bertram Mills the circus owner. His tomb stands beside the war memorial in the churchyard of St Giles.

Milton's House, Chalfont St Giles

Around Chalfont St Giles

JORDANS

1 mile S of Chalfont St Giles off the A40

This secluded village, reached down a quiet country lane, is famous as the burial place of William Penn, Quaker and founder of Pennsylvania. He and members of his family are buried in the graveyard outside the Quaker meeting house, which is among the earliest to be found in the country and has been described as the Quaker Westminster Abbey. In the grounds of nearby Old Jordans Farm is the **Mayflower Barn**, said to have been constructed from the timbers of the ship that took the Pilgrim Fathers to America.

Chiltern Open Air Museum

Newland Park, Gorelands Lane, Chalfont St. Giles, Buckinghamshire HP8 4AB
Tel: 01494 871117
web site: www.coam.org.uk

Visit **Chiltern Open Air Museum** in the parish of Chalfont St Peter, explore more than 30 rescued historic buildings and roam through 45 acres of beautiful woods and parkland.

Don't miss the chance to stroll along the woodland walk and relax at Wood End Cafe, where you can purchase light refreshments. The Museum organises a wide range of hands-on activities, demonstrations and special events for all the family to enjoy throughout the season. During the school holidays there are a series of themed weeks, special activities and demonstrations that focus on one aspect of the history of the buildings.

CHALFONT ST PETER

2 miles S of Chalfont St Giles on the A413

Hawk & Owl Trust

Now a commuter town, Chalfont St Peter dates back to the 7th century and, as its name means 'the spring where the calves come to drink', there is a long history here of raising cattle in the surrounding lush meadows. First mentioned in 1133, the parish Church of St Peter was all but destroyed when its steeple collapsed in 1708. The building seen today dates from that time as it was rebuilt immediately after the disaster.

Housed in a barn at Skippings Farm is the **Hawk and Owl Trust's National Education and Exhibition Centre**. Dedicated to conserving wild birds of prey in their natural habitats, the Trust concerns itself with practical research, creative conservation and imaginative educational programmes.

Stoke Park, Stoke Poges

STOKE POGES

6 miles S of Chalfont St Giles off the A355

Gray Monument

The ploughman homeward plods his weary way
And leaves the world to darkness and to me.

It was in the churchyard of this surprisingly still rural village that Thomas Gray was inspired to pen his *Elegy Written in a Country Churchyard.* He often visited Stoke Poges to see his mother and aunt who lived in a large late-Georgian house built for the grandson of the famous Quaker, William Penn, and he was seated beside his mother's tomb when he wrote the classic poem. The house is now the clubhouse of Stoke Poges Golf Club, where James Bond met Auric Goldfinger in the film *Goldfinger.* The statues seen in the film – one of them beheaded by Oddjob's bowler hat – are still there. To the east of the church is the imposing **Gray Monument**, designed by James Wyatt and erected in 1799. The Church of St Giles itself is very handsome and dates from the 13th century, but perhaps its most interesting feature is the unusual medieval bicycle depicted in one of the stained glass windows. Dating back to the 1600s, the window depicts a naked man with a horn astride a vintage hobby horse. Behind the church is an Elizabethan manor house where Elizabeth I was entertained and Charles I was imprisoned.

BEACONSFIELD

3 miles SW of Chalfont St Giles on the A40

Bekonscot · Odds Farm Park

This is very much a town in two parts: the old town, dating back to medieval times; and, to the north, the new town, which grew up following the construction of the Metropolitan line into central London and consisting chiefly of between-the-wars housing. The old town is best known for its wealth of literary connections. The poet and orator Edmund Waller was born in the nearby village of Coleshill in 1606 and had his family home just outside Beaconsfield. His best-known lines are perhaps the patriotic

Others may use the ocean as their road
Only the English make it their abode.

Waller's tomb in the churchyard of St Mary and All Saints is marked by a very tall, sharply pointed obelisk with a tribute from fellow poet John Dryden. The church itself is one of the finest in the county and contains the grave of the statesman and political theorist Edmund Burke (1729–1797). Beaconsfield was also the home of the writer of the *Father Brown* books GK Chesterton (his grave is in the nearby Catholic church), the poet Robert Frost and the much loved children's author Enid Blyton.

For a unique step back in time to the 1930s, or for anyone wanting to feel like Gulliver in Lilliput, a trip to the model village of **Bekonscot** is a must. The oldest model village in the world, Bekonscot was begun in the 1920s by Roland Callingham, a London accountant, who started by building models in his garden. As the number grew, Callingham purchased more land and, with the aid of a friend from Ascot who added a model railway, created the village seen today. Within the 1½-acre site are six distinct miniature villages. When the model village first opened, people would throw coins into buckets for charity; the tradition continues and, even today, all surplus profits go to charity. Enid Blyton's house Green Hedges is depicted in Bekonscot, and she wrote a story about two children who visit the model village. Call: 01494 672919.

South of Beaconsfield, on the other side of the M40 at Wooburn Common, an entertaining day out is guaranteed at **Odds Farm Park**, home to many rare and interesting animals. The park was created with children in mind and the regular events include pigs' tea time, pat-a-

Bekonscot Model Village, Beaconsfield

pet, bottle-feeding lambs and goat milking. As one of 20 approved rare breed centres in the country, the farm combines the family attractions with the breeding and conservation of many of Britain's rarest farm animals. Open from 10am all year round.

Cliveden, Taplow

BURNHAM BEECHES

5 miles SW of Chalfont St Giles off the A355

A stretch of land bought in 1880 by the Corporation of the City of London for use in perpetuity by the public, and since then a favourite place for Londoners to relax. Burnham Beeches was designated a National Nature Reserve in 1993 and this extensive area of ancient woodland and heathland includes an important collection of old beeches and pollarded oaks.

TAPLOW

8 miles SW of Chalfont St Giles off the A4

Cliveden Octagonal Temple

The name of Taplow is derived from Taeppa, a Saxon warrior whose grand burial site high above the Thames was excavated in 1883. Nothing is known of Taeppa himself, but the items discovered at the site are on display in the British Museum. To the north of the village lies the country house of **Cliveden** (National Trust), once the home of Lady Nancy Astor, the first woman to take her seat as a Member of Parliament. The first house on the site was built in 1666 for the Duke of Buckingham, but the present magnificent mansion, most of which is now a hotel, dates from the 19th century. It was in 1740 that *Rule Britannia* was first performed, in the presence of Frederick, Prince of Wales. Thomas Arne set to music words written by James Thomson. The splendid grounds include a great formal parterre with fountains, temples and statuary, a water garden and a wonderful rose garden. Some of the great names in architecture and garden design had a hand in the Cliveden of today: the house and terrace are the work of Sir Charles Barry, the rose garden was designed by Sir Geoffrey Jellicoe, and the renowned Italian country house architect Giacomo Leoni was responsible for the **Octagonal Temple**, now a chapel, where the American-born millionaire William Waldorf Astor, his son Waldorf and the ashes of Waldorf's wife Nancy are buried.

PENN

4 miles NW of Chalfont St Giles on the B474

A centre of the tiling industry after the Norman Conquest, Penn provided the flooring for Windsor Castle, the Palace of Westminster and many churches. But the village is best known as the ancestral home of William Penn, the Quaker and American pioneer. There are several memorials to the family in the village church of the Holy Trinity. In the churchyard is the grave of the diplomat spy Donald Maclean, who died in Moscow in 1983. His ashes, contained in an urn decorated with a hammer and sickle, were brought back to England by his brother and buried in the family grave.

AMERSHAM

3 miles N of Chalfont St Giles on the A413

Museum

Another town with a split personality. Top Amersham is a thriving commercial centre; Old Amersham is a popular tourist spot with a wide sweeping High Street, half-timbered buildings and picturesque period cottages. Set beside the River Misbourne, the Old Town boasts many fine old buildings, including Sir William Drake's Market Hall of 1682 and the Church of St Mary with some fine stained glass and monuments to the Drake family. The Old Town is well known for its shopping – there's a wide selection of antique and craft shops, designer boutiques, and an impressive range of restaurants, snack bars and coaching inns.

The Romans were farming around Amersham in the 3rd and 4th centuries, the Saxons called it Agmodesham and to the Normans it was Elmondesham. So the town has plenty of history, much of which is told in the **Amersham Museum**, which occupies a Tudor timber-framed building, Hall House, which is more than 500 years old. In 2009 the museum acquired a long-case clock made by Joseph Rogers of Amersham.

The town was an important staging post in coaching days, and The Crown Hotel, one of many coaching inns here, was featured in the film *Four Weddings and a Funeral.* Close to the town is Gore Hill, the site of a battle between the Danes and the Saxons in AD921. It is recorded that in 1666 the Great Fire of London could be seen raging from the hill.

CHENIES

3 miles E of Amersham off the A404

Chenies Manor

This picturesque village, with a pretty green surrounded by an old school, a chapel and a 15th-century parish church, is also home to **Chenies Manor**, a fascinating 15th-century manor house. Originally the home of the Earls (later Dukes) of Bedford, before they moved to Woburn, this attractive building has stepped gables and elaborately patterned high brick chimneys. Built by the architect who enlarged Hampton Court for Henry VIII, the house played host not only to the king, but also to his daughter Elizabeth I, whose favourite oak tree still stands in the garden. Naturally, there is a ghost here, that of none other than Henry, whose footsteps can be heard as he drags his ulcerated leg around the manor house in an attempt to catch Catherine Howard in the act of adultery with one of his entourage, Tom Culpeper. The house has much to offer, including tapestries, furniture

Chenies Manor House

and a collection of antique dolls. The elaborate gardens contain a Tudor-style sunken garden, some fine topiary, a turf maze, a kitchen garden and a physic garden with a variety of herbs that were used for both medicinal and culinary purposes.

Little Market House, High Wycombe

High Wycombe

Little Market House Museum

The largest town in Buckinghamshire, High Wycombe is traditionally known for the manufacture of chairs and, in particular, the famous Windsor design. It is still a centre of furniture manufacture today, as well as being a pleasant town in which to live for those commuting to London. Originally an old Chilterns Gap market town, High Wycombe still has several old buildings of note. The **Little Market House** was designed by Robert Adams in 1761 and is of a rather curious octagonal shape, while the 18th-century Guildhall is the annual venue for a traditional ceremony showing a healthy scepticism for politicians when the mayor and councillors are publicly weighed – to see if they have become fat at the expense of the citizens.

Located in an 18th-century house with a flint facade, the **Wycombe Museum** has displays that give the visitor an excellent idea of the work and crafts of the local people over the years. There is, of course, a superb collection of chairs, including the famous Windsor chair. Several skills and several woods were involved in the making of this classic chair: bodgers used the ubiquitous beech for the legs; benders shaped ash for the bowed backs; and bottomers made use of the sturdy elm for the seats.

In the landscaped grounds of the museum is a medieval motte, which would normally indicate that a castle once stood here but, in this case, the structure was probably little more than a wooden tower. The oldest standing building in the town is All Saints Church, a large, fine building dating from the 11th century.

Around High Wycombe

MARLOW

4 miles S of High Wycombe on the A4155

An attractive commuter town on the banks of the Thames, Marlow is famous for its suspension bridge built in 1832 to the design of Tierney Clarke, who built a similar bridge linking Buda and Pest across the Danube. The High Street is lined with elegant houses, and Marlow has a good supply of riverside pubs. In one of them, The Two Brewers, Jerome K Jerome wrote his masterpiece, *Three Men in a Boat*. Other literary connections abound: Mary Shelley completed *Frankenstein* while living here after her marriage to the poet Percy Bysshe Shelley, and TS Eliot lived for a while in West Street, as did the author Thomas Love Peacock while writing *Nightmare Abbey*. Marlow hosts an annual regatta and is one of the places the Swan Uppers visit each year counting and marking the swans belonging to the Queen and to two London Livery Companies.

BOURNE END

4 miles SE of High Wycombe on the A4155

A prosperous commuter town on the banks of the Thames, Bourne End began to expand in the late 19th century as the Victorians developed a passion for boating on the river. It was once the home of the writer Edgar Wallace, who died in Hollywood during work on the screenplay for *King Kong*. He is buried in the village cemetery at nearby Little Marlow.

HAMBLEDEN

6 miles SW of High Wycombe off the A4155

Church of St Mary

This much-filmed village was given to the National Trust by the family of the bookseller WH Smith, who later became Viscount Hambleden. He lived close by at Greenlands, on the banks of the River Thames, and is buried in the village churchyard. The unusually large **Church of St Mary**, known as the Cathedral of the Chilterns, dates from the 14th century and, though it has been altered over the years, it still dominates the area with its size and beauty. Inside the building's 18th-century tower is a fascinating 16th-century panel, which is believed to have been the bedhead of Cardinal Wolsey – it certainly bears the cardinal's hat and the Wolsey arms.

WEST WYCOMBE

2 miles NW of High Wycombe on the A40

West Wycombe Park & Caves

Church of St Lawrence

Dashwood Mausoleum

This charming estate village, where many of the houses are owned by the National Trust, has a main street displaying architecture from the 15th through to the 19th century. Close by is **West Wycombe Park**, which, although owned by the National Trust, is still the home of the Dashwood family, local landowners who built it in the 1760s. The magnificent house has appeared in several film and TV productions, including BBC-TV's 2008 production of *Cranford*.

Of the various members of the Dashwood family, it was Sir Francis who had most influence on both the house and the village. West Wycombe house was originally built in the early 1700s, but Sir Francis boldly remodelled it several years later as well as having the grounds and park landscaped by Thomas Cook, a pupil of Capability Brown. Very much a classical landscape, the grounds contain temples and an artificial lake shaped like a swan, and the house

West Wycombe Park

The Hell-Fire Caves

West Wycombe Caves, High Wycombe, Buckinghamshire HP14 3AJ
Tel: 01494 533739
website: www.hellfirecaves.co.uk

The **Hell-Fire Caves** at West Wycombe offer a totally unique experience. The Caves are owned by Sir Edward Dashwood, a direct descendent of Sir Francis Dashwood, who originally excavated them in the 1750's on the site of an ancient quarry. Throughout the 1700's and 1800's, the caves, which are quarter of a mile underground, were reputed to have hosted the Hell-Fire Club whose membership included some of Britain's most senior aristocrats and statesmen.

Today, the caves are a popular tourist attraction and a wonderful insight into our history. A tour of the caves includes a long winding passage that leads past various small chambers to the Banqueting Hall, down over the River Styx to the Inner Temple, which is about 300 feet beneath the church at the top of the hill. The Caves are scattered with statues in costume and a commentary with sound effects are included throughout the tour.

has a good collection of tapestries, furniture and paintings.

Hewn out of a nearby hillside are **West Wycombe Caves** (Hell-Fire Caves – see panel above), which were created, possibly from some existing caverns, by Sir Francis as part of a programme of public works. After a series of failed harvests, which created great poverty and distress amongst the estate workers and tenant farmers, Sir Francis employed the men to extract chalk from the hillside to be used in the construction of the new road between the village and High Wycombe.

The village **Church of St Lawrence** is yet another example of Sir Francis' enthusiasm for remodelling old buildings. Situated within the remnants of an Iron Age fort on top of a steep hill, the church was originally constructed in the 13th century. Its isolated position, however, was not intentional as the church was originally the church of the village of Haveringdon, which has long since disappeared. Dashwood remodelled the interior in the 1760s in the style of an Egyptian hall and also heightened the tower, adding on the top a great golden ball where six people could meet in comfort and seclusion.

The **Dashwood Mausoleum** near the church was built in 1765; a vast hexagonal building without a roof, it is the resting place of Sir Francis and other members of the Dashwood family. Sir Francis had a racier side to his character. As well as being remembered as a great traveller and a successful politician, he was the founder of the Hell-Fire Club. This group of rakes, who were also known as the Brotherhood of Sir Francis or Dashwood's Apostles, met a couple of times a year to engage in highly colourful activities. Though their exploits were legendary, and probably loosely based on fact, they no doubt consumed large quantities of alcohol and enjoyed the company of women. Traditionally, the group meetings were held in the caves, or possibly the church tower, though between 1750 and

PARK PARADE SHOPPING CENTRE

Western Dean, Hazelmere, Buckinghamshire HP15

CARMEN LADIES FASHIONS

Tel: 01494 716555

This ladies fashion clothing store has a range of clothes on offer for ladies of 30 and above, from seasonal general day wear, to evening and cruise wear, from t-shirts to posh frocks. Whatever your style, Carmen Ladies Fashion has it all. Exclusive hand crafted jewellery can be found here, made by a local designer to suit individual tastes, giving it a truly unique look. Suppliers include: Poppy, Fabrizo, Casamia, In Town, Signature, Saloos, Paramount and many more.

THAMESIDE CARPETS AND GIFTS

Tel: 01494 711726 / 01494 714775

Thameside Carpets and Gifts have been offering a friendly and professional service for over thirty years. The business is family owned and offers their own fitting team and installation service for all flooring needs. An impressive range of quality floors is available with wood grain patterns, stone tiles, bathroom, kitchen, hall and landing styles to choose from. The family also stocks an interesting range of clocks, lamps and other items for gifts or to help guests complete the perfect look for their home.

THE CUTTING STUDIO

Tel: 01494 714204

We warmly welcome you to one of Buckinghamshires premier salons. Established over 19 years ago, our reputation is built on fantastic service, brilliant hairdressing, and fabulous value for money. With on going training, all our team specialise in creative hairdressing and client care.

As a way of introduction, we would like to offer you 25% discount off your first visit to us, just call our reservation team.

CHILDS TOYS

Tel: 01494 711425

Alan took over **Child's Toys** in 2004 from one of the country's most reputable toy retailers, continuing a 125 year tradition for quality and fun. Alan offers a friendly and knowledgeable service about all the toys he stocks, which are displayed over the shop's two floors. Children can expect to find all the best brands with various Scalextric, Lego and Mechano sets alongside an adorable range of teddy bears and the largest range of jigsaws and board games in the area. Open Monday to Saturday 9am-5:30pm and on Sundays in the run up to Christmas.

The shopping centre is just 10 minutes from High Wycombe and Beaconsfield with free parking, coffee shops and other retail outlets.

1774, their meeting place was nearby Medmenham Abbey.

HUGHENDEN

2 miles N of High Wycombe off the A4128

Hughenden Manor · Bradenham Woods

This village is famous for being the home of Queen Victoria's favourite Prime Minister, Benjamin Disraeli; he lived here from 1848 until his death in 1881. He bought **Hughenden Manor** (National Trust) shortly after the publication of his novel *Tancred*. Though not a wealthy man, Disraeli felt that a leading Conservative politician should have a stately home of his own. In order to finance the purchase, his supporters lent him the money so that he could have this essential characteristic of an English gentleman. The interior is an excellent example of the Victorian Gothic style and contains an interesting collection of memorabilia of Disraeli's life as well as his library, pictures and much of his furniture. The garden is based on the designs of Disraeli's wife Mary Anne; the surrounding park and woodland offer some beautiful walks. Disraeli, who was MP for Buckinghamshire from 1847 to 1876, and Prime Minister in 1868 and from 1874 to 1880, is buried in the churchyard of St Michael. In the chancel of the church is a marble memorial erected in his memory by Queen Victoria. Disraeli was the son of a writer and literary critic, Isaac d'Israeli, who lived for a time in the village of Bradenham on the other side of High Wycombe. The Bradenham Estate, also owned by the National Trust, includes **Bradenham Woods**, an area of ancient beech that is among the finest in the whole Chilterns region. Although beech predominates, other trees, including oak, whitebeam, ash and wild cherry are being encouraged.

Bradenham Woods, Hughenden

Chesham

A successful combination of a commuter town, industrial centre and country community, Chesham's growth from a sleepy market town was due mainly to its Metropolitan underground railway link with central London. Chesham was the birthplace of Arthur Liberty, the son of a haberdasher and draper, who went on to found the world famous Liberty's department store in London's Regent Street in 1875.

Another resident of note was Roger Crabbe who, having suffered head injuries during the Civil War, was sentenced to death by Cromwell. After receiving a pardon, Crabbe opened a hat shop in the town where he is reputed to have worn sackcloth, eaten turnip tops and given his income to the poor. Perhaps not surprisingly, Crabbe was used by Lewis Carroll as the model for the Mad Hatter in *Alice in Wonderland*.

Around Chesham

LACEY GREEN

8 miles W of Chesham off the A4010

Smock Mill Home of Rest for Horses

Rupert Brooke

Lacey Green is home to one of the county's preserved windmills, this one a **Smock Mill**, in which only the cap carrying the sails rotates to meet the wind. As a result, the body of the mill where the machinery is housed can be bigger, heavier and stronger. Built in the mid 1600s, and moved from Chesham to this site in 1821, it is the oldest Smock Mill in England.

It was at Lacey Green that the young poet **Rupert Brooke** used to spend his weekends in the company of friends at a local pub. The son of a master at Rugby School, and a student at Cambridge University, Brooke began writing poetry as a boy and travelled widely in the years leading up to the First World War. Early on in the war his poetry showed a boyish patriotism, but his later works were full of bitter disillusion. He died in 1915 while on his way to the attempted landings at the Dardanelles in Turkey.

Close to the village is Speen Farm and the **Home of Rest for Horses**, whose most famous patient was Sefton, the cavalry horse injured in the Hyde Park bomb blast of the early 1980s. A society was founded in 1886 as a retreat and rescue for working horses from the streets of London. It moved here in 1971 and each year some 200 horses, ponies and donkeys pass through, some to rest, others, like Sefton, to retire.

historic building museum and heritage historic site scenic attraction flora and fauna

GREAT MISSENDEN

3 miles W of Chesham off the A413

Old Court House

Roald Dahl Museum & Story Centre

Great Missenden boasts an attractive medley of 16th and 17th-century buildings, which have been adapted over the years to changing needs and tastes. At the southern end of the village High Street is the medieval George Inn, behind which is the old manorial **Court House**. Also in the village is a handsome flint and stone church and the site of Missenden Abbey, which was founded in 1133 by the Augustinian order. A daughter community of St Nicholas's Abbey in Normandy, the abbey has long since gone and in its place stands a fashionable Gothic mansion dating from 1810.

Great Missenden is probably best known as being the home of Roald Dahl, the internationally recognised author particularly loved for his children's books. He lived here for 30 years and is buried on the hillside opposite his home, Gipsy House, in the churchyard of St Peter and St Paul. His daughter Olivia, who died at the age of seven, is buried at Little Missenden in a plot that was intended for Dahl himself and his first wife, the actress Patricia Neal. But this plan was changed when Dahl and Neal were divorced in 1983, seven years before his death.

At the **Roald Dahl Museum & Story Centre**, aimed at six to 12-year-olds, visitors can delve into the author's archives on touch-screen monitors, visit his writing hut and make up 'phizz-whizzing' words and stories using the interactive exhibits. A charity was established in 2001 to promote education in literature, and a sister charity, the Roald Dahl Foundation, was founded by his widow Felicity, providing grants to individuals, charities and hospitals, and assistance to children and families in the fields of neurology and haematology. There's also a shop and café on site.

PRINCES RISBOROUGH

9 miles W of Chesham on the A4010

Manor House

A busy little town with many 16th century cottages, 17th and 18th-century houses and, at its centre, a brick Market House of 1824. The ground floor is an empty space providing shelter for occasional market stalls. The Prince in the name of this Chilterns Gap market town is the Black Prince, the eldest son of Edward III, who held land and had a palace here. The town stands on the Icknield Way and was a major stopping place during the stage coach era. The last regular stage-coach service to run in England ended its journey from London here in 1898. Off the market square, opposite the church, the **Princes Risborough Manor House** (National Trust) is a 17th-century redbrick house with a handsome Jacobean staircase. Viewing appointments can be made by contacting nearby Hughenden Manor. More details can be found at the Risborough Information centre on Horns Lane.

Manor House, Princes Risborough

WENDOVER

6 miles NW of Chesham on the A413

Wendover Woods Coombe Hill Go Ape

This delightful old market town is situated in a gap on the northern escarpment of the Chiltern Hills, in the Metropolitan Green Belt and the Chilterns Area of Outstanding Natural Beauty. It has an attractive main street of half-timbered, thatched houses and cottages of which the best examples are Anne Boleyn's Cottages. A picturesque place, often seen as the gateway to the Chilterns, Wendover has a fine selection of antique and craft shops, tearooms and bookshops. In 1300 the town was granted the right to send two representatives to Parliament; these have included John Hampden, George Canning and Edmund Burke. The right was extinguished by the Reform Act of 1832. The town is twinned with Liffre in Brittany, and the Twinning Stones outside the library are permanent reminders of the close ties.

The town also offers visitors an opportunity of seeing the glorious countryside through the medium of **Wendover Woods**. Created for recreational pursuits – there's a mountain bike course at Aston Hill – as well as for conservation and timber production, these Forestry Commission woods offer visitors numerous trails through the coniferous and broadleaved woodland. It is one of the best sites in the country to spot the tiny firecrest, a bird that is becoming increasingly rare. **Go Ape** is an award-winning high wire forest adventure course of rope bridges, Tarzan swings and zip slides, all set high up in the treetops.

Off the B4010 a short drive west of Wendover, **Coombe Hill** is the highest point in the Chilterns and affords superb views across the Vale of Aylesbury, the Berkshire Downs and the Cotswolds. On the summit is a monument dedicated to the men who died in the Boer War. The National Trust has introduced a flock of sheep on to the hill to control the invasion of scrub and to encourage the grass.

Aylesbury

County Museum

Roald Dahl's Children's Gallery

Founded in Saxon times and the county town since the reign of Henry VIII, Aylesbury lies in rich pastureland in the shelter of the Chilterns. Post-war development took away much of the town's character, but some parts, particularly around the market square, are protected by a conservation order. At various times in the Civil War, Aylesbury was a base for both Cromwell and the King, and this period of history is covered in the splendidly refurbished **County Museum & Art Gallery**. The museum, housed in a splendid Georgian building, also has an exhibit on Louis XVIII of France, who lived in exile at nearby Hartwell House. Also within the museum is the award-winning **Roald Dahl Children's Gallery**, an exciting hands-on gallery for children that uses Dahl's characters to introduce and explain the museum's treasures.

Around Aylesbury

MENTMORE

6 miles NE of Aylesbury off the B488

Mentmore Towers

The village is home to the first of the Rothschild mansions, **Mentmore Towers**, which was built for Baron Meyer Amschel de Rothschild between 1852 and 1855. A splendid building in the Elizabethan style, it

Mentmore Towers

was designed by Sir Joseph Paxton, the designer of Crystal Palace, and is a superb example of grandiose Victorian extravagance. However, the lavish decoration hides several technologically advanced details for those times, such as central heating, and, as might be expected from Paxton, there are large sheets of glass and a glass roof in the design. In the late 19th century the house became the home of Lord Rosebery, and the magnificent turreted building was the scene of many glittering parties and gatherings of the most wealthy and influential people in the country. However, in the 1970s the house was put up for auction and, while the furniture and works of art were sold to the four corners of the world, the building was bought by the Maharishi Mahesh Yogi and became for a time the headquarters of his University of Natural Law.

IVINGHOE

7 miles E of Aylesbury on the B488

Ford End Watermill · Ivinghoe Beacon

Ridgeway National Trail

As the large village church would suggest, Ivinghoe was once a market town of some importance in the surrounding area. In this now quiet village can be found **Ford End Watermill**, a listed building that, though probably much older, was first recorded in 1616. It is the only working watermill with its original machinery in Buckinghamshire, and on milling days stone-ground wholemeal flour is on sale. The farm in which it stands has also managed to retain the atmosphere of an 18th-century farm. Limited opening times – call 01442 825421.

To the east lies the National Trust's **Ivinghoe Beacon**, a wonderful viewpoint on the edge of the Chiltern Hills. The site of an Iron Age hill fort, the beacon was also the inspiration for Sir Walter Scott's *Ivanhoe.* The Beacon is at one end of Britain's oldest road, the **Ridgeway National Trail**. The other end is the World Heritage Site of Avebury in Wiltshire, and the 85-mile length of the Ridgeway still follows the same route over the high ground used since prehistoric times. Walkers can use the whole length of the trail (April to November is the best time) and horse riders and cyclists can ride on much of the western part.

PITSTONE

7 miles E of Aylesbury off the B489

Pitstone Windmill · Pitstone Green Museum

Though the exact age of **Pitstone Windmill** (National Trust) is not known, it is certainly one of the oldest post mills in Britain. The earliest documentary reference to its existence was made in 1624. It is open to the public on a limited basis – call 01442 851227. Also in the village is **Pitstone Green Museum**, where all manner of farm and barn machinery, along with domestic bygones, are on display in farm buildings dating from 1831. There are two model railways and a full-size reconstruction of a section of a Second World War Lancaster bomber, and additional entertainment includes tractor rides, pottery demonstrations and occasional craft fairs.

A delightful hour or two can be spent cruising from Pitstone Wharf along a lovely stretch of the Grand Union Canal.

Pitstone Windmill

STOKE MANDEVILLE

2 miles S of Aylesbury on the A4010

Bucks Goat Centre

The village is best known for its hospital, which specialises in the treatment of spinal injuries and burns. Just south of Stoke, on Old Risborough Road, **Bucks Goat Centre** has the most comprehensive collection of goat breeds in the country, along with llamas, donkeys, rabbits, guinea pigs, sheep, pigs and birds. Visitors can groom, cuddle and feed the goats with vegetables from the Farm Shop. Also here are the famous Aylesbury ducks and other poultry.

GREAT KIMBLE

5 miles S of Aylesbury on the A4010

Chequers

Though the village is home to a church with an interesting series of 14th-century wall paintings, its real claim to fame is the nearby 16th-century mansion, **Chequers**, the country residence of the British Prime Minister. Originally built by William Hawtrey in 1565, but much altered and enlarged in the 18th and 19th centuries, the house was restored to its original form by Arthur Lee in 1912. Later, in 1920, as Lord Lee of Fareham, he gave the house and estate to the nation to be used as the prime minister's country home. The first Prime Minister to make use of Chequers was Lloyd George, and many who came to know the house later moved to the area: Ramsay MacDonald's daughter lived at nearby Speen; Harold Wilson bought a house in Great Missenden; and Nye Bevan owned a farm in the Chilterns.

WOTTON UNDERWOOD

8 miles W of Aylesbury off the A41

Wotton House

In this secluded village stands the privately owned **Wotton House**, a charming early 18th-century building said to be practically identical to the original Buckingham Palace. The gardens, which feature more than a dozen follies, were laid out between 1757 and 1760 by Capability Brown.

BOARSTALL

12 miles W of Aylesbury off the B4011

Boarstall Tower Duck Decoy

A curious feature here is the 17th-century **Duck Decoy** (National Trust) set on the edge of a lake to catch birds for the table. There are

Boarstall Tower

regular demonstrations by the Warden and his dog of how the device works. The site also contains a nature trail and exhibition hall. The National Trust is also responsible for **Boarstall Tower**, an imposing 14th-century stone gatehouse of a long demolished fortified house. The gatehouse was updated in 1615, and the exterior and many rooms remain virtually unchanged. There are guided tours around the atmospheric rooms with some colourful tales from the 11th century to the present day. Call: 01280 822850.

WADDESDON

4 miles NW of Aylesbury on the A41

Waddesdon Manor

The village is home to another of the county's magnificent country houses, in this case **Waddesdon Manor** (National Trust). Built between 1874 and 1889 for Baron Ferdinand de Rothschild, in the style of a French Renaissance château, the house is set in rolling English countryside and borrows elements from several different French châteaux. The Manor is surrounded by formal gardens and the landscaped grounds contain, among many treasures, a French-style aviary in a part of the gardens designed by the popular 20th-century American landscape artist Lanning Roper. Also within the grounds are hundreds of trees both native and foreign, a fabulous parterre, Italian, French and Dutch statuary, and a huge pheasant named Ferdinand made from 15,000 bedding plants on a steel frame. The French influence even extended to the carthorses used on the site – powerful Percheron mares that were imported from Normandy. The house contains one of the best collections of 18th-century French decorative art in the world, including Sèvres porcelain, Beauvais tapestries and fine furniture. There are also paintings by Gainsborough, Reynolds and 17th-century Dutch and Flemish masters. The Manor has two restaurants, a coffee shop, gift shop, a wine and food shop, and a plant centre.

QUAINTON

5 miles NW of Aylesbury off the A41

Tower Mill Buckinghamshire Railway Centre

A pleasant village with the remains of an ancient cross on the green, a number of fine Georgian houses, and a row of almshouses built in 1687. Here, too, is another of the county's windmills, **Quainton Tower Mill**, built in the 1830s and 100 feet high. Quite early in its life it was fitted with a steam engine, but despite this innovation the mill's working life extended barely 50 years. Just south of the village, at Quainton Railway Station, is the **Buckinghamshire Railway Centre** (see panel on page 64), a working steam museum where visitors can relive the golden age of steam. The centre boasts one of the largest collections of preserved steam and diesel locomotives in the country, including

Buckinghamshire Railway Centre

Quainton Road Station, Quainton, Aylesbury, Buckinghamshire HP22 4BY
Tel: 01296 655450
website: www.bucksrailcentre.org.uk

A working steam museum set in a 25-acre site, the **Bucking-hamshire Railway Centre** was established in 1968 and boasts one of the largest collections of preserved steam and diesel locomotives in the country, including items from South Africa, the USA and Egypt as well as from Britain. Visitors can ride behind full-sized stream locomotives and on the extensive miniature railway. The Railway Centre is also home to the beautifully restored Rewley Road Station, which dates from 1851 and was moved here from Oxford, and is now the main visitor centre. Open Wednesdays to Sundays from March to the end of October, the steam trains operate on Sundays and on Wednesdays in the school holidays.

engines from South Africa, the USA and Egypt, as well as from Britain (a Hall, a Castle and a pannier tank from the GWR and an ancient well tank from the LSWR). Rolling stock on show includes a coach from the Royal Train of 1901 and another used by Winston Churchill and General Eisenhower for wartime planning meetings in 1944. Visitors can ride behind full-sized steam locos and on the extensive miniature railway. The beautifully restored Rowley Road Station (1851), moved here from Oxford, also serves as the main visitor centre. Call: 01296 655720.

Buckingham

Chantry Chapel · Old Gaol Museum

This pleasant town, the centre of which is contained in a loop of the River Ouse, dates back to Saxon times and was granted a charter by Alfred the Great. Although it became the county town in AD888, when Alfred divided the shires, from an early date many of the functions of a county town were performed by the more centrally located Aylesbury.

Thanks to a disastrous fire in 1725, this lively little market town is characterised by a fine array of Georgian buildings, including Castle House in West Street, the impressive Old Gaol, one of the first purpose-built county gaols in England (built in 1748 in the style of a castle, with additions by George Gilbert Scott), and the Town Hall, located at either end of the Market Square. The **Old Gaol Museum** not only illustrates the building's history, but also has displays on the town's past and the county's military exploits. A high-tech glass roof was added in 2000, spanning the original prisoners' exercise yard to create a new light-filled area for special exhibits and an educational resource centre. The recently added exhibition about local author Flora Thompson has attracted visitors from all over the world. There is an annual craft fair, occasional talks, and children's activity days are held throughout the year. One building that did survive the devastating fire of 1725 is the **Buckingham Chantry Chapel**

Old Gaol, Buckingham

(National Trust). The chapel was constructed in 1475 on the site of a Norman building whose doorway has been retained. Well worth a visit, the chapel was restored by George Gilbert Scott in 1875.

A more recent addition to this delightful town is the University of Buckingham, which was granted its charter in 1983.

Around Buckingham

MIDDLE CLAYDON

5 miles S of Buckingham off the A413

Claydon House

The village is home to **Claydon House** (National Trust), a Jacobean manor house that was remodelled in the 1750s at a time of great enthusiasm for all things Oriental. The home of the Verney family for more 350 years, the house contains a number of state rooms with magnificent carved wood and plaster decorations on an Oriental theme. What makes the house particularly interesting is its associations with Florence Nightingale. Florence's sister married into the Verney family, and the pioneer of modern hospital care spent long periods at the house, especially during her old age. Her bedroom and a museum of her life and experiences during the Crimean War can be seen here. Florence died in 1910 after a long career that embraced concerns of public health as well as the training of nurses; she was the first woman to be awarded the Order of Merit.

WINSLOW

5 miles SE of Buckingham on the A413

Keech's Meeting House

A small country town of ancient origin, where Offa, the King of Mercia, stayed in AD752. The village's most prominent building is Winslow Hall, a delightful Wren house set in beautiful gardens. House and gardens are open for visits by appointment only. Another building of interest is **Keech's Meeting House**, a minuscule Baptist Chapel, which has remained virtually unaltered for 300 years.

STEWKLEY

10 miles SE of Buckingham on the B4032

Church of St Michael

Stewkley, renowned as being the longest village in England, is even better known for its wonderful **Church of St Michael**, one of the finest Norman churches in the land, with spectacular zigzag atterns and a massive tower. Built between 1150 and 1180, this mighty building has remained virtually unaltered. In the 1970s, when neighbouring Cublington was being considered as the site for London's third airport, the government proposed to move it elsewhere, stone by stone.

WING

12 miles SE of Buckingham on the A418

All Saints Church · Ascott

Wing's church faced the same threat as Stewkley with the proposed Cublington Airport development. **All Saints Church**, standing on a rise above the Vale of Aylesbury, retains most of its original Saxon features, including the nave, aisles, west wall, crypt and apse. The roof is covered in medieval figures, many of them playing musical instruments. This remarkable church also contains numerous brasses and monuments, notably to the Dormer family who came to Ascott Hall in the 1520s.

Just east of the village, **Ascott** (National Trust) was bought in 1874 by Leopold Rothschild who virtually rebuilt the original farmhouse round its timber-framed core. The house contains a superb collection of fine paintings, Oriental porcelain and English and French furniture. The grounds are magnificent too, with specimen trees and shrubs, a herbaceous walk, lily pond, Dutch garden, an evergreen topiary sundial and two fountains, one in bronze, the other in marble, sculpted by the American artist Thomas Waldo Story.

THORNBOROUGH

3 miles E of Buckingham off the A422

This lively and attractive village is home to Buckinghamshire's only surviving medieval bridge. Built in the 14th century, the six-arched structure spans Claydon Brook. Close by are two large mounds, which were opened in 1839 and revealed a wealth of Roman objects, many of which are on display at the Old Gaol Museum in Buckingham. Though it was known that there was a Roman temple here, its location has not been found.

STOWE

3 miles N of Buckingham off the A422

Stowe School & Gardens

Stowe School is a leading public school that occupies an 18th-century mansion that was once the home of the Dukes of Buckingham. Worked upon by two wealthy owners who both had a great sense of vision, the magnificent mansion house, which was finally completed in 1774, is open to the public during school holidays. Between 1715 and 1749, the owner, Viscount Cobham, hired various well-known landscape designers to lay out the fantastic **Stowe Landscape Gardens** (National Trust – see panel opposite) that can still be seen. Taking over the house in 1750, Earl Temple, along with his nephew, expanded the grounds and today they remain one of the most original and finest landscape gardens in Europe. Temples, alcoves and rotundas are scattered around the grounds, strategically placed to evoke in the onlooker a romantic and poetic frame of mind. It is one of the more intriguing quirks of fate that Lancelot

Brown, always known as Capability Brown because he told his clients that their parks had capabilities, was head gardener at Stowe for 10 years. He arrived here in 1741 and began to work out his own style, a more natural style of landscape gardening, which was to take over where gardens like the one at Stowe left off.

SILVERSTONE

5 miles N of Buckingham off the A43

The home of British motor racing, Silverstone is best known as the venue for the British Formula I Grand Prix, now secure after Donington Park was briefly considered as its successor. The first Grand Prix was held here in 1948 on the former RAF Bomber Command airfield, with victory going to the Italian Luigi Villoresi in a Maserati. In 1950, the first World Championship Formula 1 race was held in the presence of King George VI and Queen Elizabeth; the winner was Giuseppe Farina at the wheel of an Alfa Romeo. The 2010 renewal was won very easily by the Australian Mark Webber in a Red Bull. Silverstone hosts many other motorsport events throughout the year, including the Silverstone Historic Festival, British F3, GT, Touring Car and Superbike championships. It is also the place of dreams for boy racers, who can try their hand at driving a wide range of cars round the circuit, including single-seaters, rally cars, 4X4s, E-type Jaguars, Lotus Elises and Porsche 911 Carrera Supercars.

Milton Keynes

Christ Church Museum

Most people's perception of this modern town is of a concrete jungle, but the reality of Milton Keynes could not be more different. The development corporation that was charged, in 1967, with organising the new town has provided a place of tree-lined boulevards, uncongested roads, spacious surroundings, and acres of parkland. It is of course a modern town, with new housing, high-tech industries, modern leisure facilities, and a large covered shopping centre. One of the town's most notable buildings is **Christ Church**, built in the style of Christopher Wren; the first purpose-built ecumenical city church in Britain, it was opened in March 1992 by the Queen. While Milton Keynes is certainly a place of the late 20th century, it has not altogether forgotten the rural past of the villages, which are now incorporated into the suburbs of the town. Housed in a beautiful Victorian farmstead, **Milton Keynes Museum** is run by a large and active group of volunteers. Its displays include a large collection of industrial, domestic and agricultural bygones illustrating the lives of the people who lived in the area in the 200 years leading up to the creation of the new town. A Victorian house features a working kitchen and laundry, and among other eye-catching exhibits are a local tramcar and an impressive collection of working telephones.

Around Milton Keynes

BLETCHLEY

2 miles S of Milton Keynes on the A421

Bletchley Park

Now effectively a suburb of Milton Keynes, Bletchley is famous for **Bletchley Park**, the Victorian mansion that housed the wartime codebreakers who beat odds of 150 million million million to 1 and cracked the Nazi Enigma cypher, the crucial key to German military and intelligence communications. Along with a display of military vehicles and a wealth of Second World War memorabilia, there is a Cryptology Trail that allows visitors to follow the path of a coded message from its interception through decoding to interpretation. At the height of the war, more than 12,000 people worked at Bletchley Park.

Volunteers have reconstructed one of the vast electro-mechanical decoders that broke the Enigma code. The first of these machines were installed in 1940, and by 1945 more than 200 were at work. Bletchley Park hosts a year-round programme of exhibitions and events. Call: 01908 640404.

The Lake, Bletchley Park

Though Bletchley is now all but merged with its larger neighbour, it still retains a distinctive air. The original village here dates back to Roman times and was first recorded as a town in 1108.

STONY STRATFORD

3 miles NW of Milton Keynes off the A5

Often considered to be the jewel in the crown of the villages around Milton Keynes, Stony Stratford was a popular staging post on the old Roman road, Watling Street. Richard III, as the Duke of Gloucester, came in 1483 to detain the uncrowned Prince Edward before committing him to the Tower of London. Other notable visitors include Charles Dickens, Samuel Johnson and John Wesley, who preached under the tree that still stands in the market place.

GAYHURST

4 miles N of Milton Keynes off the B526

Built during the reign of Elizabeth I, Gayhurst House was given to Sir Francis Drake in recognition of his circumnavigation of the world, though the building seen today was not the one that Drake lived in. It was later occupied by Sir Everard Digby, one of the conspirators behind the Gunpowder Plot of 1605.

OLNEY

8 miles N of Milton Keynes on the A509

Church of St Peter & St Paul

Emberton Country Park · William Cowper

Cowper and Newton Museum · Pancake Race

Variety's the spice of life; Monarch of all I survey; God made the country and man made the town…

All these familiar phrases are now embedded in the language but how many could name the writer? In fact, they all came from the pen of the 18th-century poet **William Cowper** who

William Cowper's Garden

Cowper and Newton Museum, Olney

spent the last 20 years of his life in the elegant market town of Olney.

He came to the town to be near his friend the Reverend John Newton, a former slave trader who had repented and become "a man of gloomy piety". The two men collaborated on a book of religious verse, the Olney Hymns, in which Cowper's contributions included such perennial favourites as *Oh! for a closer walk with God; Hark, my soul! It is the Lord;* and *God moves in a mysterious way.*

The house in which Cowper lived from 1768 to 1786 is now the **Cowper and Newton Museum**, a fascinating place that concentrates on Cowper's life and work, but also has some exhibits and collections concerned with the times in which he lived and the life of Olney. Each of the rooms of the large early 18th-century town house has been specially themed and there are numerous displays of Cowper's work, including the *Olney Hymns*. Cowper was also a keen gardener and the summerhouse, where he wrote many of his poems, can still be seen in the rear garden. Here he experimented with plants that were new to 18th-century England. Also at the museum is the nationally important Lace Collection, and items particular to the shoemaking industry, which was another busy local trade in the 19th and early 20th century.

When Cowper died in 1800 he was buried at East Dereham in Norfolk, but his associate Newton, the reformed slave-trader, is interred in the churchyard of **St Peter and St Paul**, where he had been the curate. This church is a spacious building dating from the mid 14th century and its spire rises some 185 feet to dominate the skyline of Olney.

For more than 300 years Olney was a centre of lace-making by hand, using wooden or bone bobbins. When lace was at its most expensive, in the 1700s, only the well-to-do could afford to buy it, but the rise in machine-made lace from Nottingham saw a fall in prices and a sharp decline in Olney lace. A

DODO ANTIQUES

The Old Cock Inn, Silverend, Olney,
Buckinghamshire MK46 4AL
Tel: 01234 240505
e-mail: info@dodoantiques.co.uk
website: www.dodoantiques.co.uk

Formerly a pub, **Dodo Antiques** opened its doors to the public in the historic town of Olney at the end of 2010. Its Georgian rooms have already been bustling with customers and word is spreading about the fine selection of antiques on offer here.

The rooms are fabulous, and each one has a theme making it easier to find the item you are looking for, be it for yourself or a gift for a friend or relative. Art deco furniture, mirrors, glass, paintings and clocks are just some of the items you will find at this excellent independent shop. It stocks an innovative collection of items from specialist antique dealers and there is something to suit all tastes and budgets.

Dodo Antiques offers a search service if you cannot find what you are after in its constantly changing stock. House clearance and restoration is also part of the shop's fully complimentary service. Ask for details.

There is plenty to see in Olney, which is close to the M1, and free parking close to Dodo Antiques and a spacious loading area to the side is a bonus.

LEO ANTIQUES

19 Market Place, Olney, Buckinghamshire MK46 4BA
Tel: 01234 240003
e-mail: shop@leoantiques.co.uk website: www.leoantiques.co.uk

Located in an impressive Georgian building overlooking the busy market place in Olney, **Leo Antiques** & Collectables is a shop that people can easily spend an hour or so browsing its homely rooms, and get a good idea of how an item would look in their own home. It opened in the historical town in October 2003 and has built up a good reputation with locals and visitors.

Inside, Leo Antiques is period decorated and many people visit to view the gallery of artwork from the 19th and 20th century. The shop stocks a good range of Dining furniture, chairs, desks and other occasional furniture.

On the ceramic side, dinner services, and decorative ornaments from the best our potteries can offer with Royal Doulton, Worcester, Crown Derby and Moorcroft to name a few. Our selection of clocks and watches are provided by a local Horologist, are fully serviced and in working order.

There is a specialist Glass section with pieces dating back to the 1700's, and a large selection of everyday glassware to grace your dining table. A good variety of mirrors to add some impact to your room, vintage costume jewellry and silver items, something for everyone. With items from as little as £5 we are sure you will find something as a souvenir of your visit to Olney. We look forward to welcoming you to Leo Antiques.

Parking in Olney is mainly free and the market place can be used with the exception of Thursday, which is market day. Open six days a week Tuesday to Saturday 10.30am to 5pm and Sundays and Bank Holidays from 11 am to 4pm.

THE OLD STONE BARN

Home Farm, Warrington, Olney,
Buckinghamshire MK46 4HN
Tel: 01234 711655 Fax: 01234 711855
e-mail: info@oldstonebarn.co.uk
website: www.oldstonebarn.co.uk

The Old Stone Barn is positioned peacefully within 600 acres of a family run arable farm. It offers four star accommodation in apartment style cottages sleeping between 2-6 people. The apartments combine old character and modern facilities with computer room and wifi available on site.

Guests can relax in the gardens and enjoy the heated outdoor swimming pool, children's play area and croquet lawn in the summer months.

revival of the trade was tried by Harry Armstrong when he opened the Lace Factory in 1928 but, although handmade lace is still produced locally, the factory only lasted until Armstrong's death in 1943.

Amongst the town's claims to fame is the annual **Pancake Race**. Legend has it that the first 'race' was run in the 15th century when a local housewife heard the Shriving Service bell ringing and ran to church complete with her frying pan and pancake.

Nearby **Emberton Country Park**, located on the site of former gravel pits, is an ideal place to relax. Not only are there four lakes and a stretch of the River Ouse within the park's boundaries, but also facilities here include fishing, sailing, and nature trails.

NEWPORT PAGNELL

3 miles NE of Milton Keynes on the A422

Modern development hides a long history at Newport Pagnell, which local archaeological finds indicate was settled in the Iron Age and during the Roman occupation. It was an important administrative centre, and in the 10th century the Royal Mint was established here. Lace-making was once an important industry, and the town is also associated with the car-maker Aston Martin, which started life in the 1820s as a maker of coaches for the nobility. The marque will be forever associated with James Bond, and as we went to press one of the original Bond DB5s – FMB 7B – was due to be sold at auction, with an estimate in excess of five million dollars.

CHICHELEY

5 miles NE of Milton Keynes on the A422

Chicheley Hall

This attractive village is the home of **Chicheley Hall**, a beautiful baroque house that was built in the early 1700s for Sir John Chester and which remains today one of the finest such houses in the country. Down the years it was used by the military and as a school, but in 1952 it was bought by the 2nd Earl Beatty and restored to its former state of grace. The earl's father, the 1st Earl, was a particularly courageous naval commander and, as well as receiving the DSO at the age of just 25, he was also a commander in the decisive battle of Jutland in 1916.

WILLEN

1 mile NE of Milton Keynes on the A509

Great Linford Manor

The village Church of St Mary Magdalene, built in the late 17th century, is an elegant building in the style of Sir Christopher Wren. Willen is also home to another house of prayer, the Peace Pagoda and Buddhist Temple, opened in 1980. It was built by the monks and nuns of the Nipponsan Myohoji, and was the first peace pagoda in the western hemisphere. In this place of great tranquillity and beauty, 1000 cherry trees and cedars, donated by the ancient Japanese town of Yoshino, have been planted on the hill surrounding the pagoda in memory of the victims of all wars.

GREAT LINFORD

2 miles NE of Milton Keynes on the A422

Situated on the banks of the Grand Union Canal, this village, which is now more or less a suburb of Milton Keynes, has a 13th-century church set in parkland, a 17th-century manor house, and a **Stone Circle**, one of only a few such prehistoric monuments in the county. Despite the encroachment of its much larger neighbour, the village has retained a distinctive air that is all its own.

The central block of the present manor house was built in 1678 by Sir William Pritchard, Lord Mayor of London. As well as making Great Linford his country seat, Pritchard also provided a boys' school and almshouses for six unmarried poor of the parish. The manor house was extended in the 18th century by the Uthwatt family, relatives of the Lord Mayor, and they used various tricks to give an impressive and elegant appearance to the building. The Grand Union Canal cuts through the estate, whose grounds are now a public park.

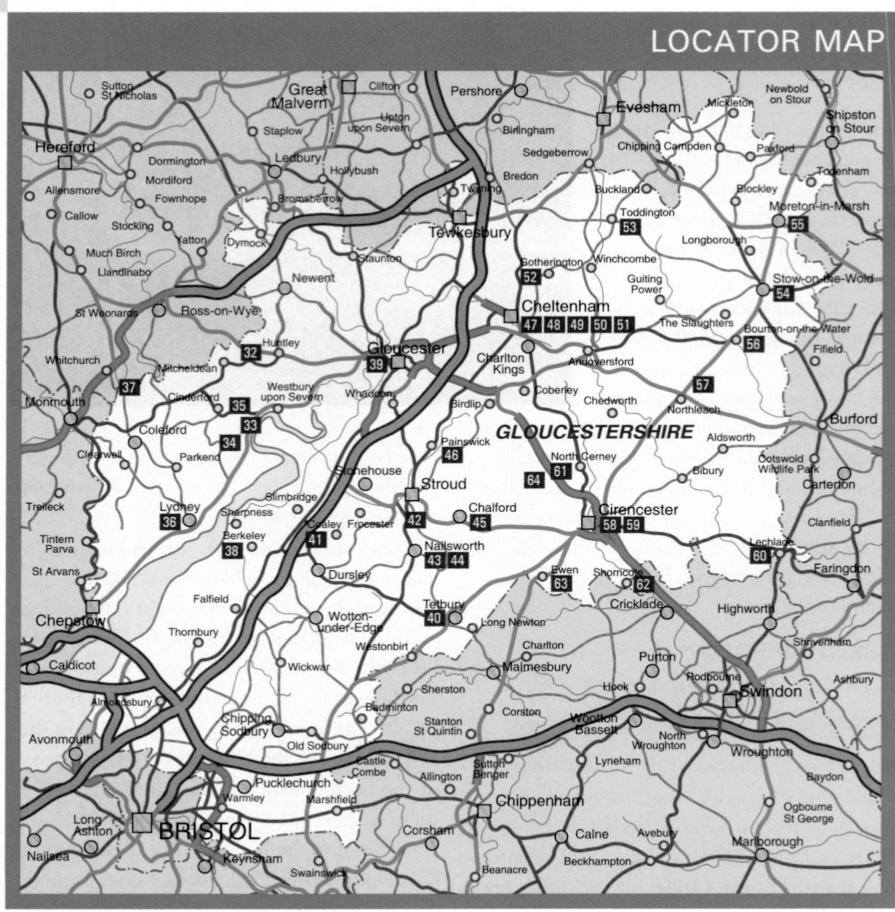

ADVERTISERS AND PLACES OF INTEREST

Accommodation, Food and Drink

34 | Dean Heritage Centre, Lower Soudley *pg 80*
35 | Littledean House Hotel, Littledean, Newnham-on-Severn *pg 81*
37 | The Rock Bed and Breakfast, Symonds Yat Rock, Coleford *pg 85*
41 | Fox & Hounds, Coaley, Dursley *pg 103*
42 | Black Horse, Amberley, Stroud *pg 105*
45 | Westley Farm Holiday Cottages, Chalford, Cirencester *pg 107*
46 | The Royal Oak Inn, Painswick *pg 108*
48 | Clematis House B&B, Cheltenham Spa *pg 110*
54 | Treebus Tea Rooms, Stow On The Wold *pg 118*
55 | Railway Cottages & Apartments, Moreton-in-Marsh *pg 119*
56 | Larks Rise, Bourton-on-the-Water *pg 122*
59 | The Thames Head Inn, Cirencester *pg 125*
61 | Bathurst Arms, North Cerney, Cirencester *pg 127*
62 | The Royal Oak, South Cerney, Cirencester *pg 128*
63 | Wild Duck Inn, Ewen, Cirencester *pg 128*
64 | Winstone Glebe Country House, Winstone, Cirencester *pg 129*

4 | Gloucestershire

For many, Gloucestershire *is* the Cotswolds, the delightful limestone hills that sweep across the county from Dyrham in the south to Chipping Campden in the north. As well as providing some of the most glorious scenery and the prettiest villages in the country, the county is also home to the historic towns of Cirencester and Cheltenham. "The most English and the least spoiled of all our countryside." So wrote J B Priestley in 1933 in his *English Journey* and, more than 70 years later, his verdict would surely have been the same.

However, Gloucestershire is not all about the Cotswolds. To the west, on the River Severn, is the ancient city of Gloucester, while further down river is the Vale of Berkeley and historic Berkeley Castle. On the opposite bank of the river lies the Forest of Dean. Wild woodland, royal hunting ground, naval timber reserve, important mining and industrial region: the Forest has been all these, and today its rich and varied landscape provides endless interest for walkers, nature-lovers and historians. Bounded by the Rivers Severn and Wye, the area has been effectively isolated from the rest of England and Wales and so has developed a character all its own.

ADVERTISERS AND PLACES OF INTEREST

stories and anecdotes famous people art and craft entertainment and sport walks

Newent

Market House · Church of St Mary

The International Centre for birds of Prey

Castle Hill Farm · Three Choirs Vineyard

Capital of the area of northwest Gloucestershire known as the Ryelands, and the most important town in the Vale of Leadon, Newent stands in the broad triangle of land called Daffodil Crescent. The rich Leadon Valley soil was traditionally used for growing rye and raising the renowned Ryelands sheep, an ancient breed famed for the quality of its wool. The town was one of the county's principal wool-trading centres, and the wealth produced from that trade accounts for the large number of grand merchants' houses to be seen here. The most distinctive building in Newent is the splendid timber-framed **Market House**, built as a butter market in the middle of the 16th. -century, its upper floors supported on 16 oak pillars that form an open colonnade. The medieval **Church of St Mary** has many outstanding features, including the shaft of a 9th-century Saxon cross, the 11th-century Newent Stone and the 17th-century nave. During the Civil War, Royalist troops had removed the lead from the roof to make bullets, an act that caused the roof to collapse during a snowstorm in 1674. A new nave was started after Charles II agreed to donate 60 tons of timber from the Forest of Dean. The church's 150ft spire is a landmark for miles around.

There aren't too many windmills in Gloucestershire, but at **Castle Hill Farm**, just outside town, is a working wooden mill with great views from a balcony at the top.

A mile south of Newent is the **International Centre for Birds of Prey** housing one of the largest and best collections of birds of prey in the world. The 110 aviaries are home to eagles, falcons, owls, vultures, kites, hawks, caracaras, secretary birds and buzzards. Between 20 and 40 birds are flown daily at the Centre, which is open every day from February to November. Also on site are a tearoom, children's play area, pets corner and picnic area. Call 01531 820286/821581.

On the road north towards Dymock, set in 75 acres of rolling countryside, the **Three Choirs Vineyard** is the country's largest wine producer. Unusually, there's also a brewery here, Whittington's, named after Dick Whittington who is believed to have been born in the nearby hamlet of Pauntley. The vineyard also has a restaurant, shop and offers bed and breakfast accommodation in rooms overlooking the rows of vines.

Market House, Newent

Around Newent

DYMOCK

3 miles N of Newent on the B4216

Dymock Poets

Dymock boasts some fine old brick buildings, including the White House and the Old Rectory near the church and, outside the village, the Old Grange, which incorporates the remains of the Cistercian Flaxley Abbey.

At the heart of the village is the early Norman Church of St Mary, whose unusual features include a tympanum depicting the Tree of Life, a 13th-century stone coffin lid, stained glass by Kempe – and the last ticket issued at Dymock station, in 1959. A corner of the church is dedicated to the memory of the **Dymock Poets**, a group who based themselves in Dymock from before the First World War. The group, which comprised Lascelles Abercrombie (the first to arrive), Rupert Brooke, John Drinkwater, Wilfred Gibson, Edward Thomas and Robert Frost, sent out its *New Numbers* poetry magazine from Dymock's tiny post office. It was also from here that Brooke published his *War Sonnets*, including *The Soldier* (*"If I should die, think only this of me: That there's some corner of a foreign field that is forever England..."*). Brooke and Thomas died in the war, which led to the dissolution of the group. Two circular walks from Dymock take in places associated with the poets.

Many other literary figures are associated with the Forest. Dennis Potter, born at Coleford in 1935 the eldest son of a Forest coal-miner, is renowned for writing the screenplays for some of TV's most memorable programmes, including *Pennies From Heaven* and *The Singing Detective*. But he also wrote with passion about the Forest in *The Glittering Coffin* and *The Changing Forest: Life in the Forest of Dean Today*. Mary Howitt, born in Coleford in 1799, is known as a translator, poet and author of children's books. It was as a translator that she met a Danish storyteller called Hans Christian Andersen who asked Mary to translate his stories into English.

St Mary's Church - Upleadon

UPLEADON

2 miles N of Newent off the B4215

Church of St Mary the Virgin

The **Church of St Mary the Virgin** features some fine Norman and Tudor work, but is best known for its unique tower, half-timbered from bottom to top; even the mullion windows are of wood. The church has a great treasure in its Bible, an early example of the Authorised Version printed by King James' printer Robert Barker. This was the unfortunate who later issued an edition with a small but rather important word missing. The so-called Wicked Bible of 1631 renders Exodus 20.14 as 'Thou shalt commit adultery'.

KEMPLEY

3 miles NW of Newent on a minor road

Church of St Mary   Dymock Woods

A village famous for its cider and for having two churches, of very different age and significance. The little **Church of St Mary** (English Heritage), now redundant, dates from the end of the 11th century and would be a gem even without its greatest treasure. That treasure, in the chancel, is an almost complete set of 12th-century frescoes, the most renowned in the region and among the finest in the land, protected by Reformation whitewash and Victorian varnish. Their subjects include St Peter and the Apostles, Christ with his feet resting on a globe, and the de Lacy family, to whom William the Conqueror granted the manor. The red sandstone Church of St Edward the Confessor was built in 1903 by the 7th Earl Beauchamp in the style of the Arts and Crafts Movement using exclusively local materials.

This is the area of **Dymock Woods**, Forestry Commission woodland, famous for its daffodils.

Cinderford

Church of St Andrew · Dean Heritage Centre

Cinderford is a former coal-mining community with evidence of the mines visible among the trees.

At Camp Hill in the nearby hamlet of Soudley is the **Dean Heritage Centre**, where four galleries open all year round tell the story of the Forest and its people. It is a perfect setting for a family day out with woodland walks, café, adventure playground and children's activity room, museum and crafts shops, farm animals and woodland crafts, including charcoal burning and woodturning. A level trail runs round Soudley Ponds, a designated Site of Special Scientific Interest.

At nearby Awre, an ancient crossing place of the Severn, the **Church of St Andrew** has changed little in its 700 years. Its most notable possession is a massive mortuary chest carved from a single piece of wood and used as a laying out place for bodies recovered from the Severn. In the churchyard are examples of headstones featuring the local speciality – cherubs.

Around Cinderford

DRYBROOK

3 miles N of Cinderford off the A4136

Mechanical Organ Museum

Hidden away at the north end of the village, at Hawthorns Cross on the edge of the Forest, is the **Mechanical Organ Museum**, with its vast collection of mechanical music spanning 150 years. The tuneful exhibits include mechanical organs, polyphons, pianolas, automatic pianos, electric organs and musical boxes. The museum is open at Easter and on Tuesday and Thursday afternoons in April, May, July and August.

MITCHELDEAN

5 miles N of Cinderford on the A4136

St Anthony's Well

Mitcheldean is a peaceful community on the northern fringe of the forest. A mile or so south of the village is **St Anthony's Well**, one of many throughout the land said to have magical curative powers. The water at this well is invariably icy cold and bathing in it is said to provide a cure for skin disease – St Anthony's Fire was the medieval name for a rampant itching disease. The monks at nearby Flaxley Abbey swore by it.

WESTBURY-ON-SEVERN

5 miles NE of Cinderford on the A48

Severn Bore · Westbury Court Garden

The village, bounded on three sides by the river, is best known for the National Trust's **Westbury Court Garden**, a formal Dutch water garden laid out between 1696 and 1705. The only restored Dutch water garden in the country and home to what is believed to be

England's oldest evergreen oak, the garden is planted with historic varieties of apple, pear and plum, along with many other species introduced to England before 1700. The house was demolished long ago, and the only building to survive is an elegant two-storey redbrick pavilion with a tower and weather vane.

Also worth a visit in Westbury is the Church of Saints Peter, Paul and Mary, with its detached tower and wooden spire. Walmore Common is winter home to thousands of swans, as well as many wading birds and unusual flora.

Westbury is an excellent spot to watch the famous **Severn Bore**. This is a tidal wave that, several times a month, makes its way along the river. The bore travels at an average speed of about 10 miles an hour and has been known to reach a height of 6½ feet. The Severn Estuary experiences the second highest tide anywhere in the world, and the difference between the lowest and highest tide in any one day can be more than 14.5 metres. These high, or spring tides, occur on several days in each lunar cycle throughout the year.

LONGHOPE

7 miles NE of Cinderford on the A4136

Harts Barn & Craft Centre

Another good starting point for a tour in and around the Forest of Dean is Longhope, a pleasant settlement south of the A40 Gloucester to Ross-on-Wye road.

Longhope is the location of the **Harts Barn Crafts Centre**, situated in a hunting lodge built by William, Duke of Normandy, and housing an array of working crafts including jewellery, pine furniture, art gallery, handmade gifts, glassware, dried flowers and picture framing.

Willow Lodge Garden and Arboretum

Longhope, Gloucestershire GL17 0RA
Tel: 01452 831211
e-mail: wood@willowgardens.fsnet.co.uk
website: www.willowgardens.fsnet.co.uk

The four acre garden is divided into separate areas giving the element of surprise as you walk from herbaceous borders and beds, to an alpine bank, to trilliums and other woodland plants in the shadier areas.

The arboretum has many rare and unusual plants from all over the temperate world. A collection of Ilex (Holly), more than a dozen different Magnolia, quite a number of Betula and Acers with coloured bark, leaves, and leaf shapes. The arboretum is also under planted with drifts of wild daffodils, bluebells, terrestrial orchids and snowdrops. Other features include a bog garden planted with many marginals and bog plants especially Asiatic primulas; also a stream and pond.

The garden has been open to the public for several years and raised considerable funds for charities both local and national. There is ample free parking for cars, plants for sale, tea and home made cakes and most areas of the garden are accessible to wheel chairs.

FOREST GUILD GIFTS AND ANTIQUES

The Old Stable, Upper High Street, Newnham-on-Severn, Gloucestershire GL14 1BB
Tel: 01594-516417
e-mail: forestguildcraftshop@yahoo.com
website: www.bigartweb.net/artist/forestguild/

Forest Guild Gifts and Antiques is hard to define but easy to love. It's a delightful mix of gifts, crafts, antiques, curios, toys, jewellery and just about anything else of interest that the owners can manage to unearth and put on display.

The shop is a charming curio itself, located in the historic village of Newnham-on-Severn, in a 15th-century former stable right by the River Severn. It's been run since 1984 by owner Elizabeth Holder, and its long life is a testimony to its quality and value-for-money. For most of that time the shop has sold Bridgewater Pottery, the popular English earthenware and has an exclusive Forest of Dean mug designed by Emma. Another talent showcased here is local jeweller Jan Fryer, whose stunning contemporary designs have caught the eye of many celebrities. There's second-hand jewellery for sale to tempt the canny bargain-hunter, while upstairs the antiques section specialises in Windsor chairs and country antiques. There are fascinating curiosities too, like old shooting sticks and tools. Truly there's something for everyone at Forest Guild Gifts and Antiques, which is open Tuesday-Saturday from 10am-1pm and 2pm-5.30pm.

DEAN HERITAGE CENTRE

Camp Mill, Soudley, Gloucestershire GL14 2UB
Tel: 01594 822170
e-mail: info@deanheritagemuseum.com
website: www.deanheritagemuseum.com

The **Dean Heritage Centre** is a must see if you are visiting the Forest of Dean. Set in a deep valley it allows visitors to discover the story of the forest in the heart of the forest.

Open all year around, there are daily walks held and family events are often hosted at weekends. The museum at the Dean Heritage Centre tells the history of the forest, which was formed by and industrial past, and there are now five galleries.

Families are given the chance to dress up in Victorian clothes and there are plenty of craft activities and trails around the museum to keep youngsters occupied.

Homemade cakes and meals can be enjoyed in the centre's cafe, which overlooks the mill pond and if you have brought your own packed lunch there are plenty of picnic areas and specially built barbeques around the site.

An impressive waterwheel and beam engine can be seen and workshops can be arranged for schools and other groups. There is also a venue space that can be hired for meetings etcetera. Ring for details.

There's also a tearoom, play area and history trail. Usually closed on Mondays.

Just to the north on the A40 is **Willow Lodge Gardens and Arboretum** (see panel on page 79). The four acre garden and arboretum, developed from a neglected plot, from 1988 onward, is open to the public most Sundays and Mondays from April to August. Call 01452 831211.

NEWNHAM-ON-SEVERN

3 miles SW of Cinderford off the A4151

One of the gateways to the Forest, and formerly a port, Newnham lies on a great bend in the river. Its heyday was at the beginning of the 19th century, when a quay was built and an old tramway tunnel converted into what was perhaps the world's first railway tunnel. The village has many interesting buildings, which can be visited by following the Millennium Heritage Walk plaques installed by the parish council with funds provided by an open-air jazz concert.

LITTLEDEAN

1 mile W of Cinderford off the A4151

Littledean Hall

Places of interest here include the 13th-century church, the 18th-century prison and, just south of the village, **Littledean Hall** (private), reputedly the oldest inhabited house in England. The house has Saxon and Celtic remains in the cellars and is thought to have been built in the 6th century. It became a Royalist garrison during the Civil War.

RUARDEAN

4 miles NW of Cinderford on the A4136

Church of St John the Baptist · Ruardean Hill

A lovely old village whose **Church of St John**

LITTLEDEAN HOUSE HOTEL

Broad Street, Littledean, nr Newnham-on-Severn, Gloucestershire GL14 3JT
Tel: 01594-822106
e-mail: littledeanhousehotel@hotmail.com
website: www.littledeanhousehotel.co.uk

Littledean House Hotel is a family-run country guesthouse in the heart of the stunning scenery of the Forest of Dean. The hotel has its own scenery too, by way of its glorious gardens nestling beneath a massive Scots pine tree, and with lovely views to the local beauty spot, May Hill. Inside the house there is lots of period charm, with a large open log fire in the old-fashioned bar area, and leather sofas and chairs for guests to relax in.

Brothers Richard and Mathew Bond, and Mathew's wife Clare, took over the running of the hotel in 2010 and have set about making it even better than it already was. Richard and Kate are the chef's who run the hotel's own restaurant, using fresh local produce to cook steaks, sausage and mash, roasted pork belly and plenty of changing daily specials too. The meals are accompanied by fine wines from the wine list, while you can also relax in the bar and treat yourself to one of the many real ciders and ales on offer, including the popular local cider, Tosher's Tipple. There are 14 ensuite rooms upstairs, with views over those gorgeous gardens, and the Wye Valley on their doorstep.

the Baptist, one of many on the fringe of the forest, has a number of interesting features. A tympanum depicting St George and the Dragon is a great rarity, and on a stone plaque in the nave is a curious carving of two fishes. These are thought to have been carved by craftsmen from the Herefordshire School of Norman Architecture during the Romanesque period around 1150. It is part of a frieze removed with rubble when the south porch was being built in the 13th century. The frieze was considered lost until 1985 when an inspection of a bread oven in a cottage at nearby Turner's Tump revealed the two fish set into its lining. They were rescued and returned to their rightful place in the church.

Ruardean was the birthplace in the 1840s of James and William Horlick, later to become famous with their Horlicks formula. Their patent for malted milk was registered in 1883, and the granary where the original experiments were carried out still remains in the village.

Forest Path to Ruardean Hill

Ruardean Hill is 951 feet above sea level and from its summit, on a clear day, Herefordshire, the Black Mountains and the Brecon Beacons can all be seen.

Lydney

- Dean Forest Railway & Norchard Railway Centre
- Forest of Dean Model Village & Gardens
- Roman Temple Site
- Lydney Park Spring Gardens

The harbour and the canal at Lydney, once an important centre of the iron and coal industries and the largest settlement between Chepstow and Gloucester, are well worth exploring, and no visit to the town should end without a trip on the **Dean Forest Railway**. A regular service of steam and diesel trains operates the 4¼-mile route on 'the Friendly Forest Line' through the Forest between Lydney Junction, St Mary's Halt, Norchard and Parkend. The fare covers unlimited travel for the day. At **Norchard Railway Centre**, headquarters of the line, are a railway museum, souvenir shop and details of restoration projects. Popular events throughout the year include Days Out with Thomas, Santa Specials and Steam Footplate Experience Courses. Resident locomotives in 2010 included ex-GWR pannier tank 9681 and Prairie (2-6-2T) 5541.

A popular family tourist attraction is the **Forest of Dean Model Village & Gardens**, which features more than 50 detailed miniatures of local landmarks and buildings in five landscaped garden zones that include an adventure play area.

DEAN FOREST RAILWAY

Norchard, Forest Road, Lydney,
Gloucestershire GL15 4ET
Tel: 01594 845840 / 843423
e-mail: info@dfr.co.uk website: www.dfr.co.uk

Even if you are not a railway enthusiast, exploration of the medieval forest should not be complete without a trip on the **Dean Forest Railway**.

It is the last remnant of the old Severn & Wye Railway and can be found nestling in a tree-lined valley in west Gloucestershire, where a regular service of mainly steam trains operates the $4^1/_4$ mile route through the forest between Lydney Junction (national network), Lydney Town, Norchard and Parkend.

A popular destination with tourists, most visitors enjoy looking around the souvenir shop and especially the railway museum at Norchard Station, the railway's headquarters and designated car park. The fare usually covers unlimited travel for the day.

During the season March to October, there are Days out with Thomas and 40's Weekends, Hallowe'en Ghost Trains and Santa Specials, with the stylish Royal Forester Dining Train running monthly on Sundays.

Restoration projects are generally centred at Norchard. Particularly impressive is the restored Great Western Railway push-pull train which is in service on Bygone Branchline Days. Some mainline diesels and railcars are also used to augment the predominantly GWR loco stud which proves to be so nostalgic against the backdrop of a mainly deciduous forest landscape. Phone or visit the website for details.

One of the chief attractions in the vicinity is **Lydney Park Spring Gardens and Roman Temple Site**. The gardens, which lie beside the A48 on the western outskirts, are a riot of colour, particularly in May and June, and the grounds also contain the site of an Iron Age hill fort and the remains of a late-Roman temple excavated by Sir Mortimer Wheeler in the 1920s. The nearby museum houses a number of Roman artefacts from the site, including the famous Lydney Dog – a bronze statuette dating from about AD365 that apparently represents a half-grown wolfhound – and a number of interesting items brought back from New Zealand in the 1930s by the first Viscount Bledisloe after his term there as Governor General. Also in the park are traces of Roman iron-mine workings and Roman earth workings.

Around Lydney

ALVINGTON

2 miles SW of Lydney on the A48

Wintour's Leap

In the churchyard at Alvington are the graves of the illustrious Wintour family, leading figures in the defeat of the Spanish Armada. Half a century after that event came Sir John Wintour's remarkable escape from Cromwell's men at what is now known as **Wintour's Leap**. Sir John was an adventurer, Keeper of the Forest of Dean and sometime secretary to Queen Maria Henrietta of the Netherlands. In 1644 he was at the head of a Royalist force defeated at Blockley, near Chepstow, by Parliamentary troops. Wintour is said to have escaped from the battlefield by riding up by the Wye and hurling himself and his horse into the river from the cliffs.

Coleford

GWR Museum   Puzzle Wood

Perrygrove Railway

Coleford is a former mining centre that received its royal charter from Charles I in the 17th century in recognition of its loyalty to the Crown. It was by then already an important iron processing centre, partly because of the availability of local ore deposits, and partly because of the ready local supply of timber for converting into charcoal for use in the smelting process. It was in Coleford that the Mushet family helped to revolutionise the iron and steel industry. Robert Forester Mushet, a freeminer, discovered how spiegeleisen, an alloy of iron, manganese, silicon and carbon, could be used in the reprocessing of burnt iron and went on to develop a system for turning molten pig iron directly into steel, a process that predated the more familiar one developed by Bessemer.

Coleford, still regarded as the capital of the Forest of Dean, is a busy commercial centre with an interesting church and a number of notable industrial relics. The Forestry Commission is housed at Bank House and has information on all aspects of the Forest. There are miles of waymarked walks and cycle trails through the Forest, and the famous Sculpture Trail starts at Beechenhurst Lodge.

Coleford is also home to the **Great Western Railway Museum**, housed in an 1883 goods shed, the last surviving part of Coleford Station, on the line that once connected the town with Monmouth and Lydney. Exhibits include several full-size steam locomotives, large scale model engines, an original signal box, a miniature railway and a wealth of railway memorabilia. There's also a craft shop and refreshment room.

Another treat for railway fans is the **Perrygrove Railway**, where a narrow gauge (15in) steam train takes a 1½ mile trip through farmland and woods. In the evening, the Ghost Train journey through the dark woods promises a few scary surprises. There are also woodland walks, picnic and play areas, and light refreshments available.

Nearby is another visitor attraction, also on the B4228 just south of the town. The **Puzzle Wood** has 14 acres of pre-Roman open-cast ore mines redesigned as a family attraction, with paths forming an unusual maze, breathtaking scenery, wooden bridges, passageways through moss-covered rocks and lots of dead ends and circles.

J R R Tolkien, author of *Lord of the Rings*, was a regular visitor to the Forest of Dean and reputedly based Middle Earth on Puzzle Wood.

Around Coleford

STAUNTON

3 miles NW of Coleford on the A4136

Buck Stone and Suck Stone   Long Stone

Lots to see here, including a Norman church with two stone fonts and an unusual corkscrew staircase leading up past the pulpit to the belfry door. Not far from the village are several enormous mystical stones, notably the **Buck Stone** and the **Suck Stone**. The former, looking like some great monster, used to buck, or rock, on its base, but is now firmly fixed in place. The Suck Stone is a real giant, weighing in at many thousands of tons.

There are several other stones in the vicinity, including the Near Harkening and Far Harkening down among the trees, and the **Long Stone** by the A4136 at Marion's Cross.

CANNOP

4 miles E of Coleford on the B4226

Hopewell Colliery | Cannop Valley

Cannop Valley has many forest trails and picnic sites; one of the sites is at Cannop Ponds, picturesque ponds created in the 1820s to provide a regular supply of water for the local iron-smelting works. Nearby is **Hopewell Colliery**, a true Forest of Dean free mine where summer visitors can see old mine workings dating back as far as the 1820s and some of the old tools of the trade, then relax with a snack from the café. Open March to October; call 01594 810706.

Hopewell Colliery - Cannop

PARKEND

3 miles SE of Coleford off the B4234

Nagshead Nature Reserve Go Ape!

This is a community once based, like so many others in the area, on the extraction of minerals. In the early years of the 19th century, before steam engines arrived and horses did all the donkey work, Parkend became a tramroad centre and laden trams ran from coalpits, iron mines, quarries, furnaces and forges to river-borne outlets at Lydbrook and Lydney. New Fancy Colliery is now a delightful picnic area, with a nearby hill affording breathtaking views over the forestscape. Off the B4431, just west of Parkend, is the RSPB's **Nagshead Nature Reserve**, with hundreds of nest boxes in a woodland site with footpaths, waymarked trails and a summer information centre.

To the east of Parkend, **Go Ape!** Is an award-winning high wire forest adventure course with rope bridges, Tarzan swings and zip slides, all set high up in the treetops. Full and half-day packages are available.

CLEARWELL

1.5 miles S of Coleford off the A466

Clearwell Caves

Clearwell Caves are part of the only remaining working iron mine in the Forest of Dean. This natural cave system became filled with iron ore around 180 million years ago and has been mined for at least 4000 years. As a result, the cave complex now consists of many miles of passageways and hundreds of caverns. Visitors can take their own self-guided tour or participate in a more strenuous adventure caving trip. Other amenities on site include a gift shop, picnic area and tearoom. Call 01594 832535. A memorable visit can be completed by wandering down to Clearwell village with its lovely French Gothic-style church and the pretty surrounding countryside.

Ventilation Shaft - Clearwell Caves

ST BRIAVELS

5 miles S of Coleford on minor roads

Castle

On the edge of a limestone plateau high above the Wye Valley, this historic village is named after a 5th-century Welsh bishop whose name appears in various forms throughout Celtic Wales, Cornwall and Brittany, but nowhere else in England. In the Middle Ages St Briavels was an important administrative centre for the royal hunting forest, and also a leading manufacturer of armaments, supplying weapons and ammunition to the Crown.

The ample Church of St Mary the Virgin, Norman in origin, enlarged in the 12th and 13th centuries and remodelled by the Victorians, is the scene of a curious and very English annual custom, the St Briavels Bread and Cheese Ceremony. After evensong, a local forester stands on the Pound Wall and throws small pieces of bread and cheese to the villagers, accompanied by the chant, "St Briavels water and Whyrl's wheat are the best bread and water King John can ever eat". This ceremony is thought to have originated more than 700 years ago when the villagers successfully defended their rights of estover (collecting wood from common land) in nearby Hudnalls Wood. In gratitude, each villager paid one penny to the church warden to help feed the poor, and that act led to the founding of the ceremony. The small pieces of bread and cheese were considered to bring good luck, and the Dean Forest miners would

St Briavels Castle

keep them in order to ward off harm.

St Briavels Castle, which stands in an almost impregnable position on a high promontory, was founded by Henry I and enlarged by King John, who used it as a hunting lodge. Two sturdy gatehouses are among the parts that survive.

NEWLAND

1 mile SW of Coleford off the A466

Cathedral of the Forest

Newland's Church of All Saints is often known as the **Cathedral of the Forest** because of its impressive size. Its aisle is almost as wide as its nave, and its huge pinnacled tower is supported by flying buttresses. Like many churches in the county, it was built during the 13th and 14th centuries and remodelled by the Victorians. Inside, it has a number of interesting effigies, including an unusual brass relief of a medieval miner with a pick and hod in his hand and a candlestick in his mouth. Other effigies depict a forester in 15th-century hunting gear with a hunting horn, a sword and knife; and, from the 17th century, an archer with wide-brimmed hat, bow, horn and dagger.

South Gloucestershire and the Vale of Berkeley

Frampton-on-Severn

Frampton Court and Frampton Manor

Cotswold Canals Arlingham Peninsula

Frampton's 22-acre Rosamund Green, incorporating a cricket ground and three ponds, is one of the largest village greens in England, formed when the marshy ground outside the gates of **Frampton Court** was drained in the 18th century. The court is an outstanding example of a Georgian country house, built in the Palladian style in the 1730s and the seat of the Clifford family ever since. Fine porcelain, furniture and paintings grace the interior, and in the peacock-strutted grounds an ornamental canal reflects a superb Orangery in Dutch-influenced Strawberry Hill Gothic. A unique octagonal tower was built in the 17th century as a dovecote.

On the other side of the green is **Frampton Manor**, the Clifford family's

Frampton Court

former home, built between the 12th and 16th centuries. This handsome timber-framed house is thought to be the birthplace of Jane Clifford, who was the mistress of Henry II and bore him two children. The manor, which has a lovely old walled garden with some rare plants, is open by written appointment.

At the southern edge of the village stands the restored 14th-century Church of St Mary with its rare Norman lead font. The church stands beside the Sharpness Canal, which was built to allow ships to travel up the Severn Valley as far as Gloucester without being at the mercy of the estuary tides. The canal has several swing bridges and at some of these, as at Splatt Bridge and Saul Bridge at Frampton, there are splendid little bridge-keeper's cottages with Doric columns.

To the west of Frampton, on a great bend in the river, is the **Arlingham Peninsula**, part of the Severn Way Shepperdine-Tewkesbury long-distance walk. The trail passes close to Wick Court, a 13th-century moated manor house. The land on which the village of Arlingham stands once belonged to the monks of St Augustine's Abbey in Bristol who believed it to be the point where St Augustine crossed the Severn on his way to converting the heathen Welsh tribes.

The Severn naturally dominated life hereabouts and at Saul, a small village on the peninsula, the inhabitants decorated their houses with carvings of sailors, some of which, in bright, cheerful colours, can be seen today. The village lies at the point where two canals cross. Two separate waterways, the Stroudwater Navigation and the Thames & Severn Canal, once linked the Severn and the Thames, a route of 37 miles. The canals, known collectively as the **Cotswold Canals**, were abandoned in 1933 and 1954 respectively, but most of the route is intact, and since 1972 the Cotswold Canals Trust has worked in partnership with local authorities on restoration work. Continuing round the bend in the river, Epney is the point from which thousands of baby eels are exported each year to the Netherlands and elsewhere to replenish their own stocks.

SLIMBRIDGE

4 miles S of Frampton on the A38

Wildfowl and Wetlands Centre

Slimbridge Wetland Centre was founded as a trust on the banks of the Severn in 1946 by the distinguished naturalist, artist, sailor and broadcaster Peter (later Sir Peter) Scott. He believed in bringing wildlife and people together for the benefit of both, and the Trust's work continues with the same aims. Slimbridge has the world's largest collection of ducks, geese and swans, and spectacular flamingoes among the exotic wildfowl. Family attractions include canoe safaris and Land Rover trips. Also at the centre are a tropical house, pond zone, a watery children's play area, wildlife art gallery, restaurant and gift shop, and there are magnificent views from the observation tower. Sir Peter died in 1989 and his ashes were scattered at Slimbridge, where he had lived for many years. A memorial to him stands at the entrance to the Centre, which is widely regarded as the birthplace of modern conservation.

BERKELEY

6 miles S of Frampton off the A38

Berekley Castle Jenner Museum

Butterfly House & Plant Centre

Gloucester & Sharpness Canal

The fertile strip that is the Vale of Berkeley, bounded on the north by the Severn and on the south by the M5, takes its name from the small town of Berkeley, whose largely Georgian centre is dominated by the Norman **Berkeley Castle**. Said to be the oldest inhabited castle in Britain, with the same family resident from the start, this wonderful gem in pink sandstone was built between 1117 and 1153 on the site of a Saxon fort. It was here that the barons of the West met before making the journey to Runnymede to witness the signing of Magna Carta by King John in 1215. Edward II was imprisoned here for several months after losing his throne to his wife and her lover. He eventually met a painful death in the dungeons in the year 1327. Three centuries later, the castle was besieged by Cromwell's troops and played an important part in the history of the Civil War. It stands very close to the Severn and once incorporated the waters of the river in its defences so that it could, in an emergency, flood its lands. Visitors passing into the castle by way of a bridge over a moat will find a wealth of treasures in the Great Hall, the

Berkeley Castle

circular keep, the state apartments with their fine tapestries and period furniture, the medieval kitchens and the dungeons.

The Berkeley family have filled the place with objects from around the world, including painted glassware from Damascus, ebony chairs from India and a cypress chest that reputedly belonged to Sir Francis Drake. Other exhibits include a four-poster bed with a solid wooden top, and a set of bells once worn by the castle's dray horses and now hanging in the dairy. The castle is surrounded by sweeping lawns and Elizabethan terraced gardens. Special features include a deer park, Queen Elizabeth I's bowling green, a beautiful lily pond and the **Butterfly House & Plant Centre**. Denizens of the Butterfly House include the Atlas moth, the world's largest moth, and the Plant Centre is stocked with unusual varieties from the Castle grounds. The 6500-acre Berkeley Estate incorporates farms, the WWT Slimbridge Wetlands Centre and part of the River Severn itself.

The parish church of St Mary, which contains several memorials to the Berkeley family, has a fine Norman doorway, a detached tower and a striking east window depicting Christ healing the sick. A curious piece of carving in the nave shows two old gossips with a giant toad sitting on their heads.

Next to the castle and church is the **Jenner**

Museum (see panel below), once the home of Edward Jenner, the doctor and immunologist who is best known as the man who discovered a vaccine for smallpox. The son of a local parson, Jenner was apprenticed to a surgeon in Chipping Sodbury at the tender age of 14. His work over several decades led to the first vaccination against smallpox, a disease that had killed or disfigured many thousands every year. His beautiful Georgian house in Church Lane has a state-of-the-art display showing the importance of the science of immunology. In the grounds of the house is a rustic thatched hut where Jenner used to vaccinate the poor free of charge and which he called the Temple of Vaccinia. The east window of the church is a memorial to Jenner, who is buried in the churchyard.

At Sharpness, a mile or so west of Berkeley, the world's first nuclear power station operated between 1962 and 1989. It marks the entrance to the **Gloucester & Sharpness Canal**, opened in 1827 to bypass the tricky waters of the lower Severn. Sixteen miles in length, it has a lock from the tidal River Severn at Sharpness and a lock back into the River Severn at the head of Gloucester Docks, from which the River Severn Navigation runs 43 miles north to Stourport. There are several interesting villages in the vicinity, including Breadstone, which has a church built entirely of tin.

The Jenner Museum

Church Lane, Berkeley,
Gloucestershire GL13 9BH
Tel: 01453 810631 Fax: 01453 811690
e-mail: manager@jennermuseum.com
website: www.jennermuseum.com

Born in Berkeley in 1749, Edward Jenner returned here after completing his medical training and his house, The Chantry, is now home the **Jenner Museum** where this pioneering doctor and immunologist's life and work is explored. Intrigued by the country lore that said that milkmaids who caught the mild cowpox could not catch smallpox, one of the most feared diseases of all time, Jenner set about developing a means of vaccinating against smallpox, which he successful did in 1798. In 1967, the World Health Organisation masterminded a final global plant to eradicate the disease and, in 1980, smallpox was declared dead.

Not only did Jenner develop the first vaccination but his discovery has now been developed into one of the most important parts of modern medicine – immunology. Along with his work on smallpox, Jenner also made several other important contributions to medicine: he was probably the first to link angina with hardening of the arteries, he described rheumatic heart disease and he purified important medicines. Both Jenner's medical work and also his work as a naturalist and geologist are described here through numerous displays and exhibits.

Thornbury

Castle

The woollen industry was important here in late medieval times, and the church, set away from the centre near the site of the old manor house, reflects the prosperity of those days. The side chapel is dedicated to the Stafford family, the local lords of the manor, whose emblem, the Staffordshire knot, is much in evidence. Edward Stafford, 3rd Duke of Buckingham, was responsible for starting work on **Thornbury Castle** in 1511 but did not live to see its completion. Charged with high treason by Henry VIII, he was beheaded on Tower Hill in London in 1522. The building was restored by Anthony Salvin in the 1850s and is now a luxury hotel.

Around Thornbury

TORTWORTH

4 miles NE of Thornbury off the B4509

Tortworth Chestnut

Overlooking the village green stands the Church of St Leonard, which contains some fine 15th-century stained glass and a pair of canopied tombs of the Throckmorton family, former owners of the Tortworth Park estate. In a field over the church wall are several interesting trees, including an American hickory, a huge silver-leafed linden and two Locust trees. Nearby, and the most famous of all, is the famous **Tortworth Chestnut**, a massive Spanish chestnut that the diarist John Evelyn called "the great chestnut of King Stephen's time". Certainly it was well established by Stephen's time (the 1130s), and a fence was put up to protect it in 1800. At that time a brass plaque was erected with this inscription:

May man still guard
thy venerable form
From the rude blasts and
tempestuous storm.
Still mayest thou flourish
through succeeding time
And last, long last,
the wonder of the clime.

And last it has; its lower branches have bent to the ground and rooted in the soil, giving the impression of a small copse rather than a single tree.

Thornbury Castle

ALMONDSBURY

6 miles S of Thornbury on the A38

The Church of St Mary has some fine windows, including a memorial to Charles Richardson, the 19th-century engineer who designed the original Severn Tunnel. A curious event took place in 1817 at nearby Knole Park when a personable young woman arrived at the door of the local squire saying that she was an Oriental princess who had been kidnapped and taken on board a ship, from which she had escaped by jumping overboard. The squire believed the story and 'adopted' Princess Caraboo, who soon became the toast of Bath. Her fame spread far enough to come to the attention of her former Bristol landlady, who identified the fake princess as a certain Mary Baker, a penniless woman from Devon. The embarrassed squire raised the money to send the impostor to Philadelphia. She returned some years later to Bristol, where she died in 1865.

Chipping Sodbury

Dodington House

This pleasant market town was one of the earliest examples of post-Roman town planning, its settlement being arranged in strips on either side of the main street in the 12th century. The town once enjoyed prosperity as a market and weaving centre, and it was during that period that the large parish church was built.

A mile or so to the east, on a loop off the A432, is **Old Sodbury**, whose part-Norman church contains some exceptional tombs and monuments. One of these is a carved stone effigy of a 13th-century knight whose shield is a very rare wooden carving of a knight. Also in the church is the tomb of David Harley, the Georgian diplomat who negotiated the treaty that ended the American War of Independence. A tower just to the east of the church marks a vertical shaft, one of a series sunk to ventilate the long tunnel that carried the London-South Wales railway through the Cotswold escarpment. Opened in 1903, the 2½ mile tunnel required its own brickworks and took five years to complete.

A lane leads south from Old Sodbury to **Dodington House**, built between 1796 and 1816 where previously an Elizabethan house stood. It was designed in lavish neo-Roman style by the classical architect James Wyatt who was killed in a carriage accident before seeing his work completed. The house, whose interior is even more ornate than the facade, is open daily in the summer. Connected to the house by an elegant conservatory is the private Church of St Mary, also designed by Wyatt, in the shape of a Greek cross.

Around Chipping Sodbury

DYRHAM

4 miles S of Chipping Sodbury on the A46

Dyrham Park

The National Trust-owned **Dyrham Park** stands on the slope of the Cotswold ridge, a little way south of the site of a famous 6th-century battle between Britons and Saxons. This striking baroque mansion, used as a location for the filming of *Remains of the Day*, houses a wonderful collection of artefacts accumulated by the original owner, William Blathwayt, during diplomatic tours of duty in Holland and North America (later he became Secretary of State to William III). Among the most notable are several Dutch paintings and some magnificent Delft porcelain. The west front of the house looks out across a terrace to lawns laid out in formal Dutch style. Much of the estate is a deer park, which perhaps it was

Dyrham Park

Thereafter they were named the Glorious Glosters. Also in the Docks area is the Gloucester Antiques Centre where more than 140 dealers buy and sell a wide variety of antiques, collectables and curios.

Elsewhere in the city **Gloucester City Museum and Art Gallery** (free) houses treasures from all over the county to reveal its history, from dinosaur bones and Roman remains to antique furniture and the decorative arts. Among the highlights are the amazing Birdlip Mirror, made in bronze for a Celtic chief just before the Roman conquest, two Roman tombstones and a section of the Roman city wall revealed under the cut-away gallery floor. The extensive art collection includes work by Jan Brueghel, Willem van der Velde, Gainsborough, Turner and Atkinson-Grimshaw.

Timber-framed Tudor buildings house **Gloucester Folk Museum**, where the exhibits include farming, fishing on the Severn, the port of Gloucester, the Civil War, a Victorian schoolroom, a dairy, an ironmongery, transport and a wheelwright's workshop.

The **House of the Tailor of Gloucester**, in College Court, is the house sketched by Beatrix Potter in 1897 and used in her tale *The Tailor of Gloucester*. It now brings that story to life, complete with Simpkin the Cat and an army of helpful mice. Apparently, the story is based on a true incident. After a Saturday night drinking spree, a Gloucester tailor's assistants returned to the shop to sleep off their over-indulgence. But they slept right through to Sunday morning and were then afraid of appearing unshaven and tousled on the street amongst the church-goers. Waiting for nightfall, they occupied themselves with finishing a waistcoat their employer had started making for the mayor but hadn't finished because he, the tailor, fell ill. They finished the waistcoat apart from one buttonhole. As in Beatrix Potter's story, they left an explanatory note saying "No more twist".

Another building of interest is the half-timbered **Parliament Rooms**. King Richard II held parliament in the older part of the building in 1378 and, at Easter, Whitsun and Christmas, the king would 'wear the crown' in Gloucester.

In the southwestern suburbs of Gloucester are the ruins of **Llanthony Priory**. The explanation of its Welsh name is an interesting one. The priory of Llanthony was originally founded in the Black Mountains of Wales at the beginning of the 12th century, but the inmates were so frightened of the local Welsh that they begged the Bishop of Hereford to find them a safer place. The Bishop passed their plea to Milo, Earl of Hereford, who granted this plot of land for a second priory bearing the same name as the first. Llanthony Secunda was consecrated in 1136. On a nearby hill the monks built St Ann's Well, whose water is believed to cure eye problems.

Around Gloucester

TWIGWORTH

2 miles N of Gloucester off the A38

Nature in Art

Twigworth is the home of **Nature in Art**, which occupies stately 18th-century Wallsworth Hall. This is the world's first museum dedicated solely to fine, decorative and applied art inspired by nature. It contains both two and three-dimensional work in all styles and media from around the world, and spans some 1500 years. Work by 600 artists from more than 50 countries is on display. Open Tuesday to Sunday.

PAUNTLEY

8 miles N of Gloucester on the A417

Pauntley Court

The penniless orphan boy, who in the pantomime fable was attracted by the gold-paved streets of London and became its Lord Mayor, was born at **Pauntley Court**. Richard Whittington, neither penniless nor an orphan, was born here about 1350, one of three sons of landowner Sir William de Whittington and Dame Joan. He became a mercer in London, then an important financier and was three times Mayor (not Lord Mayor – that title had not been invented). He married Alice Fitzwarren, the daughter of a wealthy landowner from Dorset. The origin of the cat connection is unclear, but an event that could have contributed to the myth was the discovery in 1862 of the carved figure of a boy holding a cat in the foundations of a house in Gloucester. The carving can be seen in Gloucester Museum.

HARTPURY

5 miles NW of Gloucester on the A417

Tithe Barn

There are two very interesting listed buildings here: a rare medieval set of bee hives in a building known as a bee bole and, in the churchyard, a Soper stone tomb with a shrouded body on top. At nearby Ashleworth is a magnificent 14th-century **Tithe Barn** with a stone-tiled roof, projecting porches and elaborate interlocking roof timbers.

REDMARLEY D'ABITOT

9 miles NW of Gloucester on the A417

This hilltop village, built on the red marle (clay) from which it takes its name, and once the property of the French d'Abitot family, was for a time the home of the actress Lily Langtry, mistress of the Prince of Wales, later King Edward VII. The link with the actress is remembered in two streets in the village – Drury Lane and Hyde Park Corner.

Tewkesbury

Abbey John Moore Countryside Museum

Battle of Tewkesbury

A town of historic and strategic importance close to the confluence of the Severn and Avon rivers. Those rivers also served to restrict the lateral expansion of the town, which accounts for the unusual number of tall buildings. (They also contributed to the disastrous floods of summer 2007.) Tewkesbury's early prosperity was based on the wool and mustard trades, and the movement of corn by river also contributed to its wealth. Tewkesbury's main thoroughfares, High Street, Church Street and Barton Street, form a Y shape, and the area between is a marvellous maze of narrow alleyways and small courtyards hiding many grand old pubs and medieval cottages. At the centre of it all is **Tewkesbury Abbey**, the cathedral-sized parish church of St Mary. One of the largest and grandest parish churches in the country, it was founded in the 8th century and completely rebuilt in the 11th. It was once the church of the Benedictine Abbey and was among the last to be dissolved by Henry VIII. In 1540, it was saved from destruction by the townspeople who raised £453 to buy it from the Crown. Many of its features are on a grand scale - the colossal double row of Norman pillars; the six-fold arch in the west front; and the vast main tower, 132ft in height and 46ft square, the tallest surviving Norman main tower in the world. The choir windows have

Tewkesbury Abbey

renovated and enhanced. The Tourist Information Centre is on the ground floor, the two upper storeys incorporate interactive displays, games, information panels and much more.

Three museums tell the story of the town and its environs: the Little Museum, laid out like a typical old merchant's house; Tewkesbury Museum, with displays on the social history and archaeology of the area; and the **John Moore Countryside Museum**, a natural history collection displayed in a 15th-century timber-framed house. The museum commemorates the work of John Moore, a well-known writer, broadcaster and naturalist, who was born in Tewkesbury in 1907.

stained glass dating from the 1300s, and the abbey has more medieval monuments than any besides Westminster. A chantry chapel was endowed by the Beauchamps, an influential family that married into another, that of Richard Neville, Warwick the Kingmaker. Other treasures include the 17th-century Milton Organ that is still in daily use. There's a cathedral shop, and the refectory has been restored to its original function as an eating place, although it is now licensed.

American visitors to the abbey may be interested in a memorial plaque to Victoria Woodhull Martin, a native of Ohio for which she served as Congresswoman and then, in 1872, became the first woman to run for President. When she failed to get elected and her second husband having died, she quit American politics and settled in Tewkesbury where, says her epitaph, "she devoted herself unsparingly to all that could promote the great cause of Anglo-American friendship". She died in 1927.

An excellent introduction to Tewkesbury and its history is provided at Out of the Hat, a recently opened heritage and visitor centre that occupies a former hat shop. The 17th-century building has been lovingly restored,

The **Battle of Tewkesbury** was one of the fiercest in the Wars of the Roses. It took place in 1471 in a field south of the town, which has ever since been known as Bloody Meadow. Following the Lancastrian defeat, those who had not been slaughtered in the battle fled to the abbey, where the killing began again. Abbot Strensham intervened to stop the massacre, but the survivors, who included the Duke of Somerset, were handed over to King Edward IV and executed at Market Cross. The 17-year-old son of Henry VI, Edward Prince of Wales, was killed in the conflict and a plaque marking his final resting place can be seen in the abbey. One of the victors of the battle was the Duke of Gloucester, later Richard III. Tewkesbury was again the scene of military action almost two centuries later during the Civil War. The town changed hands several times during this period and on one occasion Charles I began his siege of Gloucester by requisitioning every pick, mattock, spade and shovel in Tewkesbury.

Around Tewkesbury

BREDON

4 miles NE of Tewkesbury on the B4080

Bredon Barn

Bredon Barn (National Trust) is a 14th-century structure built of Cotswold stone, with a splendid aisled interior that gives it the atmosphere of a church. Unusually, it has five porches, one of which has a rare stone chimney cowling. Call 01451 844257.

DEERHURST

3 miles S of Tewkesbury off the A38

Odda's Chapel

Set on the eastern bank of the Severn, Deerhurst is a village whose current size and status belies a distinguished past. The church, with a distinct Celtic feel, is one of the oldest in England, with parts dating back to the 7th century, and its treasures include a unique double east window, a 9th-century carved font, a Saxon carving of the Virgin and Child and some fine brasses dating from the 14th and 15th centuries. One depicts the Cassey family, local landowners, and their dog, Terri.

Another Saxon treasure, 200 yards from the church, is **Odda's Chapel**, dedicated in 1056 and lost for many centuries before being gradually rediscovered after 1885 under a half-timbered house. The connection was then made with a stone inscribed with the date of consecration discovered in 1675 and now on view in the Ashmolean in Oxford.

FORTHAMPTON

3 miles W of Tewkesbury off the A438

Forthampton Court

This unspoilt Severn Vale village is dominated by the ancient Church of St Mary and by **Forthampton Court**, sometime home to the abbots of Tewkesbury and still retaining its fine 14th-century banqueting hall, chapel and a medieval wood-based picture of Edward the Confessor. Near the churchyard can be seen relics of harsher times – a set of stocks and a whipping post complete with manacles.

Tetbury

Chavenage House Police Museum

A really charming Elizabethan market town, another to have prospered from the wool trade. Its most famous building is the stone-pillared 17th-century Market House in the heart of town, but a visit should also take in the ancient Chipping Steps connecting the market house to the old trading centre, and the Church of St Mary, an 18th-century period piece with high-backed pews, huge windows made from recovered medieval glass, and slender timber columns hiding sturdy iron uprights.

Tetbury Police Museum (free), housed in the original cells of the 1884 police station, has a fascinating collection of artefacts, memorabilia and uniforms from the Gloucestershire Constabulary. The original courtroom has been restored and a realistic model display shows a court scene with magistrates and the accused in the dock.

Two miles northwest of Tetbury, west of the B4014, stands **Chavenage House** (see panel opposite), a beautiful Elizabethan mansion built of grey Cotswold stone on earlier monastic foundations in the characteristic E shape of the period. The elegant front aspect has remained virtually unchanged down the years, and the present owners, the Lowsley-Williams family, can trace their lineage back to the original owners. Two rooms are covered with rare 17th-

Chavenage House

Tetbury, Gloucestershire GL8 8XP
Tel: 01666 502329 Fax: 01453 836778
e-mail info@chavenage.com.
website: www.chavenage.com

Chavenage, is a wonderful family owned Elizabethan Manor House, hidden away in the magnificent South Cotswolds. Originally monastic, only two families have occupied the house since the reign of Elizabeth I. The house and its interior have changed little since it was reconstructed in 1576. The main historical interest is centred upon the English Civil War, at which time the house was owned by Col. Nathaniel Stephens M.P. One of the feature rooms is the completely tapestried Oliver Cromwell Room. From this period the 'Legend of Chavenage' has arisen with the headless ghost of Charles I, coming to the house to collect the soul of Col. Stephens with a coach and four, which subsequently disappears into a fireball at the gates of the Manor House.

Tours are lead by a member of the family, with the majority of the tour on the ground floor. The house is open to the general public from May to September on Thursday and Sunday afternoons, 2 pm to 5pm as well as Easter Sunday and Monday and Bank Holiday Mondays. The Lowsley-Williams are also happy to open the House, on any day of the week, at any time throughout the year to groups numbering between 15 and 100. Joanna Gouriet, the Prue Leith trained daughter of David Lowsley-Williams, runs the in-house catering and can produce any meal to suit pre-arranged groups.

century tapestries, and the house contains many relics from the Cromwellian period. Cromwell is known to have stayed at the house and, during the Civil War he persuaded the owner, Colonel Nathaniel Stephens, a relative by marriage, to vote for the King's impeachment. According to the Legend of Chavenage, Stephens died after being cursed by his

Chavenage House, Tetbury

daughter and was taken away in a black coach driven by a headless horseman. The present owner, who conducts tours round the property, welcomes visitors to 'Gloucestershire's second most haunted house' (Berkeley Castle is the most haunted!). In 1970, an astonishing find was made in the attic – a portfolio of watercolours by George IV of plans for the restoration of Windsor Castle. Call 01666 502329 for visiting times.

Around Tetbury

BEVERSTON

2 miles W of Tetbury on the A4135

The same Robert Stayner Holford who started the Westonbirt Arboretum built the model village of Beverston in conjunction with the architect Lewis Vulliamy. Their aim was to combine rural practicality with improved standards of accommodation, and the limestone terraces and model farms can be seen from the main road. The village also had a castle, once occupied by Earl Godwin, father of King Harold; the earthworks are still visible.

WOTTON-UNDER-EDGE

10 miles W of Tetbury on the B4508

Heritage Centre

A hillside former wool town with a number of interesting buildings: Berkeley House with its stone Jacobean front; the terraced house that was the family home of Isaac Pitman and where he devised his renowned method of shorthand; the Perry and Dawes almshouses; and the Church of St Mary with memorials to Lord Berkeley and his wife Margaret. The **Wotton-under-Edge Heritage Centre**, housed in a former fire station, provides an excellent introduction to the town and the surrounding Area of Outstanding Natural Beauty.

OZLEWORTH

11 miles W of Tetbury on minor roads

Newark Park Nan Tow's Tump

Midger Wood Nature Reserve

A secluded hamlet with a very unusual circular churchyard, one of only two in England. The church itself has a rare feature in a six-sided Norman tower. Also at Ozleworth is the National Trust's **Newark Park**, built as a hunting lodge by the Poyntz family in Elizabethan times. James Wyatt later converted it into a castellated country house. It stands on the edge of a 40ft cliff with superb views across to the Mendips. Attractions include a 14-acre woodland garden, countryside walks across the estate and two new waymarked woodland walks connected to the Cotswold Way.

This is great walking country, and one of the finest walks takes in the **Midger Wood Nature Reserve** on its way up to **Nan Tow's Tump**, a huge round barrow whose tomb is said to contain the remains of Nan Tow, a local witch.

Dursley

Cam Long Down

One of the most notable buildings in this former centre of the cloth-making trade is the 18th-century market hall standing on 12 pillars at a busy town-centre junction. It has a bell turret on its roof and a statue of Queen Anne facing the fine parish church. William Shakespeare reputedly spent some time in Dursley after being spotted poaching, and there is a reference to a bailiff from the town in *Henry IV*. Cloth is still produced in the mill at Cam on the northern edge of the town, continuing a tradition started in the 16th century.

Local legend is rich in stories about **Cam Long Down**, a small, isolated peak that is sometimes claimed to be the scene of King Arthur's last battle. One story concerns the

Cam Long Down, Dursley

FOX AND HOUNDS

The Street, Coaley, nr Dursley, Gloucestershire GL11 5EG
Tel: 01453 890366
e-mail: foxandhounds2010@gmail.com

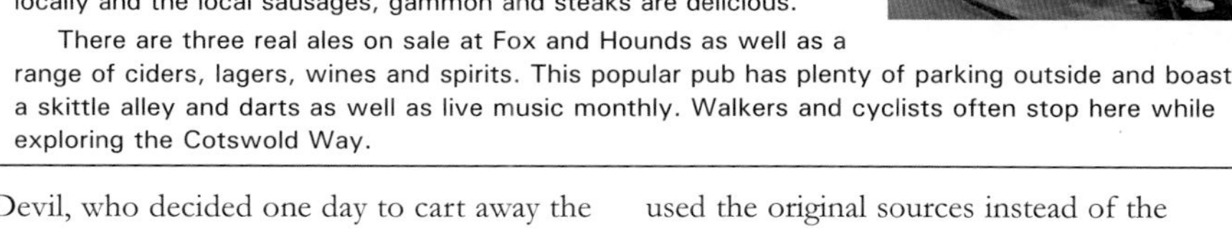

Fox and Hounds is a fantastic country pub serving the very best in traditional English pub grub. A lot of the produce used here is sourced locally and the local sausages, gammon and steaks are delicious.

There are three real ales on sale at Fox and Hounds as well as a range of ciders, lagers, wines and spirits. This popular pub has plenty of parking outside and boasts a skittle alley and darts as well as live music monthly. Walkers and cyclists often stop here while exploring the Cotswold Way.

Devil, who decided one day to cart away the Cotswolds and dam the Severn. On setting out with his first cartload he met a cobbler and asked him how far it was to the river. The cobbler showed him one of the shoes he was taking home to mend and replied, "Do you see this sole? Well, I've worn it out walking from the Severn." This persuaded the Devil, who was obviously a lazy devil, to abandon his task; he tipped out his load, creating the hill that can be seen today.

Around Dursley

STINCHCOMBE

3 miles W of Dursley off the A4135

Stancombe Park, on the southern edge of Stinchcombe, is a handsome country house built in 1880 on the site of a Roman villa, whose mosaic floor can be seen in Gloucester Museum. The gardens at Stancombe are occasionally open to the public.

NORTH NIBLEY

2 miles SW of Dursley on the B4060

Tyndale Monument

This village was the birthplace, around 1494, of William Tyndale, the first man to translate and print the Old and New Testaments. He used the original sources instead of the approved Latin, for which heresy he was burnt at the stake in Belgium in 1536. Three-and-a-half centuries later, the imposing **Tyndale Monument**, paid for by public subscription, was erected on the ridge above the village to commemorate his life and work. Standing 111 feet high on the escarpment, it is one of the most prominent landmarks on the Cotswold Way and offers superb views. North Nibley is also the site of the last 'private' battle in England, which took place in 1471 between rival barons William Lord Berkeley and Viscount de Lisle.

ULEY

11 miles NE of Chipping Sodbury on the B4066

Owlpen Manor | Uley Bury | Coaley Peak
Hetty Pegler's Tump | Nympsfield Long Barrow

Even in this part of the Cotswolds where almost every prospect pleases, Owlpen is uniquely lovely – "a breathtaking ensemble of truly English beauty" enthused one visitor; Prince Charles called it "the epitome of the English village". Manor house, church, mill and cottages of pearl-grey stone are framed by a natural amphitheatre of steep, wooded hills, a timeless setting for this beautiful village.

The jewel in the crown of this enchanting village is **Owlpen Manor**, a romantic Tudor building built between 1450 and 1616 and set in formal Queen Anne terraced yew gardens. Inside, contrasting with the ancient polished flagstones and the putty-coloured plaster, are fine pieces of William Morris-inspired Arts and Crafts furniture; there's also a rare beadwork collection and some unique 17th-century painted cloth wall hangings. Within the grounds are a Courthouse dated 1620, an 18th-century Mill and a licensed restaurant in a medieval Cyder House, complete with a massive cider press.

The village lies in the shadow of **Uley Bury**, a massive Iron Age hill fort that has thrown up evidence of habitation by a prosperous community of warrior farmers during the 1st century BC. Another prehistoric site, a mile along the ridge, is Uley Long Barrow, known locally as **Hetty Pegler's Tump**. This chambered long barrow, 180 feet in length, takes its name from Hester Pegler, who came from a family of local landowners. Adventurous spirits can crawl into this Neolithic tomb on all fours, braving the dark and the dank smell to reach the burial chambers, where they will no longer be scared by the skeletons that terrified earlier visitors. The walls and ceilings of the chamber are made of huge stone slabs infilled with drystone material.

A little further north, at the popular picnic site of **Coaley Peak** with its adjoining National Trust nature reserve, is another spectacular chambered tomb, **Nympsfield Long Barrow**.

Stroud

Museum in the Park · Stratford Park

The capital of the Cotswold woollen industry, Stroud stands on the River Frome at a point where five valleys converge. The surrounding hill farms provided a constant supply of wool, and the Cotswold streams supplied the water-power. By the 1820s there were more than 150 textile mills in the vicinity. Six survive, one of them specialising in green baize for snooker tables; another, Snow Mill, has cornered a niche market producing more than 160 types of snowflake for films and other entertainments. A stroll round the centre of town reveals some interesting buildings, notably the Old Town Hall dating from 1594 and the Subscription Rooms in neo-classical style.

An easy walk from the centre is **Stratford Park**, a large park containing dozens of trees both ordinary and exotic, and a lake with ducks. The **Museum in the Park** is a family-friendly place in a 17th-century wool merchant's mansion with innovative and colourful displays that include dinosaur remains, a Roman temple – and the world's first lawnmower, invented in 1830 by local entrepreneur Edwin Buddings. It required two operators, one pulling and one pushing.

Around Stroud

MINCHINHAMPTON

4 miles SE of Stroud off the A419

Minchinhampton and Rodborough Commons

A scattered community on a ridge between two picturesque valleys, Minchinhampton acquired its market charter as far back as 1213. The area is good for walking and exploring, with the old stone quarries at Ball's Green and the National Trust woodland and grassland at **Minchinhampton and Rodborough Commons**. The majority of the commons are open to walkers and riders, and nature lovers

BLACK HORSE

Littleworth, Amberley, nr Stroud, Gloucestershire GL5 5AL
Tel: 01453 872556
e-mail: enquiries@blackhorseamberley.co.uk
website: www.blackhorseamberley.co.uk

The Black Horse is a real hidden gem of a pub perched on the edge of Minchinhampton Common above Stroud Valley.

Dating back 400 years this traditional country pub in The Cotswolds, owned by Sharyn O'Flynn, offers a relaxed environment and the very best in professional service.

It offers award winning real ales, excellent wines and home cooked, hearty pub food. Homemade soup of the day with warm rustic bread and pan fried fillet of red mullet with red onion and sweet corn salsa are among the starters on the menu. Main courses include pan seared fillet of sea bass, new potatoes, sugar snap peas and white wine, and butternut squash & blue cheese risotto with rocket and parmesan salad. There is also a wide range of pub classics and salads to choose from.

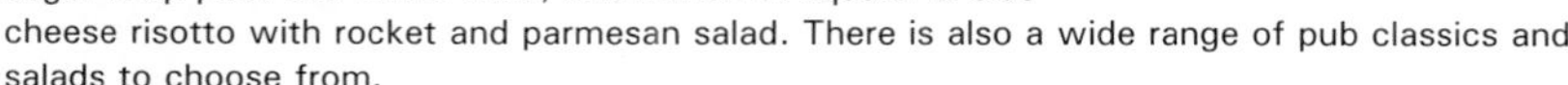

The Black Horse is very popular with locals and visitors. Keen walkers often stop off here during, or following, their exploration of The Cotswolds and there are always plenty of stories to be shared. On warm summer evenings customers can enjoy the beautiful gardens and breathtaking views across The Cotswolds and in the winter cosy log fires provide a relaxing and homely environment. The Black Horse is an ideal venue for weddings and private parties.

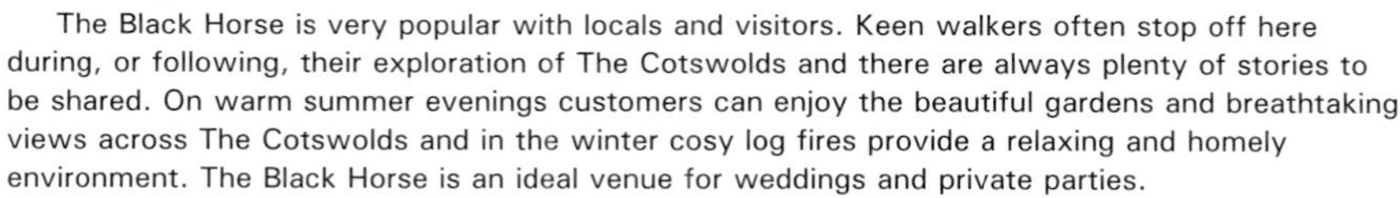

might spot rare butterflies such as the Chalkhill Blue, the tiny Green Hairstreak and the Duke of Burgundy Fritillary. The Commons are also famous for their grassland species, including the lovely Pasque flower, whose resurgence has been assisted by the introduction of a small herd of Belted Galloways to help manage the rich grassland areas of the lower slopes.

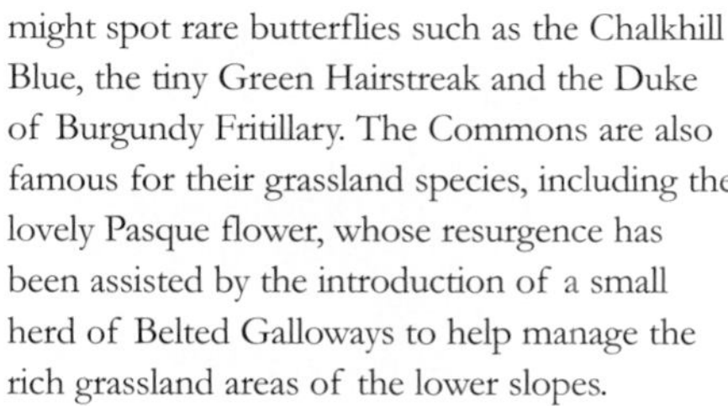

WOODCHESTER

2 miles S of Stroud off the A46

Woodchester Park Mansion

Woodchester Park Mansion is one of Britain's most intriguing Victorian country houses. Building started in 1854 and was halted abruptly in 1868, three-quarters finished, with the scaffolding in place and the workmen's tools abandoned. What stands now, as in 1868, is a vast shell with gargoyles and flying buttresses on the Gothic facade, and all the props and stays and tools inside.

SELSLEY

2 miles S of Stroud off the A46

All Saints Church

All Saints Church, built in the 1860s by wealthy mill-owner Sir Samuel Marling, is notable chiefly for its exceptional stained glass. This was commissioned from William Morris and Company and features designs by many of the Morris partnership, including Philip Webb, Burne-Jones, Ford Madox Brown, Dante Gabriel Rossetti and Morris himself.

NAILSWORTH

4 miles S of Stroud on the A46

Stokescroft Ruskin Mill

This small residential and commercial town was once, like so many of its neighbours, a centre of the wool trade. Several of the old

PAINT-A-POT

5 Cossack Square, Nailsworth, nr Stroud, Gloucestershire GL6 0DB
Tel: 01453 835043
e-mail: enquiries@paint-a-pot.co.uk
website: www.paint-a-pot.co.uk

The name sounds fun and that is just what you can look forward to when you visit **Paint-A-Pot**. Owner Deborah Pearson ensures that there always something for all the family to paint, including kitchen, and tableware, vases and ornaments. Inside the colourful shop there is plenty to do including 'Decopatch', a simple version of decoupage using papier mache shapes which are then covered in a choice of beautiful papers. There are a variety of animal figures, boxes, frames and letters.

Hand and footprint keepsakes are extremely popular and imprints in clay can be done with prior booking. Also hand and foot prints can be made into sterling silver jewellery including pendants, charms and cuff links. The party room is available for larger groups and children's parties, hen parties etc and commissions can be made for special celebrations or gifts.

For those who want something to do on a rainy day there is an option to take away pottery painting or buy a range of Decopatch including all the necessary materials or in ready made kits which also make an ideal gift and are great for party bags. Paint-a-Pot is open Tuesday to Thursday 9.30am - 5pm and Friday & Saturday 10am - 5pm.

COUNTRY QUALITY MEATS

10 Old Market, Nailsworth, Gloucestershire GL6 0DU
Tel: 01453 835058

Over a period of 20 years **Country Quality Meats** has established a reputation as one of the best butchers in the Cotswolds for quality, reliability and friendly, personal service. Paul Dowdeswell and his staff sell only the best, usually locally sourced meat, hung for 28 days to ensure maximum flavour and tenderness in the cuts and joints and chops. They prepare their own bacon, dry-cured or oak-smoked, and make their own sausages with a variety of flavours. The shop sells seasonal game both furred and feathered, along with old favourites like faggots, oxtails and pigs' trotters, and a selection of prepared frozen meats to take home for year-round availability.

mills have been modernised, some playing new roles, others plying their original trades. **Ruskin Mill** is a thriving arts and crafts centre; **Stokescroft** an unusual 17th-century building on Cossack Square. During restoration work in 1972, scribblings found on an attic wall suggested that soldiers had been billeted there in 1812 and 1815. Perhaps this is why it is known locally as the Barracks. It is thought to have housed Russian prisoners during the Crimean War, which accounts for the name of the square.

About half a mile north of the town, the Dunkirk Mill Centre contains a fulling mill, which lays on demonstrations of the finishing of fine woollen cloth.

FROCESTER

4 miles SW of Stroud off the A419

Tithe Barn

In the grounds of the chapel at the centre of the village stands the wonderful **Frocester Tithe Barn**, a massive 186 feet in length and looking much as it did when built on the instructions of Abbot John de Gamages between 1284 and 1306.

BISLEY

4 miles E of Stroud on minor roads

All Saints Church The Bisley Boy

Country roads lead across from Stroud or up from Oakridge Lynch to the delightful village of Bisley, which stands 780 feet above sea level and is known as Bisley-God-Help-Us because of the winter winds that sweep across the hillside. Bisley's impressive **All Saints Church** dates from the 13th century and was restored in the early 19th by Thomas Keble, after whose poet and theologian brother John, Keble College in Oxford was named. The font has two carved fish inside the bowl and a shepherd and sheep on the base. In the churchyard is the Poor Souls' Light, a stone wellhead beneath a spire dating from the 13th century. It was used to hold candles lit for souls in purgatory. Below the church are the Seven Wells of Bisley (also restored by Thomas Keble), which are blessed and decorated with flowers each year on Ascension Day. At the top of the village is a double lock-up built in 1824, with two cells beneath an ogee gable.

The village's main claim to fame is the story of the **Bisley Boy**. When Bisley was a rich wool town it had a royal manor, Over Court, where the young Princess Elizabeth (later Queen Elizabeth I) often stayed. The story goes that during one of those visits the princess, then aged 10, caught a fever and died. Fearing the wrath of her father Henry VIII, her hosts looked for a substitute and found a local child with red hair and remarkably similar physical characteristics except for the rather important fact that the child was a boy called John Neville. Could this explain the Virgin Queen's reluctance to marry, her problem with hair loss and her "heart that beats like a man's", or was the story made up to fit those facts?

Vale of Gloucester and the Central Cotswolds

SLAD

2 miles N of Stroud on the B4070

Immortalised by Laurie Lee in his autobiographical *Cider With Rosie*, the sprawling village of Slad in the valley of the same name was for centuries a centre for milling and the production of fruit. Cider gave way to champagne on 13 March 2002, after a Polish-bred horse called Galileo, trained by Tom George at Slad, was successful in one of the big novice hurdles at the Cheltenham Festival. A Roman villa was found in the valley, and the votive tablets discovered at the site are now in Gloucester Museum.

PAINSWICK

4 miles N of Stroud on the A46

St Mary's Church · Prinknash Abbey Park

Painswick Rococo Garden

Gloucestershire Guild of Craftsmen Gallery

This beautiful little town, known as the Queen of the Cotswolds, prospered with the wool trade, which had its peak in the second half of the 18th century. At that time 30 mills provided power within the parish, and the number of fine houses and farms in and around the town are witness to those days. Many of them are built of the pale grey limestone that was quarried at Painswick Hill.

St Mary's Church, which dates from around 1380, was the site of one of many local skirmishes in the Civil War when a party of Parliamentary soldiers came under cannon fire, which did considerable damage to the building. A later fire, a lightning strike, Victorian 'restoration' and more recent modernisation, have left little of note inside the church apart from a fine 18th-century reredos and some 300 modern kneelers depicting biblical scenes, views of the town, animals, birds and memorials to local people. The project involved around 60 people and took four years to complete.

But if St Mary's interior is generally disappointing, its churchyard is one of the must-see sights of the county. In the 1790s local people planted 99 yews – it was said that whenever a 100th was planted it would wither away – and these now stand sentinel over the graveyard's other extraordinary feature, the 33 richly carved table tombs all dating from the wool trade's boom years in the 17th and 18th centuries. The craftsman who created these striking rhapsodies in stone, John Bryan, is himself buried here beneath a pyramidal tomb.

Other buildings of interest include Court House, where King Charles I spent a night in 1643 before setting off for the siege of Gloucester, and the Post Office, dating back to the 1400s and the only surviving wooden-framed house in the town. In Bisley Street, the **Gloucestershire Guild of Craftsmen Gallery** provides a showcase for pieces made by members of the guild, which is one of the oldest in the country. This feast of creative design includes jewellery, glass, velvet and silk, turned wood, greeting cards and more.

In the grounds of early 18th century Painswick House, on the B4073 at the northern edge of town, **Painswick Rococo Garden**, hidden away in magnificent Cotswold countryside, is a unique restored 18th-century garden with plants from around the world and a maze planted in 1999 with a path structure in the shape of 250 to commemorate the garden's 250th anniversary. Other attractions are carpets of snowdrops in early spring, a kitchen garden, a children's nature trail, a gift shop and a licensed restaurant.

A little further north, at Cranham, **Prinknash Abbey Park** (pronounce it Prinnage) comprises an active monastery, chapel, replica of a Roman mosaic, gift shop and tearoom. The Benedictine monks of Caldey Island moved here in 1928 when the old house was made over to them by the 20th Earl of Rothes in accordance with the wishes of his grandfather. They no longer occupy the old house, having moved into the impressive new monastery in 1972. The abbey chapel is open daily for solitude and contemplation. Part of the abbey gardens are given over to the Prinknash Bird & Deer Park, where visitors can feed and stroke the fallow deer and see the waterfowl, the peacocks and the African pygmy goats. By the lake is a charming two-storey Wendy House.

EDGE

4 miles N of Stroud on the A473

Scottsquarr Common

Straddling a hilltop across the Spoonbed Valley, Edge has two delightful village greens and the mid 19th-century Church of St John the Baptist with an ornate spire. To the west of the village lies **Scottsquarr Common**, an Area of Special Scientific Interest with an abundance of wild flowers and butterflies and spectacular views.

MISERDEN

5 miles NE of Stroud off the B40470 or A417

Miserden Park Gardens

Miserden Park Gardens, with views over the lovely Golden Valley, were created in the 17th century and are known for their spectacular spring bulbs, perennial borders, roses, topiary and an avenue of Turkish hazels.

CHELTENHAM ANTIQUES MARKET

54 Suffolk Road, Cheltenham Spa,
Gloucestershire GL50 2AQ
Tel: 01242 529812 website: www.antiquecrystalchandeliers.co.uk

When visiting Cheltenham you simply must visit **Cheltenham Antique Market** if you are looking for lighting or furniture dating back to the 19th or 20th century.

With more than three hundred old chandeliers displayed over three floors there is sure to be something to meet most people's taste and budget in this Aladdin's Cave.

Cheltenham Antiques Market offers one of the largest selections of affordable chandeliers in the country. There is plenty to look at and antique lovers spend hours here, returning time and time again to see what is new on offer.

There are lights in a variety of sizes and ages from Italy, France, Holland, Belgium and England. They are all individually rewired to comply with current EU regulations.

Once you have worn yourself out at Cheltenham Antiques Market why not treat yourself to something to eat at one of the welcoming eateries nearby.

CLEMATIS HOUSE B&B

246 Gloucester Road, Cheltenham Spa, Gloucestershire GL51 8NR
Tel: 01242 690246
e-mail: kas-shave@hotmail.com
website: www.bedandbreakfastcheltenham.co.uk

If you are looking for a modern B&B in Gloucestershire with good railway links and beautiful gardens look no further than **Clematis House B&B**.

Owned by Karen Shave, this delightful family-run B&B offers smart, well appointed bedrooms with en-suite facilities. A relaxing and comfortable stay is offered here, perfect for those who have spent the day sightseeing, shopping or exploring the Cotswolds.

For those visiting the town on business, several major business parks are situated nearby. The B&B has the additional benefit of good public transport links and there are plenty of shops in the nearby Montpellier district.

Ken and Karen are only too happy to help tourists with their local knowledge.

Cheltenham

Art Gallery & Museum · Holst Museum
Pittville Pump Room · Racecourse
Gloucestershire-Warwickshire Railway

Smart, fashionable Cheltenham was a small, insignificant village until a mineral spring was accidentally discovered in 1716. According to tradition, the first medicinal waters were discovered when locals saw pigeons pecking at salty deposits that had formed around a spring. A local man, William Mason, built a pump room and began Cheltenham's transformation into one of Europe's leading Regency spa towns. Mason's son-in-law was the astute Captain Henry Skillicorne who added a meeting room, a ballroom and a network of walks and carriageways, and called it a spa. A number of other springs were soon discovered, including one in the High Street around which the first Assembly Rooms were built. In 1788 the Royal seal of approval came in the shape of King George III who spent five weeks taking the waters with his family and made Cheltenham a highly fashionable resort. An entirely new town was planned based on the best features of neoclassical Regency architecture, and as a result very few buildings of any antiquity still stand. One of these is the Church of St Mary, with parts going back to the 12th century and some very fine stained glass.

Skillicorne's walks and rides are now the tree-lined Promenade, one of the most beautiful boulevards in the country, its crowning glory the wonderful Neptune's Fountain modelled on the Fontana di Trevi in Rome and erected in 1893. Housed in Pittville Park, overlooking picturesque gardens and ornamental lakes north of the town centre, is the magnificent **Pittville Pump Room**. Concerts and special exhibitions are held here throughout the year. **Cheltenham Art Gallery and Museum** has an acclaimed collection of furniture and silver, much of it made by Cotswold craftsmen and inspired by William Morris' Arts and Crafts movement, as well as some fine paintings by Dutch and British artists, Oriental porcelain and English ceramics.

Gustav Holst, of Latvian-Russian descent, was born in 1874 in a terraced Regency house in Clarence Road. It is now the **Holst Birthplace Museum and Period House** where the original piano of the composer of *The Planets* is the centrepiece of the story of the man and his works. There's also a working Victorian kitchen, an elegant Regency drawing room and a nursery. The Museum was founded in 1974 by Holst's daughter Imogen. (Other notable natives of Cheltenham include Sir Arthur 'Bomber' Harris, Sir Frederick Handley-Page, Sir Ralph Richardson and the Polar explorer Edward Wilson.)

Two remarkable modern pieces of public art take the eye in the centre of town. The Wishing Fish Clock in the Regent Arcade is a work in metal by the famous artist and craftsman Kit Williams: below the clock, from which a mouse pops out when disturbed by the arrival of an egg laid by a duck on high, is suspended a 12ft-long fish, which celebrates the hour by swishing its tail and blowing bubbles, to the delight and fascination of shoppers below. The mechanical parts of the clock are the work of the renowned local clockmaker Michael Harding.

Off the High Street are the Elephant Murals, which portray an event that occurred in 1934 when three elephants from a travelling circus escaped and raided a provision shop stocked with corn – an incident that older

THE SUFFOLKS INDEPENDENT SHOPS

EDWARD COX (GOLDSMITH)

28 Suffolk Parade, Montpellier, Cheltenham, Gloucestershire GL50 2AE
Tel: 01242 577573

In the 20 years that **Edward Cox (Goldsmith)** has been trading in Montpellier it has built up a fantastic reputation among locals and visitors. The independent store is owned by Peter and Val Russell and sells a wide selection of bespoke jewellery in gold, silver and platinum. Customers spend hours browsing the unusual gemstones in the splendid showroom and a personal one-to-one service is offered. Repeat customers are frequent here and once you have paid a visit yourself it won't be hard to understand why.

There are also a variety of items from specialist independent designers, which compliment the collection of Edward Cox (Goldsmith). It is open Wednesday – Saturday between 10am and 4pm.

THE OLD GROCERS DECORATIVE ANTIQUES

34 Suffolk Parade, Montpellier, Cheltenham, Gloucestershire GL50 2AE
Tel: 01242 230974

The Old Grocers Decorative Antiques is a pleasantly unusual antique shop with a modern slant. There is a whole variety of items on sale including upholstery fabrics on role, soft furnishings and furniture such as wooden tables and bookshelves.

This delightful shop can be found in the Suffolks district of Cheltenham Spa and is popular with visitors to the area. The five minute walk from the town centre is definitely worth it as you can spend a long while exploring this wonderful shop. It is full of colour and decorative pieces, furniture of English / French country style, as well as hand painted items.

STUDIO 33

marc@whitenoiseimages

33 Suffolk Parade, Cheltenham, Gloucestershire GL50 2AE
Tel: 01242 580334

'Purveyor of Beauty' is the statement echoed throughout **Studio 33**. Her colours drawn from travels to remote places, paintings and architecture - leaving one breathless.

The studio where creativity thrives supports interior design as featured. Product development for celebrated brands always a secret.

Silken cloths, chantilly lace aching for form exclusively designed for memorable moments. Rare furniture to embellish your home for generations.

Studio 33 is owned by Linda Hewitt. She lives between London and Cheltenham.

locals with long memories still recall.

Cheltenham Boys College was used for the anarchic 1968 film *If*, directed by former pupil Lindsay Anderson after he persuaded the headmaster that it would be a respectable film!

Cheltenham Racecourse, two miles north of town, is the home of National Hunt Racing, staging numerous top-quality races highlighted by the March Festival when the Gold Cup and the Champion Hurdle find the year's best steeplechaser and best hurdler. Several other festivals have their home in Cheltenham, including the International Jazz Festival (April), the International Festival of Music (July), the International Festival of Literature (April) and the Cheltenham Festival of Science (June).

Within the racecourse grounds is the southern terminus of the **Gloucestershire-Warwickshire Railway**, which offers a 20-mile scenic round trip to Toddington on trains hauled by preserved steam locomotives. En route, the train passes through the Greet Tunnel, which, at 693 yards, is the second longest on a heritage railway. Locomotives in use in 2010 included 3717 *City of Truro*, 7903 *Foremarke Hall*, 2-6-2T 5542 and 9F 92203. Call 01242 621405 for details of timetables, events and driving courses.

Around Cheltenham

PRESTBURY

1 mile NE of Cheltenham on the A46

Prestbury Park

Racing at Cheltenham started at Cleeve Hill but moved to land belonging to **Prestbury Park** in 1819, since when all the great names in steeplechasing and hurdling have graced the Prestbury turf. But Prestbury's greatest son was not a jump jockey but the amazing Fred Archer, undisputed champion of flat race jockeys, born in the village in 1857. In The King's Arms hangs a plaque with this inscription:

'At this Prestbury inn lived
FRED ARCHER the jockey
Who trained upon toast,
Cheltenham water & coffee.

The shoe of his pony
hangs in the bar
Where they drink to his prowess
from near and from far

But the man in the street
passes by without knowledge
That 'twas here Archer
swallowed his earliest porridge.'

CLEEVE HILL

3 miles NE of Cheltenham on the B4632

Belas Knap   Cleeve Cloud

The Cotswolds rise to their highest point, over 1000 feet above sea level, at **Cleeve Cloud** above Prestbury and a mile from the village of Cleeve Hill. The views from here are magnificent, and also worth the climb to see a massive Neolithic long barrow known as **Belas Knap**, where excavations have revealed the bones of more than 30 people. It is very unusual in having a false entrance at the north end that does not lead to any chambers.

GOTHERINGTON

5 miles NE of Cheltenham on the A435

Prescott Hill Climb   The Bugatti Trust

This is the location of the famous **Prescott Hill Climb**, scene of hill climb championships and classic car meetings, as well as the location of **The Bugatti Trust** (see panel on page 114), a charitable trust whose aims are to preserve

The Bugatti Trust

Prescott Hill, Gotherington,
nr Cheltenham,
Gloucestershire GL52 9RD
Tel: 01242 677201
Fax: 01242 674191
e-mail: trust@bugatti.co.uk
website: www.bugatti.co.uk/trust

The Bugatti Trust is recommended to visitors with an interest in design and art in engineering as well as the history of the motor car. Ettore Bugatti designed and built beautiful and world leading racing and sports cars in the 1920's and 1930's. There were numerous other sensational Bugatti products from the 'Royale' to world speed record trains and aircraft. The whole story of the Bugatti family from Carlo, Ettore's artist father, to the sad demise of the family control of the Molsheim factory in the 1950's, can be seen at the Bugatti Trust. The Trust is a Bugatti research centre and small museum, containing an amazing collection of drawings, documents, photographs, artefacts and a few cars. This history is an inspirational combination of art and engineering. Open Monday-Friday 10.00am-4.30pm. Free entry.

and make available for study the works of Ettore Bugatti. The whole fascinating story of the Bugatti family and its cars can be seen here: the little museum contains an amazing collection of drawings, documents, photographs and artefacts, including a few Bugatti cars. Open from 10am to 4pm Monday to Friday and on Hill Climb days.

WINCHCOMBE

6 miles NE of Cheltenham on the B4632

Sudeley Castle · Folk & Police Museum

Railway Museum · Hailes Abbey

Winchcombe Pottery

This delightful little town was the Saxon capital of Mercia. In medieval times it prospered as pilgrims made their way to the shrine of St Kenelm who had been martyred here by his jealous sister in the 8th century. His shrine was second only to that of Thomas à Becket as a destination for pilgrims. Winchcombe grew in importance into a walled town with an abbot who presided over a Saxon parliament. The abbey was destroyed in 1539 after the Dissolution of the Monasteries and all that remains today is a section of a gallery that is part of the George Inn. As well as pilgrims, the abbey gave rise to a flourishing trade in wool and sheep.

One of the most famous townsmen of the time was Jack Smallwood, the Jack o' Newbury who sponsored 300 men to fight at Flodden Field in 1513, and was a leading producer of woollen goods. Silk and paper were also produced, and for a few decades tobacco was grown locally – a fact remembered in place names such as Tobacco Close and Tobacco Field. This activity ceased in 1670 when a law was passed banning home-produced tobacco in favour of imports from the struggling colony of Virginia.

The decline that followed had the effect of stopping the town's development, so many of the old buildings have survived largely unaltered. These include St Peter's Church, built in the 1460s and known particularly for its 40 grotesques and gargoyles, the so-called Winchcombe Worthies. **Winchcombe Folk & Police Museum**, in the Tudor-style Town Hall by the Tourist Information Centre, tells the history of the town from neolithic times to the present day, and also keeps a collection of British and international police uniforms and equipment.

A narrow passageway behind an ordinary house front leads to **Winchcombe Railway Museum and Garden**, a wonderland full of things to do: the railway museum contains one of the largest collections of railway equipment in the country, and visitors can work signals and clip tickets and generally get misty-eyed about the age of steam. The Cotswold garden is full of old and rare plants.

Winchcombe Pottery was established in 1926 on the site of an old country pottery dating back to the early 1800s. The pieces were fired in a bottle-kiln, which is still standing but is not now used. Visitors are welcome to look around the showroom and, at most times, the workshop. As well as the standard range of domestic ware, a number of individual pots are sold in the showroom.

A mile or so north of Winchcombe stand the ruins of **Hailes Abbey**, founded in 1246 by Richard, Earl of Cornwall. Richard, caught in a storm at sea, vowed that he would found a religious house if he survived, and in 1245 his brother Henry III gave him the manor at Hailes to do it. It was built on such an ambitious scale that the Cistercian monks were hard pressed to maintain it, but after Richard's son, Edmund, donated a phial said to contain

Winchcombe Church

the blood of Christ (later proved to be a fake) the abbey soon became an important place of pilgrimage and was even mentioned in Chaucer's *The Canterbury Tales*. The closure of the abbey in 1539 brought great distress to the town: merchants lost the custom of the pilgrims and the poor no longer received their 'doles' from the monks.

The abbey fell into disrepair and today shattered walls and arches are all that remain of this mighty Cistercian foundation, yet the atmosphere of a 13th-century monastery lingers most powerfully. Some of the many artefacts found at the site, including medieval sculptures and decorated floor tiles, are on display in the abbey's museum. Some of the medieval glass from the abbey is now in the church at Stanton.

One mile south of Winchcombe, and set

against the beautiful backdrop of the Cotswold Hills, is **Sudeley Castle**, which has royal connections going back 1,000 years. This magnificent palace was the last home of Catherine Parr, sixth and last wife of Henry VIII. King Charles I stayed at the castle, and his nephew, Prince Rupert, established his garrison headquarters here during the Civil War. The interior of the castle, restored by the Dent family in sumptuous Victorian style, is a treasure house of old masters (Turner, Rubens, Van Dyck), tapestries, period furniture, costumes and toys, and the beautiful grounds include a lake, formal gardens and a 15 foot double yew hedge. Among the many other attractions are an exhibition on the evolution of the gardens, The Lace and Times of Emma Dent, a gift shop, plant centre, restaurant and adventure playground.

TODDINGTON

8 miles NE of Cheltenham on the B4632/B4077

Gloucestershire-Warwickshire Railway

Toddington Station is the northern terminus of the restored **Gloucestershire-Warwickshire Railway** (see panel below) from where steam or diesel trains run a scenic round trip of 20 miles through delightful countryside by way of Winchcombe and Gotherington to Cheltenham racecourse. The line is open all year and there is a programme of special events and gala days.

STANWAY

9 miles NE of Cheltenham on the B4077

Stanway House Tithe Barn

A charming village clustered round Jacobean **Stanway House**, which is surely one of the most perfect of Cotswold mansions. Built

Gloucestershire and Warwickshire Railway

The Railway Station, Toddington, Gloucestershire GL54 5DT
Tel: 01242 621405
website: www.gwsr.co.uk

The railway offers a 20-mile round trip between Toddington and Cheltenham Race Course through some of the most spectacular scenery in the Costwolds.

As you leave Toddington, once a major fruit distribution centre, the train passes the workshops where the steam and diesel locomotives are maintained and restored. The journey provides good views of the Cotswolds before arriving at Winchcombe station.

The Station which originally stood at Monmouth Troy and was painstakingly dismantled, moved and rebuilt by volunteers. This is also the headquarters of the carriage and wagon department. Shortly after leaving Winchcombe the train enters Greet tunnel which, at 693 yards, is the second longest on a preserved railway.

As the line approaches Cheltenham Race Course, views of Cleeve Hill (the highest point of the Cotswolds) open up. The station once again fulfils its original purpose - bringing race-goers for important meetings such as the Cheltenham Gold Cup. A new 2 mile extension north towards Broadway opens in 2011.

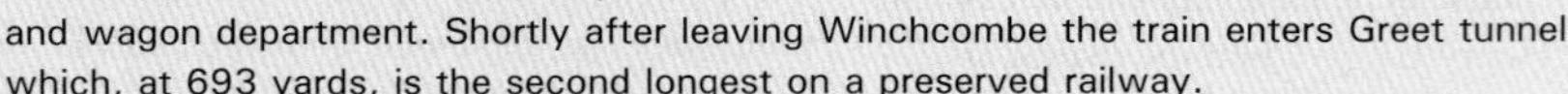

Stanway House

using the warm, honey-coloured local stone, surrounded by gardens and landscaped grounds, Stanway is a dwelling-place at peace with the world and with itself. Its towering bay window looks across a scene where for centuries the only changes have been those ordained by the passing of the seasons.

The present house was built in the 1580s with the Great Hall at its heart, a glorious room whose function changed by the hour – from business room to manorial court to dining room. The raised dais on which the Lord of the Manor and his family took their meals is still in place as is a 23-feet-long 16th-century shuffleboard carved from a single piece of oak. The house's other treasures include fine paintings, two superb Broadwood pianos, and a Chippendale exercising chair on which keep-fit enthusiasts of the time would bounce for half an hour a day.

The grounds are equally interesting. Nearby stands an immense **Tithe Barn**, which was built in 1370 when the Manor of Stanway was a small satellite of Tewkesbury Abbey. Four monks dedicated themselves in prayer for the souls of the two Saxon nobles who had presented the land to the abbot in AD715.

Stanway's water gardens are regarded as the finest in England and their beauty has recently been enhanced with the installation of a 165-foot-high fountain – Britain's highest fountain and the tallest gravity fountain in the world.

Also of note in Stanway is a thatched cricket pavilion resting on mushroom-shaped stones. The pavilion was a gift from J M Barrie, the author of *Peter Pan*, who was a regular visitor to the village.

STANTON

10 miles NE of Cheltenham on the B4632

Stanton Court · Snowshill Manor

One of the prettiest spots in the Cotswolds, an attractive village of steeply-gabled limestone cottages dating mainly from the 16th and 17th centuries. The whole village was restored by the architect Sir Philip Scott in the years before the First World War; his home between 1906 and 1937 was **Stanton Court**, an elegant Jacobean residence built by Queen Elizabeth I's Chamberlain. The village church, dedicated to St Michael and All Angels, has many interesting features, including some stained glass from Hailes Abbey and a number of medieval pews with scarred ends caused perhaps by the leashes of dogs belonging to local shepherds. Most of the glass is the much more modern work of Sir Ninian Comper (1864-1960), the Aberdeen-born architect and prolific designer of church fittings and furnishings; stained glass was one of his specialities. John Wesley is said to have preached in the church.

Beyond Stanton, on the road to Broadway, the National Trust-owned **Snowshill Manor** is an elegant manor house dating from Tudor times; once the home of Catherine Parr, it contains a fascinating collection of crafts and artefacts assembled by the last private owner, Charles Paget Wade.

GUITING POWER

8 miles E of Cheltenham off the A436

Cotswold Farm Park

A neat collection of Cotswold stone cottages

round a triangular green. Noteworthy features include the part-Norman St Michael's Church and a First World War memorial cross. Close by is **Cotswold Farm Park**, which was the first Rare Breeds Farm in England when it opened in 1971 and is now home to more than 50 flocks and herds of British farm animals. Using the hand-held audio guide, visitors can discover the animals' tales of survival. Among the many other attractions are shearing and spinning demonstrations, fleece sales, safari rides, an indoor tractor school, adventure playground, pets corner, woodland walk and a host of other activities guaranteed to keep children happy for hours.

Stow-on-the-Wold

Toy & Collectors Museum

At 800 feet above sea level, this is the highest town in the Cotswolds, and the winds sometimes prove it. The town's main source of wealth in earlier times was wool; twice-yearly sheep fairs were held on the Market Square, and at one such fair Daniel Defoe records that over 20,000 sheep were sold. Those days are remembered in Sheep Street and Shepherds Way. The square holds another reminder of the past in the town stocks, used to punish minor offenders. The sheep fairs continued until they were replaced by an annual horse fair, which was held until 1985.

The Battle of Stow, in 1646, was the final conflict of the Civil War, and after it some of the defeated Royalist forces retreated to St Edward's Church, while others were cut down in the Market Square. The church, which suffered considerable damage at the time, has been restored many times down the centuries, not always to its advantage, but one undoubted treasure is a painting of the crucifixion in the south aisle, thought to be the work of the 17th-century Flemish artist Gaspard de Craeyer. The church is dedicated to King Edward the Martyr, who was murdered at Corfe Castle by his stepmother Elfrida. Other buildings of note in the town are the 15th-century Crooked House and the 16th-century Masonic Hall. On Digbeth Street stands The Royalist Hotel, said to be the oldest inn in England; an inn has certainly stood on the site since AD947. And outside the Town Hall, somewhat incongruously, is a medieval-style statue of Edward the Confessor. It cost £4000 but Stow's ratepayers didn't pay a penny of that – the funds came from unclaimed deposits in the local savings bank.

In Park Street is the **Toy and Collectors Museum**, housing a charming display of toys, trains, teddy bears and dolls, games and books, along with textiles and lace, porcelain and pottery. Call 01451 830159.

Around Stow-on-the-Wold

UPPER & LOWER SWELL

1 mile W of Stow on the B4077 & B4068

A couple of Swells, neighbouring villages on the banks of the River Dikler. Lower Swell's focal point is the triangular village green, while the large mill pond is one of Upper Swell's many delights. Nearby, in Condicote Lane, is Donnington Trout Farm with a hatchery, smokery, farm shop and a lake for fly fishing.

MORETON-IN-MARSH

4 miles N of Stow on the A429

Wellington Aviation Museum

Batsford Park   Cotswold Falconry Centre

Moreton-in-the-Marsh is the scene, every Tuesday, of the biggest open-air street market in the Cotswolds. This attractive old town stands at the junction of the A44 and the A429 Fosse Way, and was once an important stop on the coaching route between London and the West Midlands. Its broad main street is lined with handsome 17th and 18th-century buildings, while from earlier days are the old town gaol, The White Hart, where Charles I took refuge during the Civil War, and the Curfew Tower with its clock and bell dated 1633.

In Bourton Road, the **Wellington Aviation Museum**, dedicated to all who served or passed through RAF Moreton-in-Marsh on training courses for RAF Bomber Command. The airfield is now a fire training station. The little museum has a collection of Second World War aircraft paintings, prints and models and a detailed history of the Wellington bomber. Outside are the propeller and wheels of a Vickers-Armstrong Wellington.

One of the town's most popular amenities is **Batsford Park**, which offers a variety of attractions. There's an arboretum set in 55 acres of typical Cotswold countryside, which contains more than 1500 species and varieties of trees, shrubs, bamboos and wild flowers. Visitors can wander along meandering paths and discover surprises at every turn – a Japanese Rest House, a hermit's cave or a number of magnificent bronze statues from the far east. Also within the park, next to the arboretum, is the **Cotswold Falconry & Birds of Prey Centre**, home to a large collection of falcons, hawks, owls, kites and vultures, which are flown at regular intervals during the day. Other attractions in the park include a gift shop, tearoom and garden centre.

A mile east of town on the A44 stands the Four Shires Stone marking the original spot where the counties of Gloucestershire, Oxfordshire, Warwickshire and Worcestershire met.

BLOCKLEY

7 miles N of Stow off the A44/A429

Mill Dene Garden

This pretty village was once a very busy place. Silk-spinning was the main industry and six mills created the main source of employment until the 1880s. As far back as the Domesday Book water mills were recorded here, and the village also once boasted an iron foundry and factories making soap, collars and pianos. The mills have now been turned into private residences and Blockley is a quieter place.

One of the chief attractions for visitors is **Mill Dene Garden**, set around a mill in a steep-sided valley. The garden has hidden paths winding up from the mill pool, and at the top there are lovely views over the Cotswolds. Also featured are a grotto, a potager, a trompe l'oeil and dye plants.

CHIPPING CAMPDEN

10 miles N of Stow on the B4081

Market Hall Cotswold Olimpicks

Old Silk Mill Court Barn

The Jewel of the Cotswolds, full of beautifully restored buildings in golden Cotswold stone. Chipping Campden was a regional capital of the wool trade between the 13th and 16th centuries, and many of the fine buildings date from that period of prosperity. In the centre of town is the Jacobean **Market Hall**, built in 1627 and one of many buildings financed by the wealthy fabric merchant and financier Sir Baptist Hicks. He also endowed a group of almshouses and built Old Campden House, at the time the largest residence in the town; it was burnt down by Royalists to prevent it falling into the hands of the enemy. All that survives are two gatehouses, the old stable block and the banqueting halls. The 15th-century Church of St James was built on a grand scale and contains several impressive monumental brasses, the most impressive being one of William Grevel measuring a mighty eight feet by four feet.

Chipping Campden has important links with the Arts and Crafts movement. CR Ashbee set up his Guild of Handicrafts here in 1902 with 150 workers imported from London's East End. His workshop in the **Old Silk Mill** in Sheep Street is now a small museum. In 1990 a group of local people formed the Guild of Handicraft Trust and in 1998 it was offered the chance to take over **Court Barn** and to turn it into a museum of local craftsmanship and design from the Arts and Crafts movement onward. The centre opened in the summer of 2007.

Dover's Hill, a natural amphitheatre above the town, is the scene of the **Cotswold Olimpicks**, founded in the 17th century by Captain Robert Dover who lived at Stanway House. The Games followed the traditions of ancient Greece and added some more down-to-earth activities such as shin-kicking and bare-knuckle boxing. The lawlessness and

Chipping Campden Church

hooliganism that accompanied the games led to their being closed down in 1852, but they were revived in a modern form in 1951 and are still a popular annual attraction on the Friday following the Spring Bank Holiday. Call 01384 274041.

BROADWAY

10 miles NW of Stow on the A44

Broadway Tower Snowshill Manor Garden

Just over the border into Worcestershire, where the Cotswolds join the Vale of Evesham, Broadway is one of the glories of the Cotswolds, a showpiece village with an abundance of scenic and historic attractions. The renowned Lygon Arms entertained both King Charles and Oliver Cromwell, and **Broadway Tower** at the top of Fish Hill affords spectacular views over the Severn Vale.

A couple of miles southwest of Broadway, **Snowshill Manor and Garden** (National Trust) is an Arts and Crafts garden designed to complement a handsome Cotswold manor house. Laid out by Charles Paget Wade as a series of outdoor rooms with terraces and ponds, the garden is now run on organic principles. The house has a spectacular collection of craftsmanship and design from around the world. Call 01386 852410.

HIDCOTE BARTRIM

13 miles N of Stowe off the B4632

Hidcote Manor Garden

Hidcote Manor Garden is one of the most famous in the country, a masterpiece created in the first years of the 20th century by the eminent horticulturist Major Lawrence Johnston. A series of small gardens, each with a different character and appeal, Hidcote is renowned for its rare shrubs and trees, herbaceous borders and unusual plant species from all parts of the globe. Visitors can refresh themselves in the tea bar or licensed restaurant.

UPPER AND LOWER SLAUGHTER

2 miles SW of Stow off the A429/B4068

Old Mill

The Slaughters (the name means nothing more sinister than muddy place) are archetypal Cotswold villages set a mile apart on the little River Eye. Both are much visited by tourists, much explored and much photographed; they are also much as they have always been, since virtually no building work has been carried out since 1904. Francis Edward Witts, author of *The Diary of a Cotswold Parson*, was the rector here between 1808 and 1854.

At Lower Slaughter, the **Old Mill**, with its tall chimney and giant waterwheel, is a prominent feature by the river. This restored 19th-century flour mill, last used for its original purpose in 1958, is open for visits and has a tearoom and organic ice cream parlour. The mill is owned by the well-known jazz singer Gerald Harris, so the gift shop has an extensive stock of jazz CDs.

Bourton-on-the-Water

BOURTON-ON-THE-WATER

4 miles S of Stow on the A429

- Model Village
- Motoring Museum
- Bourton Model Railway Exhibition
- Perfumery Factory
- Birdland Park & Gardens

Probably the most popular of all the Cotswold villages, the willow-fringed River Windrush flows through the centre, crossed by several delightful low-arched pedestrian bridges, two of which date from the late 18th century. The golden stone cottages are pretty as a picture, and among the notable larger buildings are St Lawrence's Church, with its 14th-century chancel and rare domed Georgian tower, and a manor house with a 16th-century dovecote.

The famous **Model Village** is a 1:9 scale replica of Bourton hand-crafted from local Cotswold stone. It comes complete with music playing in the church and even a model of the model village in the model village.

Covering 400 square feet, **Bourton Model Railway Exhibition** has more than 40 British and Continental trains running on three main displays in OO, HO and N gauge. There's also a large shop with a good range of quality toys, models, trains and accessories.

The **Cotswold Motoring Museum and Toy Collection**, in an 18th-century water mill, has a fascinating collection of antique toys, a display of historic advertising signs and 30 or so (full-size) cars and motorcycles, including James Hunt's last Formula 1 car, a Wolf WR7. Bourton is also known for its **Cotswolds Perfumery Factory**, where a guided tour includes the Perfume Garden, the Perfume Laboratory, the Compounding Room mixing raw materials to make the concentrate, and the Factory, where the processes comprise filtering, bottling, labelling, coding, cartoning and despatch.

A five-minute walk from the town centre brings visitors to **Birdland Park & Gardens** set in seven acres of woodland, water and gardens. The natural setting is home to more than 500 birds, including flamingos, pelicans, cranes, storks and waterfowl; there are over 50 aviaries of parrots, falcons, pheasants, hornbills, toucans, touracos and many others, and tropical, temperate and desert houses are home to the more delicate species. Open all year, Birdland has a café and facilities for children, including a play area, pets' corner and penguin feeding time.

NORTHLEACH

10 miles SW of Stow on the A429

- Church of St Peter and St Paul
- Chedworth Roman Villa
- Keith Harding's World of Mechanical Music

A traditional market town with some truly magnificent buildings. It was once a major wool-trading centre that rivalled Cirencester in importance and, as a consequence, possesses what now seems a disproportionately large church. The **Church of St Peter and St Paul**, known as the Cathedral of the Cotswolds, is a fine example of Cotswold Perpendicular, built in the 15th century with pinnacled buttresses, high windows and a massive square castellated tower. Treasures inside include an ornately carved font and some rare monumental brasses of which rubbings can be made (permits obtainable from the Post Office).

The town's most popular attraction is **Keith Harding's World of Mechanical Music**, which occupies a handsome period house in the main street. Keith's love of mechanical music goes back some 40 years and he has accumulated the finest collection of automata, both antique and modern, to be found anywhere. The exhibits range from a tiny singing bird concealed in a snuff box, to a mighty Welte Steinway reproducing piano of 1907. The instruments are introduced and played by the guides in the form of a live musical entertainment show and the tours include demonstrations of restored barrel organs, barrel pianos, musical boxes, polyphons, gramophones and antique clocks. Many of the clocks, musical boxes and automata on show are for sale.

Close to the pretty village of **Chedworth**, a couple of miles west of Northleach, is what must be the region's oldest stately home, the National Trust's **Chedworth Roman Villa**, a large, well-preserved Romano-British villa discovered by chance in 1864 and subsequently excavated to reveal more than 30 rooms and buildings, including a bath house and hypocaust. Some wonderful mosaics are on display, one depicting the four seasons, another showing nymphs and satyrs. The villa lies in a beautiful wooded combe overlooking the valley of the Colne. A natural spring rises at the head of the combe – probably the main reason for choosing this site.

BIBURY

15 miles S of Stow on the B4425

Arlington Row

William Morris, founder of the Arts and Crafts movement, described Bibury as "the most beautiful village in England" and, apart from the tourists, not a lot has changed since he made the claim. The Church of St Mary, with Saxon, Norman and medieval parts, is well worth a visit, but the most visited and most photographed buildings in Bibury are **Arlington Row**, a superb terrace of medieval stone cottages built as a wool store in the 14th century and converted three centuries later into weavers' cottages and workshops.

Cirencester

Corinium Museum   Church of St John Baptist

Brewery Arts House   Open Air Swimming Pool

The Capital of the Cotswolds, a lively market town with a long and fascinating history. As Corinium Dobonnorum it was the second largest Roman town in Britain (Londinium was the largest). Few signs remain of the Roman occupation, but the award-winning **Corinium Museum** (01285 655611) features one of the finest collections of antiquities from Roman Britain, and reconstructions of a Roman dining room and garden give a fascinating and instructive insight into life in Cirencester almost 2000 years ago.

The main legacy of the town's medieval wealth is the magnificent **Church of St John Baptist**, perhaps the grandest of all the Cotswold wool churches, its 120ft tower dominating the town. Its greatest treasure is the Anne Boleyn Cup, a silver and gilt cup made for Henry VIII's second wife in 1535, the year before she was executed for adultery. Her personal insignia – a rose tree and a falcon holding a sceptre – is on the lid of the cup, which was given to the church by Richard Master, physician to Queen Elizabeth I. The church has a unique three-storey porch, which was used as the Town Hall until 1897.

Cirencester today has a thriving crafts scene, with workshops in the **Brewery Arts and Craft Centre**, a converted Victorian brewery that re-opened in 2008 after a £2.7 million refurbishment. Up to 18 resident craftworkers create or restore pieces of art on site; they include a basket maker, jeweller, textile weaver, ceramicist and stained glass artist. A shop in the centre sells the best in British work, and

ALL MY BEAUTIFUL THINGS

62B Cricklade Street, Cirencester,
Gloucestershire GL7 1JN
Tel: 01285 655719
e-mail: allmybeautifulthings@gmail.co.uk
website: www.allmybeautifulthings.co.uk

All My Beautiful Things is a fantastic gallery, home to mermaids, fairies, dragons and other magic and mystical creatures. Many people are drawn through its doors by the colourful pieces on display and others come here purely to take in the tranquil atmosphere and browse the shelves.

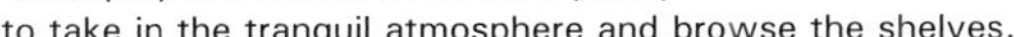

That said it is hard to leave this shop full of treasures without buying something to take home. It is an ideal shop for buying an unusual gift – so why not treat a loved one or spoil yourself? All My Beautiful Things has plenty on display including ceramic pieces and jewellery created by Chyna De La Mer, a talented sculptress who specialises in beautiful, intricate ceramic sculptures inspired by folklore, fables and changing moods and seasons of nature. The fine sculptures and objects d'art here are created especially to bring the magic back to any home or work place. If you want something totally individual then why not commission one of the shop's resident artists to create a piece of magic just for you.

The stock at All My Beautiful Things is forever changing and there will always be something new to browse – it is perhaps why so many people return time again.

THE THAMES HEAD INN

Tetbury Road, Cirencester, Gloucestershire GL7 6NZ
Tel: 01285 770259
website: www.thamesheadinn.co.uk

The Thames Head Inn is a charming establishment serving excellent food in a friendly, relaxed atmosphere with a large, well stocked central bar surrounded by various nooks and crannies and open fires.

This unique Gloucestershire pub has plenty of history and is renowned in the area for being one of the best in the county. With its extensive landscaped gardens and ample car parking, it has four guest bedrooms available in a beautifully converted barn. All of the rooms have en-suite facilities and are ideal for business accommodation or midweek and weekend breaks.

The fresh homemade food here is cooked by an award winning chef. It is absolutely delicious and the inn's specialities include fish, and perfectly cooked steaks, which can be enjoyed with a good selection of fine real ales. As well as the dishes listed on the printed menu there is a regularly updated specials board. The Thames Head Inn has a large function room with its own private bar and is available for fully catered private parties and corporate events. The inn is ideal for business meetings and regular club meetings.

there are galleries, a coffee house, arts and crafts classes and workshops.

Cirencester Open Air Swimming Pool, next to the park, was built in 1869 and is one of the oldest in the country. Both the main pool and the paddling pool use water from a private well. Other sites of interest include St Thomas' Hospital – 15th-century almshouses for destitute weavers – the Barracks of 1857, and a Yew Hedge that was planted in 1720. It now stands 40 feet high and is reputed to be the loftiest in Europe. It can be found in Cirencester Park, a 3000-acre expanse, which was designed by the poet Alexander Pope.

Cirencester certainly lives up to its reputation as a market town with street markets on Monday and Friday, a craft market in the Corn Hall on Saturdays, and regular antiques markets on Fridays.

Around Cirencester

FAIRFORD

9 miles E of Cirencester on the A417

Church of St Mary Air Tattoo

A welcoming little town in the valley of the River Coln that has many fine buildings of the 17th and 18th centuries and an abundance of inns as evidence that this was an important stop on the London-Gloucester coaching run. John and Edmund Tame, wealthy wool merchants, built the superb late-Perpendicular **Church of St Mary**, whose greatest glory is a set of 28 medieval stained glass windows depicting the Christian faith in picture-book style. John Tame's memorial stone, along with those of his wife and son, are set into the floor of the church. In July, nearby RAF Fairford hosts the annual **Royal International Air Tattoo**, the world's largest military air show, which attracts thousands of visitors. The date for 2011 is 16/17 July, and for 2012, 7/8 July.

INGLESHAM

12 mile E of Cirencester off the A361

Church of St John the Baptist

The splendidly unspoilt **Church of St John the Baptist** dates mainly from the 13th century, with some notable later additions. The chief features are important wall paintings, 15th-century screens, 17th- and 18th-century pulpit and box pews and, perhaps its greatest treasure, a Saxon carving of the Virgin and Child blessed by the Hand of God. This is one of many churches in the care of the Churches Conservation Trust, formerly known as the Redundant Churches Fund. The trust was established to preserve churches, which though no longer needed for regular worship, are of historic or architectural importance.

LECHLADE-ON-THAMES

12 miles E of Cirencester on the A417

Halfpenny Bridge

Now part of the Cotswold Water Park, Lechlade is the highest navigable point on the Thames and head of the Thames towpath walk. In and around the town visitors can hire rowing boats, go sailing or windsurfing, and enjoy lake and river fishing.

A statue of Old Father Thames, originally created for the Great Exhibition of 1851, overlooks St John's Lock, where barges loaded with building stone bound for Oxford and London have given way to pleasure craft. This bustling market town, surrounded by green meadows, boasts a fine 15th-century church with a slender spire and a structure that has remained unaltered since the early

CUTLER AND BAYLISS

Oak Street, Lechlade, Gloucestershire GL7 3AX
Tel: 01367 252451
website: www.cutlerandbayliss.co.uk

Cutler and Bayliss is a traditional family butchers, deli and greengrocers located in Lechlade, Gloucestershire. There is a strong focus on sourcing traditional quality meat and a lot of the meat on sale here is sourced from local suppliers and farmers.

Traditionally reared beef, Gloucester Old Spot pork, Cotswold lamb, free range poultry and home cured bacon are just some of the meats that can be bought at Cutler and Bayliss. Owners Tony and Shane also have handmade sausages, burgers and seasonal products available for their customers.

This fantastic shop has a well stocked delicatessen counter serving a range of home baked pies and pasties, cheese, cooked meats, olives and antipastos. There is also a greengrocery section with plenty of fresh fruit and vegetables to choose from.

Cutler and Bayliss is one of the Cotswold's best butchers and greengrocers and has been offering a personal and quality service for the past 15 years. It is well worth a look.

BATHURST ARMS

North Cerney, Cirencester, Gloucestershire GL7 7BZ
Tel: 01285 831281

This lovely Cotswold pub serves some of the finest pub food in the area and has a fantastic selection of real ales on offer. **Bathurst Arms** has been owned by James Walker for the past eight years and he has built up a superb reputation here, having won numerous awards.

James has eight en-suite rooms available to guests and with the inn's close location to Cirencester and its adjacent restaurant, which serves top quality bar food it isn't hard to see why visitors to the area choose to stay here.

There is a wide selection of dishes to choose from including traditional favourites such as beer battered day boat haddock as well as more unusual dishes such as pan fried ox liver.

Meals can be enjoyed in the beautifully decorated restaurant, which can serve 40 diners, or in the bar area, which is traditionally decorated with wooden tables. On warmer days customers can enjoy refreshments or al fresco dining in the lovely garden.

THE ROYAL OAK

High Street, South Cerney, nr Cirencester GL7 5UP
Tel: 01285 860298 e-mail: gemjar99@hotmail.com

The Royal Oak is a traditional village pub, dating back in parts to the 16th century, and can be found in South Cerney. Owners Gemma and Tommy have recently taken over, and they are doing a splendid job. Inside this family-friendly establishment you will find traditional log fires, ideal for keeping you warm on a cold winter day. In the summer you can enjoy a relaxing drink in the garden area. There is a big focus on homemade food and among the most popular dishes are the homemade delicious pies that are made with locally sourced meat and vegetables.

1500s. In its lovely churchyard, in 1815, the poet Shelley was inspired to write his *Stanzas in a Summer Evening Churchyard.* The verses are inscribed on a stone at the churchyard entrance.

Another interesting building is the **Halfpenny Bridge**, built in 1792, which crosses the Thames in the town centre and has a tollhouse at its eastern end. The toll was last charged for pedestrians in 1839, and for cattle in 1885.

SOUTH CERNEY

3 miles S of Cirencester off the A419

- Cotswold Water Park
- Keynes Country Park

Two areas of flooded gravel workings form

WILD DUCK INN

Drakes Island, Ewen, nr Cirencester, Gloucestershire GL7 6BY
Tel: 01285 770310
e-mail: wduckinn@aol.com
website: theduck.co.uk

A hidden gem in the little village of Ewen showcases what can be done with picturesque surroundings and passionate owners. The **Wild Duck Inn's** owners, Dino and Tina Mussell have successfully blended "16th century character and 21st century luxury", it possesses all the charm of a bygone age with modern all conveniences.

If you are looking to relax and unwind for a while this Inn has available twelve charming and individually designed en-suite bedrooms. The bedrooms are superior to that of many other inns due to the decadent addition of four-poster beds fit for royalty! The four-poster bed was originally designed to keep the draught off its slumbering inhabitants and the insects and dirt off their heads. Since medieval times are long past, we no longer have to worry about such things falling on our heads. All the same, the four-poster bed has remained popular.

With the emphasis on relaxed informality, lunch and supper can be taken in either the bar or the restaurant, or during much of the summer, in the delightfully enclosed courtyard canopied by a huge apple tree. The deep-red walls and soft high backed chairs all work to provide a truly tasteful, relaxing environment. The memorable quality of food, service and ambience is complemented with the very best wine from a well-stocked cellar and five real ales that are always on tap.

Cotswold Water Park, South Cerney

the **Cotswold Water Park**, an increasingly important wetland area with a greater expanse of water than the Norfolk Broads. The area, which includes **Keynes Country Park**, is a centre for water sports, fishing, bird-watching, walking and cycling.

KEMBLE

4 miles SW of Cirencester on the A429

Bristol Aero Collection

Located close to the source of the River Thames, Kemble is best known for the **Bristol Aero Collection** at Kemble Airfield. In a hangar given by Airbus UK, exhibits include Bristol helicopters, the only Britannia in working condition, Bloodhound guided missiles, aero engines, a full scale Giotto satellite, scale models of various military aircraft – and a small road transport collection featuring a Bristol tram, bus and lorry.

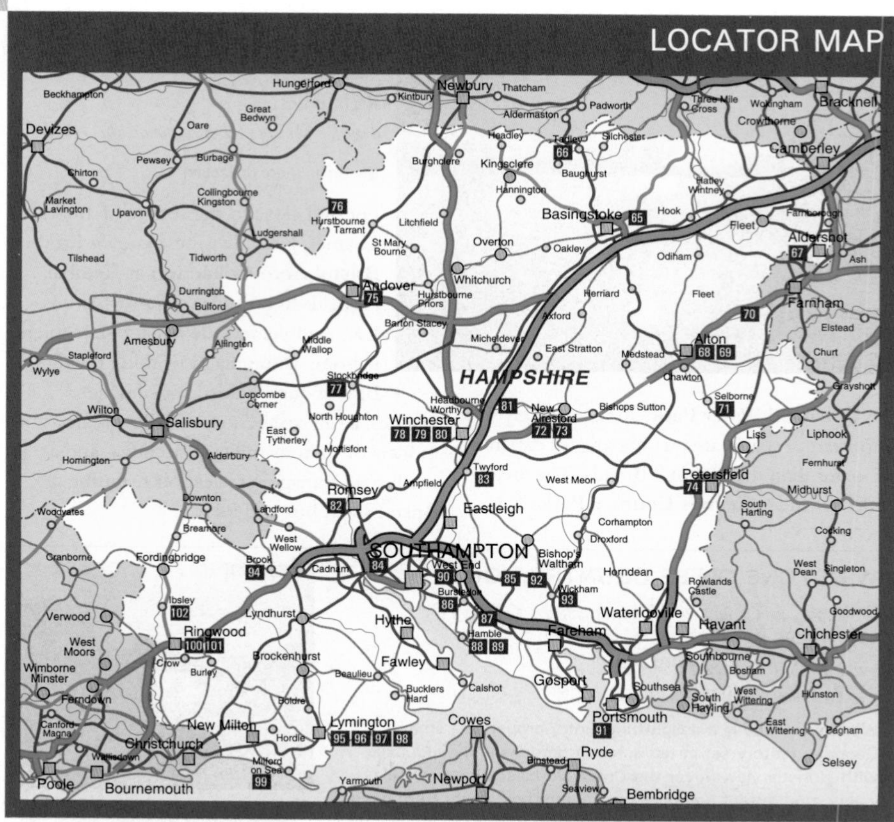

ADVERTISERS AND PLACES OF INTEREST

historic building museum and heritage historic site scenic attraction flora and fauna

5 | Hampshire

As the crow flies, the northeastern corner of Hampshire is little more than 30 miles from central London. So it's not surprising that this corner of the county is quite heavily populated, dotted with prosperous, sprawling towns such as Farnborough, Farnham and Basingstoke, plus the army enclave of Aldershot. What *is* surprising is that once you turn off the busy main roads, you can find yourself driving along narrow country lanes with very little traffic.

To the south of this area are the North Downs. Honouring the perverse tradition of English place-names, the Downs are actually uplands, softly rolling, wooded hills in whose folds lie scores of picturesque villages and small towns. Further south is the historic city of Winchester with its glorious cathedral, and further south still, the heavily populated coastal area extending from Havant through Portsmouth with its magnificent maritime heritage, to Southampton, which boasts one of the finest natural harbours in the world.

Oddly, there are comparatively few grand houses in Hampshire although The Vyne near Basingstoke, and the Duke of Wellington's home, Stratfield Saye House, are both very imposing. Two smaller dwellings, however, attract many thousands of visitors to this corner of the county: Jane Austen's House at Chawton, near Alton, and a few miles to the south, in the village of Selborne, The Wakes, home of the celebrated naturalist Gilbert White. Lovers of steam railways can combine a visit to these two houses with a ride on the Watercress Line, which runs between Alton and Alresford.

Created a National Park in 2005, the New Forest has been a Royal Forest for more than 900 years. It acquired its name after William the Conqueror proclaimed it as his hunting ground and began a programme of planting thousands of trees. The area is famous for its wildlife, in particular the ponies, and now that it has the status of a National Park, its 222 square miles will be protected from "inappropriate development" in the future.

ADVERTISERS AND PLACES OF INTEREST

Basingstoke

Basing House · The Vyne · Milestones

Willis Museum · Southview Cemetery

Chapel of the Holy Ghost · Viables Craft Centre

A vibrant, modern town whose name goes back to Saxon times when a farmer with a name something like Base, along with his extended family, or 'ing', established a 'stok', (stock or farmhouse) beside the River Lodden.

It comes as something of a surprise to discover that this busy, prosperous town with its soaring multi-storey buildings can boast no fewer than 25 parks and open spaces. A useful leaflet available from the Tourist Information Centre gives details of them all, ranging from the 16-hectare War Memorial Park, an 18th-century park complete with bandstand, aviary and sports facilities, to **Southview Cemetery**, a site with a fascinating history. Some 800 years ago, during the reign of King John, England languished under an interdict pronounced by the pope. Throughout the six years from 1208 to 1214, any baby christened, or dead person buried, lacked the official blessing of Mother Church. At Basingstoke during those years, the deceased were interred in a graveyard known as the Liten, and when the interdict was finally lifted, the ground was consecrated and a chapel built, the **Chapel of the Holy Ghost**. Today, it's a striking ruin surrounded by a well-managed site, which provides a peaceful refuge from the bustling town.

As befits such a thriving place, Basingstoke offers visitors a wide choice of attractions: theatre, cinema, a vast Leisure Park and Festival Place, whose one million square feet of shopping and leisure contains some 165 shops, 26 bars, restaurants and cafés, and a 10-screen cinema.

The Old Town area offers a lively cosmopolitan mix of bars, theme pubs and restaurants. Here, too, housed in the old Town Hall of 1832, is the excellent **Willis Museum**, which charts the town's history with lively displays featuring characters such as Fred, a Roman skeleton, and Pickaxe, a 19th-century farm worker "forced to scrape a living from the streets of Basingstoke as a scavenger". The museum, which is open every day except Sunday, is named after George Willis, a local clockmaker and former mayor of Basingstoke who established the collection in 1931. Naturally, locally-made grandfather clocks feature prominently in the displays.

Basing House

Redbridge Lane, Basing, Basingstoke,
Hampshire RG24 7HB
Tel: 01256 467294
website: www.hants.gov.uk/museum/basinghouse

Built on a massive scale inside the walls of a medieval castle, **Basing House** was once the largest private residence in the country. The ruins, the riverside walk, the dovecotes and the spectacular 16th century grange barn add up to an attraction of great appeal, and the beauty is enhanced by the re-created 17th century garden inside the Tudor walls. The house was sacked by Cromwell's men, with Cromwell himself present, after a long and arduous siege and the ruins include the historic Garrison gateway.

A more recent attraction is **Milestones**, a living history museum with reconstructed shops, factories, cobbled streets and staff in period costume. Highlights include the Tasker and Thorneycroft collections of agricultural and commercial vehicles and the fascinating AA collection. At the nearby **Viables Craft Centre**, visitors can watch craftspeople at work. A notable former resident of Basingstoke was the draper Thomas Burberry. It was while running his shop in the town that he devised a new method for waterproofing garments, which he called gabardine. His shop in Winchester Street is still there.

Just to the east of Basingstoke, **Basing House** (see panel opposite) was once one of the grandest residences in the realm. Built during the reign of Henry VIII, it rivalled even the king's extravagant mansions. Less than 100 years later, during the Civil War, Cromwell's troops besieged the house for an incredible three years, one of them reporting that the mansion was "as large as the Tower of London". When Basing House was finally captured, the victorious New Army burnt it to the ground, but a magnificent 16th-century barn survived, its timber roof a marvel of the carpenter's craft.

The Vyne (National Trust), four miles north of Basingstoke, has a much happier history.

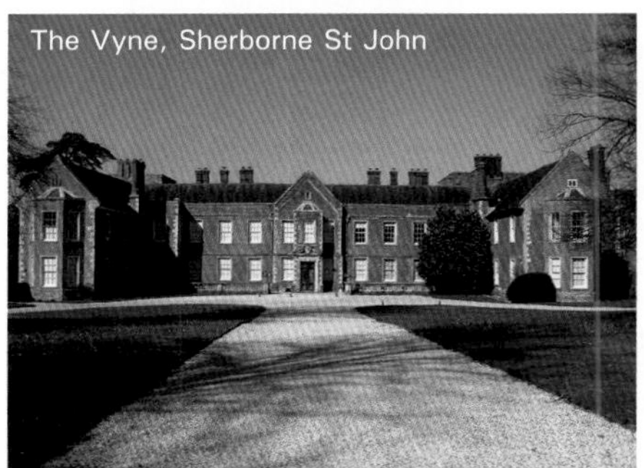

The Vyne, Sherborne St John

Built in the early 1500s for Lord Sandys, Lord Chamberlain to Henry VIII, the house enjoys an idyllic setting with lawns sweeping down to a shimmering lake. A classical portico was added in 1654, the first of its kind in England. The Vyne's treasures include a fascinating Tudor chapel with Renaissance glass, a Palladian staircase, and a wealth of linenfold panelling and fine furniture.

Around Basingstoke

STEVENTON

6 miles SW of Basingstoke, off the B3400

At Steventon Rectory on 16 December 1775, Cassandra Austen presented her husband, George, with their seventh child, Jane. George was the rector of Steventon and Jane was to spend the first 25 years of her short life in the village. There is now very little evidence of her time here. The rectory was later demolished, but there are memorials to the Austen family in the church where George Austen served for 44 years. It was at Steventon that Jane wrote *Pride and Prejudice*, *Sense and Sensibility* and *Northanger Abbey*. When the Rev George retired in 1800, the family moved to Bath. After her father's death, five years later, Jane and her mother took the house in Chawton that is now the Jane Austen Museum.

OVERTON

8 miles W of Basingstoke, on the B3400

Watership Down

A large village near the source of the River Test, Overton has a broad main street lined with handsome houses. During the stage coach era, it was an important staging post on the London to Winchester route, and the annual sheep fair was one of the largest in the county, selling at its peak up to 150,000 lambs and sheep. The fair flourished for centuries only coming to an end in the early 1930s.

To the north of the village, set high on a ridge, is **Watership Down**, immortalised in Richard Adams' book of the same name. It is now a nature reserve. The down lies on the long distance footpath, the Wayfarer's Walk, which runs from Inkpen Beacon (just over the border in Berkshire) to Emsworth on the Hampshire coast.

KINGSCLERE

8 miles NW of Basingstoke, on the A339

Collectors of curiosities might like to make a short excursion to the little town of Kingsclere where the weather vane on top of the parish church has baffled many visitors. With its six outstretched legs and squat body, the figure on the vane has been compared to a skate-boarding terrapin. Local historians, however, assert that it actually represents a bed bug and was placed here at the command of King John. The King had been hunting in the area when a thick fog descended and he was forced to spend the night at the Crown Hotel in Kingsclere. Apparently, he slept badly, his slumber continually disturbed by the attentions of a bed bug. The next morning, he ordered that the townspeople should forever be reminded of his restless night in Kingsclere by erecting this curious memorial to his tormentor.

SILCHESTER

7 miles N of Basingstoke, off the A340

Calleva Atrebatum · Church of St Mary

Excavation of the town, which the Romans called **Calleva Atrebatum**, took place at the turn of the 19th century and revealed some

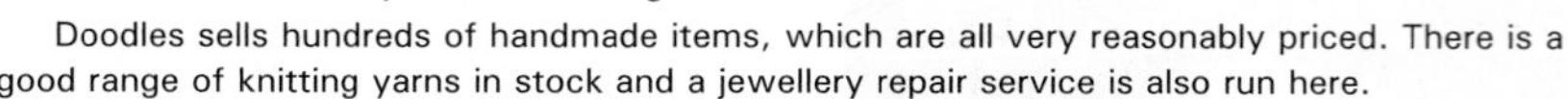

remarkable treasures, most of which are now on display at Reading Museum. The dig also revealed the most complete plan of any Roman town in the country but, rather oddly, the site was 're-buried' and now only the 1½ mile city wall is visible – the best-preserved Roman town wall in Britain. Also impressive is the recently restored 1st-century amphitheatre, which lay just beyond the town walls.

Tucked in next to part of the Roman wall is the pretty **Church of St Mary**, which dates from the 1100s. It boasts a superb 16th-century screen with a frieze of angels and some unusual bench-ends from 1909 executed in Art Nouveau style.

PAMBER HEATH

7 miles N of Basingstoke, on minor road off the A340

Priory Church

There are three Pambers set in the countryside along the A340. At Pamber End stand the picturesque ruins of a once-magnificent 12th/13th-century **Priory Church**, idyllically sited in sylvan surroundings. Set apart from the village, they invite repose and meditation.

HARTLEY WINTNEY

9 miles NE of Basingstoke, on the A30

West Green House Old Church

Mildmay Oaks

Riding through Hartley Wintney in 1821, William Cobbett, the author of *Rural Rides* and a conservationist long before anyone had thought of such a creature, was delighted to see young oaks being planted on the large village green. They were the gift of Hartley Wintney's Lady of the Manor, Lady Mildmay, and were originally intended to provide timber for shipbuilding. Fortunately, by the time they matured they were no longer needed for that purpose and today the **Mildmay Oaks** provide the village centre with a uniquely beautiful setting of majestic oak trees.

Anyone with an interest in horticulture should also visit the magnificent gardens of **West Green House**, about a mile to the west of Hartley Wintney. Owned by the National Trust, this pretty early 18th-century house is surrounded by lovely gardens planted with a dazzling variety of trees, shrubs and plants. One of its interesting features is a stone column surmounted by an elaborate finial, which was erected in 1976. It bears a Latin inscription that declares that a large sum of money was needed to put the column in place, money "which would otherwise have fallen, sooner or later, into the hands of the Inland Revenue". This quintessentially English manor house in warm red brick hosts an annual opera season.

While you are in Hartley Wintney, a visit to the **Old Church**, south of the village, is well worth while. Parts of the building date back to medieval times, but the fascination of old St Mary's lies in the fact that, after being completely renovated in 1834, it has remained almost totally unaltered ever since. High-sided box pews line the main aisle, there are elegant galleries for choir and congregation spanning the nave and both transepts, and colourful funeral hatchments add to St Mary's time-warp atmosphere.

EVERSLEY

10 miles NE of Basingstoke, on the A327

Stratfield Saye House

Wellington Country Park

Charles Kingsley, author of such immensely popular Victorian novels as *The Water Babies* and *Westward Ho!*, was Rector of the village for 33 years from 1842 until his death in 1875, and is buried in the churchyard here. The gates of the village school, erected in 1951 for the Festival of Britain, include a figure of a boy chimney sweep, the main character of *The Water Babies.* Kingsley was an attractive character with a burning passion for social justice, but modern readers don't seem to share the Victorian enthusiasm for his works. It's a sad fate for a prolific man of letters, although perhaps not quite so dispiriting as that met by one of Kingsley's predecessors as preacher at Eversley. He was hanged as a highwayman.

About four miles west of Eversley, **Stratfield Saye House** was just one of many rewards a grateful nation showered on the Duke of Wellington after his decisive defeat of Napoleon at Waterloo. The Duke himself doesn't seem to have been reciprocally grateful: only lack of funds frustrated his plans to demolish the gracious 17th-century house and replace it with an even more impressive mansion, which he intended to call Waterloo Palace. Quite modest in scale, Stratfield Saye fascinates visitors with its collection of the Duke's own furniture and personal items such as his spectacles, handkerchiefs and carpet slippers. More questionable are the priceless books in the library, many of them looted from Napoleon's own bibliotheque. A good number of the fine Spanish and Portuguese paintings on display share an equally dubious provenance, 'relieved' during the Duke's campaign in those countries as 'spoils of war'. That was accepted military practice at the time and, these quibbles apart, Stratfield Saye House is certainly one of the county's leading attractions.

Within the estate is the **Wellington Country Park** where there are numerous attractions, including walks and nature trails, a children's animal farm, an adventure playground and a miniature railway.

ODIHAM

7 miles E of Basingstoke, on the A327

Castle

Odiham Castle must have a very good claim to being one of the least picturesque ruins in the country. It looks like something rescued from a giant dentist's tray, with gaping window holes and jagged, crumbling towers. Back in 1215, though, Odiham Castle was a state-of-the-art royal residence. Great pomp and circumstance attended King John's stay at the castle, then just seven years old, the night before he set off to an important meeting. The following day, in a meadow beside the River Thames called Runnymede, John reluctantly subscribed his name to a bill of rights. That document, known as Magna Carta, proved to be the embryo of democracy in western Europe.

Odiham itself is one of the most attractive villages in the county, with a handsome High Street and a 15th-century church, the largest in Hampshire, in which those interested in curiosities will be pleased to find a rather rare item, a hudd. A portable wooden frame covered with cloth, the hudd provided Odiham's rector with graveside shelter when he was conducting burials in inclement weather. In a corner of the graveyard stands

Odiham Castle

the Pest House, built around 1625 as an isolation ward for patients with infectious diseases. From 1780 until 1950, it served as an almshouse and is now open to visitors on most weekends.

ALDERSHOT

14 miles E of Basingstoke on the A331

- Military Museum · Heroes Shrine
- Army Medical Services Museum
- Army Physical Training Museum
- Queen Alexandra's Royal Army Nursing Corps Museum

Back in 1854, Aldershot was a village of some 800 inhabitants. Then the Army decided to build a major camp here and the population has grown steadily ever since to its present tally of around 60,000. The story of how Aldershot became the home of the British Army is vividly recounted at the **Aldershot Military Museum** (see panel below), which stands in the middle of the camp and is a must for anyone with an interest in military history. Housed in the last two surviving Victorian barrack blocks, dating back to 1854, its tiny appearance from the outside belies the wealth of fascinating displays contained inside. For example, there's a detailed cutaway model of a cavalry barracks showing how the soldiers' rooms were placed above the stables, an economic form of central heating described as "warm, but aromatic".

There are other military museums to be found here: the **Army Medical Services Museum**, telling the story of medical services from 1660 to the present day; **Queen Alexandra's Royal Army Nursing Corps Museum**; and the **Army Physical Training Corps Museum** where the Corps history is recounted with the help of numerous exhibits, pictorial records – and some Victorian gymnastic equipment.

In the town's Manor Park, the **Heroes Shrine** commemorates the dead of the First World War, while a nearby walled and sunken garden, shaded by deodar trees, honours the fallen of the Second World War. Another celebrated military figure, the Duke of Wellington, is represented by an imposing bronze statue crowning Round Hill, just outside the town. The statue originally stood

Aldershot Military Museum

Queens Avenue, Aldershot, Hampshire GU11 2LG
Tel: 1252 314598
website: www.hants.gov.uk/museum/aldershot

The Museum covers the histories of Aldershot military town and the adjoining civil towns of Aldershot and Farnborough. The complex contains a rich mixture of buildings, objects, displays, vehicles and archives, and each of the several galleries has a different theme and character.

The John Reed Gallery covers the history of the Army in Aldershot from its arrival in 1854, and includes a rare example of a Victorian barrack room displayed in its original setting.

Aldershot Park

atop the Triumphal Arch at Hyde Park Corner in London, but was moved to Aldershot in 1885.

FARNBOROUGH

14 miles E of Basingstoke on the A331

Air Sciences Trust Museum

St Michael's Abbey

The town is best known for the Farnborough Air Show, held every other year. The town's unique aviation heritage is explored at the **Farnborough Air Sciences Trust Museum (FAST)**, which holds an extensive collection of exhibits, records and artefacts, including whole aircraft, parts and scale models. The museum is open at weekends and at other times by appointment. Call 01252 375050.

Less well-known is **St Michael's Abbey**, now a Benedictine foundation but with a curious history. After the fall of Napoleon III, his wife, the Empress Eugenie, came to live at a large house called Farnborough Hill where she was later joined by her husband and her son, the Prince Imperial. Napoleon died at Chislehurst after an operation to remove bladder stones; her son was killed in the Zulu War. The heartbroken Empress commissioned the building of an ornate mausoleum for their tombs and a monastery in the flamboyant French style. The first monks arrived in 1895 from Solesmes Abbey, France, and they are still here continuing their regime of liturgy, study and manual work. The abbey is open to the public and has a small farm and apiary that supplies not only the monks, but also the abbey shop. Guided tours are available on Saturday and Bank Holiday afternoons.

Alton

St Lawrence's Church | Curtis Museum

Grave of Fanny Adams | Allen Gallery

Alton Sculpture Trail

Surrounded by hop fields and some of Hampshire's loveliest countryside, Alton is an appealing market town with a history stretching back far beyond Roman times. (The name actually means Old Town.) Its market, held every Tuesday, has a history going back more than 1000 years and was the most valuable market recorded in the Domesday Book.

Alton boasts a large number of old coaching inns, and the impressive, partly-Norman **St Lawrence's Church**, which was the setting for a dramatic episode during the Civil War. A large force of Roundheads drove some 80 Royalists into the church where 60 of them were killed. The Royalist commander, Colonel Boles, made a last stand from the splendid Jacobean pulpit, firing repeatedly at his attackers before succumbing to their bullets. The church door and several of the Norman pillars are still pockmarked with bullet holes inflicted during this close-combat conflict. More cheerful, are the comical carvings on these pillars of animals and birds,

BOTTEGA COFFEE SHOP

8 High Street, Alton, Hampshire GU34 1BN
Tel: 01420 88988
website: bottegadeisapori.co.uk

This cosmopolitan coffee shop is worth investigating on account of its fairly unusual menu and rather special location, amongst superb 18th century architecture. The food is marvellous and the atmosphere one of the best around. **Bottega Coffee Shop** is more about food, and has an interesting menu of canapés, buffet platters, cakes, gateaux, tarts, petit fours and homemade Italian ice creams, as well as providing other Italian delights and lunches.

The *"Shop of Flavours"* is cheerful and relaxed – a healthy antidote to the latest crop of production-line coffee 'outlets'. It feels homey and is a great place to sit and chat. The aroma of coffee subtly, deliciously scents the air, giving everyone a chance to unwind. There is a fluid flow of customers yet people aren't deafened by the sound of everyone coming and going. People can have a decent conversation, a heart to heart or a casual chat as they feel like it either in the coffee shop or the outside garden area. Cleary, Maggie and Tiziano Tesolin, proprietors, have an excellent family run business that is well worth a visit!

MARKET STREET GALLERY

19 Market Street, Alton, Hampshire GU34 1HA
Tel: 01420 88482
e-mail: marketstgallery@btconnect.com
website: www.marketstgallery.co.uk

In the centre of the historic Hampshire market town of Alton is the **Market Street Gallery**, whose belief is firmly that art is to be enjoyed. The work of local artists can certainly be appreciated here, and those from further afield, with changing exhibitions and some whose work is permanently displayed. These include wonderful pieces of glass-making, pencil sketches, oils, watercolours and some official collector's edition prints including Quentin Blake's Roald Dahl illustrations.

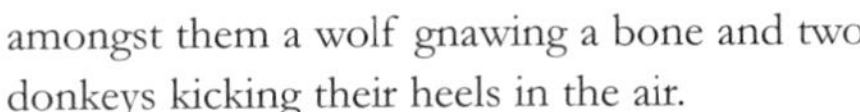

amongst them a wolf gnawing a bone and two donkeys kicking their heels in the air.

Nearby is the old cemetery and the well-tended **Grave of Fanny Adams**. The expression 'Sweet Fanny Adams' arose from the revolting murder in 1867 of an eight-year-old girl in the town who was hacked into pieces by her assassin. With macabre humour, sailors used the same phrase to describe the recently-introduced tinned mutton for which they had a certain mistrust. Over the years, the saying became accepted as a contemptuous description for anything considered valueless: a poor way to remember an innocent girl.

There's a different sort of monument in Amery Street, a narrow lane leading off the market place. On a small brick house is a plaque commemorating the Elizabethan poet Edmund Spenser, who came to Alton around 1590 to enjoy its "sweet delicate air".

Well worth a visit while you are in Alton is the **Allen Gallery** in Church Street, home to an outstanding collection of English, Continental and Far Eastern pottery, porcelain and tiles. Housed in a group of attractive 16th and 18th-century buildings, the gallery's other attractions include the unique Elizabethan Tichborne Spoons, delightful watercolours and oil paintings by local artist William Herbert Allen, and a comfortable coffee lounge. During the summer months, the charming walled garden at the rear of the gallery provides a lovely setting for sculpture exhibitions. More sculpture can be seen if you follow the **Alton Sculpture Trail**, although the word 'sculpture' is broadly defined to include a rare Edward VIII postbox and an early 19th-century mile plate.

Across the road from the Allen Gallery, the **Curtis Museum** concentrates on exploring 100 million years of local history with displays devoted to the "shocking tale of Sweet Fanny Adams"; other local celebrities

MILL FARM ORGANIC

Mill Farm, Isington, nr Alton, Hampshire GU34 4PN
Tel: 01420 22331 Fax: 01420 22331
e-mail: info@millfarmorganic.com
website: www.millfarmorganic.com

Mill Farm, and the delightful Mill Farm Shop, is set in the idyllic Hampshire countryside on the banks of the River Wey. Grazing on the farm's clover-rich pastures and traditional water meadows are their proud herds of Pedigree South Devon Cattle, Wiltshire Horn and Black Welsh Mountain sheep. These breeds have been specially selected for their taste, and their resilience and suitability in the British climate. The two breeds of sheep, the locally native Wiltshire Horn and smaller hardy Black Welsh Mountain, allow Mill Farm to sell lamb year round. The real star of the show however is the pedigree South Devon cow, which are a native British breed, and produce the most amazingly full of flavoured and meltingly tender beef.

Every cut of beef sold at Mill Farm, from the filet steak to the mince and stewing steak, is prepared in the traditional way by being hung for three and a half weeks, allowing the meat to mature and invest flavour and tenderness. In addition to beef, Mill Farm shop offers a huge range of local and organic produce, including their lamb and Hampshire pork as well as award winning 'Old English' pork sausages. Customers are also able to take one of the Farm Trails and get a real feel for this beautiful piece of countryside. After your walk you can enjoy a nice cup of tea with a delicious homemade pasty.

Opening hours are Wednesday to Friday 9am-5pm and Saturday 9am-4pm.

such as Jane Austen, Lord Baden Powell and Montgomery of Alamein; and a colourful Gallery of Childhood with exhibits thoughtfully displayed in miniature cases at a suitable height for children. Open Tuesday to Saturday 10am to 5pm.

On the western edge of the town lies The Butts, a pleasant open area of grassland that was once used for archery practice. Today, it is the setting for events such as the annual Victorian Cricket Match.

A good time to visit the town is mid-July when the Alton Show takes place. Established in 1840, this is one of southern England's most important agricultural gatherings with a wide range of events featuring such attractions as heavy horses, llamas, beagles, gun dogs and birds of prey.

Around Alton

SELBORNE

4 miles SE of Alton on the B3006

The Wakes and Oates Museum

Church of St Mary Selborne Pottery

Like the neighbouring village of Chawton, Selborne also produced a great literary figure. **The Wakes** (see panel below) was the home of Gilbert White, a humble curate of the parish from 1784 until his death in 1793. He spent his spare hours meticulously recording observations on the weather, wildlife and geology of the area. A percipient publisher to whom Gilbert submitted his notes recognised the appeal of his humdrum, day-to-day accounts of life in what was then a remote

GILBERT WHITE'S HOUSE & GARDEN AND THE OATES COLLECTION

The Wakes, High Street, Selborne, Hampshire GU34 3JH
Tel: 01420 511275
e-mail: info@gilbertwhiteshouse.org.uk
website: www.gilbertwhiteshouse.org.uk

Gilbert White's House & Garden and The Oates Collection celebrate three remarkable Englishmen. The Rev. Gilbert White (1720-1793), author of the world-famous *Natural History of Selborne,* cited by Darwin as his inspiration, lived at The Wakes for most of his life. The rooms have been restored following descriptions in White's own correspondence and contain items of his furniture, family portraits, and beautiful bed hangings embroidered by white by family members. On display in the Library is White's original hand-written manuscript of the *Natural History*. The 20 acres of garden and parkland at The Wakes was well-documented by White and has been largely restored to its 18th century form.

The Oates Collection commemorates the Oates family and their exploits. In particular, it celebrates Captain Lawrence Oates who accompanied Scott to the South Pole in 1911. Rare items from the expedition are a poignant reminder of these ill-fated men and their valiant endeavours.

Also on site is a shop which specialises in unusual and inexpensive gifts, many of them local in origin, and a licensed award winning tea parlour in a period dining room.

corner of England. *The Natural History and Antiquities of Selborne* was first published in 1788, has never been out of print, and still provides what is perhaps the most entertaining and direct access to late 18th-century life, seen through the eyes of an intelligent, sceptical mind. Visitors to The Wakes can see the original manuscript of his book along with other personal belongings, and stroll through the peaceful garden with its unusual old plant varieties.

The house also contains the **Oates Museum**, which celebrates Francis Oates, the Victorian explorer, and his nephew Captain Lawrence 'Titus' Oates who was with Captain Scott on his doomed expedition to the South Pole. Titus' last words – "I am just going outside. I may be some time" – are known around the world, as is Scott's diary entry describing Oates' selfless deed as "the act of a very gallant gentleman". The Wakes and the Oates Museum are open daily, and there's an excellent book and gift shop, and a tearoom specialising in 18th-century fare.

Gilbert White is buried in the graveyard of the pretty **Church of St Mary**, his final resting place marked by a stone bearing the austere inscription "GW 26th June 1793". A fine stained-glass window depicts St Francis preaching to the birds described in Gilbert's book. Outside in the churchyard, is the stump of a yew tree, which was some 1400 years old when it succumbed to the great storm of January 1990.

From the village centre there are several walks, one which leads to the Zig-Zag path constructed by Gilbert and his brother in 1753. It winds its way up to the Hanger (a wood on a steep hillside) that overlooks the village. The land at the summit is part of an area of meadow, woodland and common owned by the National Trust – the spot provides panoramic views across the South Downs.

Back in the village, the **Selborne Pottery** was established by Robert Goldsmith in 1985. Each piece of pottery made here is hand-thrown and turned, and the distinctive pots are not only functional, but also decorative, with rich copper red and cobalt blue glazes.

CHAWTON

2 miles SW of Alton, off the A31

Jane Austen's House

Jane Austen's House at Chawton is where the writer spent the last eight years of her life from 1809 to 1817. Jane was 33 years old when she moved in and none of her works had been published, but her eight-year stay at Chawton saw the publication of *Sense and Sensibility*, *Pride and Prejudice*, *Mansfield Park* and *Emma*. She also completed *Northanger Abbey* and *Persuasion*, which were published in 1818 shortly after her death. Now a museum, the house contains some fascinating artefacts connected with Jane and her family. Jane's music lies on the piano, her donkey cart stands in the outhouse, and the flowers mentioned in her letters still flourish. Jane died in Winchester and is buried in the cathedral there; her mother and sister Cassandra lie in the little churchyard in Chawton. Chawton village itself is a delightful spot with old

Jane Austen's House, Chawton

cottages and houses leading up to the village green outside Jane's house.

HINTON AMPNER

9 miles SW of Alton on the A272

Hinton Ampner Gardens

Itchen Way

The River Itchen, renowned for its trout and watercress beds, rises to the west of the village to begin its 25-mile journey to the sea at Southampton; the **Itchen Way** footpath follows the river throughout its course. Also to the west of the village are **Hinton Ampner Gardens** (National Trust), created by Ralph Dutton who inherited the house in 1936. The superb garden combines formal and informal planting and the design produces several delightful walks with some unexpected vistas.

ALRESFORD

10 miles SW of Alton, off the A31

Manor House   Watercress Line

Mary Russell Mitford

Alresford – pronounced Allsford – was created around 1200 by a Bishop of Winchester, Geoffrey de Lucy, as part of his grand plan to build a waterway from Winchester to Southampton. Where the river Arle flows into the Itchen, he constructed a huge reservoir covering 200 acres, its waters controlled to keep the Itchen navigable at all seasons. The Bishop's reservoir is now reduced to some 60 acres, but it's still home to countless wildfowl and many otters. Known today as Old Alresford Pond, it's one of the most charming features of this dignified Georgian town. Alresford can also boast one

of the county's most beautiful streets, historic Broad Street, lined with elegant, colour-washed Georgian houses interspersed with specialist shops and inviting hostelries.

Alresford's most famous son was Admiral Lord Rodney, a contemporary of Lord Nelson, who built the grand **Manor House** near the parish church, but the town can also boast two famous daughters. One was Mary Sumner, wife of the Rector of Alresford, who founded the Mother's Union here in 1876. The other was **Mary Russell Mitford**, author of the fascinating collection of sketches of 18th-century life, *Our Village,* published in five volumes between 1824-1832. Mary's prolific literary output was partly spurred on by the need to repay the debts of her spendthrift father. Dr Mitford managed to dissipate his own inherited fortune of many thousands of pounds. His wife's lavish dowry, which almost doubled that income, disappeared equally quickly, and when Mary at the age of 10 won the huge sum of £20,000 in a lottery, the good doctor squandered that as well. Mary's classic book tells the story.

One of Alresford's attractions that should not be missed is the **Watercress Line**, Hampshire's only preserved steam railway, so named because it was once used to transport watercress from the beds around Alresford to London and beyond. The line, which was saved in 1973, runs through 10 miles of beautiful countryside to Alton where it links up with main line services to London. Vintage steam locomotives make the 35-minute journey up to eight times a day, and there are regular dining trains as well as frequent special events throughout the year. Engines used in 2010 include Black Five 45379, Bulleid Pacific 34007, 850 *Lord Nelson* and BR Standard locomotives 76017, 73096, 80150 and 92212.

TICHBORNE

12 miles SW of Alton off the A31

The Titchborne Dole and Titchborne Claimant

Two intriguing stories are associated with this lovely village of thatched and half-timbered cottages. The legend of the **Tichborne Dole** dates from the reign of Henry I. At that time the owner of Tichborne Park was the dastardly Sir Roger Tichborne. As his crippled wife, Mabella, lay dying, her last wish was to provide food for the poor. Sir Roger agreed – but only from an area she could crawl around. The brave woman managed to encircle an area of more than 20 acres of arable land, carrying a flaming torch as she did so. Ever since then the Park's owners have provided bags of flour every year to the villages of Tichborne and Cheriton. The field is still known as 'The Crawls'.

Equally notorious is the episode of the **Tichborne Claimant**. In 1871, a certain Arthur Orton, son of a Wapping butcher, returned from Wagga Wagga, Australia, claiming to be the heir to the estate. Although he bore no resemblance to the rightful heir who had disappeared while sailing round the world, Arthur was 'recognised' by the widow as her son and supported in his claim. She, apparently, detested her late husband's family. Arthur's claim was rejected in a trial that lasted 100 days, and he was then put on trial for perjury. After a further 188 days he was found guilty and sentenced to 14 days in prison.

CHERITON

13 miles SW of Alton on the B3046

The pretty village of Cheriton has a church that is believed to stand over a prehistoric burial ground. In 1644, the Battle of Cheriton, fought near Cheriton Wood, resulted in the deaths of 2000 men as the Roundheads defeated the Royalists.

Petersfield

Church of St Peter · Physic Garden

Butser Hill · Flora Twort Gallery

Petersfield Heath · B Museum

An appealing market town, Petersfield is dominated by the bulk of **Butser Hill**, 900 feet high and the highest point of the South Downs. It provides grand panoramic views over the town and even, on a clear day, to the spire of Salisbury Cathedral, some 40 miles distant. In the 1660s, Samuel Pepys noted his stay in Petersfield, at a hotel in which Charles II had slept before him. Another king is commemorated in The Square where William III sits on horseback, incongruously dressed in Roman costume. Unusually, the statue is made of lead.

Most of the elegant buildings around The Square are Georgian, but the **Church of St Peter** is much older, dating back to Norman times and with a fine north aisle to prove it. Just off The Square, the **Flora Twort Gallery** was once the home and studio of the accomplished artist of that name who moved to Petersfield at the end of the First World War. Her delightful paintings and drawings capture life in the town over some 40 years – "reminders of some of the things we have lost" as she put it shortly before her death at the age of 91 in 1985.

From the gallery, a short walk along Sheep Street (which has some striking timber-framed 16th-century houses and Georgian cottages) brings you to The Spain, a pleasant green surrounded by some of the town's oldest houses. It apparently acquired its rather unusual name because dealers in Spanish wool used to hold markets there.

Petersfield Physic Garden

Visitors with an interest in gardening will want to see the **Physic Garden** in the centre of the town. Set in an ancient walled plot, the garden has been planted in a style and with plants that would have been familiar to the distinguished 17th-century botanist, John Goodyer, who lived in Petersfield.

Other attractions include the Dragon Gallery, providing a showcase for contemporary artists; and the **Petersfield Museum**, housed in the former Courthouse.

Just a short walk from the town centre is **Petersfield Heath**, an extensive recreational area with a cricket ground and a pond for boating and fishing. The town's annual Taro Fair is held here in October and the heath is also notable as the site of one of the most important groups of Bronze Age barrows, or burial mounds, in the country.

Petersfield is set on the Western edge of the newly designated South Downs National Park, which is laced with footpaths and cycle trails. The Hayes Way passes through the town, linking with the South Downs Way at the Queen Elizabeth Country Park. The 100-mile South Downs Way winds along the chalk escarpment and ridges of the South Downs between Winchester and Eastbourne.

Around Petersfield

STEEP

1 mile N of Petersfield, off the A3

Appropriately, the village is reached by way of a steep hill. The village is famous as the home of the writer and nature poet Edward Thomas who moved here with his family in 1907. It was while living at 2 Yew Tree Cottages that he wrote most of his poems. In 1909 he and his wife Helen moved to the Red House (private) where his daughter Myfanwy was born in 1913. Many years later, in 1985, she unveiled a plaque on the house. Her former home featured in two of her father's poems, *The New House* and *Wind and Mist*. Thomas was killed in action during the First World War. His death is commemorated by two engraved lancet windows installed in 1978 in All Saints Church, and by a memorial stone on Shoulder of Mutton Hill above the village.

It was at Steep in 1898 that the educational pioneer John Badley established Bedales, the first boarding school for both sexes in the country. His "preposterous experiment" proved highly successful. Members of staff and pupils at Bedales call each other by their first names and there is no formal school uniform. There is an absence of petty rules and, says the school brochure, "because the pupils are listened to, they learn to listen to each other".

BURITON

2 miles S of Petersfield, on minor road off the A3

Uppark

An old church surrounded by trees and overlooking a tree-lined duck pond is flanked by an appealing early 18th-century Manor House (private) built by the father of Edward Gibbon, the celebrated historian. The younger Gibbon wrote much of his magnum opus *Decline and Fall of the Roman Empire* in his study here. He was critical of the house's position "at the end of the village and the bottom of the hill", but was highly appreciative of the view over the Downs: "the long hanging woods in sight of the house could not perhaps have been improved by art or expense".

About five miles southeast of Buriton, **Uppark** (National Trust), is a handsome Wren-style mansion built around 1690 and most notable for its interior. Uppark was completely redecorated and refurnished in the 1750s by the Fetherstonhaugh family and that work has remained almost entirely unchanged – not only the furniture but even some of the fabrics and wallpapers remain in excellent condition. The servants' rooms are as they were in 1874 when the mother of HG Wells was housekeeper here – the writer's recollections of life at Uppark with his mother are fondly recorded in his autobiography.

CHALTON

5 miles S of Petersfield off the A3

Butser Ancient Farm

Situated on a slope of chalk down, Chalton is home to **Butser Ancient Farm,** a reconstruction of an Iron Age farm that has received worldwide acclaim for its research methodology and results. There's a magnificent great roundhouse, prehistoric

Buster Ancient Farm, Chalton

and Roman crops are grown, ancient breeds of cattle roam the hillside, and metal is worked according to ancient techniques. The latest project here is the construction of a replica Roman villa, complete with hypocaust, using the same methods as the Romans. A wonderful living laboratory, the farm is open one weekend each month when there are themed events. Courses providing hands-on experience in ancient crafts and archaeological techniques are available. All necessary tools are provided and course prices include materials.

HAMBLEDON

8 miles SW of Petersfield, off the B2150

A village of red brick Georgian houses and well-known for its vineyard, Hambledon is most famous for its cricketing connections. It was at the Hambledon Cricket Club that the rules of the game were first formulated in 1774. The club's finest hour came in 1777 when the team, led by the landlord of the Bat and Ball Inn, beat an All England team by an innings and 168 runs! A granite monument stands on Broadhalfpenny Down where the early games were played.

The village itself featured in the Domesday Book and, in the 13th century, was granted a licence to hold a market. About this time, the church was extensively rebuilt around the original Saxon church. Many of the village houses have their 16th-century origins concealed by the striking Georgian facades.

EAST MEON

5 miles W of Petersfield, on minor road off the A3 or A272

Tournai Font

Tucked away in the lovely valley of the River Meon and surrounded by high downs, East Meon has been described as "the most unspoilt of Hampshire villages and the nicest". As if that weren't enough, the village also boasts one of the finest and most venerable churches in the county. The central tower, with walls four feet thick, dates back to the 12th century and is a stunning example of Norman architecture at its best. Inside, the church's greatest treasure is its remarkable 12th-century **Tournai Font** of black marble, exquisitely carved with scenes depicting the Creation and the fall of Adam and Eve. Only seven of these wonderful fonts are known to

East Meon Village

exist in England (four of them in Hampshire) and East Meon's is generally regarded as the most magnificent.

In the churchyard are buried Thomas Lord, founder of the cricket ground in London, and the mother of the spy Guy Burgess. Her son's ashes were sprinkled on her grave in a suitably clandestine night-time ceremony.

Just across the road is the 15th-century Courthouse, which has walls four feet thick. It's a lovely medieval manor house where for generations the Bishops of Winchester, as Lords of the Manor, held their courts. It would have been a familiar sight to the "compleat angler" Izaac Walton, who spent many happy hours fishing in the River Meon nearby.

Northwest Hampshire

Some of Hampshire's grandest scenery lies in this part of the county as the North Downs roll westwards towards Salisbury Plain. There's just one sizeable town, Andover, and one major city, Winchester. The rest of the region is quite sparsely populated (for southern England) with scattered villages bearing evocative names such as Hurstbourne Tarrant and Nether Wallop. Winchester is, of course, in a class of its own with its dazzling Cathedral, but there are many other attractions in this area, ranging in time from the Iron Age Danebury Hill Fort, through the Victorian extravaganza of Highclere Castle, to Stanley Spencer's extraordinary murals in the Sandham Memorial Chapel at Burghclere.

Andover

St Mary's Church   Museum

Heritage Trail   Museum of the Iron Age

Finkley Down Farm Park

Andover is a growing market town well served with leisure and cultural facilities that include a five-screen cinema, The Light Theatre and a new arts centre. But the core of this ancient town, which was already important in Saxon times, retains much of interest. One outstanding landmark is **St Mary's Church**, completely rebuilt in the 1840s at the expense of a former headmaster of Winchester College. The interior is said to have been modelled on Salisbury Cathedral, and if it doesn't quite match up to that sublime building, St Mary's is still well worth a visit.

Equally striking is the Guildhall of 1825, built in classical style, which stands alone in the Market Place where markets are still held every Tuesday and Saturday. Andover has also managed to retain half a dozen of the 16 coaching inns that serviced 18th-century travellers at a time when the fastest stagecoaches took a mere nine hours to travel here from London. As many as 50 coaches a day stopped at these inns to change horses and allow the passengers to take refreshments.

For a fascinating insight into the town's long history, do pay a visit to the **Andover Museum** in Church Close. There are actually two museums here, both of them housed in buildings that began life as elegant Georgian town houses in 1750 and were later extended to

ACE FRAMING & ART GALLERY

122 The Commercial Centre, Picket Piece,
Andover, Hampshire SP11 6RU
Tel: 01264 353677
e-mail: vince.mcgarry@ntlworld.com
website: www.aceframing.co.uk

Art lovers are in their element at **Ace Framing & Art Gallery**, which can be found in the ancient town of Andover. Andover is home to St Mary's Church, which was completely rebuilt in the 1840s at the expense of a former headmaster of Winchester College and the interior is said to have been modelled on Salisbury Cathedral.

Many visitors to Andover enjoy exploring the culture and history of the town and as well as visiting Andover Museum many spend a fair time at Ace Framing & Art Gallery, which is described by its owners as a 'wonderful sanctuary of calm'. And that is exactly what it is. It is easy to lose track of time viewing the original works of art here and browsing the many paintings on display.

Vince McGarry is in charge of the gallery and it is him you will need to contact if you would like to display your own work here, which is what a lot of local and visiting artists do. There is an extensive range of famous artists displaying their works in the beautiful gallery, including wildlife artist Pip McGarry.

The framing service offered here is second to none and is very popular in the area. Full time artists and professional photographers come here constantly to frame their work. They demand the very best for their work and that is exactly what they get. Ace Framing & Art Gallery only deal in top quality work and specialise in framing original works of art, professional photographs and one off specials like signed football shirts, memorobilia and certificates.

If you are after a personal one-to-one service with high standard execution then a visit here is definitely recommended. Once you have finished looking around here you can explore the historic town of Andover including the Guildhall of 1825, built in classical style, which stands alone in the Market Place where markets are still held. The town has also managed to retain half a dozen of the 16 coaching inns that serviced 18th-century travellers at a time when the fastest stagecoaches took nine hours to travel here from London. As many as 50 coaches a day stopped at these inns to change horses and allow the passengers to take refreshments. Alterntatively there are plenty of eateries nearby where you can relax and enjoy something to eat or drink.

serve as Andover's Grammar School from the 1840s to 1925. The Andover Museum traces the story of the town from Saxon times to the present day, with a range of colourful exhibits that include a 19th-century Period Room. There's also a fascinating display evoking Victorian Andover and a workhouse scandal of the time. The museum hosts an exciting programme of temporary exhibitions with subjects including art, craft, photography, history and much more. The museum is home to a 1500-year-old Roman mosaic depicting the god Mars, discovered at nearby Fullerton. Former classrooms of the grammar school now house the **Museum of the Iron Age**, which tells the story of Danebury, an Iron Age hillfort that lies six miles southwest of Andover.

A good way of getting to know the town is to join one of the guided tours along the **Andover Heritage Trail**. Scheduled tours, lasting about 90 minutes, take place on Tuesday and Saturday afternoons, but can also be arranged for groups at other times.

Two miles east of Andover, **Finkley Down Farm Park** provides a satisfying day out for families with young children. Youngsters can feed and handle the animals, groom a pony, ride on a mini-tractor, and expend any excess energy in the well-equipped playground. Romany caravans and farming bygones are on display, and other attractions include a tearoom, gift shop and picnic area with a sandpit.

Around Andover

FACCOMBE

12 miles N of Andover, on minor road off the A343

Highclere Castle

This appealing little village, which is owned by the Faccombe Estate, is tucked away in the Hampshire countryside close to the Berkshire border. It is set on chalk downs some 750 feet above sea level with the highest points of the North Downs, Pilot Hill and Inkpen Beacon, both nearby. An extra attraction for walkers is the Test Way, a long-distance footpath that runs from Inkpen Beacon to the south coast following the track of the disused Sprat & Winkle railway.

About five miles west of Faccombe, **Highclere Castle** is a wondrous example of Victorian neo-Gothic architecture at its most exuberant. If the central tower reminds you of another well-known building, that may be because the castle was designed by Sir Charles Barry, architect of the Houses of Parliament. It stands on the site of a former palace of the Bishops of Winchester, overlooking an incomparably lovely park, one of Capability Brown's greatest creations. Highclere is the family home of the 8th Earl and Countess of Carnavon. It was the 5th Earl who was with Howard Carter in 1922 at the opening of Tutankhamun's tomb. A small museum in the basement of the castle recalls that breathtaking moment. Another display reflects the family's love of, and success in, the racing and breeding of horses. In addition to the superb parkland, there's also a walled garden

Highclere Castle, Faccombe

THE GEORGE INN

Vernham Dean, Andover, Hampshire SP11 0JY
Tel: 01264 737279 / 07733225912
e-mail: contact@thegeorgeatvernhamdean.co.uk
website: www.thegeorgeatvernhamdean.co.uk

Dating back to the 17th century, **The George Inn** is an old fashioned village pub full of character with fireplaces and oak beams. James and Nicky Haigh welcome locals and visitors to this fine public house, which has an attractive beer garden where you can sit on warmer days.

The George Inn can be found in a pretty village on the Hampshire/Wiltshire border, in an Area of Outstanding Beauty surrounded by beautiful countryside. There are many footpaths, bridleways and mountain biking routes from the village of Vernham Dean including a route up to an ancient hillfort at Fosbury.

After hours spent exploring the countryside, The George Inn provides an ideal place to relax, enjoy refreshing drink and sample some home cooked food.

The food here is of the highest quality and can be enjoyed all day alongside some fantastic real ales. It is all freshly prepared from quality ingredients and James' steak, fish and chips, and salmon fishcakes are always popular. A traditional roast lunch of beef or pork and all the trimmings can be had on a Sunday for a very affordable £8.50. The dishes are reasonably priced and favourites with diners include smoked duck salad, homemade burgers with homemade chips, and home cooked ham, egg and chips. For those with a lighter appetite there is a selection of sandwiches available. There will always be daily specials on offer such as rack of lamb, dauphinoise potatoes and sloe gin jus and pan-fried fillet of seabass and seasonal vegetables. But make sure you leave room for one of the many tempting desserts.

The George Inn is famous with the locals for holding different events throughout the year, a few to mention are the **sloe gin competition, the pub quiz, live music, BBQ's** and there is always a lot going on over Christmas. See the website for details.

Closed on Mondays, The George Inn is open 4.30pm – 11pm on Tuesdays, 12pm – 11pm Wednesday – Saturday and 12pm – 9pm on Sundays. Private functions can be held at the inn. Ring for details.

planted entirely with white blooms, a gift shop, restaurant and tearooms.

PENTON MEWSEY

2 miles NW of Andover, on minor road off the A342 or A343

For those who enjoy deciphering the cryptic place names of English villages, Penton Mewsey offers a satisfying challenge. The answer goes like this: Penton was a 'tun' (enclosure or farm) paying a 'pen' (penny) as annual rent. That's the Saxon part. Later, in the early 1200s, Penton was owned by Robert de Meisy so his surname provided the second part of the village's name.

The town of Andover has now expanded to Penton Mewsey's parish boundaries, but the village itself remains more rural than urban, with a field at its centre.

Another unusually named village is the nearby **Enham Alamein**. Enham village became Enham Alamein in 1945, when the Egyptian government gave Britain £225,000 in gratitude for the victory at the Battle of El Alamein in October 1942. A special service is held here every year on the Sunday nearest the date of the battle.

APPLESHAW

4 miles NW of Andover, off the A342

The houses in the village of Appleshaw sit comfortably along both sides of its broad, single street. Many of them are thatched and a useful old clock in the middle of the street, placed here to celebrate Queen Victoria's Jubilee, adds to the time-defying atmosphere. The former Vicarage, built in Georgian times, is as gracious as you would expect of that era, and the neo-Gothic architecture of the parish church, rebuilt in 1830, is in entire harmony with its earlier neighbours.

TANGLEY

5 miles NW of Andover, on minor road off the A342 or A343

For the best views, approach Tangley from the east, along the country lane from Hurstbourne Tarrant. Its mostly Victorian church is notable for its rare font, one of only 38 in the whole country made of lead and the only one in Hampshire. Dating back to the early 1600s, it is decorated with Tudor roses, crowned thistles and fleur-de-lys.

The old Roman road from Winchester to Cirencester, the Icknield Way, runs through the parish of Tangley. Most of this part of the county is designated an Area of Outstanding Natural Beauty and the scenery is enchanting.

WEYHILL

3 miles W of Andover on the A342

Hawk Conservancy

In its day, the October Weyhill Fair was an event of some importance. In Thomas Hardy's *Mayor of Casterbridge* it appears as the Weydon Priors Market where the future mayor sells his wife and child.

A good family day out can be enjoyed at the **Hawk Conservancy Trust** where there are more than 150 birds of prey to see in 22 acres of woodland and wildflower meadows. The Hawk Conservancy is one of the largest collections of raptors in the world. Flying demonstrations take place three times daily and include species such as owls, eagles, vultures and condors, falcons, kites, hawks and secretary birds. The grounds here are also home to Shire horses, Sika deer, Hampshire Down sheep and red squirrels that have been given their own aerial runway. Weyhill is also home to the Fairground Craft & Design Centre, with craft studies, demonstrations and tuition and a varied programme of the Exhibition Gallery.

THRUXTON

4 miles W of Andover off the A303

Motor Racing Circuit

This large village with many thatched cottages is well known for its **Motor Racing Circuit**, which is built on a Second World War airfield. Home to the British Automobile Racing Club, the circuit hosts eight events a year for the country's top championships, including Formula Three, Touring Cars, British Super Bikes, Trucks and Historic and BARC Club racing. Call 01264 882200 for full details.

NETHER WALLOP

8 miles SW of Andover, on minor road off the A343

St Andrew's Church

The names of the three Wallops (Over, Middle and Nether), have provided a good deal of amusement to visitors over the centuries, so it's slightly disappointing to discover that Wallop is just a corruption of the Old English word waell-hop, meaning a valley with a stream. At Nether Wallop the stream is picturesquely lined with willow trees, while the village itself is equally attractive with many thatched or timbered houses. The most notable building in Nether Wallop is **St Andrew's Church**, partly because of its Norman features and handsome West Tower of 1704, but also because of its striking medieval wall paintings, which provide an interesting contrast with Stanley Spencer's at Burghclere. Some 500 years old, these lay hidden for generations under layers of plaster and were only rediscovered in the 1950s. The most impressive of them shows St George slaying the dragon. Outside St Andrew's stands an item that ranks high on the list of churchyard oddities. It's a dark grey stone pyramid, 15ft high, with red stone flames rising from its tip. This daunting monument was erected at his own expense, and in memory of himself, by Francis Douce, Doctor of Physick, who died in 1760. Dr Douce also left an endowment to build a village school on condition that the parishioners would properly maintain the pyramid.

St Andrew's Church, Nether Wallop

MIDDLE WALLOP

7 miles SW of Andover on the A343

Museum of Army Flying | Danebury Ring

Danebury Vineyards

The village of Middle Wallop became famous during the Battle of Britain when the nearby airfield was the base for squadrons of Spitfires and Hurricanes. Many of the old buildings have been incorporated into the **Museum of Army Flying**, which traces the development of Army Flying from the balloons and kites of pre-First World War years, through various imaginative dioramas and two flight simulators in which visitors can test their own skills of "hand and eye" coordination. The Museum has more than 35 fixed-wing and rotary aircraft on display, and other attractions include a museum shop, licensed café and restaurant, and a grassed picnic area.

In the 1990s, Middle Wallop, with its picturesque timber-framed thatched buildings became familiar to television viewers when it provided the main location for the *Miss Marple* mysteries.

Situated about a mile to the east of the village, **Danebury Vineyards** welcomes groups of visitors by arrangement for a guided tour of the six acres of vines and winery. Tastings and dinners can also be arranged. The vineyard was planted in 1988 on south-facing slopes of free draining chalk, an excellent siting for the varieties of grape grown here. The British climate generally results in a late-ripening crop producing grapes that are most suitable for the white wines with which Danebury Vineyards has made its name.

About three miles east of Middle Wallop, **Danebury Ring** is Hampshire's largest Iron Age hill fort. Intensively occupied from about 550BC until the arrival of the Romans, the site has been meticulously excavated over the past 30 years and the finds are now displayed at the Museum of the Iron Age in Andover. Visitors can wander the 13-acre site and with the help of explanatory boards reconstruct the once-bustling community with its clearly defined roads, shops, houses and what were probably temples.

Danbury Ring, Middle Wallop

STOCKBRIDGE

7 miles S of Andover on the A3057/A30

Houghton Lodge Gardens

The trout-rich River Test flows through, under and alongside Stockbridge's broad main street, which reflects the street's earlier role as part of a drover's road. The town attracts many visitors for its famous antique shops, art galleries and charming tearooms. Two exclusive clubs strictly control fishing on the River Test at this point, but visitors may be lucky enough to catch glimpses of the fish from the bridge on the High Street.

Just to the south of Stockbridge are **Houghton Lodge and Gardens**, the spacious gardens of an 18th-century cottage ornée, which have the tranquil beauty of the River Test as their border. Chalk cob walls shelter a kitchen garden with ancient espaliered fruit trees, glasshouses and herb garden, while in the hydroponicum greenhouse, plants are grown "without soil, toil or chemical pesticides". The lovely setting has made the Lodge and Gardens popular with makers of costume dramas and also with wedding parties. Call 01264 810502.

A short drive to the south is the village of Little Somborne and its redundant All Saints Church dating back to Saxon times. In the churchyard is the grave of Sir Thomas Octave (Tommy)

STOCKBRIDGE GALLERY – DOGS IN ART

High Street, Stockbridge,
Hampshire SO20 6EU
Tel: 01264 810142
website: www.dogsinart.com

Specialising in depictions of the dog in art, **Stockbridge Gallery** offers a very wide selection of both fine and decorative artworks with a canine theme. Owned by the Armstrong family, the gallery opened its doors two years ago and has since become a honey pot attraction for animal lovers and art lovers alike.

Original artworks and limited edition pieces can be purchased here with an extensive array of both period and contemporary work on display. Paintings and sculptures are exhibited alongside an exclusive range of ceramics, glassware, textiles and objet d'art and are all available to purchase from both the gallery and its website.

Stockbridge Gallery, or Dogs in Art as it is otherwise known, can be found in the village of Stockbridge between Salisbury and Winchester. The village attracts many visitors for its famous antique shops, art galleries and charming eateries. It is also well know for the River Test, which runs through the town and is rich with trout that can often be glimpsed from the bridge in the High Street.

Artists' work is showcased throughout the year and regular exhibitions are held. A speciality of the gallery is its bespoke portraiture service which offers the opportunity to have your dogs drawn, painted, photographed or sculpted by some of the UK's foremost artists.

The gallery is situated in the Old Post Office on the High Street and makes good use of the old building's features to help create a warm, intimate space in which to display their much loved collection of gifts and artworks. The welcome from the dog-loving staff is friendly and the service exceptional making this an altogether great destination.

Sopwith, the pilot and aircraft designer who founded the Sopwith Aviation Company in 1912. The company, which produced the famous Sopwith Pup and Sopwith Camel, developed into the Hawker Siddeley company.

WHITCHURCH

6 miles E of Andover on the B3400

Silk Mill

This small market town was once an important coach stop on the London to Exeter route. The coaching inns have gone, but the town still boasts a unique attraction – the **Whitchurch Silk Mill**, the last such working mill in the south of England. Built in 1800 and located on Frog Island in the River Test, the mill's waterwheel has been fully restored although today's power is provided by electricity. The mill now functions as a museum making silks for interiors and costume dramas such as the BBC's acclaimed production of *Pride and Prejudice*. Visitors can see the working waterwheel, watch the late 19th-century looms weave the silk, view the costume exhibition and enjoy the riverside garden. There's also a tearoom and gift shop.

To the east of Whitchurch is Bere Mill**,** a weather-boarded construction where a Frenchman, Henri Portal, set up a paper-making business in the early 18th century. By 1742, Portal's mill had won the contract to supply banknote paper to the Bank of England and he moved his operation upstream to Laverstoke. Now in Overton, the business continues to make paper for banknotes and supplies it to more than 100 countries.

LONGPARISH

6 miles E of Andover, on the B3048

Living up to its name, Longparish village straggles alongside the River Test for more than two miles. This stretch of the river is famously full of trout, but no one has yet beaten the record catch of Colonel Peter Hawker who lived at Longparish House in the early 1800s. According to his diary for 1818, this dedicated angler relieved the river of no less than one ton's weight of the succulent fish during that year. A previous owner of the colonel's house had actually captured double that haul in one year, but the bounder had cheated by dragging the river.

Longparish Upper Mill, in a lovely location on the river, is a large flour mill with a working waterwheel. Visitors can see the restoration work in progress.

BURGHCLERE

11 miles NE of Andover, off the A34

Sandham Memorial Chapel

A couple of miles northeast of Highclere Castle, at Burghclere, the **Sandham Memorial Chapel** (National Trust) is, from the outside, a rather unappealing construction, erected in 1926 by Mr and Mrs JL Behrend in memory of a relation, Lieutenant Sandham, who died in the First World War. Their building may be uninspired, but the Behrends can't be faulted on their choice of artist to cover the walls with a series of 19 murals. Stanley Spencer had served during the war as a hospital orderly and 18 of his murals represent the day-to-day life of a British Tommy in wartime. The 19th, covering the east wall of the Chapel, depicts the Day of Resurrection with the fallen men and their horses rising up. The foreground is dominated by a pile of white wooden crosses the soldiers have cast aside. The whole series is enormously moving, undoubtedly one of the masterpieces of 20th-century British art.

Winchester

Cathedral · College · The Great Hall
Wolvesey Castle · Jane Austen's House
The Brooks Experience · Hospital of St Cross
Marwell Zoological Park · Keats' Walk
Hyde Abbey Garden

One of the country's most historic cities, Winchester was adopted by King Alfred as the capital of his kingdom of Wessex, a realm that then included most of southern England. There has been a settlement here since the Iron Age, and in Roman times, as Venta Belgarum, it became an important military base. **The Brooks Experience**, located within the modern Brooks Shopping Centre, has displays based on excavated Roman remains with its star exhibit a reconstructed room from an early 4th-century town house.

When the Imperial Legions returned to Rome, the town declined until it was refounded by Alfred in the late 800s. His street plan still provides the basic outline of the city centre, and a striking bronze statue of him dominates the Broadway.

A Saxon cathedral had been built in the 7th century, but the present magnificent **Cathedral**, easily the most imposing and interesting building in Hampshire, dates back to 1079. It's impossible in a few words to do justice to this glorious building and its countless treasures such as the famous Winchester Bible, a 12th-century illuminated manuscript that took more than 15 years to complete using pure gold and lapis lazuli from Afghanistan. Winchester Cathedral boasts the longest nave in Europe, a dazzling 14th-century masterpiece in the Perpendicular style, a wealth of fine wooden carvings, and gems within a gem, such as the richly decorated Bishop Waynflete's Chantry of 1486. Sumptuous medieval monuments, like the effigy of William of Wykeham, founder of Winchester College, provide a striking contrast to the simple black stone floor slabs that separately mark the graves of Izaak Walton and Jane Austen. One of the memorials is to William Walker, a diver who spent seven years, from 1906, laboriously removing the logs that had supported the cathedral for 800 years and replacing those rotting foundations with cement.

Just south of the cathedral, on College Street, are two other buildings of outstanding interest. 8 College Street, a rather austere Georgian house with a first-floor bay window, is **Jane Austen's House** in which she spent the last six weeks of her life in 1817. The house is private, but a slate plaque above the front door records her residence here. Right next door stands **Winchester College**, the oldest school in England, founded in 1382 by Bishop William of Wykeham to provide education for 70 "poor and needy scholars". Substantial parts of the 14th-century buildings still

Winchester Cathedral

BRIDGE PATISSERIE LTD.

20 Bridge Street, Winchester,
Hampshire SO23 9BH
Tel: 01962 890767
website: www.bridgepatisserie.co.uk

Founded in 2000 by Moira Windsor, the **Bridge Patisserie** was recently extended, and now gives customers more space and seats so that you can enjoy your coffee and cakes in comfort. The food is equally enjoyable either eaten in or out. The shop's sumptuous coffee lounge and lovely décor make this the perfect place to meet friends, escape the office and unwind.

As soon as you enter you are faced with a mouth-watering display of home made goodies. Choose from a fine selection of coffees, cakes, savoury items and quality chocolates. Their savoury items are the perfect choice for a great lunch at a great price, while the delicious French tarts and pastries are made on the premises using flour supplied by Winchester City Mill. With so much on offer, all equally tempting, the choice is difficult, but the very friendly staff are more than willing to offer advice.

Chocolates are another speciality here. Once you try one of these delicious treats, a high street brand will never compare. Visit their website and make sure you stay well informed!

REFLEX

151a High Street, Winchester, Hampshire SO23 9AY
Tel: 01962 865566

Located opposite Winchester's historic Guildhall in the pedestrianised centre of the town, **Reflex** has been established for some 25 years and is probably the smallest shop in Winchester. Owners Jane Winson and Claire Barker work hard to provide an extensive range of fun and quirky gifts. There are retro telephones from the 1930s to the 1950s; the Alessi range of kitchen items and watches; Leatherman tools; the Roberts range of retro radios; a selection of Ledco torches; stylish clocks from Karlsson; and the elegant Storm and Ted Baker ranges of watches. You'll also find a large choice of fascinating and unusual greeting cards.

The shop now has an engraving machine which enables them to personalise your gifts with a photo and text. The knowledgeable staff at Reflex are always happy to help with ideas and suggestions for that difficult to buy for person.

stand, including the beautiful Chapel. The Chapel is always open to visitors and there are guided tours around the other parts of the college from April to September. If you can time your visit during the school holidays, more of the college is available to view.

Two years after Jane Austen was buried in the cathedral, the poet John Keats stayed in Winchester and it was here that he wrote his timeless *Ode to Autumn – Season of mists and mellow fruitfulness.* His inspiration was a daily walk past the cathedral and college and through the Water Meadows beside the River Itchen. A detailed step-by-step guide to **Keats' Walk** is available from the Tourist Information Centre.

The city's other attractions are so numerous one can only mention a few of the most important. **The Great Hall**, off the High Street, is the only surviving part of the medieval castle rebuilt by Henry III between 1222 and 1236. Nikolaus Pevsner considered it "the finest medieval hall in England after Westminster Hall". A striking feature here is the legendary Round Table of Arthurian legend, which was made on the

The Great Hall, Winchester

orders of Edward I some 700 years ago. Originally, the huge table was unpainted, but Henry VIII had it painted to depict himself as Arthur's descendant.

Located within the castle grounds are no fewer than six military museums, including the Gurkha Museum, the King's Royal Hussars Museum, whose displays include an exhibit on the famous Charge of the Light Brigade, and the Royal Green Jackets Museum, which contains a superb diorama of the Battle of Waterloo.

Other buildings of interest include the early 14th-century Pilgrim Hall, part of the Pilgrim School, and originally used as lodgings for pilgrims to the shrine of St Swithun, and **Wolvesey Castle** (English Heritage), the residence of the Bishops of Winchester since AD963. The present palace is a gracious, classical building erected in the 1680s, flanked by the imposing ruins of its 14th-century predecessor, which was one of the grandest buildings in medieval England. It was here, in 1554, that Queen Mary first met Philip of Spain and where the wedding banquet was held the next day. Also well worth a visit is the 15th-century **Hospital of St Cross**, England's oldest almshouse. Founded in 1132 by Henri du Blois, grandson of William the Conqueror, it was extended in 1446 by Cardinal Beaufort, son of John of Gaunt. It is still home to 25 Brothers and maintains its long tradition of hospitality by dispensing the traditional Wayfarer's Dole of a piece of bread and a mug of beer to any traveller who requests it.

The city's newest public garden was opened in 2003 to commemorate the Queen's Golden Jubilee. **Hyde Abbey Garden**

follows the shape of the former abbey, which was the burial place of Alfred the Great, his wife and their son.

Just to the west of the city is a very modern attraction, **Intech**, which explores the technologies that shape our lives today – how light can be bent, for example, and how humans produce electricity. There are more than 100 exhibits, all of which have been designed to provide a genuine hands-on experience. In 2008, Intech added to its attractions the largest Planetarium in the UK. Intech is open daily all year round.

Around Winchester

SUTTON SCOTNEY

6 miles N of Winchester, on the A34

Standing at a crossroads, Sutton Scotney was once a busy little place. Today, it is bypassed by the A34 so visitors can peacefully explore its picturesque side streets lined with thatched cottages and Georgian houses. Unusually, the village has no church, but the clock tower of the Jubilee Hall, erected in 1897, has a distinctly ecclesiastical air about it.

CRAWLEY

5 miles NW of Winchester off the B3049

Crawley is a possibly unique example of an early 20th-century model village. The estate was bought in 1900 by the Philippi family who then enthusiastically set about adding to the village's store of genuine traditional cottages a number of faithful fakes built in the same style. (They also provided their tenants with a state-of-the-art bath house and a roller-skating rink.) Sensitive to tradition and history, they did nothing to blemish the partly Norman church, leaving its unusual interior intact.

Instead of stone pillars, St Mary's has mighty wooden columns supporting its roof, still effective more than 500 years after they were first hoisted into place.

AMPFIELD

8 miles SW of Winchester on the A3090

Sir Harold Hillier Gardens

One of the most important modern plant collections in the world, **Sir Harold Hillier Gardens** were established in 1953. More than 42,000 plants are set in a variety of themed landscapes within the 180-acre site. There are 11 National Plant Collections, more than 250 Champion Trees and the largest Winter Garden in Europe. A £3.5 million Visitor Pavilion has a licensed restaurant with an open air terrace, a gift shop and an interpretation area. During the summer months, the Gardens host a series of concerts, plays and operas.

ROMSEY

10 miles SW of Winchester, on the A27/A3090

Abbey · Broadlands · King John's House

Moody Museum · Romsey Signal Box

"Music in stone", and "the second finest Norman building in England" are just two responses to **Romsey Abbey**, a majestic building containing some of the best 12th and 13th-century architecture to have survived. Built between 1120 and 1230 as a nuunery, the Abbey is remarkably complete. Unlike so many monastic buildings that were destroyed or fell into ruin after the Dissolution, the abbey was fortunate in being bought by the town in 1544 for £100 – the bill of sale, signed and sealed by Henry VIII, is displayed in the south choir aisle. Subsequent generations of townspeople have carefully maintained their bargain purchase. The abbey's most spectacular feature is the soaring nave,

ALLSORTS SWEET SHOP

17 Bell Street, Romsey, Hampshire SO51 8GY
Tel: 01794 518131 / 07542211767
e-mail: moiraabrown@hotmail.com website: www.allsorts.me.uk

Located in the main road leading into the heart of Romsey, **Allsorts Sweet and Gift Shop** is a fantastic independent old fashioned sweet and gift shop. The shop is owned and run by Moira Brown and there is over 500 types of sweets. The walls are lined with sweety jars just like you remember from your child hood, why not come in and see how many you remember.

Moira also sells online and by phone just give her a ring or send her a email telling her the sweets you would you like and she will box them up for you. UK p&p is free but there is a charge for posting overseas.
At the back of this wonderful shop is a Aladdin's cave of gifts such as wind chimes, jewellery,dream catchers, incense sticks, candles and much more. Visitors often describe the shop as enchanting and few leave without a gift or sweets for themselves or a loved one. This little shop is a veritable delight for the senses.

If you then venture upstairs you will find BELLES MASSAGE CENTRE which is run by Jenny. As a ex nurse, Jenny knows just how to sort out those stress and tension areas. Just book yourself or a loved one in for a relaxing sensual massage. Allsorts is open every day from 9.30am until 5.30pm apart from Sun when opening hours are noon until 4pm. Belles Massage Centre is open 10am until late Mon to Sat apart from Sun when opening hours are noon until 4pm.

which rises more than 70ft and extends for more than 76ft. Amongst the abbey's many treasures is the 16th-century Romsey Rood, which shows Christ on the cross with the hand of God descending from the clouds.

Romsey Abbey

Just across from the Abbey, in Church Court, stands the town's oldest dwelling, **King John's House**, built around 1240 for a merchant. It has served as a royal residence but not, curiously, for King John who died some 14 years before it was built. He may though have had a hunting lodge on the site. The house is now a museum and centre for cultural activities; the garden has been renovated and replanted with pre 18th-century plants.

The **Moody Museum** occupies the Victorian home of the Moody family who were cutlers in Romsey from the 18th century up until the 1970s. Visitors are greeted by (models of) William Moody and his sister Mary in a reconstruction of the family parlour, and the exhibits include fixtures and fittings from the family's gun shop.

Train enthusiasts will want to seek out the

curious exhibit located behind the infants' school in Winchester Road. **Romsey Signal Box** is a preserved vintage signal box in working order, complete with signals, track and other artefacts. Until 1982 it controlled the junction at Romsey and was saved by the Romsey & District Buildings Preservation Trust.

Romsey's most famous son was undoubtedly the flamboyant politician Lord Palmerston, three times Prime Minister during the 1850s and 1860s. Palmerston lived at Broadlands, just south of the town, and is commemorated by a bronze statue in the town's small triangular Market Place.

Broadlands is a gracious Palladian mansion that was built by Lord Palmerston's father in the mid 1700s. The architect was Henry Holland, the landscape was modelled by Capability Brown. The important collections of furniture, porcelain and sculpture were acquired by the 2nd Viscount Palmerston. The house passed to the Mountbatten family, and it was Lord Louis Mountbatten who first opened Broadlands to the public shortly before he was killed in 1979. The present owner, Lord Romsey, has established the Mountbatten Exhibition in tribute to his grandfather's remarkable career as naval commander, diplomat, and last Viceroy of India. An audio-visual film provides an overall picture of the Earl's life and exhibits include his dazzling uniforms, the numerous decorations he was awarded, and an astonishing collection of the trophies, mementoes and gifts he received in his many roles. As we went to press Broadlands was about to close for major refurbishment/ restoration, to be re-opened in July 2012. The grounds will remain open for hosting a programme of events.

TWYFORD

3 miles S of Winchester, on the B3335

Waterworks Museum

Hampshire churchyards are celebrated for their ancient yew trees, but the one at Twyford is exceptional. A visitor in 1819 described the clipped tree as resembling "the top of a considerable green hillock, elevated on a stump". The grand old yew is still in apparently good health and provides a dark green foil to the trim Victorian church of striped brick and flint, which was designed by Alfred Waterhouse, architect of the Natural History Museum in London.

Three well-known historical figures have strong associations with the village. Benjamin Franklin wrote much of his autobiography while staying at Twyford House; Alexander Pope attended school here until he was expelled for writing a lampoon on the Master; and it was at the old Brambridge House that Mrs Fitzherbert was secretly married to the Prince Regent, later George IV, in 1785.

An interesting example of our industrial heritage is the **Twyford Waterworks Museum**. It is housed in Twyford Waterworks, which opened in 1898 to supply water to the surrounding rural area. Between 1903 and 1969 the water was also softened, which explains the lime kilns found on the site. The present steam engine dates from 1914; the electric pumps were installed in 1951. Despite being scheduled as an Ancient Monument, the waterworks still extract more than five million gallons of water from the wells every day. The museum concentrates on the evolution of water supply during the 20th century. Call 01962 714716 for opening times.

About two miles south, at Colden Common, **Marwell Zoological Park** is home to more

TWYFORD STORES LTD AND BEAN BELOW

High Street, Twyford, Hampshire SO21 1NH
Tel: 01962 711353
e-mail: twyfordstores@msn.com

All of your newspaper needs are catered for here and an extensive range of wines, beers, tobacco products, confectionary and toiletries are stocked. Twyford Stores receives flower and plant deliveries several times a week, ensuring quality and freshness for any occasion. The shop also has a Post Office and there is a hair a beauty salon upstairs. You can buy everything from fresh local fruit to handmade curry sauce.

Proprietors Simon Cooper and Richard Sellars work closely with Hampshire Fair to ensure consistent quality and the finest local produce. It is this fine produce that is used by the chefs at Bean Below restaurant, which is definitely a must see if you're looking for a relaxed atmosphere and superb food. Charming and professionally managed - this restaurant continues to regale Twyford and beyond with its much talked about cuisine. The popularity of dishes such as the New Season English Lamb and the fresh fish items denotes increasing customer satisfaction at this underground restaurant. The seasonal menu is small, yet covers every main food type. This means that you are not spoiled for choice, but can be assured that whatever takes your fancy you will be well catered for. The friendly approach and personal service that you wouldn't get from many establishments is what gives this restaurant its unsurpassable charm.

In addition to the high quality of the food and service, Bean Below now has another string to its bow, by way of entertainment. For the foreseeable future, there will be a live singer on a Thursday evening, adding atmosphere and a touch of cabaret to your meal.

than 200 species of animals, from meerkats and red pandas to snow leopards and rhinos. Set in a 100-acre park, Marwell has the largest collection of hoofed animals in the UK, nine species of cat, a family of pygmy marmosets – the smallest monkey in the world – and many endangered species. The park is owned and run by Marwell Wildlife, a registered charity dedicated to the conservation and wildlife and its natural habitats.

Mottisfont Abbey

EAST WELLOW

12 miles SW of Winchester, off the A27

Church of St Margaret

The **Church of St Margaret** is the burial place of Florence Nightingale who lies beneath the family monument bearing the simple inscription "FN 1820-1910". While a memorial service was being held in St Paul's Cathedral, her body was being transported to St Margaret's Church, East Wellow. Among the mourners was Private John Kneller from Kings Somborne, whom she had nursed in the Crimea when he was serving with the Royal Welch Fusiliers. The church itself has several interesting features, including 13th-century wall paintings and Jacobean panelling. Close to the village is Headlands Farm Fishery where there are two lakes available for fishing for carp, tench, perch, roach, pike and trout. Other facilities include rod hire, flies for sale and hot drinks.

MOTTISFONT

10 miles W of Winchester, off the A3057

Abbey

Mottisfont's little Church of St Andrew boasts a wealth of 15th-century stained glass, including a superb Crucifixion, and should not be overlooked on a visit to **Mottisfont Abbey** (National Trust). Built as an Augustinian priory in the 12th century, the abbey was converted into a country mansion after the Dissolution, and was further modified in the 1700s. Some parts of the original priory have survived, amongst them the monks' cellarium – an undercroft with vast pillars – but the main attraction inside is the drawing room decorated with a Gothic trompe l'oeil fantasy by Rex Whistler. He was also commissioned to design the furniture but the Second World War intervened and he was killed in action.

The superb grounds contain the National Collection of Old-Fashioned Roses, established in 1972, a lovely pollarded lime walk designed by Sir Geoffrey Jellicoe, and some superb trees, including what is thought to be the largest plane tree in England.

Southeast Hampshire

With a population of 1.2 million, Hampshire is the fifth most populous county in England. A goodly proportion of those 1.2 million people live along the coastal crescent that stretches from Southampton through Fareham and Portsmouth to Havant. Inland, though, there are parts of the South Downs as peaceful and scenic as anywhere in the county.

Southampton boasts one of the finest natural harbours in the world and has been the leading British deep-sea port since the days of the Norman Conquest. Portsmouth did not develop as a port until the 16th century, but makes up for its shorter history by its romantic associations with such legendary ships as *HMS Victory,* the *Mary Rose,* and *HMS Warrior.* Portsmouth is also a popular seaside resort providing, together with its neighbour, Hayling Island, some seven miles of sandy beaches. Southsea Castle and massive Portchester Castle have interesting historical associations, and the ruins of Netley Abbey and the Bishop's Palace at Bishop's Waltham are both outstandingly picturesque.

Like most major ports, Southampton and Portsmouth have something of a cosmopolitan air about them, providing an intriguing contrast with the rural charms of the inland villages.

Southampton

Medieval Merchant's House · Solent Sky
Maritime Museum · Tudor House Museum
City Art Gallery · Bargate

From this historic port, situated on one of the finest natural harbours in the world, Henry V's army set sail for Agincourt in 1415, the Pilgrim Fathers embarked on their perilous journey to the New World in 1620 and, on 10 April 1912, the *Titanic* set off on its maiden voyage, steaming majestically into the Solent. Of the 1500 who lost their lives when the ship struck an iceberg in the freezing Atlantic in 1912, around 500 were Southampton-based crew members. The city's seafaring heritage is vividly recalled at the excellent **Maritime Museum**, housed in the 14th-century Wool House. The museum tells the story of the port from the age of sail to the heyday of the great ocean liners.

As a major sea port, Southampton was a prime target for air raids during the Second World War and suffered grievously. But the city can still boast a surprising number of ancient buildings. Substantial stretches of the medieval Town Walls have miraculously survived, its ramparts interspersed with fortifications such as the oddly-named 15th-century Catchcold Tower and God's House Gate and Tower, which now houses the city's archaeological museum. Perhaps the most impressive feature of the walls is **Bargate**, one of the finest medieval city gates in the country. From its construction around 1200 until the 1930s, Bargate remained the principal entrance to the city. Its narrow archway is so low that Southampton Corporation's trams had to be specially modified for them to pass through. In a niche above the entrance is a statue of George III, cross-dressing as a Roman Emperor. Bargate now stands in its own pedestrianised area, its upper floor, the former Guildhall, a museum of local history and folklore.

Another remarkable survivor is the **Medieval Merchant's House** (English Heritage) in French Street, which has been expertly restored and authentically furnished, now appearing just as it was when it was built around 1290. One of the most popular visitor attractions in Southampton is the **Tudor House Museum and Garden**, a lovely 15th-century house with an award-winning Tudor Garden complete with fountain, bee skeps (baskets) and 16th-century herbs and flowers.

Southampton City Art Gallery (see panel

below) is a treasure house of some 3500 works ranging over six centuries, while the John Hansard Gallery and the Mallais Gallery specialise in contemporary art. The painter Sir John Mallais was a native of Southampton, as was Isaac Watts, the hymnologist whose many enduring hymns include *O God, Our Help In Ages Past.*

There's so much history to savour in the city, but Southampton has also proclaimed itself "A City for the New Millennium". Major developments include the flagship shopping area of West Quay, the enhancement of the city's impressive central parks, the superbly appointed Leisure World, the state-of-the-art Swimming and Diving Complex, which incorporates separate championship, diving and fun pools, and Ocean Village, an imaginatively conceived waterfront complex with its own 450-berth marina, undercover shopping, excellent restaurants and a multi-screen cinema.

As you'd expect in a city with such a glorious maritime heritage, there's a huge choice of boat excursions, whether along the River Hamble, around the Solent, or over to the Isle of Wight. Blue Funnel Cruises operate from Ocean Village; Solent Cruises from Town Quay.

The city also occupies an important place in aviation history. A short step from Ocean Village, **Solent Sky** commemorates the pioneering work of the Spitfire's creator RJ Mitchell. Mitchell lived and worked in Southampton in the 1930s and designed not only the Spitfire, but also the S6 Seaplane, which won the coveted Scheider Trophy. The centrepiece is the spectacular Sandringham Flying Boat, which you can board to sample the luxury of air travel in the past – very different from the cattle-class standards of today's mass travel. Over the years 26 aircraft companies were based in and around Southampton, including Short Bros, Supermarine, Airspeed,

Southampton City Art Gallery

Civic Centre, Southampton, SO14 7LP
Tel. 023 8083 2743
e-mail. esta.mion-jones@southampton.gov.uk
website: www.southampton.gov.uk/art

Southampton City Art Gallery is the most outstanding gallery in the South of England and is internationally renowned for its impressive collection and temporary exhibitions programme. Housed within a beautiful example of 1930's municipal architecture, the Gallery is fortunate in possessing a rich and varied collection of fine art. It's located in the Civic Centre, adjacent to Watt's Park and within easy walking distance of the City's shopping area. The visitor facilities are excellent and it's fully wheelchair accessible, including the Gallery Shop.

The shop stocks a wide range of greetings cards, stationery, wrapping paper, postcards and crafts. Entrance to the Gallery is free of charge. Opening times: Tues – Sat 10am - 5pm and Sundays 1pm - 4pm, Closed on Mondays.

Folland and Saunders-Roe.

Around Southampton

BOTLEY

7 miles E of Southampton on the A334

Set beside the River Hamble, Botley is an attractive village of red-brick houses, which remains as pleasant now as when William Cobbett, the 19th-century writer and political commentator, described it as "the most delightful village in the world....it has everything in a village I love and none of the things I hate". The latter included a workhouse, attorneys, justices of the peace – and barbers. The author of *Rural Rides* lived a very comfortable life in Botley between 1804 and 1817, and he is honoured by a memorial in the Market Square.

NETLEY

5 miles SE of Southampton, off the A3025

Netley Abbey Netley Hospital

Royal Victoria Country Park

A Victorian town on the shores of the Solent, Netley was brought into prominence when a vast military hospital was built here after the Crimean War. The foundation stone of **Netley Hospital** was laid by Queen Victoria in 1856 (who became a frequent visitor) and the hospital remained in use until after the Second World War. A disastrous fire in the 1960s caused most of the buildings to be demolished, but the hospital's Chapel, with its distinctive 100ft tower, did survive and now houses an exhibition about the hospital from the time of Florence Nightingale. The rest of the site has been developed as the **Royal Victoria Country**

Park offering woodland and coastal walks, waymarked themed and nature trails, and trips around the park on a miniature steam railway.

Bursledon Windmill

Heritage of a different kind can be found at ruined **Netley Abbey** (English Heritage), a wonderfully serene spot surrounded by noble trees. "These are not the ruins of Netley," declared Horace Walpole in the mid-1700s, "but of Paradise." Jane Austen was equally entranced by the abbey's romantic charm and she made many visits. Dating back to 1300, the extensive ruins provide a spectacular backdrop for open-air theatre performances during the summer.

BURSLEDON

6 miles SE of Southampton, off the A3024

Windmill Brickworks

Anyone interested in England's maritime heritage should pay a visit to Bursledon. Ships have been built here since medieval times, the most famous being the *Elephant*, Nelson's flagship at the Battle of Copenhagen. The yard where it was built, now renamed the Elephant Boatyard, is still in business. On a rise to the north of the village stands **Bursledon Windmill** (see panel below) the only working windmill in Hampshire. Built in 1814 at a cost of £800, its vanes ground to a halt during the great agricultural depression of the 1880s. Happily, all the machinery remained intact, and after a lengthy restoration between 1976 and 1991, the sails are revolving once again whenever a good northerly or southerly wind is blowing. The mill produces stoneground flour for sale and is open to visitors at weekends, or whenever the sails are turning.

The village can boast another unique

Bursledon Windmill

Windmill Lane, Bursledon, Southampton, Hampshire SO31 8BG
Tel: 023 8040 4999
e-mail: stensethhouse@aol.com
website: www.hants.gov.uk/museum/windmill

The last surviving working windmill in Hampshire was built by a Mrs Phoebe Langtry in 1814 at a cost of £800. Inactive from the time of the depression in the 1880s, the tower mill was restored to full working order between 1976 and 1991. Its sails revolve whenever a good northerly or southerly wind blows, producing stoneground flour for sale. Next to the mill is the Windmill Wood Nature Trail, a woodland habitat supporting a wide range of wildlife including woodpeckers. Open all year.

THE SPINNAKER INN

286 Bridge Rd, Swanwick, Southampton SO31 7EB
Tel: 01489 572 123 Fax: 01489 577394
e-mail: mail@thespinnaker.co.uk
website: www.thespinnakerinn.co.uk

If you are looking for somewhere to stay overnight in the beautiful area of Swanwick then **The Spinnaker Inn** is a must see. Located on the South Coast of Hampshire, near the River Hamble, the inn overlooks the harbour and has a lovely restaurant and bar area.

There are 23 rooms available here, all with en-suite facilities. The comfortable rooms vary in price and breakfast can be arranged as an extra.

The restaurant offers a wide range of light bites, salad dishes, traditional favourites, fish dishes, grills and there is a special menu for younger diners. Local produce is used where possible and on the main menu favourites include tasty home cooked gammon ham served with chips and chargrilled tuna topped with garlic cream sauce, served with new potatoes and vegetables.

The bar area has a boating theme throughout and is tastefully decorated and furnished with seats as well as more comfortable sofas, ideal for customers wanting to spend the evening relaxing and taking in the friendly atmosphere. The Spinnaker is well known for regularly hosting live bands and other entertainment and private functions can be arranged. Ring for details.

industrial site. When **Bursledon Brickworks** was established in 1897, the machinery installed was at the very forefront of brick-making technology. The works closed in 1974, but a charitable trust has now restored its gargantuan machines, thus preserving the last surviving example of a steam-driven brickworks in the country. Special events are held here from time to time, but the works are open only on Thursdays, except in December.

HAMBLE

8 miles SE of Southampton off the B3397

The Hamble Valley runs over eight miles upstream with beautiful scenery and walks with access to many nature reserves, including alongside saltwater marches. The river is a nationally and internationally important site for nature conservation, and a bird-watchers' paradise. As well as the countryside and coastal exploring, and fishing available, Hamble is a major centre for all types of boating.

There are many sailing and yacht clubs – the Royal Southern Yacht Club, Warsash Sailing Club, Hamble River Sailing Club and the Royal Air Force Yacht Club who welcome visitors warmly – and one can get expert tuition in boat handling of all sorts.

The Hamble River discharges into Southampton Water, and on either side of its mouth, are beaches of golden shingle, from which you can watch some of the largest ships in the world leaving from Southampton Docks as well as see the Isle of Wight. A short ride in the Pink Ferry from Hamble takes one across the river to Warsash and back.

Hamble is of great historical importance, particularly in the building of boats and aircraft used in many wars over the centuries.

Boat building is still a thriving industry, with

BONNE BOUCHE DELICATESSEN

Bonne Bouche, High Street, Hamble, Hampshire SO31 4HA
Tel: 02380 455771
e-mail: info@bonne-bouche.co.uk
website: www.bonne-bouche.co.uk

The attractive cobbled high street that runs through the centre of the charming village of Hamble is home to **Bonne Bouche** Delicatessen. It's bright and cheerful frontage matches its light and airy interior, open to all seven days a week from 8am – 5pm. Handsome wooden floors, stylish shelving and contemporary furniture all work to create a relaxed but fresh feeling environment. It's owned and run by Carol Hill who offers a warm and friendly service to all who walk through her doors. She serves up a delicious range of freshly prepared baguettes, salads and homemade soups, popular with both local residents and workers in the area at lunchtimes. A good selection of teas and coffees are also available, which can also be enjoyed on the outdoor decking area in sunnier weather.

Bonne Bouche also functions as a delicatessen, as Carol proudly stocks an exciting array of locally produced cheeses and meats. Convenient for shoppers and diners, Bonne Bouche is also located just a stone's throw from the River Hamble, making a lunchtime snack the perfect respite from a scenic walk in the area. Hamble is also well known for its sailing community, which affords guests plenty of opportunities to try their hand at the helm.

ARTAMAIN

High Street, Hamble, Hampshire SO31 4HA
Tel: 02380 454341
e-mail: hello@artamain.com

Artamain is a thriving art gallery and gift shop in the cobbled High Street in the old part of Hamble, down by the river. Local artists are featured in the gallery, which does particularly well with seascape and boat orientated paintings, and yacht carvings. There is also exciting work from South African artists and other handcraft artists representing beaded and metal work, wooden carvings, painted ceramics, beautiful items made using ostrich eggshell mosaic, hand worked and individually blown glass pieces, jewellery and more.

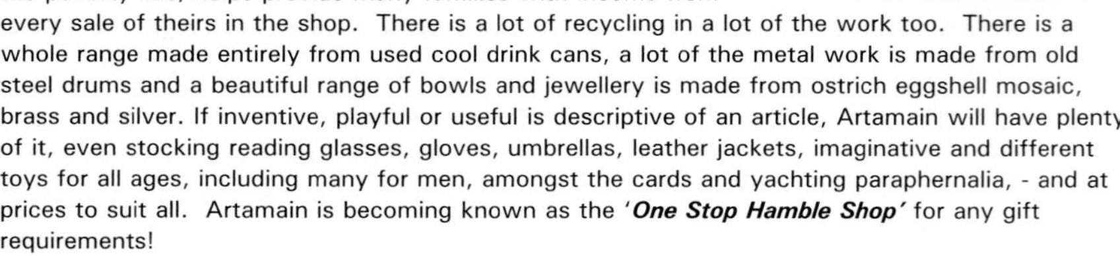

Artamain, by directly importing the goods of a number of Southern African artists and craftsmen who live perilously close to the poverty line, helps provide many families with income from every sale of theirs in the shop. There is a lot of recycling in a lot of the work too. There is a whole range made entirely from used cool drink cans, a lot of the metal work is made from old steel drums and a beautiful range of bowls and jewellery is made from ostrich eggshell mosaic, brass and silver. If inventive, playful or useful is descriptive of an article, Artamain will have plenty of it, even stocking reading glasses, gloves, umbrellas, leather jackets, imaginative and different toys for all ages, including many for men, amongst the cards and yachting paraphernalia, - and at prices to suit all. Artamain is becoming known as the ***'One Stop Hamble Shop'*** for any gift requirements!

world-class repair and servicing yards. Hamble deep water, easy access to the famous Solent Waters and is a yachtsman's paradise, being a major base for yachting competitions such as Cowes Week and the National, European and World Championships, with numerous small regatta taking place all the year round.

Hamble has many B&B's and is overflowing with excellent pubs and restaurants to cater for visitors.

PARK GATE

8 miles SE of Southampton on the A27

Back in the days when strawberries were truly seasonal, Park Gate was the main distribution centre for the produce of the extensive strawberry farms all around this area. During the season, scores of special trains were contracted to transport the succulent fruit to London, some 3000 tons of it in 1913 alone. By the 1960s, housing had taken priority over fruit farms, and today the M27 marks a very clear division between the built-up areas to the south, and the unspoilt acres of countryside to the north.

WEST END

2 miles NE of Southampton on minor road off the A27

Itchen Valley Country Park

An ideal destination for a family outing, **Itchen Valley Country Park** (see panel below) lies on the outskirts of Southampton. Its 440 acres of water meadows, ancient woodland, conifer plantations and grazing pasture lie either side of the meandering River Itchen, famous for its clear waters and excellent fishing. The Park is managed by Eastleigh Borough Council's Countryside Service to provide informal recreation, enhance and conserve wildlife habitats, and as an educational resource. The best place to begin your visit is the High Wood Barn Visitor Centre, an attractive timber structure built in the style of a 17th-century Hampshire Aisle Barn. From the Visitor Centre, waymarked trails help you to discover

Itchen Valley Country Park

High Wood Barn, Allington Lane,
West End, Southampton,
Hampshire SO30 3HQ
Tel/Fax: 023 8046 6091
e-mail: ivcp@eastleigh.gov.uk

A superb family day out is guaranteed at **Itchen Valley Country Park**, whose 440 acres of water meadows, ancient woodland, conifer plantations and grazing pasture span the River Itchen between Eastleigh and Southampton. The various areas support a great variety of bird life, insect and plant life and there are trails, cycle routes, picnic sites and a host of children's activities. The High Wood Barn Visitor Centre, built in 17th century style from timber recovered from the great storm of 1987, contains information, interactive exhibits, a café and a shop.

the different areas of the Park, and an informative leaflet reveals the history and wildlife of a landscape shaped by hundreds of years of traditional farming and woodland management. Children are well provided for at the park. In High Hill Field there's an adventure play area for the under-12s that includes an aerial runway, and behind the Visitor Centre a play area for the under-5s has giant woodland animals designed by local school children and built by sculptor Andy Frost.

EASTLEIGH

5 miles NE of Southampton on the A335

Museum · Point Dance & Arts Centre

Lakeside Country Park · Beatrice Royal Gallery

Eastleigh is first mentioned in a charter of AD932 but it wasn't until some 900 years later that it began to expand. That was when the Eastleigh Carriage and Engine Works was established in the town. At one time the works covered 60 acres and employed 3600 people. The town's railway connection is commemorated by Jill Tweed's sculpture, The Railwayman, which stands in the town centre.

Nearby, in the old Salvation Army Citadel on the High Street, is the **Eastleigh Museum** whose exhibits concentrate on the town's railway heritage. Visiting heritage, art, craft and photography exhibitions are also held here. The **Point Dance and Arts Centre** stages a full programme of theatre, dance, cinema and music events, while the **Beatrice Royal Contemporary Art and Craft Gallery** offers exhibitions of art, sculpture, ceramics, jewellery and textiles.

Just outside the town is the **Lakeside Country Park**, home to a variety of wildlife and also a place for model boating, windsurfing and fishing. Here, too, is the Eastleigh Lakeside Railway, a miniature steam railway that provides trips around the park.

To the south of Eastleigh lies Southampton International Airport, the home of Carill Aviation where you can take off for a scenic flight over the Solent, or sign up for a trial flying lesson.

BISHOP'S WALTHAM

10 miles NE of Southampton on the B2177/ B3035

Palace · Northbrook Springs Vineyard

Bishop's Waltham is a charming and historic small town. It was the country residence of the Bishops of Winchester for centuries, and through the portals of their sumptuous **Palace** have passed at least 12 reigning monarchs. Amongst them were Richard the Lionheart returning from the Crusades, Henry V mustering his army before setting off for Agincourt, and Henry VIII entertaining Charles V of Spain (then the most powerful monarch in Europe) to a lavish banquet. The palace's days of glory came to a violent end during the Civil War when Cromwell's troops battered most of it to the ground. The last resident bishop was forced to flee, concealing himself beneath a load of manure.

Set within beautiful moated grounds, the ruins remain impressive, especially the Great Hall with its three-storey tower and soaring windows. Also here are the remains of the bakehouse, kitchen, chapel and lodgings for visitors. The Palace is now in the care of English Heritage and entrance is free.

The town itself offers visitors a good choice of traditional and specialist shops, amongst them a renowned fishmonger, butcher, baker – even a candlemaker. And just north of the town you can visit one of the country's leading vineyards. Visitors to

Northbrook Springs Vineyard are offered a tour of the vineyard, which explains the complex, labour-intensive process of planting, growing, pruning and harvesting the vines, and free tasting in the Vineyard Shop.

Portsmouth

Mary Rose Museum · Royal Naval Museum
Royal Armouries · HMS Victory, HMS Warrior
Charles Dickens Birthplace Museum
D-Day Museum · Spinnaker Tower
Southsea Castle

Currently, any brochure promoting Portsmouth always adds the words "Flagship City". With good reason, since the port is home to the most famous flagship in British naval history, **HMS Victory**. From the outside it's a majestic, three-masted ship, inside it's creepily claustrophobic, except for the Admiral's and Captain's spacious, mahogany-panelled quarters. Visitors can pace the very same deck from which Nelson masterminded the decisive encounter with the French navy off Cape Trafalgar in 1805. Standing on this deck, ostentatiously arrayed in the gorgeous uniform of a British Admiral of the Fleet, Nelson presented a clear target to a sharp-sighted French sniper. The precise spot where Nelson fell, and the place on the sheltered orlop (lowest) deck where he died, are both marked by plaques.

The death of Nelson was a tragedy softened by a halo of victory: the loss of the *Mary Rose,* some 260 years earlier was an unmitigated disaster. Henry VIII had ordered the ship, the second largest in his fleet, to be built. He was standing on Southsea Common above Portsmouth in 1545, watching the *Mary Rose* manoeuvre, when it suddenly heeled over and sank. All 700 men on board drowned. "And the King he screeched right out like any maid, 'Oh, my gentlemen! Oh, my gallant men!'" More than four centuries later, in 1982, the hulk of the *Mary Rose* was carefully raised from the seabed where it had lain for so long. The impressive remains are now housed in the timber-clad **Mary Rose Museum**. The Ship Hall containing the Mary Rose is closed until 2012, when a new boat-shaped museum will open, financed by a £35 million Heritage grant.

Another ship you can see at Portsmouth doesn't possess the same historical glamour as the *Victory* or the *Mary Rose,* but **HMS Warrior** merits a visit because when this mighty craft was commissioned in 1860, she was the Navy's first iron-clad warship. A great advance in technology, but the distinctions between the officers' and crew accommodation show little difference from those in Nelson's day.

Also within the dockyard area are the **National Museum of the Royal Navy**, which has a marvellous exhibition on the life and exploits of Nelson; and The Dockyard Apprentice, where visitors can become a new apprentice for a day and learn the skills that helped construct the mighty Dreadnought battleships.

Other exhibitions not to be missed include Action Stations, Trafalgar Sail, the Trafalgar Experience and the Dockyard Apprentice.

A precious part of Portsmouth's history, the Cathedral is set in the heart of historic Old Portsmouth, close to the seafront and the Millennium Walkway. The most recent notable addition to the seafront buildings is the slim 170-metre **Spinnaker Tower**, where lifts take visitors to the viewing platforms.

Like Southampton, Portsmouth suffered badly during the Second World War, losing most of its 17th- and 18th-century buildings.

Portsmoth Historic Dockyard

College Road, HM Naval Base, Portsmouth, Hampshire PO1 3LJ
Tel: 023 9286 1533 Fax: 023 9229 5252
e-mail: mail@historicdockyard.co.uk
website: www.historicdockyard.co.uk

Portsmouth Historic Dockyard is home port to three of the greatest ships ever built, but has many other attractions. The latest of these is the blockbusting Action Stations, where visitors can test their skills and abilities through a series of high-tech interactive displays and simulators.

The most famous of the ships is undoubtedly *HMS Victory*. From the outside it's a majestic three-master, but inside it's creepily claustrophobic except for the Admiral's and Captain's spacious, mahogany-panelled quarters. Visitors can pace the very same deck from which Nelson masterminded the decisive encounter with the French navy off Cape Trafalgar in 1805. Standing on the deck arrayed in his Admiral's finery, Nelson was an easy target for a keen-eyed French sniper; the precise spot where he fell and the place on the lower deck where he later died (knowing that the battle was won) are both marked by plaques.

The *Mary Rose*, the second largest ship in Henry VIII's fleet, was putting out to sea, watched proudly by the King from Southsea Common, when she suddenly heeled over and sank. All 700 men on board lost their lives. More than 400 years later, in 1982, the ship was raised in an amazingly delicate operation from the seabed. The impressively preserved remains of the ship are now housed in the timber-clad Mary Rose Museum. (One of the tombs in Portsmouth Cathedral is that of one of the Mary Rose's crew.) *HMS Warrior* was the Navy's first iron-clad warship and the most formidable fighting ship the world had seen in 1860: bigger, faster and more heavily armed than any warship afloat, built of iron and powered by both sail and steam. Her size and might proved to be a deterrent to potential enemies and she never actually had to go to war.

Boat trips round the harbour give a feel of the soul of the city that has been home to the Royal Navy for more than 800 years, and the most attractive part, picturesque Old Portsmouth, can be seen to advantage from the little ferry that plies the short route to Gosport.

The Royal Naval Museum is the most fascinating of its kind, with a marvellous exhibition of the life and deeds of Nelson, and the interactive Dockyard Apprentice Exhibition explains the skills and crafts of 1911 that went into the building of the world's finest fighting ships, the Dreadnoughts. A relatively new addition is Action Stations, an exciting insight into the modern high-tech Royal Navy of today. Five interective areas offer physical or electronic challenges and a ride on the 19 seat simulator is an experience not to be missed.

Spinnaker Tower, Portsmouth

St George's Church, a handsome Georgian building of 1754 with large galleries, was damaged by a bomb but has been fully restored, and just to the north of the church, the barn-like Beneficial Boy's School, built in 1784, is another survivor of the bombings.

One of the most interesting buildings is to be found in Southsea, the city's resort area. **Southsea Castle** was built in 1544 as one of Henry VIII's series of forts protecting the south coast from French attacks. It has been modified several times since then, but the original Keep is still intact and there are good views across the Solent from the gun platforms.

Portsmouth also offers visitors a wealth of varied museums, three of which deserve special mention: the **Royal Armouries**, housed in the huge Victorian Fort Nelson, claims to be Britain's Loudest Museum, with live firings every day; the **Charles Dickens Birthplace Museum**, at 393 Old Commercial Road, has been restored and furnished to show how the house looked when the great novelist was born here in 1812; and the **D-Day Museum** in Southsea, which commemorates the Allied invasion of Europe in 1944, is most notable for the 83-metre-long Overlord Tapestry, a 20th-century equivalent of the Bayeux Tapestry.

Around Portsmouth

HAYLING ISLAND

4 miles E of Portsmouth on the A3023

Hayling Billy Leisure Trail

A traditional family resort for more than a century, Hayling Island manages to provide all the usual seaside facilities without losing its rural character. Much of the foreshore is still open ground with wandering sand dunes stretching well back from the four-mile-long shingle beach. Bathing is safe here and West Beachlands even boasts a European Blue Flag, which is only awarded to beaches meeting 26 environmental criteria. One of Hayling's more unusual beach facilities is the line of old-fashioned beach huts, all of which are available to rent.

A good way to explore the island is to follow the **Hayling Billy Leisure Trail**, once the Hayling Billy railway line, which provides a level footpath around most of the 14 miles of shoreline.

Hayling is something of a Mecca for board sailors. Not only does it provide the best sailing in the UK for beginners and experts alike, but it also is the place where board-sailing was invented. Many places claim that honour, but Peter Chilvers has a High Court ruling to prove it. In 1982, a judge decided that Mr Chilvers had indeed invented the sailboard at Hayling in 1958. As a boy of 10, he used a sheet of plywood, a tent fly-sheet, a pole and some curtain rings to sail up an island creek.

GOSPORT

2 miles W of Portsmouth on the A32

Fort Brockhurst Holy Trinity Church

Royal Naval Submarine Museum

Explosion! The Museum of Naval Firepower

Gosport Museum & Gallery

Gosport is home to another of Palmerston's forts – the circular **Fort Brockhurst** (English Heritage), which is in almost mint condition and open to visitors on summer Sundays, when they can see the parade ground, the gun ramps and the moated keep. At the **Royal Naval Submarine Museum**, located at *HMS Dolphin*, visitors can experience a century of submarines. Stories of undersea adventures and the heroism of the Royal Navy's submarine services are recounted, and there are also guided tours around *HMS Alliance*, a late Second World War submarine.

The town's connections with the Royal Navy are further explored at **Explosion! The Museum of Naval Firepower**, which is dedicated to the people who prepared armaments used by the Navy from the Battle of Trafalgar to the Falklands War. As well as browsing through the unique collection of small arms, cannons, guns, mines and torpedoes, visitors can experience the pitch and roll of a moving gun-deck, help move barrels of gunpowder, and dodge mines on the seabed.

Away from the Navy's influence on the town, there is Gosport's splendid **Holy Trinity Church**, which contains an organ that was played by George Frederick Handel when he was music master to the Duke of Chandos. The town bought the organ after the Duke's death. Gosport also boasts one of the county's best local museums – **Gosport Museum and Gallery** – where the history of the area from prehistoric times is brought to life through a series of fascinating exhibits.

PORTCHESTER

3 miles NW of Portsmouth on the A27

Castle Portchester Church

Standing at the head of Portsmouth Harbour, **Portchester Castle** is not only the grandest medieval castle in the county, but also stands within the best-preserved site of a Roman fort in northern Europe. Sometime around AD280, the Romans enclosed eight acres of this strategic headland and used it as a base for their ships clearing the Channel of pirates. The original walls of the fort were 20ft high and 10ft thick, their depth much reduced later by local people pillaging the stone for their own buildings.

Portchester Castle

The medieval castle dates back to 1120, although the most substantial ruins are those of the royal palace built for Richard II between 1396 and 1399. Richard was murdered in 1399 and never saw his magnificent castle. Also within the walls of the Roman enclosure is **Portchester Church**, a superb Norman construction built between 1133 and 1150 as part of an Augustinian Priory. For some reason, the Priors moved inland to Southwick, and the church remained unused for more than five-and-a-half centuries until Queen Anne personally donated £400 for its restoration. Apart from the east end, the church is entirely Norman and, remarkably, its 12th-century font of wondrously carved Caen stone has also survived the centuries.

FAREHAM

6 miles NW of Portsmouth on the A27

Westbury Manor Museum

Royal Armouries at Fort Nelson

Fareham has expanded greatly since Thackeray described it as a "dear little Hampshire town". It still has considerable charm and the handsome houses on the High Street reflect its prosperous days as a ship-building centre. Many aspects of the town's history are featured in **Westbury Manor Museum**, which occupies a large 17th-century town house in the centre of Fareham. This old market town is also home to **The Royal Armouries at Fort Nelson** whose displays of artillery dating from the Middle Ages form one of the finest collections of its kind in the world. Among the 350 big guns and weapons on show are a Roman catapult; a wrought-iron monster of 1450 that could fire a 60 kilogram granite ball almost a mile; Flemish guns captured at Waterloo; and parts of the notorious Iraqi 'Supergun'. Visitors can see some of the guns in action at daily firings and at special event days when the dramatic interpretations include accounts of the defence of Rorke's Drift, experiences under shellfire in the First World War trenches, and a Royalist account of the execution of Charles I. The guns are all part of the National Collection of Arms and Armour.

TITCHFIELD

7 miles NW of Portsmouth on the A27

Abbey Wriothesley Monument

Just to the north of the village are the ruins of the 13th-century **Titchfield Abbey**, its presence reflecting the former prominence of Titchfield as an important market town and a thriving port on the River Meon. The parish church contains a notable treasure in the form of the **Wriothesley Monument**, which was carved by a Flemish sculptor in the late 1500s. This remarkable and massive work is a triple tomb chest depicting Thomas Wriothesley, 1st Earl of Southampton, and Lord Chancellor to Henry VIII, along with his wife and son. It was the 1st Earl who converted part of the now ruined abbey into a house – and it was there that his grandson, the 3rd Earl, entertained William Shakespeare.

WICKHAM

8 miles NW of Portsmouth on the A334

Wickham Vineyard

This village was the home of William of Wykeham (1324-1404), Chancellor of England, Bishop of Winchester, founder of Winchester College and New College, Oxford.

The mill by the bridge over the River Meon will be of interest to American visitors since it contains beams from the American frigate, *Chesapeake*, which was captured in 1813 off Boston by the British frigate *Shannon*.

To the northwest of the village is **Wickham**

WICKHAM VINEYARD

Botley Road, Shedfield, Hampshire SO32 2HL
Tel: 01329 834042
e-mail: info@wickhamvineyard.co.uk
website: www.wickhamvineyard.co.uk

Discover the pleasures of English wine and experience a taste of the Hampshire countryside. Our multi award winning vineyard is situated on the south coast between Southampton and Portsmouth, and is the perfect place to enjoy a fantastic day out. You can also discover the culinary delights of Vatika restaurant, run by Michelin Star and celebrity chef Atul Kocchar.

During the early 1980's a collection Roman wine containers were discovered on the site which was proof of wine production in this area during these times and was one of the reasons why Wickham Vineyard was created. So, in 1984 further investigation into the suitability of the area was carried out and 6 acres of vines were planted. This has now been increased to 18 acres in the 40 acre estate and further plantings are in the planning stage.

We grow ten different grape varieties here which include Pinot Noir, Rondo, Triomphe and Dornfelder for the reds and Bacchus, Reichensteiner, Faber, Wurtzer, Schoenburger and Kerner for the whites. With a gentle south facing slope and a soil mixture consisting of clay gravel and chalk, this makes ideal conditions for the production of quality grapes.

The winery is housed in a converted barn which dates back to late 1800's. It is one of the most well equipped wineries in the country with temperature controlled stainless steel tanks and French oak barrels used to age our Fume and the Special Reserve Red. We currently produce approximately 90,000 bottles per year.

Tours and Tastings.

Our renowned audio tour is the perfect way to discover Wickham up close and takes you through the vineyard and into the winery describing the history and our wine making practices. Afterwards you can enjoy a free tasting in the shop which also has a large selection of gifts and local produce.

For larger groups (15+) we can organise a guided tour and tutored tasting which covers the work involved in more detail, perfect for parties or entertaining clients. The vineyard also makes the ideal setting for weddings which we can assist you in organising and our 7 acre nature reserve is perfect for a leisurely stroll, viewing the abundance of wildlife that inhabit the area.

Opening Times: 10.30 am – 5.30pm Monday - Saturday, 11.30 am – 5.00pm Sunday

THE KING'S HEAD

The Square, Wickham, Hampshire PO17 5JN
Tel: 01329 832123

A former coaching inn, **The King's Head** is a popular pub located at the heart of Wickham. The town is famous for its historic annual horse fair and English festivals, while the pub is well-known for its home cooked food and fine real ales. Traditional ales include the award-winning London Pride and many other refreshments are available from the well-stocked bar.

The King's Head is child friendly and with a children's play area in the garden and a function room complete with a skittle alley (available for private hire) many people living in the area choose to drink and dine here.

Vineyard (see panel opposite), which was established in the 1980s and has expanded over the years. The vineyard and modern winery are open to visitors who can take advantage of an audio tour, sample the wines and browse through the gift shop.

The New Forest

The New Forest, as is the way with many English place names, is neither New nor a Forest, although much of it is attractively wooded. Some historians believe that 'forest' is a corruption of an ancient British word, gores or gorest, meaning waste or open ground – 'gorse' comes from the same root. The term New Forest came into use after William the Conqueror proclaimed the area a royal hunting ground, seized some 15,000 acres that Saxon farmers had laboriously reclaimed from the heathland, and began a programme of planting thousands of trees. To preserve wildlife for his sport (the deer especially), William adopted all the rigorous venery laws of his Saxon royal predecessors, and added some harsh measures of his own. Anyone who killed a deer would himself be killed. If he shot at the beast and missed, his hands would be cut off. And, perhaps most savage of all, anyone who disturbed a deer during the breeding season had his eyes put out.

Created a National Park in 2005, the Forest still has plenty of wild deer roaming its 145 square miles, confined within its boundaries by cattle grids (known to Americans as Texas Gates). You are much more likely though to see the famous New Forest ponies, free-wandering creatures that nevertheless are all privately owned. They are also something of a hazard for drivers, so do take care, especially at night.

The largest wild area in lowland Britain, the Forest is ideal walking country with vast tracts virtually unpopulated but criss-crossed by a cat's cradle of footpaths and bridleways. The Forestry Commission has also established a network of waymarked cycle routes, which make the most of the scenic attractions and are also designed to help protect the special nature of the Forest. A map detailing the cycle network is available, along with a vast amount of other information about the area, from the New Forest Centre in Lyndhurst. Visitors can watch an audio visual show, see life-sized models of Forest characters, make use of its Resource Centre and Library, and explore a gift shop specialising in locally-made Forest crafts. The only town of any size within the New Forest, Lyndhurst is generally regarded as its 'capital', a good place then to begin a tour of the area.

Lyndhurst

Church of St Michael · Grave of Alice Liddell

New Forest Centre

The most striking building in this compact village is the **Church of St Michael**, rebuilt in mid-Victorian times in what John Betjeman described as "the most fanciful, fantastic Gothic style that I ever have seen". The rebuilding coincided with the heyday of the Pre-Raphaelite movement, so the church contains some fine stained glass by Burne-Jones, produced by the firm of William Morris, as well as a splendidly lush painting by Lord Leighton of *The Wise and Foolish Virgins.*

In St Michael's churchyard is the **Grave of Alice Liddell** who, as a young girl, was the inspiration for Lewis Carroll's *Alice in Wonderland.* As Mrs Reginald Hargreaves, Alice lived all her married life in Lyndhurst and was very active in local affairs.

Next to the church is the Queen's House which, rather confusingly, is re-named the King's House whenever the reigning sovereign is male. Originally built as a royal hunting lodge, its medieval and Tudor elements are still visible. Many Kings and Queens have lodged here and the last monarch to stay, George III, graciously allowed loyal villagers to watch through the window as he ate dinner. The house is now the headquarters of the Forestry Commission and is also home to the Verderer's Court, an institution dating back to Norman times that still deals with matters concerning the forest's ancient commoning rights. The verderers (forest officials) sit in public 10 times a year and work closely with the Commission in managing the forest. They also appoint agisters, or stockmen, who are responsible for the day-to-day supervision of the 5000 ponies and cattle roaming the forest.

At the **New Forest Centre**, in the heart of the town, visitors can learn about the history and the wide variety of plants and animal life that the forest supports. There's also a display on the mysterious death in 1100 of William Rufus, son of William the Conqueror, who was killed by an arrow while out hunting. It was officially described as an accident, but some believe that it was murder. Visitors can explore the new Family Fun Tree, see the Impressions of the New Forest film, take a look in a traditional cob cottage and marvel at the richly coloured New Forest Embroidery.

This little town is noted for its variety of small shops, many of them located in the High Street, an attractive thoroughfare of mostly Edwardian buildings that slopes gently down the hill to Bolton's Bench, a tree-crowned knoll where grazing ponies can usually be found. The spot enjoys excellent views over Lyndhurst and the surrounding forest. At the other end of the town, Swan Green, surrounded by picturesque thatched cottages, provides a much-photographed setting where cricket matches are held in summer.

Around Lyndhurst

MINSTEAD

2 miles NW of Lyndhurst off the A337

Church of All Saints · Furzey Gardens

Rufus Stone

The village of Minstead offers two interesting attractions, one of which is the **Church of All Saints**. During the 18th century, the gentry and squirearchy of Minstead seem to have regarded church attendance as a necessary duty, which, nevertheless, should be made as agreeable as possible. Three of the village's most affluent residents paid to have the

THE BELL INN

Brook, nr Lyndhurst, Hampshire SO43 7HE
Tel: 02380 812214 e-mail: bell@bramshaw.co.uk
website: www.bellinnbramshaw.co.uk

The Bell Inn is located within the popular Southern holiday destination of the New Forest. Known for its selection of picturesque villages, stunning countryside views and abundance of moorland ponies and horses, the New Forest makes an ideal short break for couples, families and groups who have ample opportunity to explore the great outdoors through a variety of mediums.

The inn itself was founded in 1782 and remains under the same family ownership as it was originally. It retains a listed status and is handsome in presentation, with beautiful brick fireplaces, and antique memorabilia decking the walls including a traditional collection of equestrian and wildlife paintings. Surrounding the inn are two eighteen hole golf courses, with a third just fifteen minutes drive away. The inn's restaurant sports stunning views across the greens and surrounding forest making it a premiere place to dine any night of the week. A full a la carte menu is offered throughout the day, sampling the very best in fresh seasonal produce. Dishes centre on a traditional theme and include many pub favourites alongside some more elegant twists on English cuisine. An exquisite wine list accompanies the menu, stocked from the inn's own large wine cellar which houses everything from affordable £14 bottles to £300 vintage wines for that special occasion. The service matches the quality of the food here and has been awarded three stars and two AA rosettes by various awarding bodies for both the restaurant and hotel services.

There are twenty-seven bedrooms to choose from at the inn, which come decadently furnished for a luxurious stay. All modern facilities are installed for convenience including en suite facilities. One room is located on the ground floor and has been fully equipped for people with disabilities. Rooms come on a bed and breakfast or full board basis, however guests have full access to the inn's facilities and many choose to dine in the restaurant independently for convenience. The inn's large tree lined gardens offer a peaceful space for guests to relax, with a selection of picnic benches, parasols and play areas available to all in the sunnier months.

The inn also has function capabilities and is licensed to hold civil ceremonies. Any event can be catered for and is made special not only by the service, but by the location and scenery which are rivalled by none. Its easy access to Southampton creates an ideal opportunity for day trips or weekend breaks, please see website for more details.

church fabric altered so that they could each have their own entrance door leading to a private 'parlour', complete with open fireplace and comfortable chairs. The squire of Minstead even installed a sofa on which he could doze during the sermon. It's easy to understand his concern since these sermons were normally expected to last for at least an hour; star preachers seem to have thought they were short-changing their flock if they didn't prate for at least twice that length. It was around this time that churches began introducing benches for the congregation. The church also has a three-decker pulpit and a two-tiered gallery; the lower tier for musicians; the upper for children from the Poor School.

Admirers of the creator of Sherlock Holmes, Sir Arthur Conan Doyle, will want to pay their respects at his grave in the churchyard here. A puzzle worthy of Sir Arthur's great detective is the idiosyncratic sign outside the Trusty Servant pub in the village. Instead of showing, as one might expect, a portrait of a dutiful domestic, the sign actually depicts a liveried figure with the feet of a stag and the face of a pig, its snout clamped by a padlock. A 10-line poem underneath this peculiar sign explains that the snout means the servant will eat any old scraps, the padlock that he will tell no tales about his master, and the stag's feet that he will be swift in carrying his master's messages.

Minstead's other main attraction is **Furzey Gardens**, eight acres of delightful, informal woodland gardens designed by Hew Dalrymple in the 1920s, and enjoying extensive views over the New Forest towards the Isle of Wight. Beautiful banks of azaleas and rhododendrons, heathers and ferns surround an attractive water garden, and amongst the notable species growing here are incandescent Chilean Fire Trees and the

Rufus Stone - Minstead

strange Bottle Brush Tree. Also within the gardens are a 16th-century thatched cottage, a craft gallery and a tearoom.

To the northwest of Minstead stands the **Rufus Stone** that is said to mark the spot where William Rufus (William II) was killed by an arrow while out hunting. William's body was carried on the cart of Purkis the charcoal burner to Winchester where William's brother had already arrived to proclaim himself King. William had not been a popular monarch and his funeral in the cathedral at Winchester was conducted with little ceremony and even less mourning.

ASHURST

2 miles NE of Lyndhurst on the A35

- New Forest Wildlife Park
- Longdown Activity Farm

Just to the east of the village, in acres of ancient woodland, is the **New Forest**

Wildlife Park. Conservation is the key word here. The park has an ongoing breeding programme for otters and barn owls, both of which are endangered species. Visitors can meander along woodland trails and encounter the otters and owls in their enclosures along with other native mammals such as deer, foxes and badgers.

There are more animals to be seen at close quarters at **Longdown Activity Farm** where visitors can handle small animals, bottle-feed goat kids and calves, and meet pigs, ponies, alpacas, ducks and more. There's a large picnic area, extensive indoor and outdoor play areas, a gift shop and a tearoom.

TOTTON

6 miles NE of Lyndhurst on the A36

Eling Tide Mill

Set beside Eling Creek, **Eling Tide Mill** has been harnessing tidal power to mill flour for a thousand years. Wholemeal flour is produced from wheat grown in the New Forest and is on sale in the Mill shop along with a selection of gifts. There's also a Heritage Centre, a café and a picnic area with a pirate ship. Eling Church on Eling Hill has an altar painting of the Last Supper in the style of Leonardo da Vinci.

Eling Tide Mill - Totton

HYTHE

8 miles SE of Lyndhurst off the A326

This is one of the very best places to watch the comings and goings of the big ships on Southampton Water, and no visit here is complete without taking a ride up the pier on the quaint little electric train, the oldest electric pier train in the world. From the end of the pier a ferry plies the short route across to Southampton. Hythe is the birthplace of the hovercraft – its inventor Sir Christopher Cockerell lived in the village. In the 1930s Hythe was the home of the British Powerboat Company, and of TE Lawrence (Lawrence of Arabia) while he was testing the RAF 200 series powerboats.

BEAULIEU

7 miles SE of Lyndhurst, on the B3056

National Motor Museum

Palace House   Bucklers Hard

The ruins of a 13th-century Cistercian Abbey, a stately home that grew up around the abbey's imposing gatehouse, and the **National Motor Museum** sited in its grounds, provide three good reasons why the captivating Georgian village of Beaulieu has become one of the county's major visitor attractions. When Lord Montagu of Beaulieu first opened his family home to the public in the 1950s, he organised a display of a few vintage motor vehicles in homage to his father who had been a pioneer of motoring in Britain. That modest clutch of cars has now expanded to include some 250 of the oldest, newest, slowest and fastest motor cars and bikes in British motoring history, plus some rare oddities. The motoring theme is continued in fun features such as Go Karts, Miniature Motors, and Fast Trax, which is promoted as the "best in

Beaulieu Abbey Cloisters

virtual racing simulators". New in 2010 is ProMotion, showcasing a number of vehicles that illustrate the imaginative and fun techniques used to promote their products. Among the vehicles on display are the Worthington Bottle truck, a Bread Loaf van, a Bird's Eye pea and a Cadbury Cream Egg car.

Montagu family treasures are on display in **Palace House**, formerly the gatehouse of the Abbey, and visitors can meet characters from Victorian days who will talk about their lives in service. The Secret Army Exhibition tells the story of wartime Beaulieu.

It was an ancestor of Lord Montagu, the 2nd Duke of Montagu, who created the picturesque riverside village of **Buckler's Hard** in the early 1700s. It was designed as an inland port to receive and refine sugar from the Duke's West Indian estates, and His Grace planned his model village on a grand scale: the streets, for example, were to be 80ft wide. Unfortunately, the enterprise failed and only a single street was built. That 18th-century street remains intact and unspoiled, and one of its buildings has been converted into the Buckler's Hard story, which illustrates the subsequent history of the village when it became a ship-building centre. More than 50 naval ships were built at Buckler's Hard, amongst them one of Nelson's favourite ships, the *Agamemnon*. Displays include models of ships, among them *Victory*, *Agamemnon* and the yacht *Bluebottle*, which Prince Philip raced with success. A special display recounts the exploits of Sir Francis Chichester, who sailed round the world in *Gypsy Moth* from his home port of Buckler's Hard, and a special exhibition tells the remarkable story of the P&O liner SS *Persia*.

A lovely riverside walk passes through Bailey's Hard, a former brickworks where the first naval vessel built on the river was completed in 1698. Henry Adams, the most distinguished of a family of shipbuilders, lived in the village in what is now the Master Builders Hotel. In the summer, half-hour cruises on *Swiftsure* depart from the pier at Buckler's Hard.

Buckler's Hard

FAWLEY

5 miles E of Beaulieu on the A326

Oil is king here, and the terminals and refineries of what is probably the largest oil plant in Europe create a science-fiction landscape. Standing bravely apart is the village church, a link with earlier days, looking out over Southampton Water. Fawley is where some islanders from Tristan da Cunha settled after fleeing a volcano that threatened their home in 1961; a model of one of the boats they used for their escape can be seen in the chapel. Also of note in Fawley is Cadland House, whose eight-acre garden overlooking the Solent was designed for the banker Robert Drummond by Capability Brown. It houses the National Collection of Leptospermums, and also features a splendid kitchen garden and a modern walled garden. Beyond the refineries a road leads off the B3053 Calshot road to Ashlett Creek and another world, the natural, unrefined world of creeks, mud flats and bird-haunted marshland.

CALSHOT

14 miles SE of Lyndhurst on the B3053

Calshot Castle

The RAF was based in both world wars at Calshot, where seaplanes were prepared and tested for the Schneider Trophy races. The hangars once used by the RAF are now the Calshot Activity Centre, whose many activities include an artificial ski slope. At the very end of a shingle spit stands one of Henry VIII's coastal defence castles, **Calshot Castle** (English Heritage), which is now restored as a pre-First World War garrison. Visitors can admire the view from the roof of the keep, walk round the barrack room that looks as it did before the First World War and see the exhibition of the Schneider air races. A little way to the west is Lepe, one of the major embarkation points for the 1944 D-Day invasion. The area at the top of the cliffs at Lepe is now **Lepe Country Park**, and there's safe swimming off the beach.

EXBURY

10 miles SE of Lyndhurst off the B3054

Church of St Catherine   Exbury Gardens

Created by Lionel de Rothschild in the 1920s, and still run by members of his family, **Exbury Gardens** fully justify the reaction of one visitor, who described them as "Heaven with the gates open". Rothschild sent expeditions to the Himalayas to find the seeds he wanted and it took 150 gardeners and workmen 10 years to create the gardens. He himself bred hundreds of varieties of plants, and the displays of rhododendrons, camellias and azaleas that he planted are renowned the world over. The 200-acre grounds are a delight to visit in spring, summer or autumn, with May perhaps the best time of all. A leisurely way of seeing the gardens is by taking a trip on the narrow-gauge steam railway's Rhododendron Line. Many varieties of the Exbury specialities are on sale in the plant centre, where there's also a gift shop, tearoom and restaurant – entry to all of these is free.

Exbury Gardens

Exbury's **Church of St Catherine** is best known for its moving, lifelike bronze memorial to two brothers who were killed in action in the First World War. The work was commissioned by the brothers' parents and executed by Cecil Thomas, a gifted young sculptor who was a friend of the brothers. The area around Exbury and Lepe is featured in Nevil Shute's sad story *Requiem for a Wren*, which describes the preparations made in the New Forest for the D-Day landings. Shute himself was an aero-engineer as well as a writer, and for a time worked here on a top-secret pilotless plane.

BROCKENHURST

3 miles S of Lyndhurst on the A337

Church of St Nicholas

A large village in a lovely setting in the heart of the New Forest. Forest ponies are frequent visitors to the main street and the village green (they naturally have right of way!). The **Church of St Nicholas** has a vast graveyard with a yew tree that is probably the oldest tree in the whole region. In the graveyard lie the soldiers, many of them from New Zealand, who died of their injuries in a nearby military hospital. But the best known grave is that of Harry Mills, known as Brusher Mills, who brushed the New Forest cricket pitch and worked as a snake-catcher.

Lymington

St Barbe Museum

An ancient seaport and market town, Lymington was once a major manufacturer of salt, with hundreds of salt pans between the quay and the tip of the promontory at Hurst Castle. Lymington is still a busy fishing point

ENIGMA FURNISHING

1 Angel Courtyard, Lymington, Hampshire SO41 9AP
Tel: 01590 688422 Fax: 01590 688422
e-mail: sales@enigma-furnishings.co.uk
website: www.enigma-furnishings.co.uk

Founded in 1996 specialising in home gifts and lifestyle, **Enigma Furnishing** in the pretty market town of Lymington is a shop passionate about gorgeous and practical home furnishing. Due to their amazing success, Enigma has recently moved to a larger shop, and has spared no time in filling this space with the most desirable pieces, from many prolific designers. A dedicated cook shop encompasses a third of the new shop, two new furniture areas have been created to show both bedroom, dining and occasional furniture ranges incorporating an extensive range of home and gift accessories. The stock is ever changing and expanding with the seasons, and with new designs and discoveries, meaning that no two visits to Enigma will ever be the same.

Their ranges include Orla Kiely home, bathroom and kitchen, Cable & Cotton innovative lighting creations, solid oak living, dining and occasional furniture, Caro Design London beautiful kimonos and accessories. Kitchen ranges include Sagaform Scandinavian designer cookware, Alessi designer kitchen and gift, Joseph Joseph, Zak Designs, Mastrad...

Opening times are Monday - Friday 9.30am - 5pm, Saturday 9am - 5.30pm and Sunday 10.30am - 4pm.

CLOUD CUCKOO LAND

6 St Thomas Street, Lymington, Hants, SO41 9NA
Tel: 01590 688840
website: www.cloudcuckooland-lymington.com

In the beautiful Georgian market town of Lymington is a unique shop certain to inspire you! The aptly named **Cloud Cuckoo Land**, contains an eclectic mix of pieces for the home, unusual gifts and inspiration to indulge yourself. Owned and run by the creative Claudia Jonkers; welcoming, and with a larger than life personality, Claudia's flair for sourcing wonderfully distinctive and unusual items has been the secret ingredient in the shop's success.

Cloud Cuckoo Land is known for its selection of opulent jewellery and with designers like Philippe Ferrandis, Bulatti, Riley Burnett, Ayala Bar, Azuni, Konplott and Leju, along with a diverse collection of gorgeous sterling silver jewellery. There is a range of plush leather belts and bags by Britains Stephen Harkin and Owen Barry and Italian designers Cosettini and Ripani. For the home, a new seasonal collection of cushions from textile designers Margo Selby, Jan Constantine and English Home. Also, lambswool throws, Kew plant pots, Culinary Concepts tableware, stunning lamps and exotic fragrance oil burning lamps by Lampeberger. Luxurious gifts of leather jewellery boxes, silver photo frames, beautiful solid animal bronzes and Royal Scott Crystal glasses.

Claudia has a range of lavish wedding and baby gifts available all year round, along with a wonderful range of hand-made cards by 5 Dollar Shake, Andrea Kett and of course Simon Drew. New to Cloud Cuckoo land is a selection of high quality limited edition prints by Paul Jonkers - only available here. Easily found next to Marks and Spencer and by the town car park, Cloud Cuckoo Land is a one-stop destination for anyone looking for that unique touch.

GLOW & CO

51 High Street, Lymington, Hampshire SO41 9AG
Tel: 01590 675617
website: www.glowandco.co.uk

This fantastic gift shop and online shop has a fine selection of inspired gifts on sale for all occasions. **Glow & Co** is run by Gary and Janet Watson and it is their aim to provide the best possible experience for all of their valued customers.

The couple do this by providing a large range of quality gifts from many of the world's leading brands including products from Archipelago Botanicals, soft toys from JellyCat and fabulous aromas from Yankee Candle.

The staff here are extremely friendly and do their very best to help everyone who comes into the shop, located in the town of Lymington. Gary and Janet have more than 40 years of retail and customer service experience and add a real personal touch that just can't be matched by larger chain stores. The couple are local to the area and opened Glow & Co in November 2008 with an extensive range of stock. If you are stuck for an idea for a unique gift, a visit here is definitely recommended.

and the cobbled streets of the old town lead to the High Street with its traditional shops and pubs.

St Barbe Museum, in New Street, tells the story of the area between the New Forest and the Solent, with special reference to the salt industry, boat-building, smuggling and the area at war. There is also a changing exhibition of the work of artists both local and world-renowned – the gallery has in the past hosted works by artists as diverse as David Hockney and Goya. The broad High Street leading up from the quay is a hive of activity on Saturdays, when the market established in the 13th century is held.

The Isle of Wight ferry to Yarmouth runs from Walhampton, just outside Lymington, where a notable building is the Neale Obelisk, a memorial to Admiral Neale erected in 1840.

Around Lymington

BOLDRE

2 miles N of Lymington, on the A337

"The village is here, there, and everywhere," wrote Arthur Mee in the 1930s, struggling to give some literary shape to an agglomeration of hamlets – Portmore, Pilley and Sandy Down, which together make up the parish of Boldre. Mee approved of the 800-year-old church, with its squat square tower, standing isolated on a hill top, and also paid due tribute to its 18th-century rector, the Rev William Gilpin, whose books describing travels around Britain achieved cult status during his lifetime, and even received a mention in Jane Austen's novel, *Sense and Sensibility*. Summing up his view of the village, Mee declared that, "The quaint simplicity of Boldre is altogether charming". Over 70 years later, there's little reason to dispute his description.

In School Lane, Spinners is a charming, informal woodland garden with a National Collection of trilliums.

SWAY

3 miles N of Lymington off the A337

Peterson's Tower · Artsway

This rural village and the surrounding countryside were the setting for much of Captain Marryat's *Children of the New Forest*, an exciting tale set in the time of the Civil War and written a year before the author died in 1848.

In Station Road, **Artsway** is a visual arts centre that was originally a coach house; the site contains a garden and a gallery. South of the village is a famous 220ft folly called **Peterson's Tower**. This curiosity was built by a retired judge, Andrew Peterson, in honour of his late wife and as proof of the efficacy of concrete. The tower was originally topped by a light that could be seen for many miles, but it was removed on the orders of Trinity House as a potential source of confusion to shipping. The judge's ashes were buried at the base of his folly, but were later moved to be next to his wife in the churchyard at Sway.

MILFORD-ON-SEA

4 miles SW of Lymington, on the B3058

Church of All Saints · Hurst Castle

This sizeable coastal village is most notable for its fine, remarkably well-preserved 13th-century **Church of All Saints**; for its grand views across the Solent to the Isle of Wight, and for the odd-looking construction called **Hurst Castle**. At the centre of Hurst Castle is a squat fort built by Henry VIII to guard the Solent entrance against incursions by the French. Its tower is flanked by two long low wings added in the 1860s for gun emplacements, the square openings making them look rather like shopping arcades. The castle was used a garrison right up until the Second World War, but is now in the care of English Heritage, which has an on-site exhibition explaining its history.

Hurst Castle - Milford-on-Sea

Hurst Castle stands at the tip of a long gravel spit that stretches out across the Solent to within three-quarters of a mile of the Isle of Wight coast. It can only be reached by a 1½ mile walk along the shingle beach or, in the summer months, by ferries operating from Keyhaven Quay, one mile east of Milford-on-Sea. The excursion makes a pleasant day or half-day trip, since in addition to the castle itself there's safe bathing north of the lighthouse, good fishing off the southern tip of the spit, and spectacular views of The Needles, as well as of huge ships making their way up The Solent.

NEW MILTON

5 miles W of Lymington on the A337

- Water Tower
- Sammy Miller Museum
- Forest Arts

If you were allowed to see only one visitor attraction in New Milton, you would have a difficult choice. One option is the town's splendid **Water Tower** of 1900. Late-Victorian providers of water services seem to have enjoyed pretending that their storage towers and sewage treatment plants were really castles dating from the Middle Ages. They built these mock-medieval structures all around the country, but the one at New Milton is particularly striking. Three storeys high, with a castellated parapet, the octagonal building has tall, narrow windows.

Devotees of vintage motorcycles will make for a very different attraction. The **Sammy Miller Museum**, to the west of the town, is widely regarded as one of the best motorcycle museums in the world. Sammy Miller is a legend in his own lifetime, still winning competitions almost half a century after his first racing victory. More than 400 rare and exotic motorcycles are on display here along with a wealth of motor-cycling artefacts and memorabilia. Also within the museum complex are two craft shops, tearooms and a children's play area.

If you are more interested in the arts, you'll be pleased to hear about **Forest Arts** in New Milton. Music of all kinds is on offer, from jazz, salsa and blues, to traditional and classical matinée concerts. Performances are conveniently timed so that you can arrive after picking up the kids from school. Other daytime events include slide talks by experts on a wide range of topics. Forest Arts also hosts some of the best contemporary dance companies around, ensembles who have performed at The Place in London and indeed all over the world. And if you enjoy the buzz and excitement of seeing new, vibrant theatre, the type of theatre, shown at the Edinburgh Fringe Festival for example, Forest Arts provides that as well.

Ringwood

Meeting House · Monmouth House

Moors Valley Country Park

Wednesday morning is a good time to visit Ringwood since that is when its market square is filled with a variety of colourful stalls, an event first established in 1226. The town has expanded greatly in recent years, but its centre still boasts a large number of elegant Georgian houses, both large and small. **Ringwood Meeting House**, built in 1727 and now a museum, is an outstanding example of an early Nonconformist chapel, complete with the original, rather austere, fittings. **Monmouth House** is of about the same period and stands on the site of an earlier house in which the luckless Duke of Monmouth was confined after his unsuccessful uprising against James II. The Duke had been discovered hiding in a ditch just outside the town and, despite his abject pleas to the King to spare his life, was beheaded at Tower Hill a few days later.

Ringwood has its own brewery and a Brewery Store where its products are available in four pint 'pottles' and up to 72-pint casks, along with bottled beers, ciders and wine from the brewery's own vineyard in the Dordogne. Tours of the brewery are available on

Lantern Centre

LANTERN COMMUNITY

Folly Farm Lane, Ringwood, Hants, BH24 2NN
Tel: 01425 473159
e-mail: emma@lanterncommunity.org.uk

The Busy Bee Café

On the edge of the New Forest, down a leafy lane, is the **Lantern Centre**. This award winning building with stunning wooden interior houses a gift shop, organic food shop, bookshop and café. Also onsite is our bakery selling freshly made organic bread, and our beautiful gardens and nursery.

Upon entering the Lantern Centre, you have the feeling of "getting away from it all", and you can breathe and relax into a space filled with peace and tranquillity.

With the Centre being very much "off the beaten track" our beautiful gardens are the perfect place to enjoy a quiet cup of coffee or a bite to eat for lunch.

Our gift shop is bursting with beautiful displays of fairly traded gifts from around the world, as well as locally made crafts. We also have a growing selection of gifts and produce from our own workshops, where we provide meaningful work opportunities for adults with a learning disability, in Pottery, Weavery, Bakery, Wood Workshop and Seasonal Crafts.

The bookshop offers a range of books covering a diverse area of subjects, and the bookshop itself is a quiet place to sit and relax.

Our wholefood section includes a variety of organic foods, and also available are natural medicines, toiletries and ecological cleaning products.

Our bakery produces fresh organic bread, pastries and biscuits on a daily basis Monday-Friday.

The Busy Bee Café is also one of our workshops .All of the café's main dishes are produced fresh on the day. The café is committed to using as many organic ingredients as possible some of which come from our own garden. Hot meals are available from 12pm till 2pm daily. Organic, fairly traded Tea and coffee and hand made organic cakes are sold throughout the day.

- Quality Gifts, Toys and Crafts
- Busy Bee Cafe
- Organic Wholefoods
- Natural Skincare
- Ecological Cleaning Products
- Fresh Organic Bread Baked Daily
- Bookshop

If you are looking for an wide selection of gifts, quality organic food and a quiet place to enjoy a walk we warmly invite you to visit us and look forward to welcoming you!

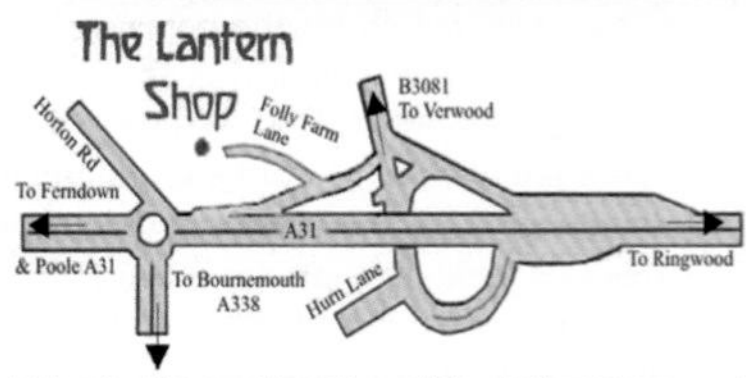

Wednesday afternoons during the summer – booking is essential.

Five miles west of the town stretch the great expanses of Ringwood Forest, which includes the **Moors Valley Country Park**. At the heart of the park stands an 18th-century timber barn, which is home to the Visitor Centre, where you will find a restaurant, a coffee shop, a gift shop and an exhibition area. A variety of other attractions including children's play areas, walks and cycle routes, and an 18-hole golf course can also be found here. Particularly popular are the Go Ape! tree top trail with its rope bridges, Tarzan swings and zip slides up to 35ft above the forest floor, and the Play Trail with its wooden structures, including Giant Ants' Nest, Snakes and Ladders and Spiders Web. Another popular attraction is the Moors Valley Railway, a delightful narrow gauge steam railway with rails just 7¼ inches apart. The railway has 11 locomotives, all in different liveries, and 33 passenger vehicles. The signal box at Kingsmere, the main station, was purpose-built, but all the equipment inside comes from old redundant signal boxes – the main signal lever frame for example came from the Becton Gas Works in East London. At Kingsmere Station, in addition to the Ticket Office and the Engine and Carriage Sheds, there's also a Railway Shop, Buffet and Model Railway Shop.

Around Ringwood

BURLEY

4 miles SE of Ringwood, on minor road off A31

At the delightfully unspoilt village of Burley, it's very clear that you are in the heart of the New Forest, with woodland running right through the village. A pleasant way to experience the peacefulness of the surrounding forest is to take a trip with Burley Wagonette Rides, which run from the centre of the village. Rides in the open wagons last from 20 minutes to 1½ hours and are available from Easter to October. The village is also home to New Forest Cider where farmhouse cider is still made the old-fashioned way from local orchard apples and cider fruit. Visitors can taste and buy draught cider from barrels stored in the former cowshed. The centre is open throughout the year although, ideally, you should time your visit to coincide with pressing time when the grand old cider press is in operation.

New Forest, nr Burley

FORDINGBRIDGE

7 miles N of Ringwood, on the A338

Alderholt Mill   Museum

The painter Augustus John (1878–1961) loved Fordingbridge, a pleasant riverside town with a graceful medieval seven-arched bridge spanning the River Avon. He spent much of the last 30 years of his life at Fryern Court, a rather austere

ST MARTIN'S GALLERY

The Old Church, Mockbeggar Lane, Ibsley, Hampshire BH24 3PP
Tel: 01425 489090
e-mail: StMartins@ibsleyhants.freeserve.co.uk
website: www.stmartinsartandcraftcentre.com
website: www.silkflowersbypost.com

St Martin's Gallery is located in the village of Ibsley, just off the A338 north of Ringwood. It is housed in the mid-17th century Church of St Martin, had fallen derelict before being bought by Pamela Denton and restored in 1998. She converted it into an art gallery while retaining the original altar, font and organ in the design. The gallery shows a wide and continually changing exhibition of local and international arts including many unique pieces, paintings and limited edition prints.

For many visitors the star of the show is the spectacular array of silk flowers and beautiful arrangements, and also featured are glassware, jewellery, pottery, ceramics, sculptures in wood and stone, furniture and some delightful bespoke teddies and gollies. Teas, coffees and delicious home-made cakes are also available. The gallery is open for visits from 11am to 5pm Thursday to Sunday.

Georgian house just north of the town (not open to the public, but visible from the road). Scandalous stories of the Bohemian lifestyle he indulged in there circulated around the town, but didn't deter the townspeople from erecting a strikingly vigorous statue to his memory near the bridge. In a former granary, **Fordingbridge Museum** has a collection donated by businessman and local benefactor John Shering, as well as an Augustus Exhibition and a Victorian dolls house.

Branksome China Works is well worth a visit. Visitors can see how the firm, established in 1945, makes its fine porcelain tableware and famous animal studies.

On the edge of the town, there's a special treat for anyone who savours daft public notices. As a prime example of useless information, it would be hard to beat the trim little 18th-century milepost that informs the traveller: "Fordingbridge: 0".

Two miles west of Fordingbridge off the B3078 – follow the signposts – is **Alderholt Mill**, a restored working water-powered corn mill standing on Ashford Water, a tributary of the Hampshire Avon. The site includes an arts and crafts shop and a tearoom selling treats made from the mill's own flour. Private fishing and B&B accommodation are also available.

BREAMORE

3 miles N of Fordingbridge on the A338

Breamore House | Countryside Museum

Breamore Down

Breamore is a lovely and largely unspoilt 17th-century village with a very interesting little church with Saxon windows and other artefacts. Most notable, in the south porch, is a Saxon rood, or crucifixion scene. **Breamore House**, set above the village overlooking the

Avon Valley, was built in 1583 and contains some fine paintings, including works of the 17th and 18th-century Dutch School, and a unique set of 14 Mexican ethnological paintings; superb period furniture in oak, walnut and mahogany; a very rare James I carpet; and many other items of historical and family interest. The house has been the home of the Hulse family for well over 250 years, having been purchased in the early 18th century by Sir Edward Hulse, Physician in Ordinary at the Courts of Queen Anne, George I and George II. In the grounds of the house, the **Countryside Museum** is a reconstructed Tudor village with a wealth of rural implements and machinery, replicas of a farm worker's cottage, smithy, dairy, brewery, saddler's shop, cobbler's shop, general store, laundry and school. Amenities for visitors include a teashop and a children's adventure play area. The museum's Millennium Project was the restoration of an extremely rare Bavarian four-train turret clock of the 16th century. On **Breamore Down** is one of those oddities whose origins and purpose remain something of a mystery: this is a mizmaze, a circular maze cut in the turf down as far as the chalk. Further north can be seen part of Grim's Ditch, built in late-Roman times as a defence against the Saxons.

ROCKBOURNE

3 miles NW of Fordingbridge off the B3078

Roman Villa

One of the prettiest villages in the region, Rockbourne lies by a gentle stream at the bottom of a valley. An attraction that brings in visitors by the thousands is **Rockbourne Roman Villa**, the largest of its kind in the region. It was discovered in 1942 when oyster shells and tiles were found by a farmer as he was digging out a ferret. Excavations of the site, which is set in idyllic surroundings, have revealed superb mosaics, part of the amazing underfloor heating system, and the outline of the great villa's 40 rooms. Many of the hundreds of objects unearthed are on display in the site's museum and souvenirs are on sale in the well-stocked museum shop.

A mile or so beyond the Roman Villa, looking out on to the downs, is the little village of Whitsbury, a major centre for the breeding and training of racehorses.

LOCATOR MAP

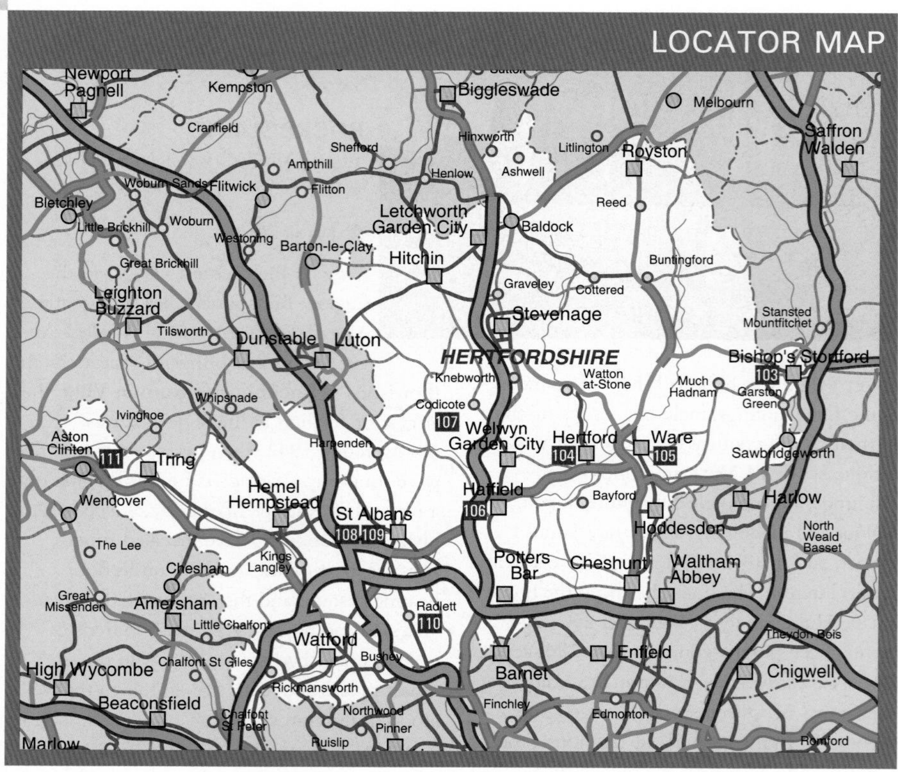

ADVERTISERS AND PLACES OF INTEREST

Accommodation, Food and Drink

105 | Hanbury Manor, Ware *pg 209*
108 | Abigails Tearoom, St Albans *pg 215*
110 | Battlers Green Farm Rural Shopping Village & Tearooms, Radlett *pg 220*

Activities

105 | Hanbury Manor, Ware *pg 209*
111 | Tring Reservoirs, Wilstone *pg 224*

Arts and Crafts

110 | Battlers Green Farm Rural Shopping Village & Tearooms, Radlett *pg 220*

Fashions

110 | Battlers Green Farm Rural Shopping Village & Tearooms, Radlett *pg 220*

Gifts

109 | Dusty Violet, St Albans *pg 215*
110 | Battlers Green Farm Rural Shopping Village & Tearooms, Radlett *pg 220*

Home & Garden

109 | Dusty Violet, St Albans *pg 215*
110 | Battlers Green Farm Rural Shopping Village & Tearooms, Radlett *pg 220*

Jewellery

110 | Battlers Green Farm Rural Shopping Village & Tearooms, Radlett *pg 220*

Places of Interest

103 | The Rhodes Museum, Bishop's Storford *pg 200*
106 | Hatfield House, Hatfield *pg 211*
107 | Shaw's House, Ayot St Lawrence, Welwyn *pg 213*
111 | Tring Reservoirs, Wilstone *pg 224*

Specialist Food and Drink Shops

104 | Foxholes Farm Shop, Hertford *pg 207*
110 | Battlers Green Farm Rural Shopping Village & Tearooms, Radlett *pg 220*

historic building · museum and heritage · historic site · scenic attraction · flora and fauna

6 | Hertfordshire

The novelist EM Forster, who lived in the county, described Hertfordshire as "England at its quietest; England meditative". When he wrote that in the 1950s, the county's population was just over 600,000; it has now topped one million. The more southerly towns expanded as residential areas for London commuters, and after the Second World War, with an acute housing shortage in the blitzed capital, New Towns such as Stevenage were created to cater for the thousands of Londoners who had lost their homes.

But the centre of the county is still largely agricultural and the southern edge lies within the precarious protection of the Metropolitan Green Belt. There is still some excellent walking and splendid scenery, most notably within the National Trust's Ashridge Estate, where the woodlands and downlands are home to a wide variety of wildlife, and the views from the highest points are magnificent.

The strongest historical ties in the county are to be found in the ancient city of St Albans, while Hatfield combines old and new elements: it was one of the designated New Towns, but the old town survives, along with the magnificent Hatfield House and part of the medieval Royal Palace, which was the childhood home of the future Elizabeth I.

Close to Hatfield lies Welwyn Garden City, conceived by Ebenezer Howard and built in the 1920s with the aim of providing working people with a pleasant and attractive place to live, with easy access to the countryside.

New River, Great Amwell

One of the best known monuments in Hertfordshire is the Eleanor Cross at Waltham Cross, one of 13 such crosses erected by Edward I to commemorate the resting places of the funeral cortege of his Queen, Eleanor of Castile.

Bishop's Stortford

St Michael's Church | Museum

Rhodes Museum

The old Roman road from St Albans to Colchester forded the river here, and some nine centuries later, the Saxon King Edward the Elder, built a castle to protect the crossing. His fortress has disappeared but the great mound on which it was built survives in the town's spacious Castle Gardens. In about 1060, the whole town was sold to the Bishops of London, hence its name. In medieval times Bishop's Stortford was a stopping place on the route between London and both Newmarket and Cambridge and became famous for its many hostelries. Even today, the town boasts three inns dating back to the 15th and 16th centuries, as well as several timber-framed buildings. In the 20th century, the building of Stansted Airport, just seven miles away, brought the town within easy reach of Europe and beyond.

In the compact town centre markets are still held twice a week, on Thursdays and Saturdays, as they have been for centuries. Standing high on a hill, **St Michael's Church** dominates the surrounding countryside. Inside the large, light building there are 18 elaborately carved misericords in the choir stalls; it is believed that they came from Old St Paul's Cathedral in London. Elsewhere, a memorial commemorates the life of Cecil Rhodes, son of a former Rector. The great imperialist's exploits are also documented in the house where he was born, Nettlewell House, now the **Rhodes Museum and Commonwealth Centre**.

The Rhodes Museum (see panel below)forms part of the Bishop's Stortford Museum, which contains an exhibit celebrating another famous son – Sir Walter Gilbey who

The Rhodes Museum

South Road, Bishop's Stortford,
Hertfordshire CM23 3JG
Tel: 01279 651746 Fax: 01279 467171
e-mail: museum@rhodesbishopsstortford.org.uk
website: www.rhodesbishopsstortford.org.uk

The Rhodes Museum was established in 1938 in two listed Victorian Buildings, one of which being the birthplace of Cecil Rhodes, Victorian Empire Builder. Today, the Rhodes Museum and the Local History Museum have merged to become the Bishop's Storford Museum. The collections are housed together and provide a new focus on the town's rich local history and unique links with the story of Cecil Rhodes, Empire and Africa.

There is also an Education Room, a Collectors corner and a Temporary Exhibition Gallery which will host a variety of exhibitions throughout the year, featuring visiting local and national artists, touring exhibitions and displays from the Museum's Reserve Collections.

River Stort, Bishop's Stortford

founded the Gilbey gin firm when he was living at nearby Elsenham Hall in the 1860s. The museum also displays a remarkable 28 foot-long mural that tells the story of the town from the Ice Age to the 1990s. Worked on canvas in wool embroidery, the project took 142 townspeople six years to complete.

Around Bishop's Stortford

MUCH HADHAM

4 miles W of Bishop's Stortford on B1004

Forge Museum

One of the county's prettiest villages, Much Hadham still retains many old timber-framed houses and cottages, the oldest of which dates back to the 15th century. The **Forge Museum and Victorian Cottage Garden** has a resident blacksmith, Richard Maynard, working in the traditional craft, as well as a display of tools, documents and photographs. A TV/video presentation shows films relating to the trade. Outside, there's a delightful cottage garden displaying and growing plants that would have been familiar to a 19th-century country gardener. The garden also contains an unusual 19th-century bee shelter.

STANDON

6 miles W of Bishop's Stortford on A120

Balloon Stone

This old village, which once had a weekly market and two annual fairs, derived its importance from the families who held the manor and from the Order of St John of Jerusalem. Though there is little evidence of it today, the order established a commandery, a hospice and a school, which is believed to be the building now known as Knights' Court.

In a field to the west of the village lies the **Balloon Stone**, a giant sandstone boulder that marks the spot where, in 1784, Vincenzo Lunardi completed the first balloon flight in England. He began his flight in Finsbury, north London, and landed here some two hours later having first touched down briefly in a field at North Mimms.

PERRY GREEN

5 miles SW of Bishop's Stortford off the B1004

Henry Moore Foundation

Perry Green became the home of Henry Moore following bomb damage to his Hampstead studio in 1941. The famous sculptor moved with his wife Irina to the peace and tranquillity of the village and he remained there for the rest of his life. **The Henry Moore Foundation**, which operates from Dane Tree House, Perry Green, and from the Henry Moore Institute in Leeds, was established in 1977 "to advance the education of the public by the promotion of their appreciation of the fine arts and in particular the works of Henry Moore". The Perry Green site comprises several studios and two converted barns containing the Foundation's collection of Moore's work, as well as tapestries based on his drawings, which were woven at West Dean College in Sussex. On the far side of the village green is a visitor centre selling books, posters, postcards and other Moore-themed merchandise, along with a limited number of original prints. The estate contains many fine trees and hedgerows, much loved by Moore and to be seen in many of his works, and it was Irina who over the years created the garden areas in which the studios and sculptures are sited. The Foundation is open to the public from April to September by appointment (call 01279 843333). Moore, who died in 1986, is buried in the village churchyard.

Stevenage

Museum Six Mills

The town grew up along the Great North Road, and as traffic increased from the 13th century it developed round its parish church, the main road becoming its High Street. Stevenage was designated the first of Britain's New Towns in 1946. The idea of New Towns grew from the severe shortage of housing following the Second World War air raids on London. The first new houses in Stevenage were occupied in 1951; the new town centre was completed in 1957. Within the new town area, by a roundabout near the railway station, rise **Six Hills**, reputed to be Roman burial mounds. The history of the town, from the earliest days to the development of the New Town and the present day, is told in the **Stevenage Museum** in the undercroft of St George's Church.

Stevenage became Hilton in the classic novel *Howards End* by EM Forster, who spent much of his childhood at Rooks Nest on the outskirts of town.

Around Stevenage

KNEBWORTH

3 miles S of Stevenage off A602

Knebworth House

Church of St Mary and St Thomas

Knebworth House has been the home of the Lytton family since 1490. The present magnificent High Gothic mansion house was built in 1843 to the design of the Victorian statesman and novelist, Edward Bulwer-Lytton, who wrote *The Last Days of Pompeii.* However, fragments of the original Tudor house remain, including parts of the Great Hall, and there is also some superb 17th-century panelling. Other members of the Lytton family of note include Constance, a leading figure in the suffragette movement, and Robert, Viceroy of India. The Raj Exhibition at the house brings to life the story of Lord Lytton's viceroyship and the Great Delhi Durbar of 1877. The house has also

Knebworth House

played host to such notable visitors as Elizabeth I, Benjamin Disraeli, Sir Winston Churchill and Charles Dickens, who took part in amateur theatrical performances here. Dickens christened his 10th child Edward Bulwer Lytton Dickens in honour of their great friendship. The grounds of Knebworth House are also well worth visiting. As well as the beautiful formal gardens laid out by Lutyens, there is a wonderful herb garden established by Gertrude Jekyll, a lovely Victorian wilderness area, a maze that was replanted in 1995, and acres of grassland that are home to herds of red and sika deer. Children will enjoy the adventure playground, where they will find Fort Knebworth, a Dinosaur Trail, a monorail suspension slide and a bouncy castle among the amusements.

Also within the grounds is the **Church of St Mary and St Thomas**, which contains some spectacular 17th- and 18th-century monuments to members of the Lytton family. Especially striking is the memorial to Sir William Lytton who died in 1705. A well-fed figure with a marked double chin and dressed in the height of early 18th-century fashion, Sir William reclines gracefully atop his tomb, his expression one of impermeable self-satisfaction.

BENINGTON

4 miles E of Stevenage off the B1037

A very attractive village, Benington has a lovely green fringed by 16th-century timber-and-plaster cottages. The village church dates from the 13th century and, next to it, on the site of a largely disappeared castle, is a spacious Georgian house known as Benington Lordship. The house is private, but the superb grounds are open at restricted times. The hilltop gardens include lakes, a Norman keep and moat (the remains of the castle), a kitchen, rose and water gardens, a charming rockery, magnificent herbaceous borders and a splendid folly dating from 1832.

CROMER

4 miles NE of Stevenage on the B1037

Cromer Windmill

Half a mile east of the village, on the B1037 towards Hare Street, stands Hertfordshire's sole surviving post mill. **Cromer Windmill** was built on an artificial mound where windmills have stood for over 600 years. The present mill dates back at least to 1720, possibly as early as 1681. Blown over in a storm around 1860 and subsequently rebuilt, it was in use until the 1920s, by which time milling by wind had become uneconomic. The mill was basically left to deteriorate until an appeal by local people in 1967 saved it. On completion of the first phase of restoration

Cromer Windmill

work, the mill was presented to the current owners, the Hertfordshire Building Preservation Trust. The first open days were held in 1991 and the mill was restored to full working order in 1998 with the help of grants from the Heritage Lottery Fund and English Heritage. The mill can be visited on Sundays, Bank Holiday Mondays and the second and fourth Saturdays from the second Sunday in May until the end of August.

ROYSTON

12 miles NE of Stevenage on A10

James I's Hunting Lodge

Royston & District Museum

Royston Cave

This light industrial town grew up at the intersection of the Icknield Way and Ermine Street and is named after a wayside cross erected by Lady Roysia. A favourite hunting base for royalty, **James I's Hunting Lodge** can still be seen, though the only original features that remain are the two large chimneys.

The man-made **Royston Cave** was discovered in 1742 below the junction of the two ancient thoroughfares. Bell-shaped and cut out of the chalk, the cave is 28 feet deep and 17 feet across. Inside the chamber is a series of crude carvings on the walls, including St Christopher and the Crucifixion; the purpose of the cave and the date of the carvings have never been determined.

The **Royston & District Museum**, in the former Congregational Schoolroom building, houses the Royston and District Local History Society collections, which relate to the history of this late medieval town and the surrounding area. Also here is a substantial collection of late 19th-century ceramics and glass.

LETCHWORTH GARDEN CITY

6 miles N of Stevenage off the A1

First Garden City Heritage Museum

Museum & Art Gallery   Standalone Farm

This attractive country town is proud to be the first Garden City where the ideals of Ebenezer Howard were put into practice. The site for Letchworth was purchased in 1903 and Barry Parker and Raymond Unwin were appointed architects. The residential cottages were designed and built by different architects for the 1905 Cheap Cottages Exhibition and, with none costing more than £150, they each demonstrated new techniques and styles of building and living accommodation.

The Letchworth architect's office, a beautiful thatched Arts and Crafts building of 1907, is now the **First Garden City Heritage Museum**, a unique place that traces the history and development of this special town; among the many displays are the original plans and drawings of Letchworth. **Letchworth Museum and Art Gallery** is home to displays of local natural history and archaeology including finds of late Iron Age and Roman origin that were unearthed at Baldock.

On the outskirts of the town, **Standalone Farm** is a working farm that welcomes anyone

Town Hall, Letchworth Garden City

who wants to learn more about farming and raising animals. A wide range of farm animals, including Shire horses, occupy the 170-acre site, which also has a recently-planted arboretum containing more than 1000 trees of 35 species, hides to view wildfowl, a natural history exhibition, a picnic area and café.

BALDOCK

7 miles N of Stevenage on the A505

Museum

A settlement of some size during the Iron Age and Roman times, the Baldock of today dates from the 12th century; it was founded by the Knights Templar and takes its name from the Old French for Baghdad. The Church of St Mary has an impressive 14th-century tower and spike steeple, and the town boasts many handsome Georgian houses, both in the tree-lined main street and in the side streets. Baldock is proud of this architectural heritage: it has more than 100 listed buildings. The local superstore has kept the historic façade of the old Kayser Bondor factory. The community-run **Baldock Museum** reflects the town's history and its connections with coaching, malting and brewing.

ASHWELL

9 miles N of Stevenage off the A505

Church of St Mary Museum

An appealing village with a wealth of attractive old houses, Ashwell was one of the five boroughs of Hertfordshire in medieval times and took its name from the ash trees around the source of the River Rhee. The village later prospered through a malting industry that only ceased in the 1950s. The 14th-century **Church of St Mary** has the highest tower in the county, at 176 feet, and inside there are several inscriptions referring to the Black Death of 1349 and the plague and great storm of 1361. **Ashwell Museum**, in the restored Tudor Town House, affords an insight into the natural history, social history and archaeology of the town. It began in 1927 as the private collection of two schoolboys who displayed their treasures in a garden shed.

HITCHIN

4 miles NW of Stevenage on A600

St Mary's Church The Biggin

The Priory Museum

Museum of Hertfordshire Imperial Yeomanry

Pevsner considered that, after St Albans, Hitchin was "the most visually satisfying town in Hertfordshire". Situated on the banks of the River Hiz, this old town was, during medieval times, a vast market area where straw was purchased for the local cottage industry of straw plaiting and where the completed plaits were sold. As the trade in straw declined, so the market at Hitchin reduced in

Swallow Fledglings - Hitchin

size, but there is still a small market place today, west of the parish church. Many of the town's older buildings have survived, if now surrounded by newer developments. The oldest parts of **St Mary's Church** date from the 12th century, though there was a minster church recorded here in the Domesday Book. The low tower is the only part of the original building to have survived an earthquake of 1298. Rebuilt in the 14th century, the grandeur of the church reflects the prosperity that Hitchin once enjoyed.

Standing on the site of a Gilbertine Priory is **The Biggin**, constructed in the early 17th century. For a while it was a private residence, then a school, before becoming, in 1723, an almshouse for "poore, auncient or middle aged women", a function that it still performs today. Another building worthy of mention is **The Priory**, which takes in fragments of a Carmelite Priory founded in the 14th century. Built in 1770 by Robert Adams as the private residence of the Radcliffe family, it was extensively renovated in the 1980s after being disused for many years.

Finally, **Hitchin Museum** (free) occupies a Georgian town house, home to the county's largest collection of period costumes and is an excellent place to visit. It shares a building with the **Museum of the Hertfordshire Imperial Yeomanry** – a band of men mustered to repel Napoleon's threatened invasion. As well as the numerous displays of local social history, part of the museum includes a Victorian Chemist Shop and Physic Garden. This re-creation of a chemist's shop uses much of the stock and fittings from Perks and Llewellyn, who ceased trading as a pharmacy in 1961; the original cabinets still contain the lavender toiletries for which the firm was world-famous. To carry the connection further between the town and pharmacy, the medical pioneer Lord Lister had family ties with Hitchin and began his education here. The Physic Garden reflects the historical and modern importance of plants as a source of medicine.

Hertford

Church of St Leonard | Quaker Meeting House | Museum | Castle | Cole Green Way | Nature Walk

Dating back to Saxon times, the town was founded at a ford across the River Lea, at that time the boundary between Saxon and Viking England. A once important waterway linking Hertford with London, the River Lea, which became the Lea (Lee) Navigation at Hertford, was used to transport flour and grain, but today its traffic is leisure cruisers. The **Hertford Nature Walk** is situated in the meadows between the Rivers Lea and Beane, and takes in the canal basin, known as The Folly.

Hertford is very much a mix of the old and new, and among the interesting buildings are the particularly beautiful Norman **Church of St Leonard**, in the area known as

Hertford Castle

FOXHOLES FARM SHOP

Foxholes Farm, London Road, Hertford,
Hertfordshire SG13 7NT
Tel: 01992 552900
e-mail: catherine@foxholesfarm.com
website: www.foxholesfarm.com

For lovers of quality local produce **Foxholes Farm Shop** is a fantastic find in the town of Hertford. Owned by Catherine Smith, all of the products are sourced as locally as possible to give customers the choice of products grown or produced from local farms, growers and small producers.

The farm shop, butchery and delicatessen has a lot to offer including home produced beef and pork, with local lamb and chicken. Home cooked meats, ready made meals, local pate and free-range eggs are also available here. There is a fine selection

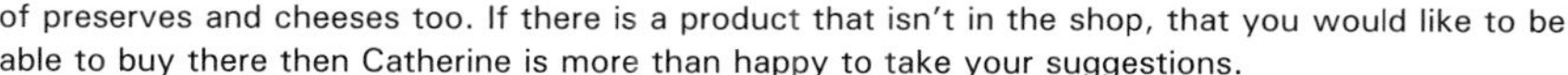

of preserves and cheeses too. If there is a product that isn't in the shop, that you would like to be able to buy there then Catherine is more than happy to take your suggestions.

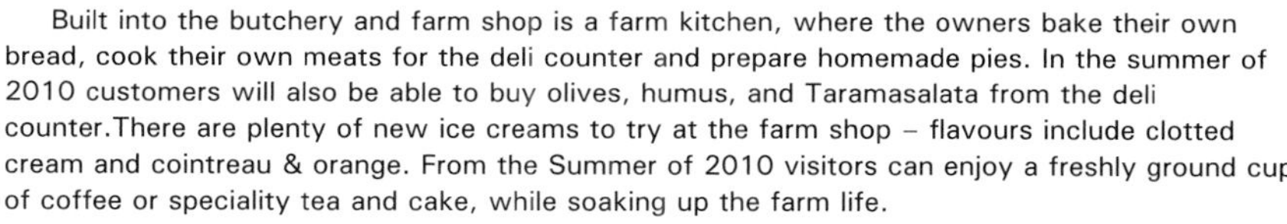

Built into the butchery and farm shop is a farm kitchen, where the owners bake their own bread, cook their own meats for the deli counter and prepare homemade pies. In the summer of 2010 customers will also be able to buy olives, humus, and Taramasalata from the deli counter.There are plenty of new ice creams to try at the farm shop – flavours include clotted cream and cointreau & orange. From the Summer of 2010 visitors can enjoy a freshly ground cup of coffee or speciality tea and cake, while soaking up the farm life.

Bengeo, and the **Quaker Meeting House**. Said to be the oldest purpose-built meeting house in the world that has been in constant use as a place of worship, the meeting house dates from 1669 and stands behind a walled courtyard; it has a unique four-tiered platform for the ministers that is screened from the entrance. The collections at **Hertford Museum** were started in the 1890s and cover a wide variety of subjects relating to the town and the surrounding area. The museum is located in a 17th-century town house that is complemented by a reconstructed Jacobean garden. The Shire Hall was where Darcy first met Elizabeth in Jane Austen's *Pride and Prejudice.*

Little remains of the original **Hertford Castle**, which was built by King Alfred's son Prince Edward to guard the ford on the river and to protect London from the Danes. However, the 15th-century gatehouse is still standing and, now modernised, is used as administrative offices for the town council. The site of the castle is now a public park and evidence of the castle's original motte and bailey can still be seen in the lie of the land. A short length of the massive Norman flint wall, complete with a 14th-century postern gate, is also preserved in the park. The town centre incorporates Salisbury Square, which features a water sculpture depicting the four rivers that meet in Hertford – the Rib, Beane, Mimram and Lea (Lee).

To the south of the town runs **Cole Green Way**, a delightful nature trail that follows the route of the now disused Hertford and Welwyn Junction Railway. Passing through attractive meadowland, the trail runs from Hertford to Cole Green, where the former station provides a pleasant picnic spot.

Around Hertford

HODDESDON

4 miles SE of Hertford on the A1010

Rye House Gatehouse · Lowewood Museum

Samaritan Woman

The town grew up around the road along the Lea Valley that replaced the Roman Ermine Street in Saxon times. In Lea Valley Park stands the 15th-century **Rye House Gatehouse**, a fascinating historic attraction, which includes an exhibition where visitors can eavesdrop on the conspirators in the Rye House Plot. In 1683, Rye House was the scene of a plot to assassinate Charles II as he passed through the town on his way back from Newmarket to London. The plot failed and the conspirators, including Richard Rumbold, the then tenant of Rye House, were executed. The Gatehouse, which dates from 1443, was once part of Sir Andrew Ogard's manor house.

Occupying a handsome Georgian building of 1750, **Lowewood Museum** (free) in the High Street depicts past local life. In a garden beside the museum there is a statue of a woman holding a water urn. Known as the **Samaritan Woman**, it stood for almost 200 years, until 1826, in Hoddesdon marketplace and was the conduit head for fresh water piped to the town.

BRICKENDON

3 miles S of Hertford off the B158

Celtic Harmony Camp · Paradise Wildlife Park

Celtic Harmony Camp is a constructed Iron Age settlement in 13 acres of beautiful woodland near the village of Brickendon. Visitors of all ages are welcomed by staff in Celtic costume and can experience life as a Celt with lots of hands-on activities and play areas for children.

A popular destination for a family outing is **Paradise Wildlife Park**, which has an amazing range of animals including tigers, lions, monkeys, zebras, camels and wolves. Visitors can get up close and personal, meeting and feeding many of the animals. There are three themed adventure playgrounds, children's rides, a woodland railway, indoor soft play areas and many other attractions. Open every day from 9.30am.

CHESHUNT

8 miles S of Hertford off the A10

Temple Bar

In 1564 Lord Burghley, Chief Minister to Elizabeth I, built his great house, Theobalds, here. Later, James I was so taken with the house that he persuaded Burghley's son Robert to exchange it for his palace at Hatfield. Theobalds was all but destroyed in the aftermath of the Civil War, and what remains of the building stands in the public Cedars Park. Also in the park is **Temple Bar**, designed by Wren and originally erected at the Fleet Street entrance to the City of London after the Great Fire of 1666. By the 1870s London's traffic had increased to the extent that the gateway was causing an obstruction, so it was removed and rebuilt in the park.

WALTHAM CROSS

9 miles S of Hertford on the A1010

Eleanor Cross · Anthony Trollope

The town takes its name from the cross built in the centre in 1291. It is an **Eleanor Cross**, one of three survivors of the 12 that Edward I erected to commemorate the resting places of the funeral cortege of his Queen,

Eleanor of Castile. Eleanor died in Lincolnshire and the cortege took 13 days to travel to Westminster Abbey where she is buried. The building materials in the cross include Caen stone, Sussex and Purbeck marble and precious stones, and it is recorded that the total cost was £95.

The other surviving crosses are at Northampton and Geddington, and a Victorian replica stands in the forecourt of Charing Cross Station. In 1859, the author **Anthony Trollope** came to live in Waltham Cross. He kept pigs, tended his garden and wrote some of his best works while he was here.

WARE

3 miles E of Hertford on the A1170

Place House Museum Scott's Grotto

Situated at the point where Ermine Street crosses the River Lea, Ware was the scene of a famous encounter between King Alfred and the Danes in AD895 and, during the Middle Ages, it became a trading rival to Hertford. The construction of a viaduct in the 1970s to carry the A10 across the valley has removed much of the traffic from the town and, despite development over the years, Ware still retains many of its original buildings. Behind the east end of the High Street, there is access to Blue Coat Yard where, on the right, stands **Place House**, possibly one of Ware's two Domesday manor houses, which was rebuilt during the 13th century as a splendid aisled hall, and in the 1680s was purchased by the governors of Christ's Hospital for use as a school for boys being fostered in Ware. Most of this building still remains, and on the opposite side of the yard stand the cottages that were built in 1698 to provide accommodation for a foster mother

Ware Gazebos & River Lea

and up to 14 boys.

The High Street crosses the River Lea at Bridgefoot, and here can still be seen some unique 18th-century gazebos, many of which have been restored to their former glory. The riverside path leads on into an attractive public garden behind what was once a Franciscan Priory, of which only a few traces remain. Founded in 1338 as a friary, the priory became a private house in 1568 and remained so for several centuries. In 1920, the owner, Mrs Page-Croft, gave the house and gardens to the town and, fully restored in 1994, the building stands pristine surrounded by seven acres of parkland.

No trip to Ware would be complete without a visit to **Scott's Grotto**, built by the poet John Scott in the late 18th century and located off the A119 Hertford Road. The son of a wealthy Quaker family, Scott devised this elaborate series of six chambers linked by passageways and air tunnels during the 1760s; they are lined with flints, fossils, minerals and thousands of shells. On a hill above the grotto is an octagonal summerhouse approached by horseshoe-shaped steps. The grotto was described by Scott's friend Dr Johnson as "a fairy hall", adding that "none but a poet could have made such a garden". The grotto was extensively restored in 1990; the replacement shells came from local donors and from as far afield as Japan. It is open on Saturdays and Bank Holiday Mondays from April to the end of September.

The history of Ware and its major role in the malting industry is explained in **Ware Museum** at Priory Lodge. The Great Bed of Ware, mentioned by Shakespeare, is in the Victoria & Albert Museum in London.

GREAT AMWELL

2 miles SE of Ware off the A10

New River

Between 1609 and 1613 the **New River** was created to carry fresh water from local springs by way of Hoddesdon and Cheshunt to the New River Head reservoir at Clerkenwell in London. Wooden pipes then carried the water to the houses and businesses of North London. This enterprise was the brainchild of Sir Hugh Myddelton, whose achievement is commemorated at Great Amwell by an island laid out by the architect of the New River Company in 1800. Just south of the village church stand the imposing buildings of Haileybury College, which was established in 1809 as a training school for the East India Company. The architect was William Wilkins, whose best known work is the National Gallery in Trafalgar Square.

Hatfield

Church of St Etheldreda

Hatfield House

This historic town grew up around the

gateway to the palace of the abbots and Bishop of Ely. Beside the palace gatehouse stands the **Church of St Etheldreda**, dedicated to the East Anglian princess and first abbess of Ely in the 7th century. The church is notable for its magnificent memorials to the Cecil family of nearby Hatfield House, the Brocket family chapel from the Tudor era, and dazzling stained glass by Burne-Jones. Also buried here are the novelist Lady Caroline Lamb and her husband Henry William Lamb, 2nd Viscount Melbourne. The viscount, who was Prime Minister in 1834 and from 1835 to 1841, has a memorial in the church, but there is no mention of Lady Caroline, whose public infatuation with Lord Byron brought about their separation in 1825.

Elizabeth I spent her early life in the Royal Palace of Hatfield, of which only the Banqueting Hall remains. This can be seen in the delightful gardens of the spectacular Jacobean mansion, **Hatfield House** (see panel below), which now stands on the site. It was built in the early 1600s for Robert Cecil (later 1st Earl of Salisbury), Chief Minister to both Elizabeth and James I. Designed with entertaining royalty in mind, no expense was spared to make Hatfield the most striking house of its time. The most impressive room

Hatfield House

Hatfield, Hertfordshire AL9 5NQ
Tel: 01707 287010
website: www.hatfield-house.co.uk

Hatfield House, where Elizabethan history began, is a superb redbrick Jacobean mansion built by Robert Cecil, Ist Earl of Shaftesbury and Chief Minister to King James I, in 1611. The house has been in the Cecil family ever since, and is the home of the Marquess of Salisbury. Superb examples of Jacobean craftsmanship can be seen throughout the house, notably in the Grand Staircase with its elaborately carved wood and in the stained-glass window in the private chapel. The state rooms are treasure houses of the finest furniture, world-renowned paintings, exquisite tapestries and historic armour; they include the fabulous Marble Hall, the Long Gallery and King James' Drawing Room.

The gardens at Hatfield House are a great attraction in their own right, laid out by John Tradescant the Elder and planted by him with many species never previously grown in England. The gardens, where restoration started in Victorian times and still continues, include herb, knot and wilderness areas which can be visited when the house is open to the public. A variety of arts and crafts events are hosted throughout the season - see website for details. Open: Easter Saturday to end September. House: 12am – 4pm, Wednesday to Sunday only. Park, West Garden, Restaurant & Shop: Daily, 11am - 5.30pm. East Garden: Open only on Thursdays (except during August).

is the superb Marble Hall, a richly-decorated version of the medieval Great Hall with a sumptuously carved Screen and Minstrel's Gallery, a specially made 30 foot long refectory table and a black and white marble floor. Here hang the two most famous paintings of Elizabeth I – Nicholas Hilliard's *Ermine Portrait* and Isaac Oliver's deeply allegorical *Rainbow Portrait*. The Cecil family still live here, in the East Wing, and the present Marchioness has taken a special interest in restoring the superb gardens to their 17th-century appearance, complete with herb and knot gardens, and a foot maze typical of the period. Visitors to the Park can also enjoy the national collection of model soldiers, five miles of marked park trails, a picnic site, children's play area, gift shop, licensed restaurant and tearoom.

Back in the centre of town lies the Eight Bells pub, which was frequented by Charles Dickens when, as a newspaper reporter for the *Morning Chronicle*, he visited Hatfield to report on the fire that not only destroyed a substantial part of Hatfield House, but also resulted in the death of the Dowager Lady Salisbury. The pub also features in Dickens' *Oliver Twist*, as following the murder of Nancy, Bill Sikes 'shaped his course' for Hatfield and, in the tap room of the Eight Bells, a fellow drinker saw the blood on Sikes' hat.

The idea of Hatfield New Town was nothing new in post Second World War Britain, as in 1848 proposals for a new town were advertised to coincide with the completion of the railway line in 1850. Though some development did take place, it was not until the 1950s that the rapid expansion began. However, the two areas remain separate, on either side of the railway line and, fortunately, much of the older part of the town has survived. Hatfield has strong links with the history of aviation and was the home of the Mosquito, Comet and Trident.

Around Hatfield

BROOKMANS PARK

3 miles S of Hatfield on the A1000

Northaw Great Wood

Brookmans Park is a quiet residential area with a large commuting population. To the east is **Northaw Great Wood**, the remains of the forest that once covered a large part of Hertfordshire. It is now preserved with conservation in mind, and visitors can wander through the woodland and perhaps spot muntjac deer, badgers, foxes and some of the 60 or so species of birds that have been sighted here.

Northaw Great Wood, Brookmans Park

WELWYN

1 mile N of Hatfield on the A1(M)

Welwyn Roman Baths

This historic town has grown up along the route of the Great North Road, which became the High Street, but, since the construction of the A1(M) took the route away from the town centre, Welwyn is now relatively traffic-free.

During the excavations for the motorway, the famous **Welwyn Roman Baths** were uncovered. Part of a 3rd-century villa or farm, the bath house is preserved in a steel vault within the motorway embankment.

WELWYN GARDEN CITY

2 miles N of Hatfield on the A1000

Mill Green Museum   Mill Green Mill

As the name of this town would suggest, Welwyn is indeed a Garden City, one of two in Hertfordshire that followed the ideas and plans of Ebenezer Howard. After seeing the squalor in which people lived in the cities, particularly London, Howard conceived the idea of providing working people with an opportunity to live in well-spaced housing with access to the clean air of the countryside as well as the industrial areas close by. The land for Welwyn Garden City was first acquired in 1919, and building began a year later, with the present station completed in 1926. Howard's ideas are still perhaps best seen here, as the railway line also acts as the demarcation line for the two areas of the town: industry to the east; the shopping and commercial areas to the west; while the residential areas, with extensive planting and many open spaces lie beyond.

Just to the south of the town lies **Mill Green Museum**, in the tiny hamlet of Mill Green. Housed in the workers' cottages for the adjoining watermill, this was, between 1911 and 1973, a private residence. There are two permanent galleries here where local items from Roman times to the present day are on display, including pottery, craft tools, underwear and school certificates. A further gallery is used for temporary exhibitions. The

Shaw's Corner

Ayot St Lawrence, nr Welwyn,
Hertfordshire AL6 9BX
Tel: 01438 829221 (Infoline)
website: www.nationaltrust.org.uk

Visit the home of George Bernard Shaw from 1906 until his death in 1950. The atmospheric rooms remain much as he left them, with many literary and personal belongings. The modest house provides a fascinating insight into the domestic life of a literary figure in the first half of the twentieth century.

Relax in the timelessly tranquil 3.5 acre garden complete with an orchard, flower meadow, rose dell and richly planted herbaceous and shrubbery beds. All the plants are pre – 1950s with traditional plants such as Phlomis, Delphinium, Allium, Achillea, Agapanthus, Acanthus and Aster.

The ashes of George Bernard Shaw and his wife Charlotte were scattered throughout the garden and around the 6ft square **Writing Hut** where most of his most famous works were written.

adjoining **Mill Green Mill** is a wonderful watermill restored to full working order. Standing on the site of one of the four such mills in Hertfordshire that featured in the Domesday Book, Mill Green Mill was originally owned by the Bishops of Ely. Reconstructed and altered many times, the mill finally ceased to grind corn at the beginning of the 20th century when the incumbent miller emigrated to Australia. Milling recommenced in 1986, after much careful restoration work by the Mill Green Water Mill Restoration Trust, and not only can it be seen working, but freshly ground flour is on sale.

AYOT ST LAWRENCE

3 miles NW of Hatfield off the B653

Shaw's Corner · Ayot Greenway

The most famous resident of the village was the playwright George Bernard Shaw, who lived here from 1906 until his death in 1950. It seems that while on a visit to the area looking for a country home, he saw a headstone in the churchyard with the inscription, "Her time was short". The lady in question had in fact died at the age of 70, and Shaw thought that if 70 was considered a short span of years, this was the place for him. The house in which he lived, **Shaw's Corner** (see panel on page 213), has been preserved by the National Trust as it was in his lifetime and contains many literary and personal mementos of the great Irish writer. All the plants in the lovely garden are pre-1950, including phlomis, delphinium, agapanthus, allium, acanthus and aster. The ashes of Shaw and his wife Charlotte were scattered throughout the garden and around the six-foot-square writing hut where GBS wrote most of his famous works. Close by, just south of Ayot St Peter, runs **Ayot Greenway**, an attractive footpath, rich in flora, that follows part of the route of the old Luton, Dunstable and Welwyn Junction Railway, which hit the buffers under the Beeching axe in 1966.

St Albans

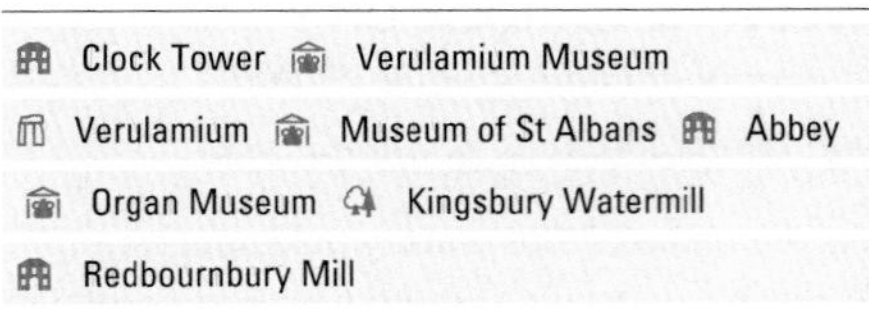

This historic cathedral city, whose skyline is dominated by the magnificent Norman abbey, is a wonderful blend of the old and new. One of the major Roman cities in Britain, the remains of **Verulamium** were excavated only quite recently, but there was a settlement here before Julius Caesar's invasion in 54BC. Attacked and ruined by Boadicea (Boudiccea) in the 1st century, the city was rebuilt and today the remains of the walls, Britain's only Roman theatre (as distinct from an amphitheatre) and a hypocaust can still be seen in Verulamium Park. Also in the park is the **Verulamium Museum**, where the story of everyday life in a Roman city is told; among the displays are ceramics, mosaic floors, personal possessions and room re-creations.

Designated as a cathedral in 1877, **St Albans Abbey** was built on the site where Alban, the first British martyr, was beheaded in AD303 for sheltering a Christian priest. Dating from the 11th century and built from flint and bricks taken from the Roman remains, the Cathedral has been added to and altered in every century since. It was the premier Abbey of medieval England until its monastic life ended in 1539, when all but the Abbey Church and Gatehouse were destroyed. Among its many notable features, the medieval paintings, said to be unique in Britain, are the

ABIGAILS TEAROOM

The Village Arcade, 7 High St,
St Albans, Hertfordshire AL3 4ED
Tel: 07970219957
e-mail: jod13@aol.com

Abigails Tearoom is a family run establishment located in the shadow of St Albans' beautiful cathedral. Plenty of visitors come here and many are drawn into the charming tearoom that is Abigails.

Abigails Tearoom was opened 17 years ago. It is a family run establishment and is owned by Brian Dawkins and his wife Jo. The waiting staff offer a friendly service and are only more than too happy to help.

The tearooms are very popular with locals as well as visitors to the area who are all welcomed to enjoy traditional English dishes and clotted cream teas. Abigails is renowned for its fine selection of homemade cakes and such is the choice it might take you a while to decide which one you want to sample. An excellent range of coffees is also served here along with plenty of other refreshments.

Abigails Tearoom can be found at the end of the charming Village Arcade and there is a large tree-covered patio and garden area, perfect for al fresco dining.

DUSTY VIOLET

14A George Street, St Albans, Hertfordshire AL3 4ER
Tel: 01727 811288
e-mail: info@dustyviolet.com
website: www.dustyviolet.com

With a delightful range of carefully selected gifts, home accessories, soft furnishings and home fragrances, **Dusty Violet** is a fantastic find in St Albans. Owned by Sharon Onley the independent shop has plenty of ideas and inspirations for those stuck for a gift idea.

Many of the products on sale here are homemade and all of them are selected with care from international, national and local suppliers. Sharon is always looking for new ideas, suppliers and products, so that there is always something new for her valued customers to see. Although the emphasis is very much on quality she likes to keep prices accessible. The shop has a very good reputation in the area and many of Dusty Violet's customers come back every time they need a gift for somebody or a treat for themselves. It is one of only a few suppliers of Sid Dickens memory blocks in the UK, whilst also providing brands such as Abode Aroma, Bronte Tweeds, Heyland and Whittle, Hogben Pottery, Thomas Kent and Newgate Clocks. Items can also be purchased from Dusty Violet's website.

most interesting. In the nearby Church of St Michael are the tomb and life-size monument of Lord Chancellor Francis Bacon (1561–1626), 1st Baron Verulam and Viscount St Albans, who lived in St Albans for the last five years of his life. The shrine of St Alban is a beautiful structure of carved Purbeck marble made in 1308. It was restored in 1993. In 2002, a bone believed to be of St Alban was given to the Cathedral by the Church of St Pantaleon in Cologne.

In the town's central market place stands the **Clock Tower**, the only medieval town belfry in England, built between 1403 and 1412. Originally constructed as a political statement by the town, it asserted the citizens' freedom and wealth in the face of the powerful Abbey, as the town was allowed to sound its own hours and ring the curfew bell. The original 15th-century bell, Gabriel, is still in place.

Clock Tower, St Albans

Close to the peaceful and tranquil Verulamium Park, on the banks of the River Ver, is **Kingsbury Watermill**, a wonderful 16th-century mill that is built on the site of an earlier mill that was mentioned in the Domesday Book. Beautifully restored, the waterwheel is still turned by the river and visitors can not only enjoy this idyllic setting, but also they can see the working milling machinery and a collection of agricultural implements.

Two other museums in the town are well worth a visit. The **Museum of St Albans** relates the fascinating history of the town from Roman times through to the present day, and among the exhibits on show is the famous Salaman collection of trade and craft tools that is considered to be the finest in the country. In **St Albans Organ Museum** visitors can enjoy the stirring sounds of an amazing collection of working mechanical musical instruments, which include two theatre organs, musical boxes, the Mills self-playing violin and reproducing pianos, all of which have been lovingly restored. All the most famous manufacturers are represented, including Mortier, Decap, Bursens, Wurlitzer and Steinway.

Two miles north of St Albans, in the tiny hamlet of Redbournbury, is **Redbournbury Mill**, an 18th-century watermill that stands on the site of a mill that was mentioned in the Domesday Book. Once owned by the Abbey at St Albans, the mill was seized by the crown following the Dissolution of the Monasteries. In 1652, it was sold to an ancestor of the present Earl of Verulam and stayed in his family until 1931 when it once again became Crown property. Now back in private hands, this splendid mill, on the banks of the River Ver, has been restored to its former glory and is in full working order, powered by a large 1935 Crossley oil engine. Open to the public on Sundays from March to October, and on other days for special events, the mill also sells its own stone-ground flour and bread.

Around St Albans

HARPENDEN

5 miles N of St Albans on A1081

Local History Centre Railway Museum

The whole of the town centre is now a conservation area and, in particular, the High Street, is lined with many listed 17th and 18th-century buildings. The **Harpenden Local History Centre** is an ideal place to find out more about this charming old agricultural community. As well as the small permanent collection, there are regularly changing themed exhibitions. The **Harpenden Railway Museum**, a small private collection that was begun in 1963, contains several thousand items of railway memorabilia, many of which originate from the county (call 01582 713524). The ashes of the comedian Eric Morecambe were scattered in the garden of remembrance next to the Church of St Nicholas. Every summer, Harpenden hosts the Harpenden Highland Gathering, one of the largest outside Scotland, featuring bagpipes, Highland dancing, Highland games and vintage cars.

MARKYATE

7 miles NW of St Albans off the A5

Markyate's narrow main street is part of the great Roman road, Watling Street, the route between London and Holyhead. A mansion in the village, built on the site of a medieval nunnery known as Markyate Cell, became famous as the home of Lady Katherine Ferrers, the notorious highwaywoman of Nomansland Common near Sandridge, just north of St Albans. Married as a teenager to a man she did not like, Katherine found escape and adventure by disguising herself as a highwayman and holding up the coaches that plied the busy Watling Street. She kept both her disguise and her booty in a secret room above the kitchen in the house. Famed and feared for her audacity, the 'Wicked Lady' always rode a jet-black horse. In her last hold-up she was mortally wounded but managed to escape and reach her house, dying at the door of her room. She was buried quietly by her husband, who had her room sealed in the hope that her secret would die with her. It did not.

CHISWELL GREEN

2 miles SW of St Albans on A414

The Royal National Rose Society Gardens

This village is home to probably one of the biggest attractions in Hertfordshire, a site that contains one of the most important rose collections in the world. The **Royal National Rose Society Gardens** can boast some 30,000 rose trees and upwards of 1700 varieties. It isn't necessary to be a horticultural enthusiast to appreciate the sheer natural beauty of gorgeous displays such as the President's Walk or the Queen Mother Rose Garden, named after the garden's original patron, which contains some of the oldest varieties of rose, including Damask, Gallicas, Albas and Portland. With the model gardens, the miniature roses, and the breathtaking pergola, it would be difficult to exaggerate the beauty of this place, which really has to be visited to be appreciated.

LONDON COLNEY

3 miles SE of St Albans off the A414

Mosquito Aircraft Museum

Among the interesting old buildings in this pleasant village on the River Colne is the late-Victorian All Saints Convent, which stands within the former Colney Park. Begun in 1899 as an Anglican establishment, with a church added in the 1920s, it was bought by the Roman Catholic Church in 1973 as a pastoral centre. A mile south of London Colney, aircraft enthusiasts will be in their element at the **Mosquito Aircraft Museum**, which is part of the de Havilland Aircraft Heritage Centre. It was here in 1940 that the first Mosquito aircraft was built and taken by road to the de Havilland airfield at Hatfield. In addition to the prototype Mosquito there is a collection of other de Havilland planes, plus various engines and displays of all kinds of aeronautical memorabilia. The museum is located within the grounds of moated Salisbury Hall (private). Built in the mid 1500s, the house was modernised a century later in order to provide a secluded but not too distant refuge for Charles II's mistress, Nell Gwynne.

SHENLEY

5 miles SE of St Albans on B5378

Lock-Up

A traditional country village with, at its centre, two inns, a pond, the site of a former pound for stray animals, and the village lock-up. One of several in Hertfordshire, this **Lock-Up** is a brick beehive-shaped construction where the village's drunks and petty criminals were locked up overnight before being brought before the magistrate the next day. On either side of the door is the warning sign: Be sober, do well, fear not, be vigilant.

The architect Nicholas Hawksmoor lived near Shenley and is buried in the churchyard of the neighbouring village of Shenleybury. Here, too, is the grave of the dashing racing driver Graham Hill, who was killed in a flying accident at Arkley, three miles from Shenley.

ALDENHAM

6 miles S of St Albans on the B462

Country Park

The greatest feature of **Aldenham Country Park**, established in 1971 on what was formerly Aldenham Common, is a large reservoir that was dug by hand by French prisoners of war in the 1790s. Designed to maintain the levels of local rivers following the building of the Grand Union Canal, it is now used for recreational purposes and also supports a wealth of wildfowl and plant life. Coarse fishing is available by permit. The park has a lakeside nature trail and woodland walks, and is home to several rare breeds of domestic animals, including Longhorn cattle. Families can have fun in Winnie the Pooh's '100 Aker Wood', where the homes of Pooh Bear, Christopher Robin, Piglet, Eyeore and Owl have been re-created in association with the Disney Corporation.

Aldenham Park

Hemel Hempstead

St Mary's Church · Charter Tower

Snook's Grave · Gadebridge Park

This is a place with two distinct identities: the charming old town centred around the ancient Church of St Mary and tranquil Gadebridge Park; and the new town, one of the first to be built following the Second World War, planned as an integrated series of communities, each with its own individual centre.

Gadebridge Park is an extensive expanse of open parkland through which runs the River Gade. The park's attractive walled garden adjoins the High Street of the old town alongside the grounds of **St Mary's**, which is an outstanding example of a large Norman parish church. Its interior has remained essentially unchanged since it was completed in 1180. St Mary's 200ft-high spire, made of oak and lead and added in 1340, is believed to be the loftiest in Europe.

Evidence of a settlement here long before the Norman Conquest can be found surprisingly close to the town's industrial area. Protected by a fenced enclosure and visible from the road, lies the mound of a Bronze Age barrow.

Charter Tower & Walled Garden, Hemel Hempstead

The **Charter Tower**, just inside one of Gadebridge Park's entrances, is reputed to be the tower from whose upper window Henry VIII handed down Hemel Hempstead's royal charter, but the tower was in fact built long after the charter was given. On the road close to the railway station is a curious stone tablet known as **Snook's Grave**, marking the spot where James Snook, a notorious highwayman, was hanged and buried. Thought to be the last person in England to be taken back to the scene of his crime for the ultimate punishment, Snook was found guilty in 1802 of robbing a postboy and killing him in the process.

The village of **Bedmond**, three miles southeast of Hemel Hempstead, was the birthplace of Nicholas Breakspear, the only British pope, who was elected in 1154 and took the name Adrian IV.

Around Hemel Hempstead

KING'S LANGLEY

2 miles S of Hemel Hempstead on the A4251

The home of Ovaltine, the drink invented in 1865 by a Swiss doctor called George Wander. His son Albert later took over the business. The King's Langley canal-side factory was built in 1912 and greatly expanded subsequently. Local farms produced eggs, barley, milk and malt for the popular drink, and the factory even had its own narrow boats on the Grand Union Canal. One of these boats has been renovated and bears the name *Albert*.

BATTLERS GREEN FARM

Common Lane, Radlett, Hertfordshire WD7 8PH
Tel: 01923 856551 Fax: 01923 857221
e-mail: paul@battlersgreenfarm.co.uk
website: www.battlersgreenfarm.co.uk

'The Gateway to Real Village Shopping'

Battlers Green Farm Rural Shopping Village has grown since 1960 from a single farm shop (which is still going strong) to a dozen or so highly distinctive stores. With its lovely farmland setting and ample free parking, the shopping village offers a unique experience.

Aga cookers and kitchenware

The Aga name has long been synonymous with good food and fine living. Its cookers are one of the world's most recognisable design icons and an Aga cooker is surprisingly easy to own!

Tel: 01923 289726

e-mail: radlett@aga-rayburn.co.uk

Andrew Brown furnishings

An eclectic mix of classic, period and contemporary pieces for the home. Centuries and styles mingle in what is quintessentially a modern space created in an old barn, dedicated to furnishings, architectural joinery and interior design.

Tel: 01923 856343

e-mail: info@andrewbrownhome.com

Battlers Green Farm Shop food & wine

After 50 years, the Farm Shop remains the anchor of the shopping village, a genuine original that stocks everything you might expect, and more.

Tel: 01923 856551

e-mail: info@battlersgreenfarm.co.uk

Brimarks Butchers butchers of quality

An independent company that maintains the highest standards of animal welfare and purity while providing top-quality meats.

Tel: 01923 853591

The Bull Pen tearooms

When visiting Battlers Green don't forget to take a break in these attractive tearooms with their specious dining area and traditional décor.

Tel: 01923 857505

e-mail: thebullpen@btinternet.com

Classic Framing bespoke picture framing

Professional picture framing of the highest quality offered in a variety of materials.

Tel: 01923 853902

e-mail: classicframing@tiscali.co.uk

Destiny Rising holistics

Destiny Rising stocks sparkly crystals from all over the planet, along with incense, salts, oils, candles, books, CDs and gifts. One section offers treatments, courses and tarot and psychic readings.

Tel: 01923 852522

e-mail: dsetinyshop@tiscali.co.uk

Suzanne Constantine Shoes style in colour

Stylish, colourful ladies shoes for that special occasion, crafted from the best quality leather and suede, with colours for all seasons. Sizes 35-42 (43-44 to order).

Tel: 07751 692592

e-mail: Suzanne.constantine@houseofcolours.co.uk

Fired Earth sanitaryware

A unique resource for people with a sense of individuality and authenticity who want to create beautiful homes in their chosen style. Tiles, paints. Flooring for kitchens and bathrooms.

Tel: 01923 855382

e-mail: radlett@firedearth.com

The Flower Grove florists

Shoppers are invited to come and browse among the beautiful displays, bouquets, bunches and plants, or enquire about the bespoke floral service for any special event.

Tel: 01923 858377

The Loose Box pet store

Hertfordshire's premier pet store supplies a range of high-quality food for all pets including many natural feedstuffs, along with collars, leads. brushes, bowls and other accessories.

Tel: 01923 852616

Maine Sail fishmongers

Daily supplies of the finest and freshest fish direct from the sister company at Billingsgate.

Tel: 01923 853177

e-mail: info@mainesail.com

WATFORD

5 miles S of Hemel Hempstead on the A411

Bedford Almshouses · Museum

Cheslyn House

Originally a country market town, Watford was transformed in the 19th century by the arrival of the railway, which brought new industry and new building. Among the few earlier buildings to survive the rapid development are the five-gabled **Bedford Almshouses**, which date back to 1580, and the early 18th-century Fuller and Chilcott school. On the high street stands the splendid Mansion House, once the offices of the Benskin Brewery and now home to **Watford Museum**, where visitors can learn about the industrial and social history of the town. The local brewing and printing industries feature prominently, along with a tribute to Watford Football Club.

In the north of the town, off the A411 Hemel Hempstead road, Watford Council manages the gardens at **Cheslyn House**. The 3½-acre garden, "Watford's Best Kept Secret", has woodland, lawns, a bog garden, rock garden, splendid herbaceous borders and an aviary, and is open from dawn to dusk every day except Christmas.

Tring

St Mary's Church · Mansion House

Natural History Museum at Tring

Market House

Situated on the edge of the Chiltern Hills and on the banks of the Grand Union Canal, Tring is a bustling little market town whose character has been greatly influenced by the Rothschild family. However, the members of this rich and famous family are not the only people of note to be associated with the town. In **St Mary's Church** can be found the grave of the grandfather of the first US president, George Washington, while the 17th-century **Mansion House**, designed by Sir Christopher Wren, was reputedly used by Nell Gwynne.

The town's narrow winding High Street, off which lead little alleyways and courtyards, contains many late-Victorian buildings, all designed by local architect William Huckvale. Of particular note is the **Market House**, built by public subscription in 1900 to commemorate, albeit a little late, Queen Victoria's Diamond Jubilee. A fine example of the Arts and Crafts style, so popular at the turn of the century, the building was later converted into a fire station and today it serves as the town council chamber.

The old Silk Mill, first opened in 1824, once employed over 600 people, but towards the end of the 19th century the silk trade fell into decline and Lord Rothschild ran the mill at a loss to protect his employees rather than see them destitute. Unable to carry on in this fashion, the mill closed to the silk trade and, after losing some of its height, the building was converted into a generating station. From 1872 to the 1940s, the Rothschild

Tring Church

family lived at Tring Park and from here they exercised their influence over the town. Perhaps their greatest gift to the town is the Walter Rothschild Zoological Museum, now the **Natural History Museum at Tring**, one of the finest collections of stuffed mammals, birds, reptiles and insects in the UK. It includes examples of several animals now extinct, and a model of a dodo. The collection was given to the nation by Lionel Walter, 2nd Baron Rothschild, on his death in 1937. An eccentric man with a great interest in natural history, Walter collected more than 4000 rare and extinct species of animals, birds and reptiles.

Tring's focal point is The Square, remodelled in 1991 and featuring an ingenious Pavement Maze in the form of a zebra's head – a tribute to Walter's work. The town's war memorial, unveiled in 1919, stands in The Square, as does the flint and Totternhoe stone Church of St Peter and St Paul. Dating chiefly from the 15th century, this parish church contains some fine medieval carvings as well as 18th-century memorials.

Extending south from close to the town centre, Tring Park provides 300 acres of excellent walking.

Around Tring

MARSWORTH

2 miles N of Tring off B489

Nature Reserve

Mentioned in the Domesday Book and situated on the banks of the Grand Union Canal, Marsworth was known as Mavvers to the canal people. The village is home to the **Tring Reservoirs National Nature Reserve** (see panel on page 224). The four reservoirs were built between 1802 and 1839 to store water for the then Grand Junction (now Grand Union) Canal, which reached its summit close by. Declared a nature reserve in 1955, this is a popular place for bird watchers,with a nature trail and a variety of trees and marshland flora.

ALDBURY

2 miles E of Tring off A4251

Ashridge Estate

Ashridge Management College

Bridgewater Monument

This picturesque village, with its green, pond, stocks, village shop, timber-framed houses and parish church, dates back to Saxon times and is often used as a film location. There was once a castle in the village that is said to have disappeared in a flash of light sometime during the 14th century. The story goes that the castle's owner, Sir Guy de Gravade, in league with the Devil, raised the dead from their graves and from them learned the secret of turning base metals into pure gold. One night a servant, having seen his master at work, decided to experiment on his own; the results were disastrous, for the castle and all the residents within were engulfed in a flash of lightning.

The village lies on the western boundary

The Stocks, Aldbury

Tring Reservoirs

Wilstone, Hertfordshire HP23 4LN
website: www.tring.gov.uk/info/reserv.htm

When the Grand Junction Canal was built, between 1793 and the early 1800s, it opened up the first cost-effective trading route between the new Industrial towns of the Midlands and London's markets and ports. Products were being mass-produced for the first time in history and the canals provided the vital link between producers and customers. Black Country coal could be delivered cheaply to London, making it affordable to poor families. Farmers could send their grain and livestock to the big cities, making farming a profitable business and reducing the fear of famine for city dwellers.

In the 1830s, new locks were dug alongside some of the existing locks to speed up boat traffic through busy sections of canal. Take a close look at the bridge at Startop's End and the dry dock at the Wendover Arm junction and you can see where these locks were located. To calculate how many locks full of water to supply to the canal each day, the Reservoir Attendant has to estimate the number of boats likely to cross the summit. This is based on the time of year and readings from automatic counters in the locks. The weather must also be checked· on a sunny day as much as 25 mm (1 inch) of water can evaporate from the summit pound.

The Reservoirs are connected to Tringford Pumping Station by a network of underground, brick-lined passageways. Water flows through these, by gravity, to deep wells beneath the station. When the pumps are switched on, water rises up the wells, into the Wendover Arm Canal and then flows to the summit. Water is usually taken from Wilstone Reservoir first with Startop's End as a back up. Tringford Reservoir is rarely used to avoid sudden drops in water level, which would disturb the wildlife and trout fishery.

of the **Ashridge Estate**, formerly part of the estate of Lord Brownlow and now owned by the National Trust. With grounds and woodland extending to some 4000 acres on the Hertfordshire-Buckinghamshire border, this is a lovely place for walking and spotting the wealth of local flora and fauna. The focal point of the area is the **Bridgewater Monument**, an impressive tower that was erected in memory of the Duke of Bridgewater, who was famous for his pioneering work in the development of canals.

To the east of Aldbury, a mile south of Little Gaddesdon off the A4146, lie the 150 acres of **Ashridge Management College**, 90 acres of gardens and the rest woodland. Designed by Humphry Repton (he presented his Red Book to the 7th Earl of Bridgewater in 1813), the gardens were actually laid out by Sir Jeffrey Wyatville. Among the highlights are an Italian garden and fountain, a circular rosarie, a large oak planted by Princess (later Queen) Victoria, an avenue of Wellingtonias, a Bible garden, a sunken garden once used as a skating pond, and a grotto constructed from Hertfordshire pudding-stone.

NORTHCHURCH

3 miles SE of Tring on A4251

Grand Union Canal

On the south wall of the Church of St Mary is a memorial plaque to Peter the Wild Boy, who is buried close to the porch. Found living wild in a wood near Hanover, Germany, in 1725, he was brought to this country by the royal family and entrusted to the care of a farmer in this parish. He died in 1785 at an estimated age of 75.

Though the full length of the **Grand Union Canal** towpath in Hertfordshire can be walked, the section of canal from Northchurch to Tring has been developed with recreational use in mind. As well as the attractive canal-side walk, there are numerous maintenance and conservation projects to preserve this magnificent waterway and the wealth of wildlife and plant life found along its banks.

BERKHAMSTED

4 miles SE of Tring on the A4251

Castle Dean John Incent's House

It was in this historic town – one of Hertfordshire's five boroughs at the time of the Domesday Book – that William of Normandy, William the Conqueror, two months after the Battle of Hastings, accepted the British throne from the defeated Saxons. Shortly afterwards, William's half-brother Robert, Count of Mortain, commenced work on **Berkhamsted Castle**, which as a precaution against the low lie of the land was surrounded by a double moat. The castle entertained many distinguished visitors down the years: the Black Prince on honeymoon with his bride Joan, the Fair Maid of Kent; King John's wife Isabel, besieged in 1216 by the Barons; Thomas à Becket when he was Lord Chancellor; Geoffrey Chaucer as Clerk of the Works. The castle was a place of considerable importance until at least the 15th century, although now all but ruined.

One of the most interesting of the town's surviving ancient buildings is **Dean John Incent's House**, an impressive black and white timbered and jettied building in the main street opposite the 13th-century Church of St Peter. A notable feature of this church is a window dedicated to the poet William Cowper, who was born at the local rectory in 1731. The town's cultural connections reach modern times through an annual festival to Graham Greene, son of Berkhamsted School's headmaster, and frequent visitor JM Barrie, creator of Peter Pan. Berkhamsted lies in the Chilterns Area of Outstanding Natural Beauty.

LOCATOR MAP

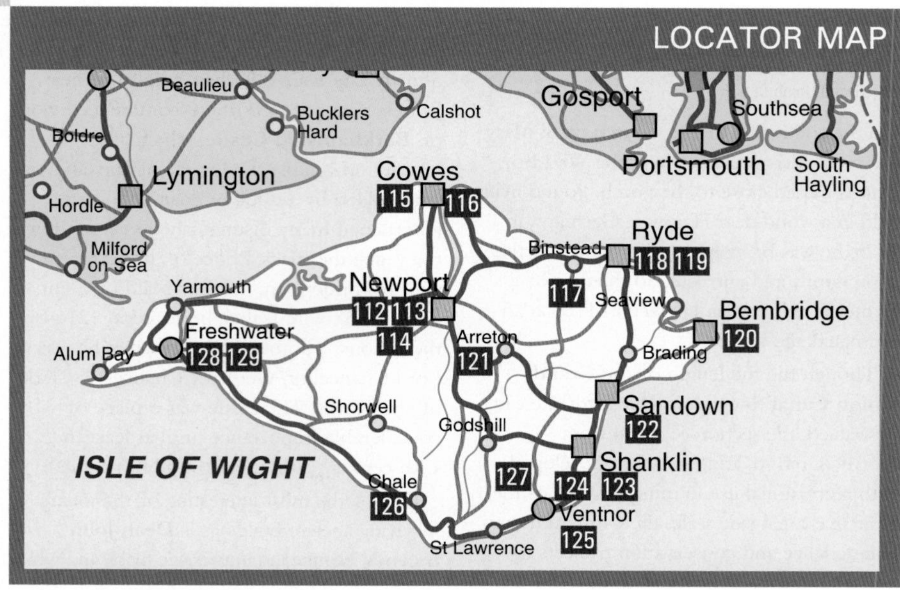

ADVERTISERS AND PLACES OF INTEREST

Accommodation, Food and Drink

120 | The Crab & Lobster Inn, Bembridge *pg 238*
123 | The Birkdale Guest House, Shanklin Old Village *pg 242*
124 | The Leconfield, Upper Bonchurch, Ventnor *pg 243*
126 | Gotten Manor, Chale, Ventor *pg 245*
127 | Little Span Farm, Wroxall, Ventor *pg 246*
128 | Braewood Bed & Breakfast, Freshwater *pg 248*
129 | Seahorses, Freshwater *pg 249*

Activities

117 | Isle of Wight Steam Railway, Havenstreet *pg 234*
122 | Dinosaur Isle, Sandown *pg 241*

Arts and Crafts

112 | Forget Me Not, Newport *pg 228*
118 | IW Natural Candle Co, Ryde *pg 235*

Giftware

118 | IW Natural Candle Co, Ryde *pg 235*

Home & Garden

118 | IW Natural Candle Co, Ryde *pg 235*
125 | Distinctive Designs, Ventnor *pg 244*

Jewellery

113 | St Thomas Jewellers, Newport *pg 229*

Places of Interest

114 | Carisbrooke Castle, Carisbrooke *pg 230*
115 | Cowes Maritime Museum, West Cowes *pg 232*
116 | Barton Manor, East Cowes *pg 233*
121 | Arreton Manor, Arreton, Newport *pg 240*

Specialist Food and Drink Shops

119 | The Kandy Box Ltd, Ryde *pg 236*

7 | Isle of Wight

The Needles

The Isle of Wight has adopted a motto that declares: All this beauty is of God. It echoes the poet John Keats, "A thing of beauty is a joy for ever", the first line of his poem *Endymion*, which he wrote while staying on the island in the hope that its crisp country air would improve his health.

Other distinguished visitors have described Wight as "The Garden Isle", and "England's Madeira", but it was quite late in the day before the island became popular as a resort. This was partly because for centuries, right up until the 1600s, the island was a first port of call for pestiferous French raiders who made the islanders' lives a misery with their constant incursions. These attacks ceased following the Napoleonic wars, but the turning point came in the 1840s when Queen Victoria and Prince Albert bought an estate near East Cowes. They demolished the existing house and Albert designed and built an Italianate mansion he named Osborne House. A few years later, the Poet Laureate, Alfred, Lord Tennyson, bought Farringford on the eastern side of the island. Socially, the Isle of Wight had arrived.

Most of the island's 125,000 residents (the mainland town of Peterborough outnumbers all of them by about 10,000), live in the northeast quadrant of the island, with its main resort towns of Sandown and Shanklin strung along the east coast. The rest of Wight is wonderfully peaceful with a quiet, unassertive charm all of its own.

Newport

Classic Boat Museum · Old Grammar School
Isle of Wight Bus Museum · Roman Villa
Quay Arts Centre · Parkhurst Forest

Set around the River Medina, Newport has a history going back to Roman times. Excavations in 1926 uncovered the well-preserved remains of a **Roman Villa**, a 3rd-century farmhouse in which one side of the building was given over entirely to baths. Visitors can follow the bather's progress through changing room, cold room, warm and hot rooms with underfloor heating systems, and integral cold and hot plunge baths. A Roman style garden has been re-created in the grounds and provides an interesting insight into the wealth of new plants the Romans introduced into Britain.

Newport received its first charter back in 1190, but the growth of the small town received a severe setback in 1377 when it was completely burnt to the ground by the French. Recovery was slow, and it wasn't until the 17th century that Newport really prospered again. Indirectly, the new prosperity was also due to the French since the island was heavily garrisoned during the Anglo-French wars of that period. Supplying the troops with provisions and goods brought great wealth to the town.

Some striking buildings have survived, amongst them God's Providence House, built in 1701 and now a tearoom; John Nash's elegant Town Hall of 1816, which is now occupied by the Museum of Island History, a charming Tudor **Old Grammar School**, and the parish Church of St Thomas, whose foundation stone was laid in 1854 by Queen

Hemel Hempstead

St Mary's Church · Charter Tower · Snook's Grave · Gadebridge Park

This is a place with two distinct identities: the charming old town centred around the ancient Church of St Mary and tranquil Gadebridge Park; and the new town, one of the first to be built following the Second World War, planned as an integrated series of communities, each with its own individual centre.

Gadebridge Park is an extensive expanse of open parkland through which runs the River Gade. The park's attractive walled garden adjoins the High Street of the old town alongside the grounds of **St Mary's**, which is an outstanding example of a large Norman parish church. Its interior has remained essentially unchanged since it was completed in 1180. St Mary's 200ft-high spire, made of oak and lead and added in 1340, is believed to be the loftiest in Europe.

Evidence of a settlement here long before the Norman Conquest can be found surprisingly close to the town's industrial area. Protected by a fenced enclosure and visible from the road, lies the mound of a Bronze Age barrow.

The **Charter Tower**, just inside one of Gadebridge Park's entrances, is reputed to be the tower from whose upper window Henry VIII handed down Hemel Hempstead's royal charter, but the tower was in fact built long after the charter was given. On the road close to the railway station is a curious stone tablet known as **Snook's Grave**, marking the spot where James Snook, a notorious highwayman, was hanged and buried. Thought to be the last person in England to be taken back to the scene of his crime for the ultimate punishment, Snook was found guilty in 1802 of robbing a postboy and killing him in the process.

The village of **Bedmond**, three miles southeast of Hemel Hempstead, was the birthplace of Nicholas Breakspear, the only British pope, who was elected in 1154 and took the name Adrian IV.

Charter Tower & Walled Garden, Hemel Hempstead

Around Hemel Hempstead

KING'S LANGLEY

2 miles S of Hemel Hempstead on the A4251

The home of Ovaltine, the drink invented in 1865 by a Swiss doctor called George Wander. His son Albert later took over the business. The King's Langley canal-side factory was built in 1912 and greatly expanded subsequently. Local farms produced eggs, barley, milk and malt for the popular drink, and the factory even had its own narrow boats on the Grand Union Canal. One of these boats has been renovated and bears the name *Albert*.

BATTLERS GREEN FARM

Common Lane, Radlett, Hertfordshire WD7 8PH
Tel: 01923 856551 Fax: 01923 857221
e-mail: paul@battlersgreenfarm.co.uk
website: www.battlersgreenfarm.co.uk

'The Gateway to Real Village Shopping'

Battlers Green Farm Rural Shopping Village has grown since 1960 from a single farm shop (which is still going strong) to a dozen or so highly distinctive stores. With its lovely farmland setting and ample free parking, the shopping village offers a unique experience.

Aga cookers and kitchenware

The Aga name has long been synonymous with good food and fine living. Its cookers are one of the world's most recognisable design icons and an Aga cooker is surprisingly easy to own!

Tel: 01923 289726

e-mail: radlett@aga-rayburn.co.uk

Andrew Brown furnishings

An eclectic mix of classic, period and contemporary pieces for the home. Centuries and styles mingle in what is quintessentially a modern space created in an old barn, dedicated to furnishings, architectural joinery and interior design.

Tel: 01923 856343

e-mail: info@andrewbrownhome.com

Battlers Green Farm Shop food & wine

After 50 years, the Farm Shop remains the anchor of the shopping village, a genuine original that stocks everything you might expect, and more.

Tel: 01923 856551

e-mail: info@battlersgreenfarm.co.uk

Brimarks Butchers butchers of quality

An independent company that maintains the highest standards of animal welfare and purity while providing top-quality meats.

Tel: 01923 853591

The Bull Pen tearooms

When visiting Battlers Green don't forget to take a break in these attractive tearooms with their specious dining area and traditional décor.

Tel: 01923 857505

e-mail: thebullpen@btinternet.com

ST THOMAS JEWELLERS

8 St Thomas Square, Newport,
Isle of Wight PO30 1SN
Tel: 01983 520515
e-mail: john@st-thomas-jewellers.co.uk
website: www.st-thomas-jewellers.co.uk

St Thomas Jewellers is a specialist in fine English and continental jewellery, porcelain and objects d'art. Proprietor John Cracknell offers a personal one-to-one service and specialises in fine diamond and gem jewellery, antique jewellery, Russian jewellery, Sitzendorf porcelain and English silver mounted claret jugs.

The attractive jewellers can be found in a lovely area of Newport town and its window displays often draws passersby in. Inside it is very elegant and it is the perfect place to shop if you are looking for a specific item or rare gift.

John buys top quality stones and has them set in London. St Thomas Jewellers is highly recommended and if you are looking to get engaged or married it is bound to have what you are looking for to ensure your partner says yes.

If it is something older you are looking for John has a wide selection of antique jewellery as well as second hand jewellery that can be had for a fraction of the price. Among the claret jugs available are silver and cranberry glass, silver and Bohemian cut glass and silver crystal glass.

Victoria's consort, Prince Albert. The church contains the tomb of the tragic Princess Elizabeth, daughter of Charles I, who died of a fever at the age of 14 while a prisoner at nearby Carisbrooke Castle.

There's also an 18th-century brewer's warehouse near the harbour, which now houses the **Quay Arts Centre**, incorporating a theatre, two galleries, a craft shop, café and bar; another old warehouse is home to the **Classic Boat Museum**. Among the highlights here are a 1910 river launch, Uffa Fox's Airborne lifeboat, Prince Philip's Flying Fox *Coweslip* and *Lady Penelope*, a fabulous speedboat once owned by the 1950s socialite Lady Docker. Other exhibits include beautifully restored sailing and power boats, along with engines, equipment and memorabilia, and a restoration project is a launch that belonged to the Beken family.

Next door to the Boat Museum is the **Isle of Wight Bus Museum**, which displays an impressive array of island buses and coaches and a former Ryde Pier tram. Housed within a former grain storage warehouse, the buses include an 1899 tramcar, 1920s Daimler, a 1950 Bedford OB and a Bristol Lodekka that completed a successful trip to Nepal.

Church Litten Park, on the site of an old churchyard whose Tudor gateway still remains, is a peaceful spot and interesting for its memorial to Valentine Gray, a nine-year-old chimney sweep, whose death in 1822 as a result of ill-usage by his master caused a national outcry.

To the northwest of Newport, **Parkhurst Forest** offers miles of woodland walks.

Around Newport

CARISBROOKE

1 mile SW of Newport, on the B3323/B3401

Carisbrooke Castle | Princess Elizabeth

Another quote from John Keats: "I do not think I shall ever see a ruin to surpass **Carisbrooke Castle**" (see panel below). The castle is set dramatically on a sweeping ridge and it's quite a steep climb up from the picturesque village to the massive gatehouse. It was built in 1598, but the oldest parts of the castle date back to Norman times, most notably the mighty keep, which, apart from Windsor Castle, is the most perfect specimen of Norman architecture in Britain. Archaeologists believe that the castle stands on the site of a Roman fort built some thousand years earlier.

Carisbrooke Castle

Carisbrooke, Isle of Wight PO30 1XY
Tel: 01983 522107

Dating from Saxon times, **Carisbrooke** is the Isle of Wight's foremost castle. Once prison to Charles I and home to Princess Beatrice, the castle is also famous for the donkeys that work in the well house. Throughout the summer costumed guides and colourful events bring the castle alive and its remarkable history is told in the museum and castle exhibitions. Open daily except 24-26 December and 1 January.

During the season costumed guides, or 'storytellers' as English Heritage prefers to call them, conduct visitors around the noble ruins. The most poignant of their stories concern Charles I and his youngest daughter, **Princess Elizabeth**. Charles was imprisoned here in the months before his trial and the guides will point out the mullioned window through which he unsuccessfully attempted to escape. After the King's execution, Cromwell's Council of State ordered that his daughter Elizabeth, "for her own safety", should also be incarcerated at Carisbrooke. The 14-year-old implored them not to send her to her father's former prison, but they were adamant. Elizabeth was a sickly child and less than a week after her arrival at the Castle she "was stricken by fever and passed away, a broken-hearted child of fourteen". The story touched the heart of Queen Victoria who set up a monument in St Thomas' Church in Newport where the Princess was buried. The effigy, in pure white Carrara marble, bears an inscription stating that it had been erected "as a token of respect for her virtues, and of sympathy for her misfortunes by Victoria R 1856".

More cheerful aspects of a visit to the Castle include the Donkey Centre. Donkeys walking a treadmill were once used to turn the huge 16th-century wheel in the well house to draw water from a well 161 feet deep. A light at the bottom of the well gives some idea of its depth. Before donkeys were trained to raise the water, the task was performed by prisoners, and nowadays visitors are invited to have a go at walking the treadmill themselves, as well as meeting the donkeys, all of whose names begin with a J.

Also within the Castle grounds are a Coach House Exhibition and Victorian Island Exhibition, the Isle of Wight Museum and a tearoom.

CALBOURNE

5 miles W of Newport off the B3401

Calbourne Mill

Calbourne Mill is a 17th-century watermill in full working order, with an overshot wheel, millstones and an 1896 roller plant. Also on site are a World War and Rural Museum, gardens, a putting green, peacocks, waterfowl and punting on the millpond.

Calbourne Water Mill

COWES

5 miles N of Newport, on the A3020

Cowes Maritime Museum · Cowes Week
Sir Max Aitken Museum · Osborne House

Cowes' origins as the most famous yachting resort in the world go back to the early 1800s. It was then a rather shabby port whose main business was shipbuilding. In 1811, the Duke of Gloucester came to stay and, as part of the rather limited entertainment on offer, watched sailing matches between local fishermen. The duke's patronage led to amateur gentlemen running their own race and founding a club. The Prince Regent joined in 1817 and, on his accession as George IV, it was first re-christened the Royal Yacht Club, and then the Royal Yacht Squadron with its headquarters in one of Henry VIII's castles. Nowadays,

Cowes Maritime Museum

Cowes Library, Beckford Road, Cowes,
Isle of Wight PO31 7SG
Tel: 01983 823433

The **Cowes Maritime Museum** is a must visit, for those exploring Cowes. It has a small exhibition area that currently displays model boats from the Maritime Collection.

The Museum has an extensive photographic and paper archive depicting yachting and the shipbuilding industry in Cowes, which is accessible by appointment only.

If you require more information about the archive collection of Cowes Maritime Museum please contact Corina Westwood - 01983 823433. You will need to make an appointment in order to access any reference materials.

The museum is situated within Cowes Library, which also houses a collection of maritime related books. Entrance to Cowes Maritime Museum is free of charge. (Contact the Isle of Wight Heritage Librarian, 01983 203880 - local.studies@iow.gov.uk)

Cowes Week is the premier yachting event of the year and a fixture in the aristocratic social calendar.

Shipbuilding was for centuries the main industry of East Cowes, making ships for the Royal Navy, lifeboats, flying boats and seaplanes. Many of the seaplanes took part in the Schneider Trophy races, which brought great excitement to the Solent in the inter-war years. Sir Donald Campbell's *Bluebird* was built here, and the hovercraft had its origins in what is now the home of Westland Aerospace. Westland's factory doors were painted with a giant Union Jack to mark the Queen's Jubilee in 1977 – a piece of patriotic paintwork that has been retained by popular demand. Two museums in Cowes have a nautical theme. The **Sir Max Aitken Museum** in an old sailmaker's loft in West Cowes High Street houses Sir Max's remarkable collection of nautical paintings, instruments and artefacts, while the **Cowes Maritime Museum** (free) charts the island's sea-faring history and has a collection of racing yachts that includes the Uffa Fox pair *Avenger* and *Coweslip.* (Uffa Fox, perhaps the best known yachtsman of his day, is buried in the Church of St Mildred at Whippingham, a few miles south of Cowes.)

Cowes

Across the River Medina, linked by a chain

ferry, East Cowes is most famous for **Osborne House**, a clean-cut, Italianate mansion designed and built by Prince Albert in 1846. Queen Victoria loved "dear beautiful Osborne" and so did her young children. They had their very own house in its grounds, a full-size Swiss Cottage, where they played at house-keeping, cooking meals for their parents, and tending its vegetable gardens using scaled-down gardening tools. In the main house itself, visitors can wander through both the State and private apartments, which are crammed with paintings, furniture, ornaments, statuary and the random bric-à-brac that provided such an essential element in the decor of any upper-class Victorian home. Osborne House possessed a special place in the Queen's affections. It had been built by the husband she adored with an almost adolescent infatuation: together they had spent many happy family days here. After Albert's premature death from typhoid in 1861, she often returned to Osborne. Her staff had instructions to lay out the Prince's clothes in his dressing-room each night, and the Queen herself retired to bed with his nightshirt clasped in her arms. In 1901 she returned to Osborne for the last time, dying here on January 22nd in her 83rd year, her death coincidentally signalling the beginning of the slow decline of the British Empire over which she had presided as Queen-Empress.

Osborne House and its grounds featured prominently in the film *Mrs Brown* (2001) starring Judi Dench and Billy Connolly, which explored the controversial relationship between the Queen and her Scottish ghillie, John Brown.

WHIPPINGHAM

3 miles S of Cowes on the A3021

Barton Manor

Queen Victoria also acquired **Barton Manor** (see panel below) at nearby Whippingham, a peaceful retreat whose grounds are occasionally open to the public. Prince Albert had a hand in the design of the gardens and of the ornate Church of St Mildred, where the contractor and co-designer was AJ Humbert, who was also responsible for Sandringham. The royal family regularly worshipped at St Mildred's, which is predictably full of royal memorials, including a monument to Victoria's son-in-law Prince Henry of Battenberg, who succumbed to malaria in Africa at the age of 38. Alfred

Barton Manor

Whippingham, East Cowes, Isle of Wight PO32 6LB
Tel: 01983 528989 Fax: 01983 528671

The estate of Barton is first mentioned in the Doomsday Book of 1086, and after a period as an Augustinian oratory was run as a farm until the 19th century. When Queen Victoria and Prince Albert bought Osborne House, **Barton Manor** became their home farm. In 1902, after the Queen's death, King Edward VII made a gift of Osborne to the nation and kept Barton Manor until 1922 when it was sold into private hands. The gardens are a real delight, with the rhododendron walk, the splendid rose maze, a water garden, a secret garden and the national collections of Watsonia and red hot pokers. The estate is open on special days in the year in aid of the local Earl Mountbatten Hospice.

Gilbert's wonderful Art Nouveau screen in the chancel arcade is a unique work of art; other notable pieces are a bronze angel and the font (both of them designed by Princess Louise, a daughter of the Queen), a memorial to Albert and a chair used by the Queen.

WOOTTON CREEK

3 miles W of Ryde, off the A3054

Butterfly World

Wootton Creek is notable for its ancient bridge and mill-pond, and as the western terminus of the **Isle of Wight Steam Railway** (see panel below) with an old wooden booking office and signal box moved from elsewhere on the island. It is also the home of **Butterfly World & Fountain World**. This complex comprises a sub-tropical indoor garden with hundreds of exotic butterflies flying free; a colourful Italian garden with computer-controlled fountains; a Japanese garden with Oriental buildings and a koi carp lake; plus a five-acre garden centre.

Quarr Abbey, Fishbourne

FISHBOURNE

2 miles W of Ryde on the A3054

Quarr Abbey

Fishbourne is the port where the car ferry from the mainland docks. Nearby **Quarr Abbey** is a handsome red brick Benedictine monastery built around 1910 near the ruins of a 12th-century Cistercian Abbey. The old abbey, founded by a certain Baldwin de Redvers, enjoyed 400 years of prestige and influence, owning much of the land and many of the grand houses, before its destruction in 1536.

The stone for the original Quarr Abbey at Fishbourne came from the quarries at nearby Binstead, where a major family draw is Brickfields Horse Country.

Isle of Wight Steam Railway

The Railway Station, Havenstreet,
Isle of Wight PO33 4DS
Tel: 01983 882204 Fax: 01983 884515
e-mail: havenstreet@iwsteamrailway.co.uk
website: www.iwsteamrailway.co.uk

The Isle of Wight Steram Railway operates a five mile stretch of historic railway, recalling the days when most of the Island was served by steam trains. Travel aboard delightfully restored carriages dating back to 1864, often hauled by a 19th century steam locomotive. Drive to Havenstreet Station with its large car park, or travel in by train via Smallbrook Junction. At Havenstreet Station you will find our well stocked railway shop, licensed cafe, museum, woodland walk and children's play area. Trains operate selected days March - October (daily June - Sept) Talking Timetable 01983 884343.

HAVENSTREET

3 miles SW of Ryde off the A3054

IOW Steam Railway · Parkwood Forest

Headquarters and nerve centre of the **Isle of Wight Steam Railway** (see panel opposite), Havenstreet has a small workshop and museum, gift shop and refreshment room. The locomotives working the line date back as far as 1876 and include a tiny A1 class engine acquired from the London, Brighton & South Coast Railway in 1913, and a W14, named *Calbourne*, which was built in 1891 and came to the island in 1925. The carriages and goods wagons are of a similar vintage. Call: 01983 882204.

The road south from Cowes to Newport (A3020) passes by the edge of **Parkwood Forest**, 1000 acres of ancient royal hunting forest now managed by the Forestry Commission. From the car park and picnic area a waymarked trail leads through the forest, which is one of the few remaining safe houses for the red squirrel.

RYDE

9 miles NE of Newport, on the A3054

St Mary's Church · Appley Tower · Waltzing Waters · Puckpool Park

Ryde is the largest town on the island and its attractions include a huge expanse of sandy beach and a half-mile-long pier, one of the first to be built in Britain. Passenger ferries from Portsmouth dock here, the hovercraft service settles nearby, and the car ferry from the mainland disgorges its cargo a couple of miles to the west. The town is essentially Victorian, a popular resort in those days for affluent middle-class families. Then, as now, visitors enjoyed strolling along the elegant Esplanade with its sea views across Spithead

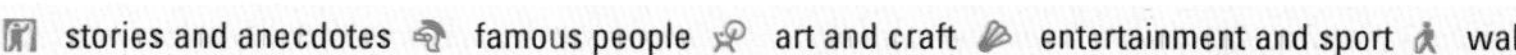

THE KANDY BOX LTD

23 Cross St, Ryde, Isle of Wight PO33 2AA
Tel: 01983 566123

If you have got a sweet tooth you will find it hard to resist the tempting delights on offer in this old fashioned sweet shop and milkshake bar. Tracy Dutch opened **The Kandy Box** seven years ago after a complete refurbishment was carried out by her husband Geoffrey.

He has done a fantastic job, and now jars full of colourful sweets draw plenty of passersby in. The shop is well known among the residents of Ryde and visitors to the town return to stock up on their favourites.

A delicious selection of sweets is available here and they are sold per 100g from the jars that line the shelves. There really is something for everyone with bon bons, sherbert lemons, coconut mushrooms, fudge, pear drops and violet creams among the many treats on offer.

Aside from the sweets, confectionary, hot savouries, sandwiches, milkshake, cup cakes and hot drinks are all sold here.

Sound to Portsmouth.

Reminders of the town's Georgian and Victorian heyday are still here in abundance, among them a fine arcade in Union Street opened in 1837, the year of Queen Victoria's accession. The town has some important churches including All Saints, which was designed by Sir George Gilbert Scott, and the Roman Catholic church of **St Mary's**, which boasts a Pugin chapel.

On the beach by Appley Park stands **Appley Tower**, built as a Victorian folly and now open to the public as a centre for fossils, crystals, natural gems, oracles and rune readings. Another public space is **Puckpool Park**, a leisure area behind the sea wall between Ryde and Seaview. It surrounds what was once a battery, built in the 19th century; its last gun was removed in 1927. At the Westridge Centre, just off the A3055 road to Brading, **Waltzing Waters** is an indoor water, light and music 40-minute spectacular performed several times daily in a comfortable modern theatre. There's also a gift shop and coffee lounge.

SEAVIEW

2 miles SE of Ryde, on the B3330/B3340

Seaview Wildlife Encounter

To the east of Ryde, the aptly named resort of Seaview has a good beach with clean firm sand, ideal for making sandcastles. There are little rock pools where small children can play in safety while trying to catch the abundant crabs and shrimps. Lines of clinker-built wooden dinghies bob about on the waves, and out to sea rise two of Palmerston's Follies – forts constructed in the 1850s as a warning signal to the French to keep away.

A short distance west of Seaview, on the B3330, lies **Seaview Wildlife Encounter**, whose colonies of flamingos, penguins, macaws and waterfowl are among the largest in the country. Visitors are encouraged to join in feeding the birds and also the giant carp and koi carp.

ST HELENS

4 miles SE of Ryde, on the B3330

Sophie Dawes' Cottage

Famed for its picturesque harbour and magnificent village green, St Helen's straggles down the hillside above the mouth of the River Yar, a quiet spot beloved by yachtsmen. It must be the only English village to be named after a Roman Emperor's wife – the Helen who was the wife of Constantine and in whose honour a church was erected here in AD704.

Another 'royal' figure, the Queen of Chantilly, was actually born in the village, and if the name is unfamiliar to you, seek out **Sophie Dawes' Cottage**, which bears a wall plaque stating that "Sophie Dawes, Madame de Fouchères, Daughter of Richard Dawes, Fisherman and Smuggler, known as the Queen of Chantilly, was born here in 1792". As a young girl, Sophie left St Helens to seek her fortune in London where she worked (non-professionally) in a Piccadilly brothel for a while before ensnaring the exiled Duc de Bourbon and becoming his mistress. The Duke paid for her education and, when he was able to return to France, took her with him, marrying her off to a compliant Baron. Eventually, she married her Duke, now Prince de Condé and having made sure that his will was in order, contrived his murder. Although she was tried for the crime, political considerations led to the case being quietly dropped. Sophie returned to England with her ill-gotten gains, but in her last years she seems to have been stricken with remorse and gave lavishly to charity.

BEMBRIDGE

5 miles SE of Ryde, on the B3350

Windmill   Maritime Museum

Roy Baker Heritage Centre

The most easterly point of the island, this popular sailing centre was itself an island until the reclamation of the huge inland harbour of Brading Haven in the 1880s. The story of that major work is one of many aspects of the town's history that features in the **Shipwreck Centre & Maritime Museum**, which also displays ship models, artefacts from shipwrecks, and diving equipment, as well as action videos of underwater footage and lifeboat rescues. Call: 01983 533079. A fascinating exhibition of life in Bembridge, past and present, is portrayed in photographs and artefacts at the **Bembridge Roy Baker Heritage Centre** in Church Road.

Also well worth a visit is the **Bembridge**

Bembridge Windmill

THE CRAB AND LOBSTER INN

32 Forelands Field Road, Bembridge PO35 5TR
Tel: 01983 872244
e-mail: info@crabandlobsterinn.co.uk
website: www.crabandlobsterinn.co.uk

Dating back in parts to the 1800s, **The Crab and Lobster Inn** is an award-winning traditional pub which specialises in seafood in addition to the usual pub menu.

Little is known about the early history of the inn, but a building without a name was shown on the 1862 map and this may have well been the inn, which became the focal point for coastguards, fishermen and smugglers.

Today, the main inn is decorated in a traditional fashion with its intimate beamed interior, wooden floors, nautical paraphernalia and open fires in the winter. The restaurant, which overlooks the patio and the sea, are lighter and more airy, but still decorated in a traditional fashion.

The Crab and Lobster Inn has a comprehensive menu with a heavy seafood influence but the traditional pub favourites and vegetarian options are all there too. At lunch time there is an additional smaller light bite menu to supplement the main menu. This coupled with an ever changing special board ensures there really is something for everyone at the pub.

Food is served from noon - 2.30pm every lunch time and from 6pm - 9pm Sunday - Thursday and 6pm to 9.30pm on Friday and Saturday. A limited menu is served from 2.30pm - 5.30pm at weekends and in holiday times.

Outside there is a wonderful patio area which directly overlooks the Solent and in particular Bembridge Ledge. Many guests like to enjoy refreshments sitting at the traditional wooden picnic tables on the patio area in the summer months when the building is adorned with a mass of hanging baskets and planters which give it a real splash of colour.

The pub has five B&B rooms, all with en-suite facilities. There are two twin doubles, one double, one small double and a family room (for two adults and two children). The two front rooms have a stunning view over the Solent and make it ideal for the perfect escape. With the award winning pub below those staying do not have to look far for a good meal but guest must make sure they leave room for the full English breakfast provided as part of the room rate.
Car parking is restricted at this cliff top location but located a minute walk behind the premises is further parking for the general public.

Windmill (National Trust). Dating from around 1700, it is the only windmill to have survived on the island and much of its wooden machinery is still intact. There are spectacular views from the top floor.

BRADING

2 miles N of Sandown on the A3055

Nunwell House & Gardens Morton Manor
Lilliput Museum Roman Villa

For what is little more than a large village, Brading is remarkably well-stocked with visitor attractions. Amongst them are a diminutive Town Hall with whipping post and stocks outside, and a fine church housing some striking tombs of the Oglander family. The most ancient of the village's sights is the **Brading Roman Villa**, which in the 3rd century was the centre of a rich and prosperous farming estate. Discovered in 1880, the villa covers some 300 square feet and has fine mosaic floors with a representation of that master-musician, Orpheus, charming wild animals with his lyre.

The Lilliput Antique Doll & Toy Museum exhibits more than 2000 dolls and toys, ranging across the centuries from around 2000BC to 1950. The collection also includes dolls' houses, tinplate toys, trains, rocking horses, and many unusual and rare playthings.

On the edge of the village stands **Morton Manor**, a lovely old house, dating back to 1249, largely rebuilt in 1680, and now set amidst one of the finest gardens in England. The landscaped grounds feature rose and Elizabethan sunken gardens, ponds and cascades, and many mature specimen trees, including the largest London Plane you are ever likely to see. Other attractions include the Stable Shop, licensed tearooms, a safe children's play area with a traditional Elizabethan turf maze, and even a vineyard. In fact, Brading has two vineyards. The other is the well-known Adgestone Vineyard, planted in 1968 and the oldest on the island. Entry is free, as is the wine-tasting, there are pony trap rides around the vineyard during the season, a gift shop and café.

A mile or so northwest of the village, **Nunwell House and Gardens** should definitely not be missed. This picturesque house has been a family home since 1522 and is of great historic and architectural interest. It was here that Sir John Oglander, an ancestor of the present owner, was host to Charles I on his last night of freedom, and today's visitors can still see the Parlour Chamber in which they met. The house is beautifully furnished, there are exhibits recalling the family's military connections, and the five acres of tranquil gardens enjoy views across the Solent.

Some of the grandest views on the island can be enjoyed from **Brading Down**, just west of the village on the minor road that leads to Downend.

ARRETON

5 miles W of Sandown on the A3056

Arreton Manor

From Downend, it's less than a mile to **Arreton Manor** (see panel on page 240), which claims, with some justification, to be "the most beautiful and intriguing house on the Isle of Wight". There was a house on this site long before Alfred the Great mentioned Arreton in his will of AD885, and the manor was owned by successive monarchs from Henry VIII to Charles I. The present house was built during the reigns of Elizabeth and James I and is a superb example of the architecture of that period, with mellow stone walls and Jacobean panelling complemented by

Arreton Manor

Main Road, Arreton, Newport,
Isle of Wight PO30 3AA
Tel: 01983 522604
e-mail arretonmanor@mac.com
website: www.arretonmanor.co.uk

The present house was built in the late Elizabethan/early Jacobean times although the east wing is considered to be 14th century and is constructed on part of the much older Manor, which belonged to "Alfred the Great" and was left to his younger son Etherward in his will of 885AD. The manor was endowed to the Monks of Quarr in the 12th century and farmed by the abbot's steward, but was snatched back by Henry VIII around 1536 during the dissolution of the monasteries. There is still a monastic screen in the Hall erected in 1396. As you enter the manor there is an overwhelming feeling of history and as a visitor to the manor you are in good company as other visitors have included Charles I, Queen Victoria and Queen Mary. The ancient stone steps, heavily worn, must have seen the passing of hundreds of thousands of feet to be in this condition.

The interior of the manor gives you an insight of how the wealthy lived in the 17th century. There is also a much older part of the manor to explore where you can follow in the footsteps of the monks; you may also find one or two surprises on the way. In the grounds you will find one of the largest Horse chestnut trees in England and the conifer, which Queen Victoria planted on the south lawn.

furniture from the same era. Perhaps the most appealing aspect of Arreton is that indefinable atmosphere of a house that has been lived in for centuries. Other attractions here include a Museum of Childhood, Lace Museum, National Wireless Museum, gift shop, tearooms and picnic area.

NEWCHURCH

2 miles W of Sandown on the A3056

Amazon World Zoo Park

Amazon World Zoo Park is a popular family attraction that tells the story of the rainforest with the help of a large number of exotic animals and birds – conservation is the name of the game here. One of the Island's most renowned products is garlic, and the annual Garlic Festival, held in Newchurch on a weekend in August, attracts many thousands of visitors. The village church and its steeple are, unusually, clad in wood.

ALVERSTONE

2 miles NW of Sandown, off the A3055

The secluded and picturesque village of Alverstone sits beside the tiny River Yar. It has everything you expect of an English village – except for a pub. The deeds of the estate's owner, Lord Alverstone, specifically forbid the sale of intoxicating liquor within the village.

Sandown

Zoological Gardens

Dinosaur Isle

"A village by a sandy shore" was how a guide-book described Sandown in the 1870s. Since then, its superb position on sweeping

Sandown Bay has transformed that village into the island's premier resort. Now a lively town, Sandown offers its visitors every kind of seaside attraction. There are miles of flat, safe sands where a Kidzone safety scheme operates during the season; a traditional pier complete with theatre; colourful gardens; a Sunday market; abundant sporting facilities; and even pleasure flights from the nearby airfield.

On the edge of the town, the **Isle of Wight Zoological Gardens** specialises in breeding severely endangered exotic species, and is home to the UK's largest variety of Royal Bengal, Siberian and Chinese tigers. The zoo is also a World Health Organisation centre for venomous snakes, their venom extracted for use in antidotes for snake bites. You may well see TV "Snake Man" Jack Corney handling these lethal reptiles, and children who are photographed with a small harmless snake are presented with a handling certificate to prove it. There are all-weather snake and parrot shows, a kiddies' play area and Pets' Corner, a seafront pub and café, the Zoofari Gift Shop, and a snack bar. A Road-Runner Train operates frequent services between the zoo and the town centre.

In Sandown's Culver Parade, **Dinosaur Isle** (see panel below) is Britain's first purpose-built dinosaur attraction, and contains many exhibits from the former Museum of Isle of Wight Geology. Dinosaur Isle is especially popular with children who love its life-sized dinosaurs – the Isle of Wight is renowned for the number and quality of the dinosaur remains that have been discovered here. The museum, "120 million years in the making", has excellent displays on all aspects of the island's geology. As part of its educational programme, museum staff will advise you on the best places to look for fossils and, when you return with your discoveries, will identify them for you.

Throughout the season, the Sandown Bay area hosts a wide range of special events – from the Regatta in August to Sunday markets, from the Isle of Wight Power Boat Festival in May to the National Strong Man finals in September.

SHANKLIN

2 miles SW of Sandown, on the A3055

Shanklin Chine Heritage Centre

Like Sandown, Shanklin was just a small village a century or so ago. The old village has survived intact, a charming little complex of thatched houses standing at the head of the

Dinosaur Isle

Culver Parade, Sandown, Isle of Wight PO36 8QA
Tel: 01983 404344
website: www.dinosaurisle.com

In a spectacular pterosaur shaped building watching over Sandown's blue flag beach is Britain's first purpose built dinosaur museum. Walk back through fossilised time to the period of the dinosaurs where you will find amongst the fossils many interactive displays. On a recreated landscape enhanced by sights, smells and sounds you will meet life sized dinosaurs including our animatronic Neovenator. Guided fossil hunts (which must be pre booked) have proved to be a popular addition to a visit. For more information regarding opening times and admission prices, please call the museum.

Shanklin Chine. The famous Chine is a spectacular ravine some 300 feet deep, 180 feet wide, noted for its waterfalls and rare flora. There's a Nature Trail to follow or you can join a guided tour. The **Heritage Centre** contains an interesting exhibit on PLUTO (the Pipe Line Under The Ocean) secretively constructed during the Second World War to transport fuel from the island to the Continent during the D-Day landings. There's also a memorial to the soldiers of 40 Commando who trained in this area for the disastrous assault on Dieppe in 1942.

The old village stands on a 150 foot cliff from which the ground slopes gently down to the safe, sheltered beach, with its long, seafront esplanade. With its scenic setting, many public gardens, and healthy climate, Shanklin has appealed to many celebrities. Charles Darwin was particularly fond of the town, the American poet Longfellow fell in love with it, and John Keats was a familiar figure in Sandown throughout the summer of 1818. The grassy open space known as Keats Green commemorates his stay here during which he wrote some of his best-known poems.

GODSHILL

4 miles W of Shanklin on the A3020

Church of All Saints · Nostalgia Toy Museum · Model Village · Natural History Centre

A short drive inland from Shanklin leads to the charming village of Godshill, which with its stone-built thatched cottages and its medieval **Church of All Saints** is one of the most popular stops on the tourist trail. The double-naved church, whose 15th-century pinnacled tower dominates the village, contains some notable treasures, including a 15th-century wall painting of Christ crucified on a triple-branched lily, a painting of Daniel in the Lions' Den and many monuments to the Worsleys and the Leighs, two of the leading island families.

Godshill has much to entertain visitors, including the magical **Model Village** with its 1/10th scale stone houses, trains and boats, even a football match taking place on the green. The miniature village was built with the help of model-makers from Elstree film studio, and after two years' preparation was opened to the public in 1952. The models are made of coloured cement and the detail is quite incredible. Real straw was prepared in the traditional way for thatching; the church on the hill took 600 hours of work before being assembled in its position; each house has its own tiny garden with miniature trees and shrubs. The airfield is in the style of small landing strips of the 1920s and 1930s, and the little railway is modelled on the older Island systems. Things get even smaller in the model garden of the model Old Vicarage, where there is another (1/100th scale) model village with yet another Old Vicarage, and within its garden another (1/1000th scale) model village – a model of a model of a model! There's also a (full-size) tearoom here with outdoor seating. The Model Village is open every day from 10am.

Also in Godshill are the **Nostalgia Toy Museum**, where 2000 Dinky, Corgi, Triang, Hornby and Matchbox toys and 1960s dolls bring back childhood memories, and the **Natural History Centre** with its famous sea-shell collection of more than 40,000 shells from both tropical and local shores. The display includes the world's tiniest shell, most poisonous shell mollusc and the most beautiful shells.

BONCHURCH

2 miles S of Shanklin on the A3055

The poet Algernon Swinburne spent some of his childhood in this lovely hilltop village and is buried in the churchyard of St Boniface.

DISTINCTIVE DESIGNS

74 High Street, Ventnor, Isle of Wight PO38 1LU
Tel: 01983 853555
e-mail: info@distinctivedesigns.co.uk
website: www.distinctivedesigns.co.uk

Distinctive Designs offers a complete interior design service. Founded in 1984, owners Michael and Jill Edwards have a showroom in Ventnor where they have an extensive library of fabric and wallpaper books for you to browse through. They also offer a home consultation service where they can gain a better understanding of your requirements.

Whether it is a single blind or pair of curtains, Distinctive Designs can assist you at every step, from the choice of fabric to make-up and fitting. Distinctive Designs offers everything you need to decorate, refurbish or renovate your home which includes furniture, lighting and an upholstery service. They are also the Isle of Wight suppliers of Zoffany fabrics, wallpaper and paint, and Duresta furniture.

Distinctive Designs also offers a management service to oversee larger projects with comprehensive quotations and plans. They have a professional, qualified team of electricians, plumbers, carpenters and decorators to assist, whether it is a bathroom refurbishment or complete house renovation.

Distinctive Designs has a vast knowledge of what is available, what works and provide detailed quotations for all work. The services they offer are of the highest standard and they are extremely professional in their approach. A personal, one-to-one service is always at hand at Distinctive Designs, so whether it is a small or larger project, visit their showroom or phone to arrange a visit.

Charles Dickens wrote part of *David Copperfield* while staying in Bonchurch. His first impressions of the place were very favourable – "I think it is the prettiest place I ever saw". He seemed likely to make it his permanent home, but he soon grew to dislike the weather and the place and returned to his familiar Broadstairs.

VENTNOR

3 miles SW of Shanklin on the A3055

Heritage Museum · Visitor Centre

Botanical Gardens · Coastal Visitor Centre

St Boniface Down

Along the southeastern corner of the island stretches a six-mile length of ragged cliffs known as Undercliffe. Clinging to the slopes at its eastern end, Ventnor has been described as "an alpinist's town" and as "a steeply raked auditorium with the sea as the stage". Promoted as a spa town in the 1830s, its distinguished visitors have included a young Winston Churchill and an elderly Karl Marx.

Ventnor Heritage Museum houses a fascinating collection of old prints, photographs and working models relating to the town's history, while **Ventnor Botanical Gardens** shelters some 10,000 plants in 22 acres of grounds, amongst them many rare and exotic trees, shrubs, alpines, perennials, succulents and conifers. The exhibits at the **Visitor Centre** include an interactive display called The Green Planet – the Incredible Life of Plants. Many unusual varieties are for sale in the shop. There's a picnic area and children's playground, and during August the Gardens host open-air performances of Shakespeare's plays.

Back in town, the **Coastal Visitor Centre** provides a fascinating and educational insight into the island's coastal and marine environment, with special features on animal and plant life, coastal defences and living with landslides – a problem very familiar to the island as well as to many parts of England's south coast.

Above the town, **St Boniface Down** (National Trust), at 785 feet the highest point on the island, provides some dizzying views across coast and countryside.

ST LAWRENCE

1 mile W of Ventnor on the A3055

St Catherine's Point · Studio Glass

Blackgang Chine

Nestling in the heart of the Undercliff, the ancient village of St Lawrence has a 13th-century church that once laid claim to being the smallest in Britain. It was extended in 1842 but remains diminutive, measuring just 20 feet by 12 feet.

Not far away, old farm buildings were converted into **Isle of Wight Studio Glass**, where skills old and new produce glass of the highest quality.

Lord Jellicoe, hero of Jutland, lived for some years in St Lawrence and often swam in Orchard's Bay, a small cove where Turner sketched.

The coast road continues through the village of Niton to **St Catherine's Point**, the most southerly and the wildest part of the island, and an Area of Special Scientific Interest. Steps lead down to St Catherine's lighthouse and a path leads up to the summit of St Catherine's Hill, where the remains of a much older lighthouse, known as the Pepperpot, can be seen. Close by is the Hoy

GOTTEN MANOR

Gotten Lane, Chale, Ventnor, Isle of Wight PO38 2HQ
Tel: 01985 551368
e-mail: carthouse@gottenmanor.co.uk

Found in the village of Chale near the more well known town of Ventnor is **Gotten Manor**. This glorious estate dates back over a thousand years when it was believed to be an early Jutish settlement named Godyngton. The manor's current owner Caroline Gurney-Champion has details of manor's history as far back as the Doomsday book, complete with a charming set of early century photographs depicting the manor's occupants. The manor is now divided into bed and breakfast accommodation in the Old House, and self catering in the Milk House and the Cart House. The Old House has been described as 'B&B heaven,' with huge lime washed bedrooms, wooden floors, cast iron roll top baths and Persian rugs to create the feeling of old fashioned opulence. Evenings can be spent soaking in bubbles, bathed in candlelight with fluffy bathrobes and a rich glass of red wine – pure indulgence. Breakfasts are equally decadent with a scrumptious selection of local and organic produce from the island including Caroline's own homemade jams, marmalades and yoghurts.

Self catering is also popular. The 200 year old Milk House sleeps 6-8 people over three bedrooms in a stylish barn conversion, complete with its own garden, a shaker style kitchen and a sitting room with stunning sea views. The Cart House dates back to the 18th century, since having been converted into two luxuriously equipped cottages sleeping 2-5 people in two bedrooms. All accommodation has access to free wifi and broadband.

Blackgang Chine, St Lawrence

Monument erected in honour of a visit by Tsar Nicholas I.

Blackgang Chine, at the most southerly tip of the island, has been developed from an early Victorian scenic park into a modern fantasy park with dozens of attractions for children. Also inside the park are two heritage exhibitions centred on a water-powered sawmill and a quayside, with displays ranging from cooper's and wheelwright's workshops to a shipwreck collection, a huge whale skeleton and a 19th-century beach scene complete with a bathing machine. The coastline here is somewhat fragile, and a large slice of cliff has been lost to storms and gales in recent years.

WROXALL

2 miles N of Ventnor on the B3327

Appuldurcombe House

Owl & Falconry Centre   Donkey Sanctuary

Owls, falcons, vultures and donkeys all call Wroxall their home. **Appuldurcombe House**, once the grandest mansion on the whole island, with gardens laid out by Capability Brown, was badly bombed in 1943 and has never been lived in since. The building has been partly restored and visitors

LITTLE SPAN FARM

Rew Lane, Wroxall, Ventnor, Isle of Wight PO38 3AU
Tel: 01983 852419
e-mail: info@spanfarm.co.uk
website: www.spanfarm.co.uk

Little Span Farm in Wroxall, is an attractive stone farmhouse dating back to the 17th century, and is part of a working arable stock farm. Set in an Area of Outstanding Natural Beauty, it is ideal for walking and family holidays. Wroxall's main attraction is Appuldurcombe House and at Little Span you couldn't be any closer to this magnificent ruin since the farm used to part of the Appuldurcombe Estate. In this lovely peaceful setting Felicity Corry offers a choice of accommodation for Bed & Breakfast and self-catering guests. The Farmhouse has two en-suite double bedrooms and a double/twin with en suite shower. All have TV/video-player, beverage tray and hairdryer. The other B&B property is Harvester Cottage, located behind the farmhouse, with a king-size double-bedded room, bunk beds, a shower room and similar amenities to the farmhouse. A hearty full English breakfast along with vegetarian options is served in the dining room in the farmhouse. WiFI is also available to guests.

For self-catering guests The Stable has been recently converted to provide comfortable 'upside down' accommodation with a roomy farmhouse kitchen, an open-plan beamed living/dining area and a first-floor sun deck. It also has its own small-enclosed garden. The Brewhouse, sleeping four (double and bunk beds), plus extra sofa bed offers the visitor every comfort. Both these properties have spiral staircases linking the living and sleeping areas. Guests are free to roam round the farm, and children can help with feeding during the lambing season.

Appuldurcombe House, Wroxhall

can stroll in the 11 acres of ornamental grounds, which provide an enchanting setting for picnics. The **Owl and Falconry Centre**, in what used to be the laundry and brewhouse, stages daily flying displays with owls, hawks, buzzards, vultures and eagles from around the world and holds courses in the centuries-old art of falconry.

Heaven for 200 donkeys and many other animals, the **Isle of Wight Donkey Sanctuary** is at Lower Winstone Farm. The rescue centre is a registered charity relying entirely on donations, and visitors have several ways of helping, including an Adopt a Donkey scheme. Open spring and summer.

SHORWELL

7 miles SW of Newport, on the B3323

St Peter's Church · Yafford Mill

Pronounced Shorell by Caulkheads, as Isle of Wight natives are known, this village of thatched stone cottages has no fewer than three venerable manor houses within its boundaries. West Court, Wolverton and North Court were built respectively during the reigns of Henry VIII, Elizabeth I and James I. They possess all the charm you would expect from that glorious age of English architecture, but sadly none of them is open to the public. However, you can visit **St Peter's Church** to gaze on its mesmerisingly beautiful 15th-century wall-painting and admire its 500-year-old stone pulpit covered by an elaborate wooden canopy of 1620. The church also has a real oddity in a painting on wood of the Last Supper, brought from Iceland in 1898.

This small village boasts another attraction. **Yafford Mill** is an 18th-century water mill in full working order (it worked commercially until 1970). It's surrounded by ponds and streams where you'll find Sophie, the resident seal, and within the grounds there are paddocks that are home to rare cattle, sheep and pigs, a collection of antique farm machinery, a steam engine and narrow-gauge railway. There are also waymarked nature walks, a playground, picnic area, gift shop, tea gardens and a licensed bar.

BRIGHSTONE

8 miles S of Newport on the B3399

Dinosaur Farm Museum

Mottistone Manor Garden · Mottistone Common

One of the prettiest villages on the island, Brighstone was once notorious as the home of smugglers and wreckers. Today, the National Trust runs a shop in a picturesque row of thatched cottages, and there's a little museum depicting village life down the years.

The island has long been known for its fossil finds, especially relating to dinosaurs. On a clifftop near the village the bones of a completely new species of predatory dinosaur were unearthed. The 15 foot carnivore, which lived in the cretaceous period about 120 million to 150 million years ago, has been named cotyrannus lengi after Gavin Leng, a local collector who found the first bone. On Military Road (A3055) near Brighstone, the **Dinosaur Farm Museum** came into being following the unearthing in 1992 of the skeleton of a brachiosaurus, at that time the island's largest and most spectacular dinosaur discovery. This unique attraction follows the tale of this and other finds. Visitors are invited to bring their own fossils for identification, and the farm also organises guided fossil tours at various locations on the Island. There are plans to relocate the Museum in 2011. Call: 01983 740844.

A mile or so west of Brighstone, the National Trust is also responsible for **Mottistone Manor Garden**, a charming hillside garden alongside an Elizabethan manor house. The garden is particularly well known for its herbaceous borders and terraces planted with fruit trees. The Mottistone Estate extends from Mottistone Down in the north to the coast at Sudmoor. On **Mottistone Common**, where New Forest ponies graze, are the remains of a neolithic long barrow known as the Longstone.

FRESHWATER

11 miles W of Newport, on the A3055

Church of All Saints · Dimbola Lodge · Old Battery · Tennyson Down · Farringford · Tennyson Trail · The Needles · Needles Park

Freshwater and the surrounding area are inextricably linked with the memory of Alfred, Lord Tennyson. In 1850, he succeeded Wordsworth as Poet Laureate, married Emily Sellwood, and shortly afterwards moved to **Farringford,** just outside Freshwater. The house, set in 33 acres of parkland, is now a hotel where visitors can relax in the luxuriously appointed drawing room with its delightful terrace and views across the downs. Tennyson was an indefatigable walker, and however foul the weather, would pace along nearby High Down dramatically arrayed in a

BRAEWOOD BED AND BREAKFAST

Afton Road, Freshwater, Isle of Wight PO40 9TP
Tel: 01983 759910
e-mail: pamelasducks@tiscali.co.uk
website: www.braewood-iow.co.uk

Braewood Bed and Breakfast is located just minutes from Yarmouth and Freshwater Bay on the outskirts of Freshwater village on the Isle of Wight. This beautiful late Victorian establishment is run and owned by Pamela Thomas who works endlessly to create the perfect environment for a weekend or short break away. She has been awarded four stars from the Tourist Board for her efforts, which keep visitors returning year after year.

Pamela opens all year round offering luxuriously comfortably guest bedrooms, with full en suite facilities, colour TV and Freeview. Rooms range from standard double and twin rooms with private bathrooms to a large en suite room with a King size bed and its own balcony which commands stunning views across the surrounding countryside. Braewood has its own beautifully maintained gardens which roll right down to the banks of the River Yar where a wildlife reserve is open to explore. Guests are also welcome to enjoy a boat trip on Pamela's boat which is moored nearby, adding another interesting dimension to any stay here.

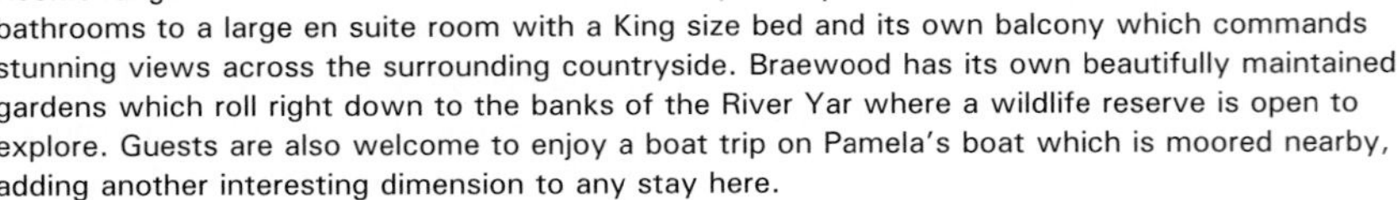

Guests can enjoy a full English breakfast with eggs from Pamela's own free range chickens and homemade jam. Home cooked meals are also available in the evenings on request. More information and photos can be found on Braewood's excellent new website.

SEAHORSES

Victoria Road, Freshwater, Isle of Wight PO40 9PP
Tel: 01983 752574
e-mail: seahorses-iow@tiscali.co.uk
website: www.seahorsesisleofwight.com

Since 1999 **Seahorses**, a four star bed and breakfast on the west side of the Isle of Wight, has been welcoming visitors to the island. Located near Freshwater Bay, where there is a thatched church and close to the ferry port and yacht harbour at Yarmouth, the guest house comes with its own art studio.

There are five guest rooms available, all of varying size. The spacious rooms offer comfortable accommodation for families and just a short drive in any direction leads to a beach for children to play. The reasonable tariff includes a hearty breakfast, which can be enjoyed in the dining room. It is also known as the 'Africa Rooms, because of the African prints, weaving, batique and embroidery on show.

Seahorses also has an attractive self-catering cottage available all year round. Studio Cottage is located next to Seahorses Art Studio and has been built as a stable conversion, with two bedrooms (one double and a twin) plus a study/bedroom. The kitchen/dining/sitting room is open plan and looks out onto a small lawn and orchard.

At Seahorses there is an opportunity to do some art and craft, beginners are welcome. Depending on your time there are various activities from T-shirt printing to sculpting. Prices vary according to materials used.

billowing cloak and a black, broad-brimmed sombrero. After his death, the area was re-named **Tennyson Down** and a cross erected high on the cliffs in his memory.

There are more remembrances of the great poet in the **Church of All Saints** in Freshwater town where Lady Tennyson is buried in the churchyard and a touching memorial inside commemorates their son Lionel, "an affectionate boy", who died at the age of 32 while returning from India. As Tennyson grew older, he became increasingly impatient with sightseers flocking to Farringford hoping to catch sight of the now-legendary figure. He moved to his other home at Blackdown in Sussex where he died in 1892.

About a mile south of the town, Freshwater Bay was once an inaccessible inlet, much favoured by smugglers. Today, the bay is the start point of the 15-mile **Tennyson Trail**, which ends at Carisbrooke, and its scenic beauty attracts thousands of visitors every year. They also flock in their thousands to **Dimbola Lodge**, one of the most important shrines in the history of early photography. It was the home of Julia Margaret Cameron (1815–1879) who bought it in 1860 to be close to her friend, Tennyson. Three years later, she was given a camera and immediately devoted herself with her usual energy to mastering the technical and artistic aspects of what was then called the 'Black Art'. (Because handling the chemicals involved usually left the photographer's hands deeply stained.) The coal-house at Dimbola Lodge was turned into a dark room and, within a year, Julia had been elected a member of the Photographic Society of London. She photographed most of the leading lights of the artistic community of the time including Thackeray, Darwin, GF Watts and his wife the actress Ellen Terry, who all at some time lived locally. Perhaps the most famous of her images is the classic portrait of Tennyson himself, a craggy, bearded figure with a visionary gaze. Dimbola Lodge was acquired by the Julia Margaret Cameron Trust in 1993 and it has been converted into a museum and galleries devoted to her photography. There's also a gift shop, antiquarian bookshop and vegetarian restaurant.

From the bay itself, there are regular cruises around the island's most spectacular natural feature, the dreaded **Needles**. The boat trip takes you through the swirling waters around the lighthouse, and past the line of jagged slabs of gleaming chalk towering some 200 feet high. The sea has gouged deep caves out of the cliffs. Two of them are known as Lord Holmes' Parlour and Kitchen, named after a 17th-century Governor of the Island who once entertained his guests in the 'Parlour' and kept his wines cool in the 'Kitchen'.

The Needles are undoubtedly at their most impressive when viewed from the sea, but they are still a grand sight from the land. There are some particularly striking vistas from the **Needles Old Battery** (National Trust), a Victorian coastal fort standing 250 feet above the sea. Visitors pass through a 200-foot long tunnel and emerge onto a platform with panoramic views.

Needles Park, Alum Bay

Alternatively, **Needles Park** at Alum Bay also has good views and offers a wide range of family entertainments, a chairlift from the clifftop to the beach, boat trips to the lighthouse, a glass-making studio and many other attractions. In the car park at Alum Bay is a monument to Marconi, who sent messages to a tug in Alum Bay and set up the first wireless station here in 1897. The first paid Marconigram was sent in the following year by Lord Kelvin.

YARMOUTH

10 miles W of Newport, on the A3054

Castle Fort Victoria Country Park

Sir Robert Holmes

A regular ferry links this picturesque little port to Lymington on the mainland. Yarmouth was once the principal port on the island, which was why Henry VIII ordered the building of **Yarmouth Castle** (English Heritage) in the

Yarmouth Castle

1540s. It was garrisoned until 1885, but is now disused, though much remains. The town also boasts a quaint old Town Hall, a working pier, and a 13th-century church rather unhappily restored in 1831. It's worth going inside to see the incongruous statue on the tomb of **Sir Robert Holmes**, Governor of the Island in the mid 17th century. During one of the

Beach next to Fort Victoria Park, Yarmouth

endless conflicts with the French, Sir Robert captured a ship on board which was a French sculptor with an unfinished statue of Louis XIV. He was travelling to Versailles to model the King's head from life. Sir Robert decided that the elaborate statue of the King (in full French armour) would do nicely for his own tomb. The sculptor was ordered to replace the Royal head with Sir Robert's. No doubt deliberately, the artist made a poor fist of the job and the head is decidedly inferior to the rest of the statue.

One mile west of this appealing little town, **Fort Victoria Country Park**, owned by the Isle of Wight Council, is one of the major leisure complexes on the island and occupies the area around one of Palmerston's forts. Set on the Solent coastline, the park offers an enormous range of attractions. There are unspoilt sandy beaches, woodland walks, and Ranger-guided tours around the park highlighting the local and natural history of the area. Within the park you'll also find the largest model railway in Britain, a state-of-the-art Planetarium and Astronomy Resources Centre, a Marine Aquarium with some 80 different species of local and tropical fish, and a Maritime Heritage Exhibition. Speedboat trips are also available from the slipway next to the Boathouse Lunch & Tea Gardens.

NEWTOWN

5 miles E of Yarmouth off the A3054

Colemans Animal Farm

Founded in the 13th century by a Bishop of Winchester, Newtown once had a large, busy harbour, but silting led to its decline as a maritime centre and the harbour is now a nature reserve. At its height, the town was the most important on the island and regularly sent two MPs to Westminster; among them were John Churchill, later the 1st Duke of Marlborough, and Prime Minister George Canning. The town's most notable building is the Old Town Hall, erected in 1699 and now owned by the National Trust. A small, unassuming building of brick and stone, it contains many interesting documents and memorabilia. The records include the exploits of Ferguson's Gang, an anonymous group of benefactors who gave donations to save selected properties. It is not recorded why this building was chosen, but in 1934 one of the gang went into the National Trust offices and discreetly dropped £500 on the secretary's desk to save the town hall.

At Porchfield, two miles east of Newtown, fun in the country for the whole family is promised at **Colemans Animal Farm**, where visitors are encouraged to stroke and feed the animals, which include goats, guinea pigs, chipmunks, chinchillas and more. Children will also love the huge wooden play area, the sandpit, the straw maze, straw fun barn, model railway and the mini-farm with pedal tractors.

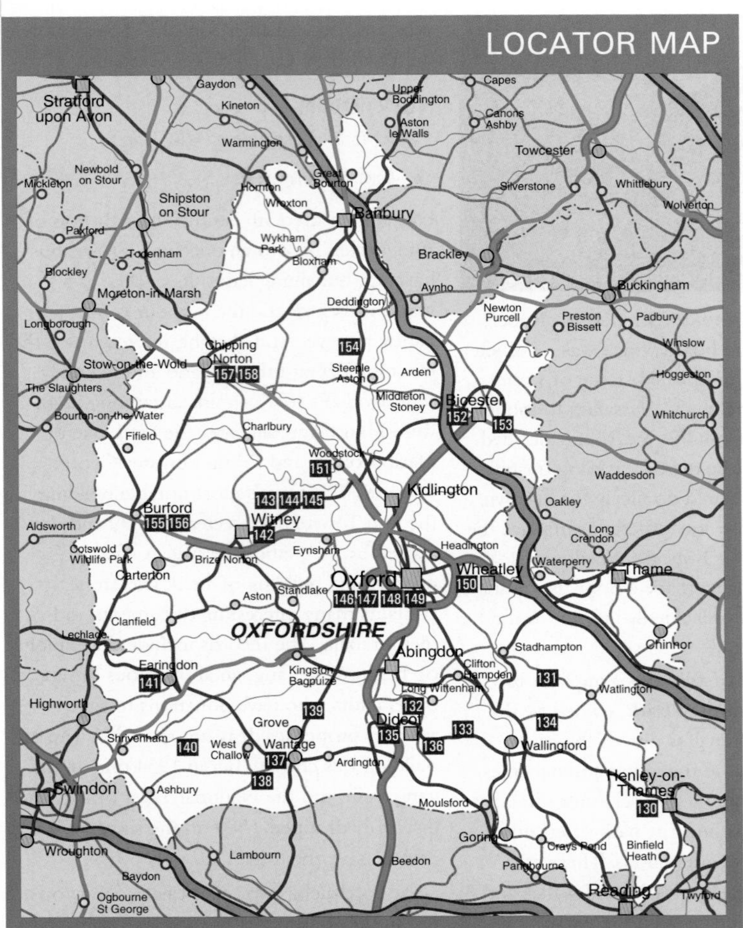

ADVERTISERS AND PLACES OF INTEREST

Accommodation, Food and Drink

131 | The Red Lion Inn, Chalgrove *pg 258*
133 | Red Lion, Brightwell-cum-Sotwell *pg 262*
134 | Fords Farm B&B, Ewelme, Wallingford *pg 263*
136 | The Bear At Home, North Moreton, Didcot *pg 264*
138 | Brook Barn Country House, Letcombe Regis *pg 267*
140 | Norton House, Uffington, Faringdon *pg 269*
149 | The Woodstock Road Deli, Oxford *pg 279*
152 | The Newland's, Bicester *pg 286*
154 | The White Horse Inn, Duns Tew *pg 288*
156 | Burford House, Burford *pg 294*
157 | The Chequers, Chipping Norton *pg 297*

Activities

135 | Didcot Railway Centre, Didcot *pg 264*

Antiques and Restoration

150 | Country Collections, Wheatley *pg 280*

Arts and Crafts

137 | Dolphin Art, Wantage *pg 266*
143 | Arts Inc, North Leigh, Witney *pg 272*
144 | Graham's Studio and Gallery, North Leigh *pg 272*
145 | Cuckoo Lane Studio, North Leigh, Witney *pg 272*
155 | Burford Woodcraft, Burford *pg 293*
158 | The Persian Shop and Art Gallery, Chipping Norton *pg 298*

historic building museum and heritage historic site scenic attraction flora and fauna

8 | Oxfordshire

Oxfordshire is a county covering about 1000 square miles, contained largely within the Thames Basin. Between Henley and Wallingford lie the beginnings of the Chiltern Hills, while in the north are the most easterly hills of the Cotswolds as well as rich farmland based on the clay soil that stretches up from Oxford to the Midlands. In the east, Henley is one of many attractive Thames-side settlements, towards the west are Faringdon and Witney, and in the north, Bicester, Chipping Norton and Banbury. The county is of course dominated by its capital, Oxford, which from the 12th century grew from a small and little known market town into one of the major seats of learning in the world. It also prospered as a central point of communication, first as a stopping point on coaching routes and later with the coming of the canals and the railways. Industry grew, too, and in the suburb of Cowley, Lord Nuffield's Morris car works were a major employer. Many palaeolithic, mesolithic and neolithic finds have been made in the county, but the most eyecatching early archaeological feature is the Uffington White Horse from the Iron Age. Dorchester and Alchester were the most important sites in Roman Oxfordshire, the Saxons built many settlements along the Thames, and the Danes over-ran the area in the 10th and 11th centuries. The county was heavily involved in the Civil War (1642-1651) and the towns of Oxford (for three years the Royalist headquarters), Banbury and Wallingford were all besieged by Parliamentary forces during the conflict.

ADVERTISERS AND PLACES OF INTEREST

stories and anecdotes · famous people · art and craft · entertainment and sport · walks

Henley-on-Thames

Greys Court | River & Rowing Museum | Fawley Court Museum | Regatta

Reputed to be the oldest settlement in Oxfordshire, this attractive riverside market town has more than 300 listed buildings from various periods. The Thames has always played an important role in its life; in 1829 the first varsity boat race, between Oxford and Cambridge, took place here on the river and, within a decade, the event was enjoying royal patronage. First held in 1839, the **Henley Regatta** takes place every year in the first week of July, is a marvellous and colourful event with teams from all over the world competing on the mile-long course. Scores of tents and striped marquees are erected on the Berkshire side of the river and champagne flows freely.

Opened in 1988, the **River and Rowing Museum** is a fascinating place that traces the rowing heritage of Henley, the river's changing role in the town's history, and even provides the opportunity to 'walk' the length of the River Thames, from source to sea, taking in all the locks. Housed in spacious, purpose-built premises designed by the award-winning architect, David Chipperfield, its exhibits include the boat in which the British duo, Steve Redgrave and Matthew Pinsent, won their gold medals at the 1996 Olympics. A major attraction re-creates Kenneth Grahame's much-loved tale *The Wind in the Willows*. In a spectacular walk-through exhibition visitors can meet all the familiar characters and places in the book, with EH Shepard's illustrations brilliantly brought to life. The Museum is open from 10am every day.

Henley was the site of Rupert's Elm, where Prince Rupert is said to have hanged a Roundhead spy. A portion of the tree is preserved in this museum. Also situated on the riverbank, beside the town's famous 18th-century five-arched bridge decorated with the faces of Father Thames and the goddess Isis, is the Leander Club, the headquarters of the famous rowing club.

Apart from the boating, which is available throughout the summer, and the pleasant walks along the riverbanks, there are many interesting shops, inns, and teashops in the town. Buildings of note include Speaker's House, home of Speaker Lenthall of the Long Parliament who lived there in the 17th century, some attractive almshouses around the churchyard, and Chantry House, which dates from the 14th century and is believed to be the oldest building in Henley.

Just down river from the town centre lies **Fawley Court**, a wonderful private house that was designed by Christopher Wren and built in 1663 for Colonel William Freeman. Now owned by the Marian Fathers, the **Museum** within contains a library, documents relating to the Polish kings, and memorabilia of the Polish army. The Court is not generally open to the public.

To the northwest of Henley, at Rotherfield Greys, is another interesting house, **Greys Court** (National Trust), dating originally from

Hart Street, Henley-on-Thames

the 14th century, but much altered down the years; a beautiful courtyard and a tower survive from the earliest building. A Tudor wheelhouse is among the interesting outbuildings, and the gardens offer many delights, notably old-fashioned roses and wisterias, an ornamental vegetable garden, a ha-ha, an ice-house, and the Archbishop's Maze, which was inspired, in 1980, by Archbishop Runcie's enthronement speech.

Mapledurham House

Around Henley-on-Thames

SONNING COMMON

3½ miles SW of Henley on the B481

Sonning Common was originally part of the manor of Sonning-on-Thames with the livestock driven up from the flooded riverside pastures to winter on the higher ground.

Widmore Pond, on the edge of the village, is said to have been a Roman silver mine: according to a 17th-century account, when the pond was emptied for cleaning out, upturned oak tree stumps were found in the bottom of the pond along with stag antlers and Roman coins.

MAPLEDURHAM

6½ miles SW of Henley off the A4074

Mapledurham House · Church of St Margaret

Watermill

A narrow winding lane leads to this famously picturesque village set beside the Thames. The cluster of brick and flint cottages and the church are overshadowed by the lovely Elizabethan mansion, **Mapledurham House**. It was built on the site of an older manor house by the Blount family and has remained with their descendants ever since. As well as viewing the great oak staircase and the fine collection of paintings, visitors will find the house's literary connections are equally interesting: Alexander Pope was a frequent visitor in the 18th century; the final chapters of John Galsworthy's *The Forsyte Saga* were set here; and it was the fictional Toad Hall in *The Wind in the Willows*. The house has also featured in films, including *The Eagle has Landed,* and the TV series *Inspector Morse.*

Another attraction on the estate is the old riverside **Watermill**, a handsome late 15th-century construction, which stands on the site of an earlier building that was mentioned in the Domesday Book. The mill remained in operation until 1947 and it was then the longest surviving working mill on the river. Now fully restored, the traditional machinery can be seen in action grinding wholemeal flour, which is then sold through the mill shop.

The **Church of St Margaret** has a number of notable features. It provided a major location for the film *The Eagle has Landed* and is believed to be the only church in the country to have had a king's son as vicar – Lord Augustus FitzClarence, one of William IV's 10 illegitimate children by the actress Mrs Jordan, was appointed to the living in 1829.

Another curiosity here is that the south aisle is owned outright by the Blount family and partitioned off from the rest of the church. Major restoration was carried out in 1863 by the architect William Butterfield who made great use of coloured brickwork and also refaced the tower with a bold chequered pattern using flint and brick.

GORING-ON-THAMES

9½ miles W of Henley on the B4009

This ancient small town lies across the River Thames from its equally ancient neighbour, Streatley, and, while today they are in different counties, they were once in different kingdoms. This is a particularly peaceful stretch of the river, with the bustle of Pangbourne and Henley-on-Thames lying downstream, and it is some distance to the towns of Abingdon and Oxford further upstream.

In the 19th century, after Isambard Kingdom Brunel had laid the tracks for the Great Western Railway through Goring Gap, the village began to grow as it was now accessible to the Thames-loving Victorians. Though there are many Victorian and Edwardian villas and houses here, the original older buildings have survived, adding an air of antiquity to this attractive place.

WATLINGTON

8 miles NW of Henley off the B480

Watlington Hill

There are superb views over the surrounding countryside from **Watlington Hill**, which rises 700 feet above Watlington Park with its woods of beech and yew. Watlington Hill and its neighbour Pyrton Hill are designated a Site of Special Scientific Interest and are home to over 30 species of butterflies and a wide

Watlington Hill

variety of chalk-loving plants.

EWELME

9 miles NW of Henley off the B4009

At the centre of this pretty village is a magnificent group of medieval buildings, including the church, almshouses and school, which were all founded in the 1430s by Alice Chaucer, granddaughter of the poet Geoffrey, and her husband, the Duke of Suffolk. There is a wonderfully elegant alabaster carving of Alice inside the church and under this effigy is another rather macabre carving of a shrivelled cadaver. In the churchyard is the grave of Jerome K Jerome, author of *Three Men in a Boat*, who moved to the village following the success of his book.

CHALGROVE

10 miles NW of Henley on the B480

Chalgrove is the site of an English Heritage registered Battlefield, where in 1643 Prince Rupert defeated John Hampden. An information board at the site gives details of the battle, and there is also a monument to John Hampden, a local squire and sometime MP for Buckinghamshire who refused to pay Ship Money to the King. He was taken to court in 1638 and incarcerated in the Tower of London. He was a cousin of Oliver Cromwell and in the Civil War became a leading opponent of the King.

THE RED LION INN

115 High Street, Chalgrove, Oxfordshire OX44 7SS
Tel: 01865 890625

The Red Lion is a Free House owned by the Church, dating back to the 15th Century, in the delightful village of Chalgrove, Oxfordshire.

Ray and Sue Sexton, the landlords, are both highly qualified chefs who have won many accolades, including being Head Chef and Patisserie Chef at one of only two pubs in Essex to gain a place in the coveted Michelin Pub Guide, and to be named Food Pub of the Year for East Anglia whilst they were at the helm.

They have built up their growing reputation based on a regularly changed a la carte menu, and a daily specials board that whets the appetite. All meals, including the desserts, are prepared in-house from the best seasonal ingredients available, with as much as possible sourced locally. Their whole ethos is, that excellently prepared and cooked food attracts customers who will return again and again; many do, travelling miles, and bringing friends or recommending them to others.

They have an excellent range of beers, real ales and wines to help you while away those convivial hours with friends.

The pub's front garden leads down to a babbling stream and to the rear there is a large garden (which can accommodate a marquee to seat 200 persons). There are plenty of tables and sun shades for eating outdoors on those balmy summer days, with plenty of space for children to play, who are most welcome. For the winter months there is the log fire to keep you warm and snug.

Ray and Sue are always willing to quote based on your budget and requirements for those special occasions, large or small, and everything will be tailored to make your event memorable.

If you are in or near South Oxfordshire and in need of sustenance, you will not better that available at the Red Lion, the diversion will be well worthwhile as countless others have found; you never know, you may well, and probably will, want to come again.

STONOR

4 miles N of Henley on the B480

Stonor

The village is the home of Lord and Lady Camoys whose house, **Stonor**, has been in the family for over 800 years. Set in a wooded valley in the Chilterns and surrounded by a deer park, this idyllic house dates from the 12th century, though the beautiful, uniform facade is Tudor and hides much of the earlier work. The interior of the house contains many rare items, including a mass of family portraits. There is also a medieval Catholic Chapel here that was in continuous use right through the Reformation. In 1581, Edmund Campion sought refuge at the house and from a secret room in the roof supervised the printing of his book *Decem Rationes* – Ten Reasons for being a Catholic. An exhibition features his life and work. The gardens, too, are well worth a visit with their lawns, orchard and lovely lavender hedges, and the splendid views they offer over the rolling parkland.

Abingdon

Church of St Helen Museum Abbey

This is an attractive town and one of the country's oldest as it grew up around a Benedictine **Abbey** that was founded in AD 675. Sacked twice by the Danes for its gold and silver, the abbey was practically derelict by the 10th century but, under the guidance of Abbot Ethelwold, the architect of the great Benedictine reform, it once again prospered and was, in its heyday, larger than Westminster Abbey. At one time the abbot here was the largest landowner in Berkshire after the Crown. Unfortunately little remains today of this great religious house, but the Gatehouse, built in the late 15th century, is a splendid reminder.

The largest town in the Vale of the White Horse, Abingdon was also the county town of Berkshire between 1556 and 1869. The prosperity this brought enabled the townspeople to build the impressive and outsize County Hall of 1678 that dominates the Market Place. This outstanding example of English Renaissance architecture was designed by a pupil of Sir Christopher Wren. In its former Assize court is the **Abingdon Museum**, which provides interesting insights into the town's history.

Another of Abingdon's pleasing buildings, set close to the lovely bridge over the Thames, is the **Church of St Helen** whose 150ft-high steeple dominates the skyline here. Originally built in the 14th century, the church was remodelled in the 15th and 16th centuries, when the town prospered from a thriving wool trade, to provide an altogether larger and

Abingdon Museum

more elaborate building. With its five aisles, it is now broader than it is long. The main glory of the church, the painted ceiling of the Lady Chapel, has been retained from the 14th century. Beside the churchyard, which contains a curious small building that was the blowing chamber for the church organ, are three sets of almshouses. The oldest, Christ's Hospital, was founded in 1446 while the other two, Twitty's Almshouses and Brick Alley Almshouses, date from the early 1700s.

Around Abingdon

DORCHESTER

5 miles SE of Abingdon off the A4074

Abbey Church | Abbey Museum

This charming little town, situated on the River Thame just before it flows into the River Thames, has been described as "the most historic spot in Oxfordshire", since it was here that Christianity was established in the southwest of England by St Birinus. Known as the Apostle of the West Saxons, Birinus was consecrated in Genoa, landed in Wessex in AD634, and converted King Cynegils of Wessex in the following year. As a mark of his devotion to the church, Cynegils gave Dorchester to Birinus and the church he built here became the cathedral of Wessex.

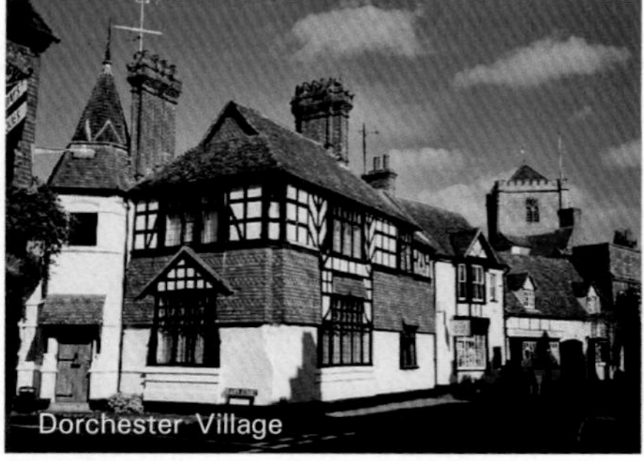
Dorchester Village

The **Abbey Church of St Peter and St Paul** was built in 1170 on the site of that Saxon church and greatly extended during the next two centuries. Its chief glory is the 14th-century choir and the huge Jesse window, showing the family tree of Jesus, which has retained its original stained glass. The story of the abbey, along with the history of settlement in the area going back to neolithic times, is told in the **Abbey Museum**, which is housed in a classroom of the former Grammar School, built in 1652. It has a series of displays, in the oak-panelled Old School Room, in the Abbey Guest House and in Abbey's Cloister Gallery.

The town itself has some attractive old houses with overhanging upper stories, a fine Georgian coaching inn, and a pleasant footpath that crosses fields to the bank of the Thames.

LITTLE WITTENHAM

5 miles SE of Abingdon off the A4130

Wittenham Clumps | Pendon Museum

This village, which has a number of pretty cottages, lies beneath the **Wittenham Clumps**, which for centuries formed an important defensive position overlooking the Thames. In the village church of St Peter are effigies of Sir William Dunch, a former MP for Wallingford, and his wife, who was the aunt of Oliver Cromwell. A little way northwest, towards the village of Long Wittenham, is the unique **Pendon Museum** (see panel opposite), which recaptures scenes showing the beauty of the English countryside through, detailed models. The main attraction is a model village built in tiny scale to resemble a typical 1930s village in the Vale of the White Horse. The model is the incredibly skilled and

Pendon Museum

Long Wittenham, Abingdon, Oxfordshire OX14 4QD
Tel: 01865 407365
website: www.pendonmuseum.com

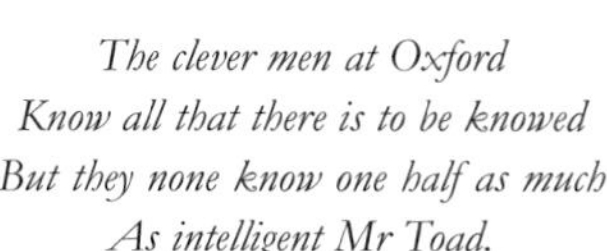

Pendon Museum at Long Wittenham in Oxfordshire is a delightful museum devoted to portraying parts of rural England as they were in the 1920s and 30s - in particular, it reflects how life was influenced by the transport infrastructure of the period. It achieves this through the medium of modelling - accurate, authentic and carried out to the highest standard at a 1:76 scale; literally art in three dimensions.

Pendon was founded in 1954 by Roye England, an Australian who first came to England in 1925 to patent an invention related to the control of model railways. It was not long before he found himself staying with a cousin in Wanborough, in the Vale of White Horse - a countryside that soon beguiled him with its rural charm. But Roye saw change in the offing, as he later wrote in the 1980s in "The Vale that Inspired Pendon".

The museum is run, and the models it displays are built, almost entirely by a number of dedicated volunteers and it is open to the public at weekends, on bank holidays and on Wednesdays in school holidays.

detailed work of Roye England, an Australian who came to this country in 1925 to study. The model incorporates a model railway (Roye England's first passion) and, as a tribute to the master, who died in 1995, there's a tiny model of himself in the 1:76 scale of the whole model. A highly detailed model of a Dartmoor scene is also in the display.

BLEWBURY

7 miles S of Abingdon on the A417

In the foothills of the Berkshire Downs, this pretty village was, and remains, a favoured spot for artists and writers. Among the latter was Kenneth Grahame, the author of *The Wind in the Willows*, who lived in a Tudor brick house in the village from 1910 to 1924. He wrote the book for his son, who tragically died while an undergraduate at Oxford. They are buried together in the churchyard of St Cross in Oxford. Mr Toad compares himself favourably with Oxford students in the book:

The clever men at Oxford
Know all that there is to be knowed
But they none know one half as much
As intelligent Mr Toad.

WALLINGFORD

8 miles SE of Abingdon on the A4130

A busy and prosperous town, Wallingford has been a strategic crossing point of the Thames since ancient times. Alfred the Great first fortified the town, against the Danes, and the Saxon earth defences can still be seen. It was here that William the Conqueror crossed the river on his six-day march to London. Wallingford was also an important trading town; it received its charter in 1155 and for several centuries had its own mint. During the Civil War, the town was a Royalist stronghold defending the southern approaches to Oxford, the site of the Royalist headquarters. It was besieged in 1646 by the Parliamentary forces under Sir

RED LION

Brightwell cum Sotwell, Oxfordshire OX10 0RT
Tel: 01491 837373
e-mail: sue@redlion.biz website: www.redlion.biz

The Red Lion is a traditional 16th century half timbered, thatched inn. It has played an integral part in village life for centuries, and continues to do so today.

Owned by Sue Robson, this charming pub and restaurant can be found nestled at the heart of one of Oxfordshire's most beautiful villages. Located in Brightwell cum Sotwell, The Red Lion was voted South Oxfordshires 'Pub of the Year' 2009 by CAMRA and is included in the 2009, 2010 and 2011 CAMRA Good Beer Guide.

The Red Lion has done well to recover from a devastating fire in December 2001 when a chimney fire set light to the thatched roof destroying much of the building and the adjoining cottage. It has re-established itself as a thriving village pub.

The staff members at The Red Lion, like Sue, are very friendly and everyone is made to feel very welcome, be they a regular or a visitor to the area. In its time the pub has even played host to royalty on two separate occasions. Firstly, George III dined there during a stag hunt in the area on November 7th 1781. In 1914 the Prince of Wales, later uncrowned Edward VIII visited it during his student days.

Sue is well known for her homemade bread, which she uses to make the wide range of sandwiches on offer. The lunch time menu offers varied choices including filo parcel stuffed with spinach & feta, and homemade chicken liver pate, served with toasted homemade bread, salad garnish and homemade chutney.

Sue and her team try to source the produce they use locally and the quality really shows. The pies are a speciality here, and are made with or without a pastry bottom with a choice of either homemade shortcrust or puff pastry top. Fillings include; roast chicken and leeks, mixed game in a red wine and juniper gravy, steak and kidney and Morrocan lamb and apricot.Sue and her team pride themselves on serving homemade pub classics with changes to the menu to reflect the seasons, such as liver and bacon, or stew and dumplings in the winter, and a range of tartlets and salads in the summer.

Drinks can be enjoyed in the light and airy bar and there is a good selection of traditional beers, fine wines and spirits available. Alternatively, on warmer days customers can sit outside at the front and watch the world go by, or relax in the beautiful Mediterranean style garden at the rear.

The Red Lion is open 12pm – 3pm and 6pm – 11pm Monday through til Saturday with evening times on a Sunday shortened to 7pm – 10.30pm. (Only basket meals are served on Sunday and Monday evenings).

FORDS FARM B&B

Ewelme, Wallingford, Oxfordshire OX10 6HU
Tel: 01491 839272
e-mail: fordsfarm@callnetuk.com
website: www.fordsfarm.co.uk

Nestled in the peaceful historic village of Ewelme near Wallingford is **Fords Farm**; the essence of Oxfordshire hospitality, surrounded by postcard-perfect countryside. The farmhouse here, part of which dates back to the 15th Century, has maintained many original features such as an inglenook fireplace and flagstone flooring, adding great character. The gardens too are traditionally styled, and have special features such as a yew hedge and crazy paving which give the feel of stepping back in time. Within a short distance from the farm is a beautiful walk along an ancient track thought to be Britain's oldest road.

For almost 20 years Fords Farm has run their successful, four star Bed and Breakfast. Even the most discerning visitors are breath-taken by the tranquillity of the village and farmhouse, and the high standard of the service. The delicately decorated rooms are spacious and filled with light; you are sure to have a comfortable night sleep, woken in the morning by the country sounds of the nearby church clock and the soft calls of collared doves. There are also two self contained self-catering cottages, fully equipped with everything you need during your stay, and opening out onto the pretty walled garden, they are perfect for a family trip or a quiet romantic getaway.

Thomas Fairfax and its walls were breached after a 12-week siege; it was the last place to surrender to Parliament. The castle built by William the Conqueror was destroyed by Cromwell in 1652, but substantial earthworks can still be seen and the museum tells the story of the town from its earliest days.

Buildings of note include the charming 17th-century Town Hall and St Mary's Church with its impressive tower.

SUTTON COURTENAY

2 miles S of Abingdon on the B4016

Church of All Saints

A pretty village that was mentioned in the Domesday Book, with an abbey that was founded in 1350. The village **Church of All Saints**, which dates back to Norman times, contains some fine stone carvings and woodwork, but the real interest lies in the churchyard. Here can be found the chest tomb of Herbert Asquith, the last Liberal Prime Minister (from 1908 to 1916) and his wife; they lived by the Thames not far from the church. Also here is the grave of Eric Blair, better known as George Orwell, author of *1984* and *Animal Farm*; several yew trees are planted here in his memory.

DIDCOT

4½ miles S of Abingdon on the A4130

Railway Centre

The giant cooling towers of Didcot's power station dominate the skyline for miles around and there is little left of the old town. But the saving grace is the **Didcot Railway Centre** (see panel on page 264), a shrine to the golden days of the steam engine and the Great Western Railway. Isambard Kingdom Brunel designed the Great Western Railway and its

Didcot Railway Centre

Didcot, Oxfordshire OX11 7NJ
Tel: 01235 817200 Fax: 01235 510621
website: www.didcotrailwaycentre.org.uk

The Great Western Railway was incorporated in 1835 to build the railway from Bristol to London and it was designed and engineered by Isambard Kingdom Brunel to be the finest in the land.

Now, at Didcot, half way between Bristol and London, members of the Great Western Society have created a living museum of the Great Western Railway. It is based around the original engine shed and depot to which have been added a typical branch line with a country station and signalling demonstrations and a recreation of Brunel's original broad gauge trackwork on which a replica of the Fire Fly locomotive dating from 1840 operates on special occasions. There is a large collection of GWR steam locomotives, carriages and wagons.

On steamdays the locomotives come to life and you can ride in the 1930s trains on one or both of the demonstration lines. Steamdays are on most weekends from March to September, public holidays (not Christmas), and Wednesdays from mid-July to the end of August. There is a programme of special events during the year, including 'Day Out with Thomas' with the children's favourite tank engine, and Family Activity Days with lots to keep the children entertained whilst mum and dad can try their hand at becoming an engine driver.

THE BEAR AT HOME

High Street, North Moreton, Oxfordshire OX11 9AT
Tel: 01235 811311
e-mail: tim@bear-at-home.co.uk
website: Bear-at-home.co.uk

The Bear at Home is a charming 500 year old country pub in the picturesque & historic village of North Moreton. The first impression is of a "homely", relaxed, pub, with low ceilings and nooks & crannies. The owners are antique dealers too, so many pieces in the pub are for sale.

Food is freshly prepared & wholesome, including fresh fish on the "specials" board, traditional steaks, salads & vegetarian dishes, as well as a range of filled baguettes. This is a popular pub with local residents & businesses, so it's wise to phone ahead to ensure you get a table.

The Bear is a regular in the Good Beer Guide, and at the end of July they run a Beer & Cricket Festival, over 4 days, with live music, so check their comprehensive website for up to date information. The cricket pitch is adjacent to the spacious beer garden, so cricket is a regular feature in the summer months- a quintessential English village scene.

route through Didcot, from London to Bristol, was completed in 1841. Until 1892, its trains ran on their unique broad gauge tracks and the GWR retained its independence until the nationalisation of the railways in 1948. Based around the engine shed, where visitors can inspect the collection of steam locomotives, members of the Great Western Society have re-created the golden age of the railway. The displays also include a beautiful re-creation of a country station, complete with level crossing. The locomotives on display include saddle tanks, pannier tanks and famous main-line engines, along with one of the very distinctive Great Western diesel railcars, this one, No 22, dating from 1940. The Firefly Trust built a reproduction of the broad-gauge Firefly locomotive of 1840. Steam days are held throughout the year when locomotives once again take to the broad gauge track and visitors can also see the Victorian signalling system and the centre's Relics Display.

NORTH MORETON

3 miles east of Didcot off the A4130

North Moreton is a quintessential English village whose spiritual heart is the 13th-century All Saints Church. Medieval stained glass panels depict 15 scenes from the lives of Christ, the Virgin Mary, St Peter, St Paul and St Nicholas.

Wantage

- Church of St Peter & St Paul
- Vale & Downland Museum

This thriving market town in the Vale of the White Horse was, in AD849, the birthplace of Alfred the Great and remained a Royal Manor until the end of the 12th century. In the central market place, around which there are

Church of St Peter & St Paul, Wantage

some fine Georgian and Victorian buildings, is a huge statue of the King with a battleaxe in one hand and a manuscript in the other, symbolising his skill as a warrior and his dedication to learning. Alfred spent much of his life (he died in AD899) defending his kingdom from the Danes in the north before being able to style himself Rex Anglo rum – King of the English.

Unfortunately, only the **Church of St Peter and St Paul** has survived from medieval times and, though it was heavily restored in 1857 by GE Street, various features have survived from the original 13th century structure. There's also a brass commemorating the life of Sir Ivo Fitzwarren, the father of Dick Whittington's wife, Alice.

Opposite the church is the **Vale and Downland Museum Centre**, which is located

DOLPHIN ART

23-24 Market Place, Wantage, Oxfordshire OX12 8AE
Tel: 01235 763030
e-mail: patrick@dolphinart.co.uk website: www.dolphinart.co.uk

Providing a friendly, informal place to browse local art and highly collectible limited editions, **Dolphin Art** is a gallery with an extremely high reputation in the art world.

Owners Patrick and Tara O'Leary offer a personal one to one service to customers, be it their first visit to the gallery or as an existing client. The couple has run the business since 1999 and recently revamped the whole shop. It is now an incredibly stylish destination shop for anyone with a fondness for art and it attracts a good number of people through its doors.

Dolphin Art is unique and as well as an impressive gallery it is an art materials stockist and picture framers. It is located in the delightful and charming market place of Wantage, Oxfordshire. This thriving market town in the Vale of the White Horse was, in 849AD, the birthplace of Alfred the Great and remained a Royal Manor until the end of the 12th century. In the central market place, around which there are some fine Georgian and Victorian buildings, is a huge statue of the King.

Dolphin Art is located nearby and its reputation as a quality picture framers draws customers in from far afield. Many return for Patrick and Tara's advice and patience as they choose from the considerable collection of bespoke frames on offer. There is also a fine selection of sculptures, glassware and ceramics, which are popular with visitors.

A wide range of materials for the professional amateur artist is stocked at this wonderful gallery. For younger artists there is a fabulous range of art materials to inspire children to get stuck in and let their creativity and imaginations flow.

Whatever your age, a visit to Dolphin Art can be highly recommended if you have a passion for art. There are frequent original art exhibitions held here as well as art demonstrations. Ring for details.

in another of the town's old buildings – a house dating from the 16th century – and a reconstructed barn. Dedicated to the geology, history, and archaeology of Wantage and the Vale of the White Horse, the displays cover the centuries from prehistoric times to the present day. The Centre has a café with a delightful terrace and garden.

It was in Wantage that the first steam tramway operated, opening in 1873 and surviving until 1948.

Just to the east of the town lies Ardington House, a beautifully symmetrical, early 18th-century building that is the home of the Baring family. Occasionally open to the public, the best feature here is the Imperial Staircase – where two flights come into one – of which this is a particularly fine example.

BROOK BARN COUNTRY HOUSE

Letcombe Regis, nr Wantage, Oxfordshire OX12 9JD
Tel: 01235 766502
e-mail: info@brookbarn.com website: www.brookbarn.com

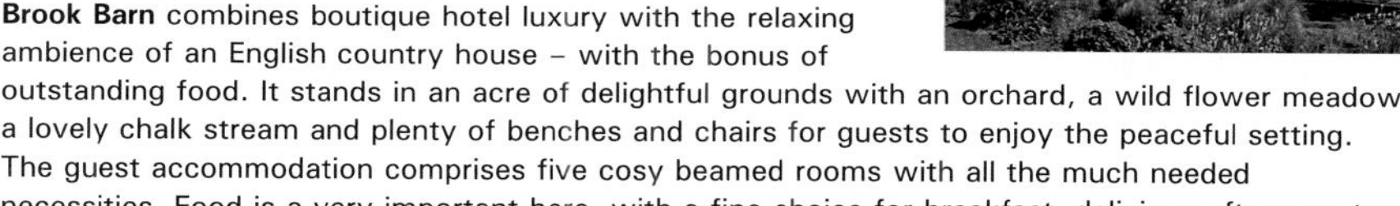

Brook Barn combines boutique hotel luxury with the relaxing ambience of an English country house – with the bonus of outstanding food. It stands in an acre of delightful grounds with an orchard, a wild flower meadow, a lovely chalk stream and plenty of benches and chairs for guests to enjoy the peaceful setting. The guest accommodation comprises five cosy beamed rooms with all the much needed necessities. Food is a very important here, with a fine choice for breakfast, delicious afternoon teas and an evening menu (optional) using fresh local produce.

DEWS MEADOW FARM SHOP

Oxford Road, East Hanney, Wantage OX12 0HP

Nestled in the grand market town of Wantage, in the Vale of White Horse, is the Dews Meadow Farm Shop; a delight for the eyes, and the taste-buds! This gloriously rustic farm shop prides itself in their delicious local produce. Dews Meadow is renowned for their pork products, which are loved by locals and visitors alike. Their range includes award-winning dry-cured green and smoked bacon, homecured hams and collars, and speciality home-made sausages and burgers, which are available in additive-free, low salt and gluten-free varieties. As well as these there are pork pies, hand-made sausage rolls, and a whole range of tempting treats. All of these pork delights are sourced from the Dews Meadow Farm, where traditional and ethical practice is a priority. The pigs are bred outside and are finished in a straw-based, unstressed system, where no growth-promoters, hormones, routine antibiotics, or added copper are used. Add the optimum mix of breeds, and the result is the flavour and tenderness of traditional pork. Having been trailblazers with additive-free pork and dry-curing of bacon since the mid-80's, Andy and Jane have developed a customer focused business, employing staff who echo their passion for quality and friendliness.

The shop is open Monday to Saturday 8:30am – 5pm (6pm on Friday).

e-mail: bowler.jane@btinternet.com

www.dewsmeadowfarm.co.uk

Around Wantage

KINGSTON BAGPUIZE

6 miles N of Wantage off the A420

Kingston Bagpuize House

The intriguing name of this straggling village goes back to Norman times when Ralf de Bachepuise, a contemporary of William the Conqueror, was given land in the area. The village grew to serve the needs of **Kingston Bagpuize House**, a fine mansion dated 1660 with superb gardens. Notable features include a magnificent cantilevered staircase, panelled rooms with some good furniture and paintings, Chinese porcelain and hand-painted wallpaper. Within the mature parkland are many noble trees and a woodland garden – a detailed map is available giving the names and precise location of almost 300 plants. There's also a tearoom and gift shop. Opening times are restricted – call 01865 820259.

STEVENTON

5 miles NE of Wantage on the A4185

Steventon is a small village of mostly modern housing, but in Mill Street stand the National Trust's Priory Cottages, former monastic buildings now converted into two houses. South Cottage contains the priory's original Great Hall, which can be visited in the summer by written appointment.

LETCOMBE BASSETT

2 miles S of Wantage off the B4001

Segsbury Camp

This tiny village, with a picturesque centre of thatched cottages, has a notable place in literary history: it appears as Cresscombe in *Jude the Obscure*, which Thomas Hardy wrote while staying here. Earlier, Jonathan Swift spent the summer of 1714 at the village's rectory where he was visited by the poet Alexander Pope.

Just to the east of the village lies **Segsbury Camp**, which is sometimes also referred to as Letcombe Castle. Set on the edge of the Berkshire Downs, this massive Iron Age hill fort encloses some 26 acres of land and provides panoramic views along the Vale of the White Horse.

KINGSTON LISLE

4½ miles W of Wantage off the B4507

The Blowing Stone

Just to the southwest of the attractive Norman Church of St John lies **The Blowing Stone** (or Sarsen Stone), a piece of glacial debris that is perforated with holes. When blown, the stone emits a fog-horn like sound and tradition has it that the stone was used by King Alfred as a

The Blowing Stone, Kingston Lisle

NORTON HOUSE

Broad Street, Uffington, Faringdon, Oxfordshire SN7 7RA
Tel: 01367 820230
e-mail: carloberman123@btinternet.com
website: www.smoothhound.co.uk/hotels/nortonfaringdon

Going that extra mile to give a personal touch that makes guests feel comfortable and relaxed from the moment they arrive is all in a day's work for owner of **Norton House** Fenella Oberman.

The guest house is charming and its beautiful garden is bursting with colour in the spring and summer. The house itself dates back to the 18th century and its quiet village location offers a relaxing getaway for those wanting to explore the local countryside with its ancient White Horse and the mysterious Waylands Smithy, linked by the Ridgeway path and offering excellent opportunities for walkers.

There are three comfortable guest rooms, one double, one twin/family (well behaved children welcome) and one single room, each with a private bathroom.

Home cooked full English breakfasts with free range local produce are definitely worth getting out of bed for and if you are after an evening meal there is a pub in the village and others nearby. Fenella makes her own bread, jam, marmalade and grows fruit in the garden – it doesn't get fresher than this.

trumpet to summon his troops.

UFFINGTON

5½ miles W of Wantage off the B4507

Tom Brown's School Museum   White Horse
Uffington Castle & Dragon's Hill

This large village was, in 1822, the birthplace of Thomas Hughes, the son of the vicar. The author of *Tom Brown's Schooldays*, Hughes incorporates many local landmarks, including the White Horse and Uffington Castle, in his well-known work. The **Tom Brown's School Museum** occupies the 380-year-old village schoolroom and tells the story of Hughes' life and works.

The village is perhaps best known for the **Uffington White Horse**. This mysteriously abstract and very beautiful figure of a horse, some 400 feet long, has been created by removing the turf on the hillside to expose the gleaming white chalk beneath. It is a startling sight, which can be seen from far and wide, and many a tantalising glimpse of it has been caught through the window of a train travelling through the valley below. Popular tradition links it with the victory of King Alfred over the Danes at the battle of Ashdown, which was fought somewhere on these downs in AD871, but modern thinking now considers that it dates from about 100BC.

Above the White Horse is the Iron Age camp known as **Uffington Castle**, and to one side is a knoll known as **Dragon's Hill,** where legend has it that St George killed the dragon.

GREAT COXWELL

8 miles NW of Wantage off the A420

Great Barn

This village is best known for the magnificent stone **Great Barn** (National Trust) of a

PRESENTATION GIFTS

6 London Street, Faringdon, Oxfordshire SN7 7AA
Tel: 01367 241111
e-mail: denise@presentationgifts.co.uk
website: www.presentationgifts.co.uk

'For the very best in Home, Interior Design, Giftware, Jewellery and Fashion'

Presentation Gifts is one of the very best places in the region to find something for the home, a personal treat or a beautiful present for a special friend. Denise Palmer bought an existing business at the beginning of 2005 and changed just about everything. With her knowledge of the local market and her eye for style and design she created a veritable oasis of wonder and luxury, a browser's delight that's guaranteed to bring a smile to all who pass through the door.

One room is given mainly to women's fashion and accessories and gifts for the home, with a small section for men, the other is filled with kids' toys and accessories aimed at 1 to 10 year olds. The choice throughout is wide and varied, always different and sometimes quirky, and many of the items would be hard to find elsewhere.

The range for ladies includes cardigans which change season to season, shoes, handbags, skincare products by Nougat, jewellery from an assortment of suppliers which includes individual peices from their Murano glass rings to handmade brooches from Shetland. The men's range is smaller but equally attractive, with luggage, table trivia, clocks and cufflinks among the items all personally chosen by Denise. For children there are table sets, cutlery, essential fairy dust, pretty dresses for the girls, pirates and monsters and vehicles for the boys, games, bunting and lots more.

There's also plenty to enhance the home, including cocktail sets, platters and dishes, jugs and mugs, Boujies soya wax candles and fun retro bunting. For putting the finishing touch to a gift the shop sells a wide range of gift wrap, tissue and ribbon, along with classic cards, invitation cards and thankyou notes. For those who can't get to the shop, Denise has created an online shop, a gorgeous showcase for finding something for everyone; gifts can be wrapped and sent with a personalised note to anywhere in the country or even worldwide.

Denise is passionate about her shop and about Faringdon, a pleasant little town between the Thames and the Ock in the Vale of the White Horse. It was the first capital of the ancient kingdom of Wessex, and Alfred the Great had a castle here. Denise has her home here and brought up her three children in the town, and is a busy and committed member of the business community.

monastic grange (farm) owned by the Cistercian Abbey at Beaulieu in Hampshire. Regarded as the finest medieval barn in England, it still has the original oak posts that have supported the roof for some 700 years. With Cotswold stone walls more than four feet thick, this huge barn was used to store the tithe – or taxes – received from the tenants of the church land.

BUSCOT

11 miles NW of Wantage on the A417

Old Parsonage and Park

This small village, in the valley of the upper Thames, is home to two National Trust properties: **Buscot Old Parsonage** and **Buscot Park** (both National Trust). The parsonage is a lovely house with a small garden on the banks of the River Thames and was built of Cotswold stone in 1703. The house is open by appointment only.

Buscot Park is a much grander affair, a classic example of a late Georgian house, built in 1780. It houses the magnificent Faringdon Art Collection, which includes paintings by Rembrandt, Murillo, Botticelli and Reynolds; one room is decorated with a series of pictures painted by Edward Burne-Jones, the pre-Raphaelite artist who was a close friend of William Morris. Painted in 1890, they reflect Burne-Jones's interest in myths and legends and tell the story of the Sleeping Beauty. The grounds of Buscot Park were largely developed in the 20th century and include a canal garden by Harold Peto, a large kitchen garden, a modern water feature and an Egyptian avenue created by Lord Faringdon in 1969 featuring sphinxes and statues based on originals in Hadrian's Villa outside Rome. Anyone interested in the work of Burne-Jones should also visit the village church, where a stained-glass window showing the Good Shepherd was designed by him in 1891, when he was working with William Morris's firm, Morris and Co. The church itself is very pleasantly situated by the river just outside the village.

Witney

St Mary's Church Museum

Cogges Manor Farm Museum

Witney Wool & Blanket Trail

Situated in rich sheep-farming land in the valley of the River Windrush, this old town's name is derived from Witta's Island and it was once of importance as the meeting place of the Witan, the council of the Saxon Kings.

From the Middle Ages onward the town became much better known for its wool and even more so for its woollen blankets – the water of the River Windrush was said to contribute to their softness. The Witney Blanket Company was incorporated in 1710, but before that there were more than 150 looms in the town working in the blanket trade and employing more than 3000 people. The Blanket Hall, in the High Street, displays the arms of the Witney Company of Weavers; it was built for the weighing and measuring of blankets in an age before rigid standardisation. An informative booklet published by the District Council, the **Witney Wool & Blanket Trail**, details a circular walk of about 2¾ miles taking in many locations associated with the trade.

En route the Trail visits **Cogges Manor Farm Museum**, which stands on the site of a now deserted medieval village of which only the church, priory, and manor house remain. The museum was not open in 2010 and as we went to press, was about to be taken over by a new trust.

Nearby St Mary's Church, Cogges, has a curious tower that is square at the base but then becomes octagonal and is surmounted by a stone pyramid.

The story of the blanket trade and other local industries, including brewing and glove-making, is recounted at the **Witney and District Museum** (see panel on page 271), housed in a traditional Cotswold stone building in a courtyard just off the High Street.

Real-life brewing can be seen at the Wychwood Brewery, which produces more than 50,000 barrels of ale each year using traditional methods. Guided tours for groups of up to 20 people are available on Saturday afternoons. The 45-minute tour concludes with a tutored tasting in the Cellar Bar.

St Mary's Church is notable for its soaring spire, which is all the more striking set amidst the surrounding level fields. Built on the scale of a mini-cathedral, the church and spire are 13th century; as Witney's wool trade prospered in the 14th and 15th centuries, chapels and aisles were added; but the interior is marred by over-enthusiastic restoration in Victorian times.

By 1278, Witney had a weekly market and two annual fairs, and in the centre of the market place stands the charming Buttercross. Originally a shrine, the cross has a steep roof with 12 rustic-looking stone columns; its precise date is unknown.

Around Witney

STANTON HARCOURT

4 miles SE of Witney off the B4449

Stanton Harcourt Manor

Church of St Michael · Pope's Tower

This beautiful village is noted for its historic manor house **Stanton Harcourt Manor**, which dates back to the 14th century. Famed for its well-preserved medieval kitchen, one of the most complete to survive in this country, the house is also renowned for its fine collection of antiques and the tranquil gardens. It was while staying here, from 1717 to 1718, that Alexander Pope translated Homer's great work, the *Iliad.* He worked in the tower, part of the original manor house and now referred to as **Pope's Tower**.

While the manor house draws many people to the village, the splendid Norman **Church of St Michael** is also worthy of a visit. Naturally, the Harcourt chapel dominates, but there are other features of interest, including an intricate 14th-century shrine to St Edburg.

STANDLAKE

5 miles SE of Witney on the A415

Newbridge

A little way south of the village is the three-arched **Newbridge,** built in the 13th century and now the second oldest bridge across the Thames. Newbridge saw conflict during the Civil War and the Rose Revived pub was used by Cromwell as a refreshment stop.

BRIZE NORTON

3 miles SW of Witney off the A40

Best known for its RAF transport base, Brize Norton village lies to the north of the airfield, the 'Home of Air Transport, Air Refuelling and Military Parachuting'. It's a long straggling village of old grey stone houses and a Norman church, which is the only one in England dedicated to a little-known 5th-century French bishop, St Brice.

RADCOT

7 miles SW of Witney on the A4095

Radcot Bridge

This tiny hamlet boasts the oldest bridge

Radcot Bridge

across the River Thames. Built in 1154, **Radcot Bridge** represents an important crossing place and, as a result, the hamlet has seen much conflict over the centuries. To the north of the bridge are the remains of a castle where, in 1141, King Stephen battled with the dethroned Queen Matilda. In the following century King John fought his barons here before finally conceding and signing the Magna Carta.

FILKINS

8 miles SW of Witney off the A361

Cotswold Woollen Weavers

Swinford Museum

This tiny Cotswold village is now the home of a flourishing community of craft workers and artists, many of whom work in restored 18th-century barns. One of these groups operates the **Cotswold Woollen Weavers**, a working weaving museum with an exhibition gallery and a mill shop. In the same village, occupying a charming 17th-century cottage, is the **Swinford Museum**, which concentrates on 19th-century domestic and rural trade and craft tools.

KELMSCOTT

9 miles SW of Witney off the A4095

Kelmscott Manor

William Morris called the village of Kelmscott "a heaven on earth", and **Kelmscott Manor**, the exquisite Elizabethan manor house he leased jointly with Dante Gabriel Rosetti, "the loveliest haunt of ancient peace that can well be imagined". Located near the River Thames, and dating from about 1570, the manor was Morris's country home from 1871 until his death in 1896. He loved the house dearly and it is the scene of the end of his utopian novel *News from Nowhere*, in which he writes of a world where work has become a sought-after pleasure. The house, which along with the beautiful garden is open to visitors during the summer, has examples of Morris's work, the four-poster in which he was born, and memorabilia of Dante Gabriel Rosetti. Rosetti is reputed to have found the village boring, so presumably the fact that he was in love with Morris's wife, Jane, drew him here. Rosetti's outstanding portrait of her, *The Blue Silk Dress*, hangs in the Panelled Room. Opening times at the manor are limited and admission is by timed ticket.

Morris is buried in the churchyard, under a tombstone designed by his associate Philip Webb on the lines of a Viking tomb house. The church itself is interesting, the oldest parts dating from the late 12th century, and the village includes some fine farmhouses from around the end of the 17th and beginning of the 18th centuries.

Oxford

The Colleges · Church of St Mary

Martyrs Memorial · Radcliffe Camera

Bodleian Library · Bridge of Sighs

Sheldonian Theatre · Modern Art Oxford

Ashmolean · Museum of Oxford

Museum of History of Science · Folly Bridge

University Museum · Pitt Rivers Museum

Bate Collection of Historical Instruments

Botanic Garden · Harcourt Arboretum

Christ Church Picture Gallery · University Parks

The skyline of this wonderful city can be seen from many of the hilltops that surround it and the view is best described by the 19th-century poet, Matthew Arnold: "that sweet city with her dreaming spires"

George Bernard Shaw was rather less effusive when he wrote: "Very nice sort of place, Oxford, I should think, for people who like that sort of place".

Oxford is not all beautiful ancient buildings, but also a town of commerce and industry, and around the academic centre there are suburbs and factories. A city that has been the centre of the country's intellectual, political, religious and architectural life for over 800 years, it is still an academic stronghold, housing some of the finest minds in some of the finest buildings in the country.

A walled town in Saxon times, Oxford grew on a ford where the River Thames meets the River Cherwell. The first students came here in the 12th century when they were forced out of Paris, at that time Europe's leading academic centre. Intellectual pursuits then were chiefly religious, and, as the town already had an Augustinian Abbey, it soon became the country's leading seat of theological thinking. However, there was considerable tension between the townsfolk and the intellectuals and in the 13th century, in a bid to protect their students, the university began to build colleges – enclosed quadrangles with large, sturdy front doors. The first colleges, University (1249), Balliol (1263) and Merton (1264) were soon joined by others, which to this day maintain their own individual style while all coming under the administration of the university.

Merton College was founded by Walter de Merton, Lord Chancellor of England, as a small community of scholars. The present buildings mostly date from the 15th to 17th centuries, with Mob Quad as the university's oldest. The key feature of the college is its splendid medieval library where the ancient

Balliol College, Oxford

books are still chained to the desks. Once considered the poor relation to other, wealthier colleges, **Balliol College** was founded as an act of penance by John Balliol, and for many years it was reserved for poor students only. Most of the college buildings now date from the 19th century when the college was instrumental in spearheading a move towards higher academic standards.

Thought by some to have been founded by Alfred the Great, **University College** was endowed in 1249, but the present college buildings are mostly 17th century. The poet Shelley was the college's most famous scholar, though he was expelled in 1811 for writing a pamphlet on atheism.

One of the most beautiful colleges in the city, **Christ Church**, was founded in 1525 as Cardinal College by Thomas Wolsey and re-founded as Christ Church in 1546 by Henry VIII after Wolsey had fallen from royal favour. The visitor entrance is at the garden gate, through the Memorial Gardens, and leads through the bottom of Tom Tower (designed by Christopher Wren and home of the Great Tom bell) into Tom Quad, the largest of the city's quadrangles. From here there is access to the rest of the college and also to the college's chapel. Christ Church Cathedral is the only college chapel in the world to be designated a cathedral and was founded in 1546 on the remains of a 12th-century building. Christ Church also has a superb **Picture Gallery** (see panel opposite) with an important collection of Old Master paintings and drawings.

Another splendid college well worth a visit is **Magdalen College**, which has extensive grounds that include a riverside walk, a deer park, three quadrangles and a series of glorious well-manicured lawns. It was founded in 1458 by William Waynflete, Bishop of Winchester, and its bell tower is one of the city's most famous landmarks.

Oxford was closely involved in the Civil War and was for three years the King's headquarters. Several of the colleges were pressed into service by the Royalists: Wadham and New College were both used as stores for arms and gunpowder; Magdalen was Prince Rupert's headquarters and the tower was used as Charles's lookout when the Earl of Essex laid siege to the city. The damage caused by Cromwell's men is dramatically illustrated by bullet holes in the statue of the Virgin in the wonderful **Church of St Mary the Virgin**. It was in this church that the trial of the Protestant martyrs Hugh Latimer, Nicholas Ridley and Thomas Cranmer was held. They were found guilty of heresy and burned to death in a ditch outside the city walls. The three are commemorated by the **Martyrs Memorial**, erected in 1841 in St Giles. If Oxford was the temporary home of countless luminaries (from Wolsey, Wesley and Wilde to more than a dozen British Prime Ministers), it is also the permanent resting place of many others. In the churchyard of St Cross are buried Kenneth

Christ Church Picture Gallery

Oxford, Oxfordshire OX1 1DP
Tel: 01865 276150
e-mail: picturegallery@chch.ox.ac.ukm website: www.chch.ox.ac.uk

Christ Church is unique among the Oxford and Cambridge colleges in possessing an important collection of Old Master paintings and drawings, housed in a purpose built gallery of considerable architectural interest in itself.

General John Guise bequeathed his collection of over 200 paintings and almost 2000 drawings to his former college, where it arrived after his death in 1765. This extraordinary gift enabled Christ Church to introduce art into Oxford education without the necessity to travel to Italy or to access to stately homes, which still held the majority of art in the country. At that date the collection was unequalled by any other Oxford institution.

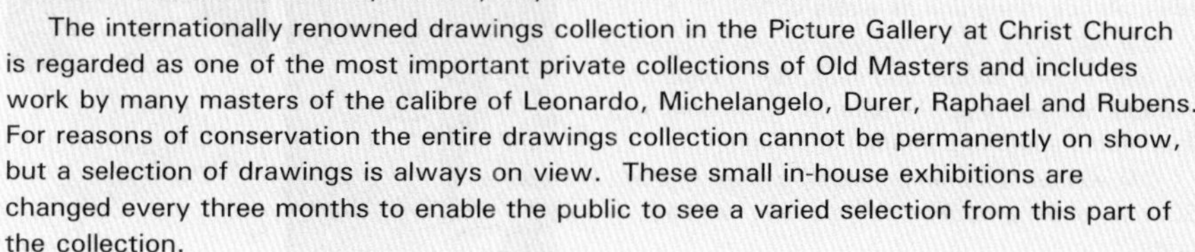

The internationally renowned drawings collection in the Picture Gallery at Christ Church is regarded as one of the most important private collections of Old Masters and includes work by many masters of the calibre of Leonardo, Michelangelo, Durer, Raphael and Rubens. For reasons of conservation the entire drawings collection cannot be permanently on show, but a selection of drawings is always on view. These small in-house exhibitions are changed every three months to enable the public to see a varied selection from this part of the collection.

Grahame (*The Wind in the Willows*), Kenneth Tynan and the composer Sir John Stainer. William Laud, 17th-century Archbishop of Canterbury, is buried in the chapel of St John's College; JRR Tolkien, Oxford professor and author of *The Lord of the Rings*, and the philosopher Sir Isiah Berlin lie in Wolvercote cemetery; and CS Lewis, critic and writer of the Narnia series of books, is at rest in the churchyard of Holy Trinity, Headington.

Many of the colleges have lovely peaceful gardens, some of them open to the public at various times, and the **University Parks** are a perfect place for a stroll at any time. As well as the college buildings, Oxford has many interesting and magnificent places to explore. At the city's central crossroads, unusually named Carfax and probably derived from the Latin for four-forked, is a tower, Carfax Tower, which is all that remains of the 14th-century Church of St Martin. A climb to the top of the tower offers magnificent views across the city. One of the most interesting buildings, the **Radcliffe Camera**, was built between 1737 and 1749 to a design by James Gibb. England's earliest example of a round reading room (camera means chamber, or room), this splendid domed building still serves this purpose for the **Bodleian Library**. Named after Sir Thomas Bodley, a diplomat and a fellow of Merton College, it contains

Bodleian Library, Oxford

over five and a half million books and is one of the world's greatest libraries. The collection of early printed books and manuscripts is second only to the British Library in London and, though members of the University can request to see any book here, this is not a lending library and the books must be read and studied on the premises.

Close by is the Clarendon Building, the former home of the Oxford University Press and now part of the Bodleian, and also in this part of the city is the **Bridge of Sighs**, part of Hertford College and a 19th-century copy of the original bridge in Venice. In Oxford, the bridge crosses a street rather than a canal. The magnificent **Sheldonian Theatre** was designed and built in the style of a Roman theatre by Christopher Wren between 1664 and 1668 while he was Professor of Astronomy at the University. It is still used today for its intended purpose, as a place for University occasions including matriculation, degree ceremonies, and the annual Encaenia, when honorary degrees are conferred on distinguished people. As well as the superb wooden interior, the ceiling has 32 canvas panels, depicting Truth descending on the Arts, which are the work of Robert Streeter, court painter to Charles II.

Founded in 1965, **Modern Art Oxford** in Pembroke Street has a programme of changing exhibitions, films, talks and activities.

Naturally, the city has a wealth of museums and a good place to start is the **Museum of Oxford**, which covers the story of Oxford through a series of permanent displays showing various archaeological finds. First opened in 1683, and the oldest museum in the country, the **Ashmolean Museum** was originally established to house the collection of the John Tradescants, father and son. On display in this internationally renowned museum are archaeological collections from Britain, Europe, Egypt, and the Middle East; Italian, Dutch, Flemish, French and English old masters; Far Eastern art, ceramics, and lacquer work and Chinese bronzes. The Ashmolean, named after the 17th-century antiquary Elias Ashmole, also features many items from the Civil War, including Cromwell's death mask, his watch, King Charles's spurs and a collection of coins, among them the famous Oxford crown and a £3 coin minted by Charles. Here, too, is the **Museum of the History of Science**, a remarkable collection of early scientific instruments including Einstein's blackboard and a large silver microscope made for George III.

In a splendid high-Victorian building, near the University Science Area, is the **University Museum** where the remains of a dodo, extinct since around 1680, and a mass of fossilised dinosaur remains are on display. Also here is the **Pitt Rivers Museum of Anthropology** with its interesting collection, from a witch in a bottle to a totem pole, taken from all over the world. Musicians will enjoy the **Bate Collection of Historical Instruments**, the most comprehensive collection in Britain of European woodwind, brass and percussion instruments and one of the top five in the country of harpsichords and clavichords.

Another place worthy of a visit, and a particularly peaceful haven in the city, is **Oxford Botanic Garden**, down by the river opposite Magdalen College. Founded in 1621, when plants were practically the only source of medicine, this was a teaching garden where the plants grown were studied for their medicinal and scientific use. Today, the garden contains 8000 species of plants in its four-and-a-half acres, including the National collection of euphorbias. Outside the entrance is a rose

garden commemorating the work of Oxford's scientists in the discovery and use of penicillin.

Under the same ownership as the Botanic Garden, the **Harcourt Arboretum** can be found at Nuneham Courtenay, six miles south of Oxford off the A4074. As well as a magnificent collection of trees, the site includes a bluebell wood.

Oxford is also the place where the River Thames changes its name to the poetic Isis (an abbreviation of the Latin Thamesis) and punts can be hired at various points along its banks.

Around Oxford

HEADINGTON

2 miles E of Oxford on the A40

Now a popular residential suburb of Oxford, Headington pre-dates the city by several centuries. It was the centre of an Anglo-Saxon royal domain with a palace where St Frideswide grew up and Henry I came to stay. From the nearby quarries came the stone used to build many of the Oxford colleges. You can enjoy a grand view of them from South Park where Parliamentary troops camped during the Civil War.

WHEATLEY

4 miles E of Oxford on the A40

Waterperry Gardens

This former quarry village retains many old buildings, of which the most interesting is a curious conical lock-up. To the west, close to the M40 (junction 8), are the famous **Waterperry Gardens** surrounding Waterperry House (the house is not open to the public). Established by Beatrix Havergal as a residential gardening school for women in the 1930s, Waterperry is now part pleasure garden and part commercial garden centre. The gardens are host each year to Art in Action, which brings together many of the world's finest craftspeople.

GARSINGTON

4 miles SE of Oxford off the B480

Garsington Manor · Church of St Mary

The most distinguished building hereabouts is **Garsington Manor**, built on a hilltop of mellow Cotswold stone in the 16th century. Between 1915 and 1927, this was the home of the socialite Lady Ottoline Morrell and her husband Philip who were hospitable to a whole generation of writers, artists and intellectuals, including Katherine Mansfield, Lytton Strachey, Clive Bell, Siegfried Sassoon, DH Lawrence, TS Eliot, Rupert Brooke, Bertrand Russell and Aldous Huxley. Huxley based an account of a country house party in his novel *Crome Yellow* on his experiences at Garsington, thereby causing a rift with his hostess. She found his description all too recognisable and they were estranged for some time. It seems that Lady Ottoline was not very lucky in the artists on whom she lavished her attention and hospitality. DH Lawrence also quarrelled with her after drawing a less than flattering, but clearly recognisable, portrait of life at her house in *Women in Love*.

Garsington's other claim to literary fame is that Rider Haggard was sent to the school run by the Rev HJ Graham at the rectory in 1866. The present house is later, built in 1872, but across the road from the Church is a 16th-century gateway from the rectory he would have known. While there Haggard became friendly with a local farmer named Quartermain whom he must have remembered with affection as he used the name for his hero, many years later, in his novel *King Solomon's Mines*.

The village **Church of St Mary** is a pleasant and cosy building with fine views to the south over the Chilterns from its hill top position, but it also looks over the industrial belt to the south of Oxford. Though the interior is chiefly Victorian, the church has retained its Norman tower and inside there is an elegant memorial to Lady Ottoline.

THAME

11 miles E of Oxford on the A418

Church of St Mary · Grammar School

Prebendal House

Founded in AD635 as an administrative centre for the Bishop of Dorchester, Thame first became a market town in the 13th century and its importance as a commercial centre is evident by the wide main street it still has today. Lined with old inns and houses, some of which go back to the 15th century, this is a delightful place to visit.

The imposing **Church of St Mary**, tucked away at one end of the High Street, was built in the 13th century, though the aisles were widened in the 14th century and the tower was heightened in the 15th century. In the centre of the chancel is a monument to Lord John Williams who was notorious for having helped burn Archbishop Thomas Cranmer in the 16th century. To the west of the church stands the **Prebendal House**, which, in its oldest parts, dates from the 13th century. A prebend was an income granted to a priest by a cathedral or collegiate church. At Thame the prebend was established in around 1140 by Lincoln Cathedral. A special residence for the holders of the office was first mentioned in 1234.

The town also has a famous **Grammar School**, housed in a Tudor building in Church Lane. The schoolmaster's house faces the road and over the doorway are the arms of Lord Williams, who founded the school in 1558. John Hampden, one of the Parliamentary leaders during the Civil War, was at school here and also died at Thame. When the Civil War broke out he raised a regiment of infantry for the Parliamentary Army and fought with great bravery at Edgehill and Reading. He was wounded at the battle of Chalgrove Field in June 1643 and was carried back to Thame, where he died some days later in an inn that stood on the High Street. A plaque on a wall denotes the site.

NUNEHAM COURTENAY

5 miles S of Oxford on the A4074

Nuneham Park

When the 1st Earl of Harcourt moved his family here from Stanton Harcourt in 1756, he built the splendid **Nuneham Park**, one of the grandest mansions in Oxfordshire. The earl commissioned Capability Brown to landscape the grounds and observing the completed work deemed it "as advantageous and delicious as can be desired, surrounded by hills that form an amphitheatre and, at the foot, the River Thames."

Nuneham House

To achieve this idyllic result, the earl had the old village moved a mile away and out of sight. It's a charming model village of 18th-century cottages facing each other in matched pairs on either side of the road. The mansion house is now a conference centre, but its parkland forms the Arboretum of Oxford University and is open to the public (see under Oxford).

ELSFIELD

2 miles N of Oxford off the A40

This small village of farms and thatched cottages was the home of the author and administrator John Buchan, 1st Baron Tweedsmuir, from 1919 until 1935 when he left to take up his appointment as Governor-General of Canada. During his time at Elsfield Manor House he wrote a number of books, including *Midwinter*, written in 1923 and partly set in the vicinity. His ashes are buried by the east wall of the churchyard of St Thomas of Canterbury. RD Blackmore, author of *Lorna Doone*, lived in Elsfield as a child while his father was the vicar.

WOODSTOCK

8 miles NW of Oxford on the A44

Blenheim Palace

Oxfordshire County Museum · Secret Garden

Situated in the Glyme Valley, in an area of land that was originally part of the Wychwood Forest, the name of this elegant Georgian market town means a place in the woods. To the north of the River Glyme is the old Saxon settlement, while on the opposite bank lies the town that was developed by Henry II in the 13th century to serve the Royal Park of Woodstock. There had been hunting lodges for the Kings of England here long before the Norman invasion, and it was Henry I who established the deer park around the manor of

Woodstock. It was while at his palace here that Henry II first seduced Rosamund, whom he is said to have housed in a bower in the park. One story tells how Henry's wife, Queen Eleanor, managed to uncover the couple by following an unravelled ball of silk that had become attached to her husband's spur.

This long since disappeared medieval palace was also the birthplace of the Black Prince in 1330, and Princess Elizabeth was held prisoner here in 1558 during the reign of her sister, Queen Mary. On ascending the throne, a grateful Elizabeth I granted the town a second weekly market and two fairs for its loyalty. The palace was damaged during the Civil War, when it served as a Royalist garrison, and the last remains were demolished in 1710.

When the new town became an important coaching centre, many inns were built and survive to this day. The town also prospered as a result of the construction of the Oxford Canal and later the railway. The old town's trade was glove-making and, traditionally, a pair of new gloves is always presented to a visiting monarch.

The town is also home to the **Oxfordshire County Museum**, which is housed in the wonderful and imposing 16th-century Fletcher's House. As well as the permanent displays on the life of the county through the centuries, the museum hosts regular exhibitions and has a sculpture court and a peaceful garden at whose entrance stand the old town stocks. Closed Monday.

It is the magnificent **Blenheim Palace** (see panel below), one of only a handful of sites in the country to be included on the World Heritage List, which brings most people to Woodstock. The estate and the cost of building the palace was a gift from a grateful Queen Anne to the heroic John Churchill, 1st Duke of Marlborough, for his victory at the

Blenheim Palace

Woodstock, Oxfordshire OX20 1PX
Tel: 01993 810555 Fax: 01993 810585
e-mail: shop@blenheimpalace.com
website: www.blenheimpalace.com

Situated just 8 miles from Oxford on the A44, **Blenheim Palace** was created a World Heritage site in 1987 and is the home of 11th duke of Marlborough and birthplace of Sir Winston Churchill.

The imposing scale of the Palace is beautifully balanced within, by the intricate detail and delicacy of the carvings, the hand painted ceilings and the amazing porcelain collections, tapestries and paintings displayed in each room. On the first floor 'Blenheim Palace: The Untold Story' brings to life enticing tales from the last 300 years.

Set in beautiful parkland Of 2,100 acres, which was landscaped by 'Capability' Brown in 1760's, the Palace is surrounded by sweeping lawns and formal gardens. The Pleasure Gardens offer plenty of fun for children and adults alike, including the Marlborough Maze, a giant Chess board and Butterfly farm.

Battle of Blenheim during the Spanish War of Succession. However, the Queen's gratitude ran out before the building work was complete and the duke had to pay the remainder of the costs himself. As his architect, Marlborough chose Sir John Vanbrugh, whose life was even more colourful than that of his patron. He was at once both an architect (although at the time of his commission he was relatively unknown) and a playwright, and he also had the distinction of having been imprisoned in the Bastille in Paris. The result of his work was the Italianate palace, built between 1705 and 1722, which is now seen sitting in a very English park that was designed by Charles Bridgeman and Henry Wise and later landscaped by Capability Brown. Unfortunately, once completed, the new house did not meet with universal approval: it was ridiculed by Jonathan Swift and Alexander Pope, and Marlborough's wife, Sarah, who seems to have held the family purse strings, delayed paying Vanbrugh as long as possible.

Blenheim is a marvellous, grand place with a mass of splendid paintings, furniture, porcelain and silver on show. Visitors will also be interested in the more intimate memorabilia of Sir Winston Churchill. Born here in 1874, Churchill was a cousin of the 9th Duke, whose family name remains Churchill.

Secret Garden at Blenheim Palace, Woodstock

The **Secret Garden** was opened in 2004, the 300th anniversary of the Battle of Blenheim. The garden was originally planted in the 1950s by the 10th duke, but after his death it became overgrown and virtually inaccessible. Now restored, this Four Seasons garden with its many unusual trees, shrubs and flowers offers an enchanting mix of winding paths, soothing water features, bridges, fountains, ponds and streams.

Blenheim Palace, Woodstock

First grown by George Kempster, a tailor from Old Woodstock, the Blenheim Orange apple took its name from the palace. Though the exact date of the first apple is unknown, Kempster himself died in 1773 and the original tree blew down in 1853. The spot where the tree stood become so famous that it is said that London-bound coaches and horses used to slow down so that passengers might gaze upon it.

BLADON

1.5 miles S of Woodstock on the A4095

Churchyard

The village lies on the southern edge of the Blenheim estate and it was in the **Churchyard** here in 1965 that Sir Winston Churchill was laid to rest in a simple grave after a state funeral. Also interred here are his parents, his brother John, and his daughters. The ashes of his wife Clementine were buried in his grave in 1977.

LONG HANBOROUGH

2 miles SW of Woodstock

Oxford Bus Museum

Located next to Long Hanborough railway station, the **Oxford Bus Museum** has some 40 vehicles on display, all of which were used at one time for public transport in and around Oxford. They range from early 19th-century horse-trams to buses from the 1980s. Here, too, is the Morris Motors Museum, with vehicles ranging from a 1925 Oxford Bullnose to a 1977 BMC Mini.

NORTH LEIGH

4.5 miles SW of Woodstock off the A4095

Roman Villa

The Saxon-towered St Mary's Church is well worth a visit, and just to the north of the village lies the **Roman Villa**, one of several known to have existed in this area. Little remains apart from the foundations and some mosaic flooring, but this is enough to measure the scale of the place; it had over 60 rooms, two sets of baths and a sophisticated underfloor heating system, all built round a courtyard and clearly the home of a prosperous farming family.

FINSTOCK

5 miles W of Woodstock on the B4022

A charming village with two notable literary associations. It was in 1927, at the 19th-century Holy Trinity Church, that TS Eliot was baptised at the age of 38 following his controversial conversion to Catholicism. The novelist and churchwoman Barbara Pym lived in retirement with her sister in a cottage in the village; she died in 1980 and is buried in the churchyard. A lectern in the church is dedicated to her memory.

CHARLBURY

5 miles NW of Woodstock on the B4026

Museum   Railway Station

Cornbury Park

Now very much a dormitory town for Oxford, Charlbury was once famous for its glove-making as well as being a centre of the Quaker Movement – the simple Friends' Meeting House dates from 1779 and there is also a Friends' cemetery. **Charlbury Museum**, close to the Meeting House, has displays in five rooms on the traditional crafts and industries of the town, and the town's charters given by Henry III and King Stephen can also be seen. Well known for its

Cornbury Park, Charlbury

THE NEWLAND'S

75 Sheep Street, Bicester, Oxfordshire OX26 6JS
Tel: 01869 816000
e-mail: info@newlandsteashop.co.uk website: www.newlandsteashop.co.uk

Tea rooms, Gift & Flower shop, Special occasion & Wedding boutique
Old fashion shopping experience, high quality, reasonable prices
and friendly service from days gone by.
All under one roof in one of the oldest buildings in Bicester.

Our Tea Room offers a great selection of teas, coffees, home made light lunches, a large selection of delicious handmade cakes and Cream teas served all day in our tea room or outside in the secluded covered courtyard.

Need a Gift our shop has something different for everyone. Two floors of wonderful items from around the world for newborns to grandmas. We also stock all occasions cards, crystal, diffusers, candles, gold and silver jewellery.

The florist shop can supply silk or fresh floral arrangements, bouquets, baskets, corsages and wreaths at very competitive prices with free delivery in Bicester. Weddings are a speciality. Flowers for any occasion anywhere in the world through our membership with Iflorists.

Special Occasions Boutique, Hand made dresses wedding or any occasion. Bridal tiaras & veils also full wedding and party planning service. Bespoke dressmaking and alterations. Ladies hats, fascinators and handbags for hire or purchase. Children's party and special occasion clothing for all ages Christenings, Holy Communion, Confirmation & Weddings.

Location: 10 minutes drive from Junction 9 off the M40. Top of Sheep Street a 10 minute walk from Bicester North Train station and 5 minutes walk up from Market Square. On the corner of the turning into Franklin's Yard long stay car park.

olde-worlde **Railway Station**, built by Isambard Kingdom Brunel, complete with a fishpond and hanging baskets, the town also has two interesting great houses.

On the other bank of the River Evenlode is **Cornbury Park**, a large estate that was given to Robert Dudley by Elizabeth I. Although most of the house now dates from the 17th century, this was originally a hunting lodge in Wychwood Forest that had been used since the days of Henry I. Glimpses of the house can be seen from the walk around the estate.

Lying just to the west of the town is Ditchley Park, a restrained and classical house built in the 1720s by James Gibbs. The interiors are splendid, having been designed by William Kent and Henry Flitcroft, and Italian craftsmen worked on the stucco decorations of the great hall and the saloon; the first treated to give an impression of rich solemnity, the second with a rather more exuberant effect. The house has associations with Sir Winston Churchill, who used it as a weekend headquarters during the Second World War. Appropriately enough, given that Sir Winston had an American mother, Ditchley Park is now used as an Anglo-American conference centre and is not open to the public.

Bicester

Bicester has a traceable history that goes back for a thousand years and a settlement here was recorded in the Domesday Book. Today it is a busy market town and home to Bicester Village – a factory designer outlet shopping village. Because it is close to the M40 motorway linking London with Birmingham

THE WHITE HORSE INN

Daisy Hill, Duns Tew,
Oxfordshire OX25 6JS
Tel: 01869 340272
e-mail: info@whitehorsedunstew.com
website: www.whitehorsedunstew.com

Set in a quaint Oxfordshire village, **The White Horse Inn** is a traditional Costwold stone pub full of charm and warmth. Owned by Christina White, this gorgeous inn, which dates back to the 17th century, offers the very best in accommodation, food and drink.

Inside the attractive building, you will find traditional flagstone floors, beamed ceilings and walls; and a real olde worlde atmosphere with open fires in each room.

The food here is absolutely delicious and with such a talented head chef it isn't surprising that The White Horse Inn is becoming well known in the area for the dishes it serves. The specials board changes weekly and there is a wide and varied choice on the printed menu. Starters include salad of pan-fried bacon & black pudding, and tempura squid. The dishes are all reasonably priced and slow roasted breast of lamb; classic steak suet pudding; and chef's honey roast & mustard glaze ham are all on the main menu. The produce used is sourced within Oxfordshire and the dishes are made freshly cooked to order.

The desserts are tempting even if you aren't known for having a sweet tooth, with choices such as chocolate eton mess, mango & vanilla crème brulee, apple & mixed fruit crumble and chilled lemon soufflé with raspberry coulis.

For those with a lighter appetite there is a tasty selection of open sandwiches and baguettes, as well as ploughman's lunch and deli boards. Food is served all day, everyday.

If you are looking for a cosy, welcoming and charming pub selling food throughout the day, then this former coaching inn can be highly recommended. As well as the homey and warm feel of the pub's dining area there is also the option to sit outside, where there is a delightful terraced area, which many visitors like to enjoy on warmer days.

There are 11 letting rooms available in separate cottages within the grounds of the pub. Ring for details.

via Oxford, the town has seen a considerable growth in size in recent years.

Flora Thompson based her trilogy *Lark Rise to Candleford* on the area northeast of Bicester, including the nearby villages of Juniper Hill, Cottisford, Fringford and Hethe.

Around Bicester

DEDDINGTON

8 miles NW of Bicester off the A423

Deddington Castle & Castle House

Visitors to this old market town might recognise it as the place that was demolished by a runaway crane in the television adaptation of Tom Sharpe's *Blott on the Landscape*. The damage was, of course, cleverly faked and Deddington, which hovers between a small town and a large village, still retains all its medieval character. Surveyed in the Domesday Book at twice the value of Banbury, the town never developed in the same way as Banbury and Bicester, but it remains a prosperous agricultural centre with a still bustling market place. Little can now be seen of the 12th-century **Deddington Castle**. This was destroyed in the 14th century and most of the building materials were put to good use in other areas of the town. However, excavations have revealed the remains of a curtain wall, a hall and a small rectangular keep.

Close by is **Castle House**, where Piers Gaveston, Edward II's favourite, was held before his execution in 1312. The house's two towers were added later, in the 1650s, when the house was in the ownership of Thomas Appletree. A supporter of Cromwell, Appletree was ordered to destroy the property of Royalists and it was material from two local houses that he used in his building work.

LOWER HEYFORD

6 miles W of Bicester on the B4030

Rousham House

Situated at a ford across the River Cherwell, which was replaced in the 13th century by a stone bridge, the delightful village of Lower Heyford lies on the opposite bank from its other half – Upper Heyford.

To the south lies **Rousham House**, a fine mansion built in the mid 1600s for Sir Robert Dormer and set in magnificent gardens. The gardens as seen today were laid out by William Kent in 1738 and include many water features, sculptures and follies. Next to the house are very attractive pre-Kent walled gardens with a parterre, herbaceous borders, a rose garden and a vegetable garden. The garden is open to the public all year round; the house has limited opening times – call: 01869 347110.

Banbury

St Mary's Church   Banbury Cross

Museum & Tooley's Boatyard

Famous for its cross, cakes and the nursery rhyme, this historic and thriving market town has managed to hang on to many of its old buildings as well as become home to Europe's largest livestock market.

The famous **Banbury Cross** can be found in Horsefair where it was erected, in 1859, replacing the previous one demolished by the Parliamentarians during the Civil War. It was built to commemorate the marriage of Queen Victoria's oldest daughter to the Prussian Crown Prince, and the figures around the bottom of the cross, of Queen Victoria, Edward VII and George V, were added in 1914.

The town's other legendary claim to fame is its cakes, made of spicy fruit pastry, which can still be bought. Banbury was also, at one time, famous for its cheeses, which were only about an inch thick. This gave rise to the expression "thin as a Banbury cheese".

On the east side of the Horsefair stands **St Mary's Church**, a classical building of warm-coloured stone and hefty pillars, which are pleasantly eccentric touches. The original architect was SP Cockerell, though the tower and portico were completed between 1818 and 1822 by his son, CR Cockerell. The style reflects the strong influence on English architecture of Piranesi's *Views of Rome*, using massive shapes and giving stone the deliberately roughened appearance, which comes from the technique known as rustication.

Banbury Museum (free) tells the story of the town's development, from the days when it came under the influence of the bishops of Lincoln, through the woollen trade of the 16th century, to the present day. Adjoining the striking modern museum is **Tooley's Boatyard**, a scheduled ancient monument that can be visited as part of a guided tour. Established in 1790 and in continuous use ever since, Tooley's is the oldest working dry dock in the country. It was designed to build and repair canal barges and narrowboats and has a boatyard, forge, chandlery and shop. It also runs various courses.

Tooley's Boatyard, Banbury

Around Banbury

BROUGHTON

2½ miles SW of Banbury on the B4035

Broughton Castle

Arthur Mee considered **Broughton Castle** "one of the most fascinating buildings in the county". As you cross the ancient bridge over a moat and approach the sturdy 14th-century gatehouse, it becomes clear that it is indeed something special, the perfect picture of a great Tudor mansion. The house has been owned by the Broughton family since 1451 – Nathaniel Fiennes, 21st Lord Saye and Sele is the present occupant. Over the years there have been several royal visitors, including Queen Anne of Denmark, wife of James I. Both James I and Edward VII used the aptly named King's Chamber, with its hand-painted Chinese wall paper. The house also played a part in the Civil War as it has a secret room where leaders of the Parliamentary forces laid their plans. Arms and armour from that period are displayed in the castle's grandest room, the Great Hall, which is also notable for its dazzling plaster ceiling installed in 1599. The castle has a walled garden, café and picnic area.

BLOXHAM

3½ miles SW of Banbury on the A361

Museum St Mary's Church

Dominated by the 14th-century **St Mary's Church**, whose spire is a highly visible local landmark, and its Victorian public school, this large village is one of narrow lanes and fine gentlemen's houses. The church has three notable features: a tower completely covered with carvings of men and beasts; the elaborately carved 15th-century Milcombe Chapel; and some exquisite stained glass byMorris, Burne-Jones and Webb.

The old court house, to the south of the church, contains the **Bloxham Village Museum**, where there is a permanent collection of items on display that tell the life of the inhabitants of the village and surrounding area.

SOUTH NEWINGTON

6 miles SW of Banbury on the A361

Church of St Peter ad Vincula

This small village of ironstone dwellings is home to the **Church of St Peter ad Vincula**, which contains the best medieval wall paintings in the county. Detail and colouring are both superb in the depictions, which include the murders of Thomas à Becket – very gory – and of Thomas of Lancaster (a rebel against Edward II). St Margaret is shown slaying a dragon and there's also a wonderful Virgin and Child.

GREAT TEW

7 miles SW of Banbury off the B4022

One of the most picturesque villages in the county, Great Tew, a planned estate village, had fallen into such disrepair by the 1970s that it was declared a conservation area in order to save it from complete dereliction. Today, the thatched cottages and houses from the 16th, 17th and 18th centuries nestle in a fold in the landscape of rolling countryside. The big house hereabouts is Great Tew Park, dating mainly from the 19th century. Only the garden walls remain of its 17th-century predecessor, owned by Lucius Carey, Lord Falkland. It was a gathering place for some of the great writers and intellectuals of the day, including Edmund Waller and Ben Jonson. In the 17th century, the 5th Viscount Falkland was Secretary to the Navy and gave his name to the Falkland Islands.

HOOK NORTON

7 miles SW of Banbury off the A361

Hook Norton Pottery and Craft Gallery

This large village is best known for its brewery, which was set up by John Harris from his farmhouse in 1849. He started there as a maltster and after years of gaining expertise and learning from experiments, he constructed a purpose-built brewery in 1872. The **Brewery**, which moved to its present premises in 1900, remains in the Harris family. Tours are available, which last about two hours and conclude with a sampling of Hook Norton brews in the visitor centre.

At the **Hook Norton Pottery and Craft Gallery** visitors can watch the internationally renowned potter, Russell Collins, at work. A wide range of hand-crafted pottery including mugs, jugs, dishes, bowls and much more is available to buy.

SWALCLIFFE

5 miles W of Banbury on the B4035

Church of St Peter and St Paul

15th-century Barn Madmarston Hill

The village is dominated by the large **Church**

of St Peter and St Paul, which towers over all the other buildings here. Founded in Saxon times, the bulk of the building dates from the 12th, 13th and 14th centuries but it is the tracery in the east window that makes the church noteworthy. However, by far the most impressive building in Swalcliffe is the **Barn**, which has been acknowledged as one of the finest 15th-century half-cruck barns in the country. Built as the manorial barn by New College, Oxford, between 1400 and 1409, it was used to store produce from the manor and never to store tithes. Today, it is home to a collection of agricultural and trade vehicles.

To the northeast of the village, on **Madmarston Hill**, are the remains of an Iron Age hill fort, which was occupied from the 2nd century BC to the 1st century AD.

WROXTON

3 miles NW of Banbury on the A422

Abbey

A charming village of brown stone cottages clustered round the village pond, from which a road leads to **Wroxton Abbey**. This impressive Jacobean mansion was built by Sir William Pope, Earl of Downe, and was the home of the North family for 300 years. The gardens and grounds of the abbey, now restored as an 18th-century park, are open to the public, but the house is not. All Saints Church contains several imposing monuments including those to Sir William and his wife, to Lord North, who was Prime Minister from 1770 to 1782, and to the banker Thomas Coutts.

Wroxton Abbey

Burford

Church of St John the Baptist

Tolsey Museum

Cotswold Wildlife Park

Often referred to as The Gateway to the Cotswolds, Burford is an enchanting old market town of honey-coloured Cotswold stone set on a hillside rising from the River Windrush. Ancient taverns and a wealth of upmarket shops, cafes and restaurants line the steepish main road.

Lying on important trade routes, north-south and east-west, the town prospered, and its first market charter was granted in 1087. In the 16th century, the town was an important centre of the woollen trade and it was used as the setting for *The Woolpack*, in which the author Celia Harknett describes the medieval wool trade in Europe. After the decline in the wool trade, Burford became an important coaching centre and many of the old inns can still be seen today.

The **Church of St John the Baptist** was built on the wealth of the wool trade and this grand building has the atmosphere of a small cathedral. Originally Norman,

BURFORD WOODCRAFT

144 High Street, Burford, Oxfordshire OX18 4QU
Tel: 01993 823479
e-mail: enquiries@burford-woodcraft.co.uk
website: www.burford-woodcraft.co.uk

Burford has drawn people to its beautiful Cotswold architecture and one of the top twenty English churches for centuries. However the diversity of its independent shops and galleries is less well known.

One of these, Burford Woodcraft has an excellent reputation for a contemporary collection inspired by wood and handmade in Britain. The first thing visitors notice the moment they walk through the door is 'the wonderful smell'. It's beeswax on wood and they are in for a real treat. The passion is obvious; it's been shared in the family run business since 1978.

Wood is a natural medium, incredibly versatile and within every variety each piece is different. The work chosen by Jayne and Robert Lewin highlights the inventiveness and expertise of the designer-craftsmen. Robert is a furniture designer-maker and like the other makers understands and combines woods' beauty and tactile quality with individuality, good design and a superb standard of craftsmanship to achieve the best.

Visitors enjoy a fascinating and wide range including pieces for home interiors and studies, kitchenware, furniture, boxes, jewellery, decorative carving and turning, toys and a great selection of cards! Whether choosing practical essentials, gifts or indulging in treats, they love the touch and warmth only wood can give.

BURFORD HOUSE

99 High Street, Burford,
Oxfordshire OX18 4QA
Tel: 01993 823151 Fax: 01993 823240
e-mail: stay@burfordhouse.co.uk
website: www.burfordhouse.co.uk

Located on the high street is the unmistakable landmark that is **Burford House**. This striking 17th century building in traditional Cotswold stone has become one of the most highly regarded small hotels in the area and stepping through the doors it is easy to see why. Burford House is furnished to an exceptional standard; the cosy sitting room with its log fire screams comfort and luxury whilst the elegant and light dining room gives a glimmer of the tempting dishes that are served there. Breakfast and light lunches are served from Monday to Saturday and dinner is available on Thursday, Friday and Saturday evenings.

Each of the eight bedrooms are decorated and furnished individually using the finest materials. Enjoy the luxury of the Egyptian bed linen whilst watching the flat screen television or relax in the large tubs in the en-suite bathrooms before slipping into the complimentary robes. All the rooms have wireless broadband access, books, mineral water and hospitality trays provided to add to the guests comfort.

The beautiful Wysteria clad courtyard is the perfect place to sample a drink from the well stocked bar that includes some rare single malts and a fine range of wines.

Burford House is the ideal place to pamper oneself whilst enjoying all this lovely area has to offer.

the church has been added to over the centuries and there are several interesting monuments and plaques to be found. In the south wall of the tower stair is a carved panel, dated around AD100, which is thought to show the Celtic fertility goddess Epona, with two male supporters and a horse. In the nave north aisle a monument erected to Edmund Harman, the barber-surgeon to Henry VIII, shows North American natives – possibly the first representation of native Americans in the country. In the south porch is a small plaque that commemorates three Leveller mutineers who were imprisoned in the church by Cromwell's men and shot in the churchyard in 1649.

The Levellers were troops from Cromwell's army who mutinied against what they saw as the drift towards the authoritarian rule they had been fighting against. While they were encamped at Burford, the Levellers were taken by surprise by Cromwell's forces. After a brief fight, some 340 prisoners were taken and placed under guard in the church. The next day a court martial was held and three of the rebels were shot as an example to the rest, who were made to watch the executions. They were spared similar punishment when their leader recanted in a sermon.

The town's old court house, built in the 16th century with an open ground floor and a half-timbered first floor, is now home to the **Tolsey Museum**. An interesting building in its own right, its displays cover the history of the town and the surrounding area. Other buildings worth seeking out include the 16th-century Falkland Hall, the home of a local wool and cloth merchant Edmund Sylvester, and Symon Wysdom's Cottages, which were built in 1572 by another of the town's important merchants.

The 160 acres of park and garden that make up **The Cotswold Wildlife Park** are home to a whole host of animals, many of whom roam freely in the wooded estate. Rhinos, zebras, ostriches and tigers are just some of the animals in the spacious enclosures, while tropical birds, monkeys, reptiles and butterflies are all given the chance to enjoy the warmth of their natural habitat by staying indoors. With an adventure playground and a narrow-gauge railway, the park has something to offer all the family. Open every day from 10am.

Around Burford

TAYNTON

1.5 miles NW of Burford off the A424

Up until the end of the 19th century, Taynton was a quarrying village. The limestone taken from the quarries was used in the construction of Blenheim Palace, Windsor Castle and St Paul's Cathedral, as well as many Oxford colleges and local buildings.

CHASTLETON

10 miles N of Burford off the A44

Chastleton House

Chastleton House

Chastleton is home to one of the best examples of Jacobean architecture in the country. In 1602, Robert Catesby, one of the Gunpowder Plot conspirators, sold his estate here to a prosperous wool merchant from Witney, Walter Jones. A couple of years later, Jones pulled down the house and built **Chastleton House**, a splendid Jacobean manor house with a dramatic five-gabled front and a garden where the original rules of croquet were established in 1865 – it features Jacobean topiary and a long-established vegetable plot. Until it became a National Trust property, Chastleton had been inhabited by the same family for more than 400 years. They became increasingly impoverished over the years and were unable to upgrade or update the property or its fixtures and fittings. By the time the National Trust acquired the house in 1991, it had become a virtual time capsule. For the first time in its history, the Trust decided to keep the house 'as found' rather than restore it to its former state of grace (the kitchen ceiling has not been cleaned since 1612!). One of the finest and most complete Jacobean houses in England, it is filled with a remarkable collection of furniture, textiles and items both rare and everyday. Visits by appointment only.

SWINBROOK

2 miles E of Burford off the A40

The Fettiplace family lived in a great manor house in this peaceful village in the valley of the Windrush. The manor has long gone, but the family is remembered in several impressive and highly distinctive monuments in the Church of St Mary. The family home of the Redesdales was also at Swinbrook, and in the churchyard are the graves of three of the six Mitford sisters, who were the daughters of the 2nd Baron Redesdale. Nancy, Unity and Pamela are buried here.

MINSTER LOVELL

4.5 miles E of Burford off the B4047

Minster Lovell Hall

One of the prettiest villages along the banks of the River Windrush, Minster Lovell is home to the ruins of a once impressive 15th-century manor house. **Minster Lovell Hall** was built in the 1430s and was, in its day, one of the great aristocratic houses of Oxfordshire, the home of the Lovell family. However, one of the family was a prominent Yorkist during the Wars of the Roses. After the defeat of Richard III at Bosworth Field, he lost his lands to the Crown. The house was purchased by the Coke family in 1602, but around the middle of the 18th century the hall was dismantled by Thomas Coke, Earl of Leicester, and the ruins became lowly farm buildings. They were rescued from complete disintegration by the Ministry of Works in the 1930s and are now in the care of English Heritage. What is left of the house is extremely picturesque, and it is hard to imagine a better setting than here, beside the River Windrush. One fascinating feature of the manor house that has survived, is the medieval dovecote, complete with nesting boxes, which provided pigeons for the table in a way reminiscent of modern battery hen houses.

Minster Lovell Hall

SHIPTON-UNDER-WYCHWOOD

4 miles NE of Burford on the A361

Shipton Court Wychwood Forest

The suffix under-Wychwood derives from the ancient royal hunting forest, **Wychwood Forest**, the remains of which lie to the east of the village. The name has nothing to do with witches – wych refers to the Hwicce, a Celtic tribe of whose territory the forest originally formed a part in the 7th century. Though cleared during the Middle Ages, it was still used as a royal hunting forest until the mid-1600s. By the late 1700s there was little good wood left and the forest was cleared to provide arable land.

The forest was one of the alleged haunts of Matthew Arnold's scholar gypsy. In the poem, published in 1853, Arnold tells the legend of the brilliant but poor Oxford scholar who, despairing of ever making his way in the world, went to live with the gypsies to learn from their way of life.

The village itself is centred around its large green, which is dominated by the tall spire of 11th-century St Mary's Church. On the green, a pyramidal memorial commemorates the 17 men, women and children of Shipton who lost their lives in the wreck of the *Cospatrick* in 1874, while on their way to a new life in

New Zealand. Here, too, can be found The Shaven Crown, now a hotel, which was built in the 15th century as a guest house for visitors to the nearby (and now demolished) Bruern Abbey. Finally, there is the superb **Shipton Court** (private) built around 1603, which is one of the country's largest Jacobean houses. It can be seen from the main road.

CHIPPING NORTON

10 miles NE of Burford on the A44

Church of St Mary Bliss Tweed Mill

Museum

The highest town in Oxfordshire, at 650 feet above sea level, Chipping Norton was once an important centre of the wool trade. King John granted the town a charter to hold a fair to sell wool. This was later changed to a Mop Fair and the tradition continues to this day when the fair is held every September.

The town's medieval prosperity can be seen in the fine and spacious **Church of St Mary**, which was built in 1485 with money given by John Ashfield, a wool merchant. The splendid east window came from the Abbey of Bruern, a few miles to the southwest, which was demolished in 1535 following the Dissolution of the Monasteries. In 1549, the minister here, the Rev Henry Joyce, was charged with high treason and hanged from the then tower because he refused to use the new prayer book introduced by Edward VI.

Still very much a market town – the market is held on Wednesdays - Chipping Norton has been little affected by the influx of visitors who come to see this charming place. **Chipping Norton Museum** is an excellent place to start any exploration and the permanent displays here cover local history from prehistoric and Roman times through to

THE PERSIAN SHOP AND ART GALLERY

18 New Street, Chipping Norton,
Oxon OX7 5LJ
Tel: 01608 646647
e-mail: art@thepersianshop.co.uk
website: www.thepersianshop.co.uk

A beautiful selection of handpicked rugs, handicraft and artwork is available at **The Persian Shop and Art Gallery**. Located in a grade two listed building in Chipping Norton, the highest town in Oxfordshire, The Persian Shop is extremely popular with locals and visitors to the area.

The town was once an important centre of the wool trade and continues to hold markets every Wednesday. The Persian Shop is one of the more individual shops in the town and everybody who comes through the door is greeted with a warm welcome. The building dates back to 1820 and it has retained plenty of character and charm from that by-gone era.

The products on sale here are very varied and all are handpicked by Sakine Khosravi who was born close to Persepolis, the capital of the Ancient Persian Empire. There is a fine range of rugs from the main weaving centres of Iran including Tabriz, Qom, Esfahan, Nain, Bijar, Kashan, Mashad, Baluchi, Bahktiari, Shiraz and Yalameh. Handicraft from Esfahan such as exquisite enamelware and luxurious block-printed cotton are also available. The jewellery and pottery displayed on the shelves make fantastic gifts for friends or relatives and such is the choice at this independent shop it would be hard not to find something you like.

The Persian Shop is also home to an art gallery, which displays work by local artists as well as artists of international repute from along the silk route. Many people come here to browse the gallery and exhibitions are held frequently. Recently, works by De Benedictis, Rusconi, Morosini and Tosi have been displayed. Ring for details or check website.

The Persian Shop and Art Gallery is open from 10am until 5pm from Monday through to Saturday. It is closed on Sundays and Tuesdays. Access for disabled customers is not a problem with a ramp leading to the entrance.

the present day, with topics including farming equipment, local industries, Chipping Norton at War, the local baseball club and Law and Order in Chipping Norton. Open Monday to Saturday afternoons Easter to October.

Found just to the west of the town is **Bliss Tweed Mill**, an extraordinary sight in this area as it was designed by a Lancashire architect, George Woodhouse, in 1872 in the Versailles style. With a decorated parapet and a tall chimney, which acts as a local landmark, this very northern-looking mill only ceased operation in the 1980s. It has since been converted into luxury apartments.

Whispering Knights

LITTLE ROLLRIGHT

13 miles NE of Burford off the A3400

To the northwest of Over Norton are the **Rollright Stones** – one of the most fascinating Bronze Age monuments in the country. These great gnarled slabs of stone stand on a ridge that offers fine views of the surrounding countryside. They all have nicknames: the **King's Men** form a circle; the **King Stone** is to the north of the circle; and, a quarter of a mile to the west, stand the **Whispering Knights**, which are, in fact, the remnants of a megalithic tomb. Naturally, there are many local legends connected with the stones and some say that they are the petrified figures of a forgotten king and his men that were turned to stone by a witch.

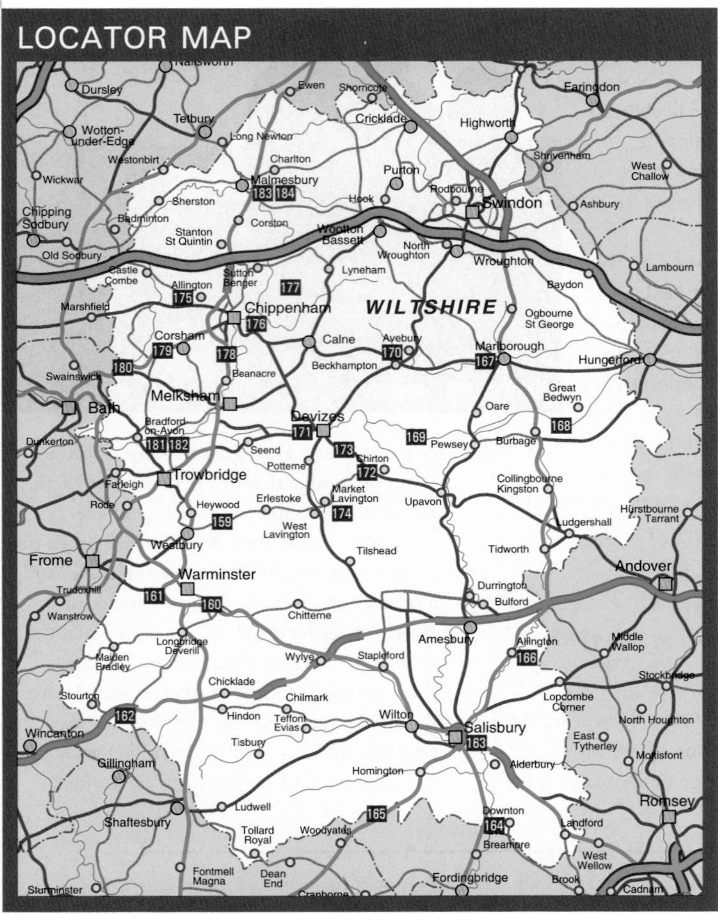

ADVERTISERS AND PLACES OF INTEREST

Accommodation, Food and Drink

159 | Duke at Bratton, Bratton, Westbury *pg 302*
160 | The Angel Coaching Inn, Heytesbury *pg 303*
162 | Angel Corner Tea Rooms, Mere *pg 306*
166 | The Old Inn, Allington, Salisbury *pg 316*
168 | The Swan Inn, Wilton, Marlborough *pg 318*
169 | The Barge Inn, Honeystreet, Pewsey *pg 320*
172 | Wiltshire Yeoman, Chirton, Devizes *pg 324*
174 | The Green Dragon, Market Lavington *pg 325*
175 | Allington Farm Shop and Café, Allington *pg 330*
176 | Dutch Cottage Tea Rooms, Chippenham *pg 331*
177 | Foxham Inn, Foxham, Chippenham *pg 332*
178 | Lacock Pottery Bed & Breakfast, Lacock *pg 333*
180 | Saltbox Farm, Box, Corsham *pg 336*
183 | Amanda's Oxford Street Bistro, Malmesbury *pg 339*

Activities

161 | Longleat, Longleat, Warminster *pg 305*
173 | Horse Country, Lydeway, Devizes *pg 324*

Arts and Crafts

162 | Angel Corner Tea Rooms, Mere *pg 306*
181 | Stained Glass Studio and Gallery, Bradford-on-Avon *pg 337*

Fashions

163 | Twenty One B, Salisbury *pg 308*
184 | Pattini, Malmesbury *pg 340*

historic building · museum and heritage · historic site · scenic attraction · flora and fauna

9 | Wiltshire

Wiltshire is a county that is rich in the monuments of prehistoric man; it also boasts one of the highest concentrations of historic houses and gardens in the country, which makes it a great place for the tourist. It's also a perfect choice for walkers, cyclists and lovers of nature, with wide open spaces, woodland and downland and a number of chalk streams that are home to a huge variety of wetland wildlife.

The industrial heritage is also strong, taking in Brunel's Great Western Railway and the railway town of Swindon, brewing at Devizes and carpet-making at Wilton. And the county has many surprises, from the white horses carved in hillsides and the mysterious crop circles, to the ancient hill forts and the greatest mystery of them all, the stone circles of Stonehenge – how *did* those stones get from the Marlborough Downs and the mountains of Pembrokeshire and what *was* their use?

The jewel in the crown of Wiltshire is the city of Salisbury, at the confluence of the rivers Avon, Wylye, Bourne and Nadder, with its glorious cathedral, a masterpiece of the Early English style, and many other fine buildings. The cathedral for the episcopal see stood originally at nearby Old Sarum, a flourishing town in medieval days that lost its status when a 12th-century bishop moved flock, stock and barrel down the hill to the more amenable surroundings of Salisbury and began to build a new cathedral. Atmospheric ruins are all that remain of Old Sarum.

Westbury, at the western edge of the chalk downlands of Salisbury Plain, was an important centre of the medieval cloth and wool trades and still boasts some handsome buildings from its days of great prosperity. Like Old Sarum, Westbury was formerly a rotten borough, returning two MPs until the 1832 Reform Act stopped the cheating (Old Sarum was the more notorious, having two MPs at a time when it had no voters). Stourhead, a beautiful Palladian mansion full of treasures, stands in magnificent grounds laid out by Henry Hoare; Longleat is another house filled with wonderful things, whose grounds contain the famous safari park. The National Trust village of Lacock, the market town of Devizes with its extraordinary flight of locks on the Kennet and Avon Canal, the historic abbey town of Malmesbury, the lovely Vale of Pewsey and the ancient 4500-acre Savernake Forest, designated a Site of Special Scientific Interest, are other attractions that no visitor to this wonderful county should miss.

ADVERTISERS AND PLACES OF INTEREST

Westbury

White Horse Woodland Park
Salisbury Plain All Saints Church

Westbury, at the western edge of the chalk downlands of **Salisbury Plain**, was a major player in the medieval cloth and wool trades, and still retains many fine buildings from the days of great prosperity, including some cloth works and mills. Westbury was formerly a rotten borough and returned two MPs until 1832, when the Reform Bill put an end to the cheating. Scandal and corruption were rife, and the Old Town Hall in the market place – a gift from a grateful victorians candidate in 1815 – is evidence of such goings-on. He was Sir Manasseh Massey Lopes, a Portuguese financier and slave-trader who 'bought' the borough to advance his political career.

All Saints Church, a 14th-century building on much earlier foundations, has many unusual and interesting features, including a stone reredos, a copy of the Erasmus Bible and a clock with no face made by a local blacksmith in 1604. It also boasts the third heaviest peal of bells in the world.

On the southern edge of town is another church well worth a visit. Behind the simple, rustic exterior of St Mary's, Old Dilton, are a three-decker pulpit and panelled pew boxes with original fittings and individual fireplaces.

To the west of the town, at Brokerswood, is **Woodland Park and Heritage Centre**, 80 acres of ancient broadleaf woodland with a wide range of trees, plants and animals, nature trails, a lake with fishing, a picnic and barbecue area, a tearoom and gift shop, a museum, a play area and a narrow-gauge railway.

By far the best known Westbury feature is

DUKE AT BRATTON

Melbourne Street, Bratton, Westbury, Wiltshire BA13 4RW
Tel: 01380 830242

Dating back to the 18th century, The Duke at Bratton is a traditional country pub run by Andy and Lyn. The quaint pub, which used to be three cottages, has many character features including a pair of whale jaw bones, which have been erected over the garden gate.

Located just outside of Westbury in the picturesque countryside village of Bratton, the pub welcomes regulars and visitors to enjoy quality drink and fine food. Real ales, brewed in Melksham, are available and the extensive food menu offers traditional homemade cuisine. All food is freshly cooked to order, and locally sourced produce is used where possible.

The restaurant caters for 38 diners and it is an ideal venue for private parties. On warmer days food can be enjoyed outside in the beer garden, where families and their dogs are more than welcome.

Food is served Monday to Thursday 12pm – 3pm and 6pm – 9pm. On Friday and Saturdays food can be ordered between 12pm and 9pm and Sunday lunch is served weekly 12pm – 4pm.

the famous **Westbury White Horse**, a chalk carving measuring 182 feet in length and 108 feet in height. The present steed dates from 1778, replacing an earlier one carved to celebrate King Alfred's victory over the Danes at nearby Ethandun (Edington) in AD878. The White Horse is well looked after, the last major grooming carried out in 2006. Above the horse's head are the ruins of Bratton Castle, an Iron Age hill fort covering 25 acres.

Around Westbury

WARMINSTER

4 miles S of Westbury on the A350

Dewey Museum Cley Hill

Arn Hill Nature Reserve

Warminster is a historic wool, corn-trading and coaching town with many distinguished buildings, including a famous school with a door designed by Wren. In addition to the 18th and 19th-century buildings, Warminster has a number of interesting monuments: the Obelisk with its feeding troughs and pineapple top erected in 1783 to mark the enclosure of the parish; the Morgan Memorial Fountain in the Lake Pleasure Grounds; and *Beyond Harvest*, a statue in bronze by Colin Lambert of a girl sitting on sacks of corn. Warminster's finest building is the Church of St Denys, mainly 14th century but almost completely rebuilt in the 1880s to the design of Arthur Blomfield. The **Dewey Museum**, in the public library, displays a wide range of local history from Iron Age times to the present day, and includes the Victor Manley collection of geology.

To the west of town is the 800-foot **Cley Hill**, an Iron Age hill fort with two Bronze

THE ANGEL COACHING INN

High Street, Heytesbury,
Warminster, Wiltshire BA12 OED
Tel: 01985 840330
e-mail: admin@angelheytesbury.co.uk
website: www.angelheytesbury.co.uk

There is plenty of history surrounding **The Angel Coaching Inn**, which dates back to the 16th century. Located in the attractive village of Heytesbury, it is full of character with beamed ceilings, log fires and antique furnishings.

Whether you want to dine in the restaurant with a three course meal or simply pop in with your dog for a pint, The Angel Coaching Inn is ready to welcome you.

The aroma of quality home cooked food often attracts people through the inn's doors and with a

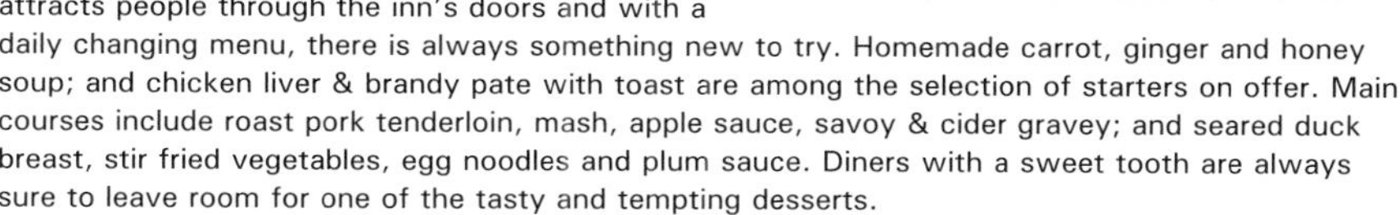

daily changing menu, there is always something new to try. Homemade carrot, ginger and honey soup; and chicken liver & brandy pate with toast are among the selection of starters on offer. Main courses include roast pork tenderloin, mash, apple sauce, savoy & cider gravey; and seared duck breast, stir fried vegetables, egg noodles and plum sauce. Diners with a sweet tooth are always sure to leave room for one of the tasty and tempting desserts.

There are currently two double en-suite rooms available to overnight guests, but in 2011 it is hoped this will increase to eight. Ring for details.

Age barrows. Formerly owned by the Marquess of Bath, the hill was given to the National Trust in the 1950s and is a renowned sighting place for UFOs. (The region is also noted for the appearance of crop circles and some have linked the two phenomena.)

On the northern edge of Warminster, **Arn Hill Nature Reserve** forms a circular walk of two miles along public footpaths through woodland and open downland. The site was donated to the town in 1920 by the then Marquess of Bath.

CODFORD ST PETER & CODFORD ST MARY

8 miles SE of Westbury on the A36

Sister villages beneath the prehistoric remains of Codford Circle, an ancient hilltop meeting place that stands 617 feet up on Salisbury Plain. The church in Codford St Peter has a historic treasure in an exceptional 9th-century Saxon stone carving of a man holding a branch and dancing. East of Malmpit Hill and visible from the A36, is a rising sun emblem carved by Australian soldiers during the First World War. In the military cemetery at Codford St Mary are the graves of Anzac troops who were based at a camp here. Anzac graves may also be seen at Sutton Veny.

WYLYE

10 miles SE of Westbury off the A36

Yarnbury Castle

Peace came to Wylye in 1977, when a bypass diverted traffic from the busy main roads. It had long been an important junction and staging post on the London-Exeter coaching route. A statue near the bridge over the River Wylye (from which the village, Wilton, and, indeed, Wiltshire get their names) commemorates a brave postboy who drowned here after rescuing several passengers from a stagecoach that had overturned during a flood.

Above the village is the little known **Yarnbury Castle**, an Iron Age hill fort surrounded by two banks and an outer bank. To the west is a triangular enclosure from Roman times, which could have held cattle or sheep. From the 18th century to the First World War, Yarnbury was the venue of an annual sheep fair.

IMBER

5 miles E of Westbury off the B3098

The part of Salisbury Plain containing the village of Imber was closed to the public in 1943 and has been used by the Army ever since as a live firing range. The evicted villagers were told that they could return to Imber after the war, but the promise was not kept and the village remains basically inaccessible. A well-marked 30-mile perimeter walk skirting the danger area takes in Warminster, Westbury, Tilshead in the east and Chitterne in the south.

LONGLEAT

7 miles SW of Westbury off the A362

Longleat House | Safari Park

Longleat House (see panel opposite), the magnificent home of the Marquess of Bath, was built by an ancestor, Sir John Thynne, in a largely symmetrical style, in the 1570s. The inside is a treasure house of old masters, Flemish tapestries, beautiful furniture, rare books and Lord Bath's racy murals. The superb grounds of Longleat House were landscaped by Capability Brown, and now contain one of the country's best known venues for a marvellous day out. In the famous **Safari Park** the Lions of Longleat, first introduced in 1966, have been followed by a veritable Noah's Ark of exotic creatures, including rhinos, zebras and white

Longleat

Warminster, Wiltshire BA12 7NW
Tel: 01985 844400
e-mail: enquiries@longleat.co.uk website: www.lomgleat.co.uk

Discover some of the world's most magnificent animals in this first Safari Park outside of Africa ... see how you measure up to a giraffe, watch out for the zebras crossing and be enthralled by the majestic lions and tigers! Continue your adventure aboard the Safari Soats for a sea lion-escorted cruise, find yourself going round in circles in the Longleat Hedge Maze, enjoy a fun-packed ride on the Longleat Railway before discovering the treasures and heirlooms within Longleat House.

Keepers at Longleat Safari Park are often kept busy during the summer with the birth of baby animals and have recently seen the arrival of wolf cubs, sea lion pups, ostrich chicks, lion cubs as well as baby giraffes, Bactrian camels and tapirs. Visitors can see the young animals on display. At birth the baby wolves measure just 15 cms in length and weigh around 500 grams. After spending the first weeks of life underground, the pups begin to emerge into the outside world. The cubs are just the latest in a string of breeding successes at the Wiltshire wildlife attraction.

As well as all the animal attractions, Longleat puts on special shows during the summer. Phone or visit the website for all details including prices and opening times.

tigers. The park also features safari boat rides, a narrow-gauge railway, children's amusement area, garden centre and the largest hedge maze in the world. The Lions of Bath project has installed its own Lions of Bath lion: On Safari is a life-size fibreglass lion created by a Longleat keeper, Jo Hawthorn.

STOURTON

13 miles SW of Westbury off the B3092

Stourhead King Alfred's Tower

The beautiful National Trust village of Stourton lies at the bottom of a steep wooded valley and is a particularly glorious sight in the daffodil season. The main attraction is, of course, **Stourhead**, one of the most famous examples of the early 18th century English landscape movement. The lakes, the trees, the temples, a grotto and a classical bridge make the grounds, laid out by Henry Hoare, a paradise in the finest 18th-century tradition. The gardens are renowned for their striking vistas and woodland walks, as well as a stunning selection of rare trees and specimen shrubs, including tulip trees, azaleas and rhododendrons. The house itself, a classical masterpiece built in the 1720s in Palladian style for a Bristol banker, contains a wealth of Grand Tour paintings and works of art, including furniture by Chippendale the Younger and wood carvings by Grinling Gibbons. On the very edge of the estate, some three miles by road from the house, the imposing **King Alfred's Tower** stands at the top of the 790-foot Kingsettle Hill. This 160 foot triangular red brick folly was built in 1772 to commemorate the King, who reputedly raised his standard here against the Danes in AD878.

MERE

14 miles SW of Westbury off the A303

Museum · Castle Hill

A small town nestling below the downs near the borders with Dorset and Somerset. The town is dominated by **Castle Hill**, on which Richard, Earl of Cornwall, son of King John, built a castle in 1253. Nothing of the castle remains, though many of the stones were used in building Mere's houses. The High-Gothic-style Church of St Michael the Archangel features some fine medieval and Victorian stained glass, carved Jacobean pews, an unusual octagonal font and a 12th-century statue of St Michael slaying a dragon. **Mere Museum**, in the public library in Barton Lane, is principally a local history collection with a good photographic archive. Displays are changed regularly, but a permanent feature is a large, detailed map of Mere drawn in colour by a local artist. It also has a mini-museum for kids. This is a great area for rambling, one of the best spots being the Whitesheet Hill Nature Trail with wonderful views and a wealth of plants and insects, including some rare chalk-loving butterflies.

EAST KNOYLE

17 miles S of Westbury on the A350

Two items of interest here. A simple stone monument marks the birthplace, in 1632, of Sir Christopher Wren, son of the village rector at that time. East Knoyle Windmill is a tower mill on a circular base, without sails and unused for over a century. It offers good views over Blackmoor Vale and has a large grassy area for picnics.

WEST KNOYLE

18 miles S of Westbury off the A303

Bush Farm Bison Centre

The major attraction at this small village is **Bush Farm Bison Centre**, where herds of bison, elk and red deer roam in their near natural state in 30 acres of old oak woodland. There are also groups of prairie dogs, chipmunks, guanacos and racoons. Bison and elk meat is on sale and there's a children's playground.

TOLLARD ROYAL

6 miles SE of Shaftesbury on the B3081

Larmer Tree

Tollard Royal is a historic village in the heart of Cranborne Chase. King John had a small estate here that he used on his hunting trips. King John's House is a part-stone, part-timber residence whose fine condition is largely due to the efforts of General Pitt Rivers, an eminent Victorian archaeologist who inherited the estate and spent the last 20 years of his life unearthing Bronze Age remains. His collection is housed in the Salisbury and South Wiltshire Museum, where a gallery is named in his honour.

The General was also responsible in 1890 for creating **Larmer Tree**, pleasure grounds for "public entertainment and enlightenment". The gardens contain a wonderful collection of ornate buildings and majestic trees and are a lovely place for a picnic. Group visits with a guided informal talk on the history of the Larmer Tree, plus a cream tea or light lunch, can be arranged.

Larmer Tree Gardens, Tollard Royal

LUDWELL

2 miles E of Shaftesbury on the A30

Win Green Hill

Near the village is the National Trust-owned **Win Green Hill**, the highest point in Wiltshire, crowned by a copse of beech trees set around an ancient bowl barrow. From the summit there are wonderful views as far as the Quantock Hills to the northwest and the Isle of Wight to the southeast.

Salisbury

Cathedral · Boy Bishop

Mompesson House · Old Sarum

Salisbury and South Wiltshire Museum

The Rifles Berkshire & Wiltshire Museum

John Creasey Museum

Edwin Young Collection · Salisbury Racecourse

The glorious medieval city of Salisbury stands at the confluence of five rivers, the Avon, Wylye, Bourne, Ebble and Nadder. Originally called New Sarum, it grew around the present

TWENTY ONE B

21b Milford Street, Salisbury,
Wiltshire SP1 2AP
Tel: 01722 410522
web: www.twentyonebsalisbury.co.uk

Opening Hours:
Monday ~ Friday 10.00am ~ 5.00pm
Saturday 9.00am ~ 5.00pm
Out of hours appointments by prior arrangement

Specialists in high quality ladies fashion, **Twenty One B** is situated at 21b Milford Street (an extension of New Canal, one of Salisbury's main shopping streets) adjacent to 'Greenfields' the gunsmiths. (*Please do not confuse us with 'Store Twenty one' further along Milford Street*).

Twenty One B's collections encompass casual, occasion, formal and evening wear, beautiful coats, and for the Mother of the Bride or Bridegroom its signature label, the exquisite Paule Vasseur of Paris.

You'll find an exciting, varied and colourful collection that aims to span the generations and to please all in presenting a wonderful selection of garments from such labels as Cocomenthe, Hugan'Co, Kapalua, Libra, Lucia, Marcona, Prêt and Zaffiri Jeans.

These are just a few of the labels that have long been the hallmark of Twenty One B.

The shop stocks a fantastic range of millinery to complement its Haute Couture and also holds an extensive range of beautiful pashmina from Indian Kashmir, imported directly and thus making these beautiful stoles and scarves very affordable.

Twenty One B takes pride in offering stress-free and totally relaxed shopping (and browsing!) which, hopefully, will make your visit a happy and memorable experience. We also provide a full alteration service from our own exceptionally talented and much valued tailoress.

Cathedral, which was built between 1220 and 1258 in a sheltered position two miles south of the site of its windswept Norman predecessor at Old Sarum. Over the years the townspeople followed the clergy into the new settlement, creating a religious and market centre whose two main aspects flourish to this day.

One of the most beautiful buildings in the world, **Salisbury Cathedral** is the only medieval cathedral in England to be built throughout in the Early English style – apart from the spire, the tallest in England, which was added some years later and rises to an awesome 404 feet. The Chapter House opens out of the cloisters and contains, among other treasures, one of the four surviving originals of Magna Carta. Six hundred thousand visitors a year come to marvel at this and other priceless treasures, including a number of magnificent tombs. The oldest working clock in Britain, and possibly in the world, is situated in the fan-vaulted north transept; it was built in 1386 to strike the hour, has no clock face and has ticked more than 500million times. The cathedral is said to contain a door for each month, a window for each day and a column for each hour of the year. A small statue inside the west door is of Salisbury's 17th-century **Boy Bishop**. It was a custom for choristers to elect one of their number to be bishop for a period in December lasting from St Nicholas Day to Holy Innocents Day. One year the boy bishop was apparently, literally, tickled to death by the other choristers; since he died in office, his statue shows him in full bishop's regalia.

Salisbury Cathedral

The Close, the precinct of the ecclesiastical community serving the cathedral, is the largest in England and contains a number of museums and houses open to the public. **Salisbury and South Wiltshire Museum**, in the 17th-century King's House, is the home of the award-winning redesigned Stonehenge Gallery and a designated archaeological collection of national importance. Displays include Early Man, the Romans and Saxons, Old Sarum with the Giant and Hob Nob, Romans and Saxons, the Pitt Rivers collection, pottery, ceramics, costume, lace, embroidery, a pre-NHS surgery and Turner watercolours.

A few doors away is **The Rifles Berkshire and Wiltshire Museum**, housed in a 13th-century building called the Wardrobe because it was originally used to store the bishop's clothes and documents. The museum tells the story of the Royal Berkshire Regiment, the Wiltshire Regiment and the Duke of Edinburgh's Royal Regiment, and the exhibits include Bobbie the Dog, the hero of Maiwand, and many artefacts from foreign campaigns. The house has a tearoom and a riverside garden with views of the famous water meadows. **Mompesson House**, a

National Trust property, is a perfect example of Queen Anne architecture notable for its plasterwork, an elegant carved oak staircase, fine period furniture and the important Turnbull collection of 18th-century drinking glasses. The house featured in the film *Sense and Sensibility* as Mrs Jennings's London home. In the Library are the **John Creasey Museum** and the Creasey Collection of Contemporary Art, a permanent collection of books, manuscripts, objects and art, and the **Edwin Young Collection** of 19th and early 20th-century watercolours, drawings and oil paintings of Salisbury and its surrounding landscape.

Also within the Close is **Arundells**, home of the former Prime Minister Sir Edward Heath, which is no longer open to the public. Although there has been a building here since the 13th century, the present house is mostly Georgian. In the mid 1900s it had deteriorated to such an extent that demolition was considered. Fortunately, it was renovated in the 1960s and refurbished by Sir Edward Heath when he came to live here in 1985. The house is surrounded by a beautiful two-acre walled garden stretching down to the River Avon.

Another building of interest is Poultry Cross, an elaborately decorated 15th-century structure that stands on eight sturdy pillars. Another lovely 15th-century building, complete with oak beams and heraldic shields, has been converted into a cinema and has been fitted with a sign proclaiming ODEON in Gothic script.

A short drive takes visitors to the ruins of **Old Sarum** (English Heritage), abandoned when the bishopric moved into the city. Traces of the original cathedral and palace are visible on the huge uninhabited mound, which dates back to the Iron Age. Old Sarum became the most notorious of the rotten boroughs, returning two Members of Parliament, despite having no voters, until the 1832 Reform Act stopped the practice. A plaque on the site commemorates Old Sarum's most illustrious MP, William Pitt the Elder who, of course, was elected by the rotten borough procedure.

Salisbury Racecourse, a short drive west of the city, is one of England's oldest racecourses – racing has taken place at this picturesque downland course since the 1500s. The course stages a number of flat racing meetings during the summer months.

Around Salisbury

BRITFORD

1 mile S of Salisbury on the A338

Lying within branches of the Wiltshire River Avon, Britford has a moated country house and a fine Saxon church with some early stone carvings. An ornate tomb is thought to be that of the Duke of Buckingham, who was beheaded in Salisbury in 1483.

DOWNTON

5 miles S of Salisbury off the A338

Moot House

The Saxons established a meeting place, or moot, on an earlier earthwork fortification, and it was in commemoration of that ancient parliament that the present **Moot House** was built on the foundations of the old castle. The building and its garden stand opposite a small 18th-century amphitheatre built to resemble the Saxon moot. In 1955, a Roman villa comprising seven rooms and a bath house was discovered nearby.

WILTON WHOLEFOODS

Sunrize House, Salisbury Road,
Downton SP5 3JJ
Tel: 01752 513122
e-mail: shop@wiltonwholefoods.com
website: www.wiltonwholefoods.com

Wilton Wholefoods is the largest wholefood supplier in the south of England and supplies more than 450 independent retailers. Brothers Solomon and Daniel Rimel run the business, which has been in the family since 1989 and is now second generation.

All types of natural and wholefood products are available here including dried fruits, nuts, seed, pulses, grains, muesli, herbs & spices, and healthy snacks. More unique products are also available. There are well over 250 lines sourced, mixed and packed by Wilton Wholefoods under its exclusive Sunrize brand. There is also an extensive range of branded oriental products including Fern's, Linghams and Mae-ploy.

A huge range of traditional baking ingredients are available from the thriving market stall at Salisbury Charter Market. The market runs every Saturday and Tuesday and is ever popular with locals and visitors to the area.

Alternatively, the website offers the same superior quality, but at exceptionally low web prices. It is well worth a look.

The Pepperbox, Lover

LOVER

6 miles SE of Salisbury off the A338

Pepperbox Hill

In the vicinity of this charmingly named village is the National Trust's **Pepperbox Hill**, topped by an early 17th-century octagonal tower known as **Eyre's Folly**. Great walking, great views, and a great place for nature-lovers, with a variety of plant and bird life.

WILTON

3 miles W of Salisbury on the A30

Carpet Factory | Wilton House

Church of St Mary & St Nicholas

The third oldest borough in England, Wilton was once the capital of Saxon Wessex. It is best known for its carpets, and the **Wilton Carpet Factory** on the River Wylye continues to produce top-quality carpets, maintaining a worldwide reputation for quality that goes back 300 years. Wilton carpets as we know them today were created by a French carpet weaver who was brought to England by the Earl of Pembroke in the early 1700s to teach the local weavers his skills. In 1835, redundant handlooms were brought from the Axminster factory in Devon and set up in Wilton. Luxurious hand-knotted Axminsters, with each tuft individually tied by hand, were made alongside traditional Wiltons up to 1958. Situated beside the factory, the Wilton Shopping Village offers high-quality factory shopping in a traditional rural setting.

Wilton House is the stately home of the Earls of Pembroke. When the original house was destroyed by fire in 1647, Inigo Jones was commissioned to build its replacement. He designed both the exterior and the interior, including the amazing Double Cube Room. The house was further remodelled by James Wyatt. The art collection is one of the very finest, with works by Rembrandt, Van Dyke, Rubens and Tintoretto; the furniture includes pieces by Chippendale and Kent.

There's plenty to keep children busy and happy, including a treasure hunt quiz and a huge adventure playground. There's a Tudor kitchen, a Victorian laundry, and 21 acres of landscaped grounds with parkland, cedar trees, water and rose gardens, and an elegant Palladian bridge. Call 01722 746714 for opening times.

The **Church of St Mary and St Nicholas** is a unique Italianate church built in the style of Lombardy by the Russian Countess of Pembroke in 1845. The interior is resplendent with marble, mosaics, richly carved woodwork

WS CLARKE (BUTCHERS)

55 High Street, Sixpenny Handley,
nr Salisbury SP5 5ND
Tel: 01752 552328
e-mail: jclarke@fsmail.net

Founded in 1915 **WS Clarke** butchers has been in the same family for almost 100 years. The traditional butchers sell locally sourced meat as well as continental cheeses and deli products.

The Clarke family has been running the butchers shop at Sixpenny Handley since William Clarke opened the shop in the early 1900s. He was followed by his sons Norman and Gordon, and now his grandson John runs WS Clarke & Sons.

This is a traditional butcher's business, selling meat that comes from farms in the area. The Clarkes run their own small abattoir which means they have real control over the quality. The Clarkes make their own sausages and the traditional bacon and much of the cheese comes from the Westcountry and smoked chicken, salmon and fish come from the Dorset smokery.

Located at the heart of a small but thriving community, locals really support the lone butchers shop in the village and many people come here from neighbouring towns and villages. The independent shops really are important to the residents of Sixpenny Handley and it is their use of them that shows their commitment to the area.

and early French stained glass.

BROAD CHALKE

7 miles W of Salisbury off the A354

A Saxon village where the 17th-century diarist John Aubrey had a small estate. A warden of the parish church, he was also a keen angler and wrote of his beloved River Ebble: "There are not better trouts in the Kingdom of England than here". The designer and photographer Cecil Beaton spent his final years in Broad Chalke and is buried in the churchyard of All Saints.

Fovant Badges

TEFFONT EVIAS

9 miles W of Salisbury off the B3089

Farmer Giles Farmstead

Teffont Evias is a quiet little village with some handsome houses built with stone from the local Chilmark quarries. Close by, on the road that connects with the A303, is **Farmer Giles Farmstead**, a 175-acre working farm where a wide variety of farm animals can be seen at close quarters. Amongst them are some very interesting rare breeds; alpacas have recently been added to the company. There are vast indoor play areas, a gift shop and a licensed restaurant.

FOVANT

8 miles W of Salisbury on the A30

Fovant Badges

The **Fovant Badges** are badges carved in the chalk hillside by troops during the First World War. They include the Australian Imperial Force, the Devonshire Regiment, 6th City of London Regiment, the London Rifle Brigade, the Post Office Rifles, the Royal Corps of Signals, the Royal Wiltshire Yeomanry, the Wiltshire Regiment and the YMCA. The badges can be seen from the A30.

DINTON

9 miles W of Salisbury off the A30

There are two National Trust properties to visit near this lovely hillside village. Little Clarendon is a small but perfectly formed Tudor manor house, with three oak-furnished rooms open to visitors; Philipps House is a handsome white-fronted neo-Grecian house with a great Ionic portico. Built by the early 19th-century architect Jeffrey Wyattville for William Wyndham, it stands in the beautiful landscaped grounds of Dinton Park.

TISBURY

12 miles W of Salisbury off the A30

Tithe Barn Old Wardour Castle

Tisbury is the most prominent of the villages strung along the River Nadder. It has a fine parish church that has a 15th-century clerestory and used to have a lofty spire. This was hit by lightning in 1742, rebuilt, and then struck by lightning again 20 years later. At this point the parishioners gave up. In the churchyard is a venerable yew tree, which carbon dating, has established is 4000 years old.

To the east of the village stands the magnificent gateway of Place Farm. It was built for the abbesses of Shaftesbury in the late 14th- and early 15th-centuries and gives a clear idea of the splendour of the farm at that time. The only building that remains is the huge **Tithe Barn**, believed to be the largest in England. Built of local stone, it has a thatched roof that was originally covered by stone tiles.

Notable sons of the village include Thomas Mayhew, a prosperous mercer in the early 1600s who emigrated to New England where he acquired the off-shore islands of Martha's Vineyard and Nantucket. He and his family also helped establish the township of Tisbury.

In the churchyard of the Wiltshire Tisbury, John Lockwood and Alice Kipling, the parents of the author Rudyard Kipling are buried. He often visited them at their home, The Gables in Hindon Lane, and wrote much of his novel *Kim* while staying in Tisbury.

To the south, **Old Wardour Castle** (English Heritage) was the scene in 1643 of a bloody battle when Parliamentarian forces besieged the castle for several weeks, causing great loss of life and extensive damage to the building. The landscaped grounds in which the castle stands include an elaborate rockwork grotto.

WOODFORD VALLEY

6 miles N of Salisbury off the A345

Heale Garden & Plant Centre

A seven mile stretch between Salisbury and Amesbury contains some of the prettiest and most peaceful villages in the county. Among them, Great Durnford with its Norman church and restored mill, Lake, with an imposing Tudor mansion, and Middle Woodford, where the internationally renowned **Heale Garden and Plant Centre** lies within the grounds of 16th-century Heale House in an idyllic setting by a tributary of the Avon. Much of the garden was designed by Harold Peto (1854-1933), whose own garden at Iford Manor is in the Italianate style that he so favoured. Highlights at Heale include a superb collection of plants, shrubs and roses, a water garden and a Japanese bridge and teahouse built in 1910 with the help of four Japanese gardeners.

AMESBURY

8 miles N of Salisbury on the A345

Stonehenge Woodhenge

Queen Elfrida founded an abbey here in AD979 in atonement for her part in the murder of her son-in-law, Edward the Martyr, at Corfe Castle. Henry II rebuilt the abbey's great Church of St Mary and St Melor, whose

Woodhenge, Amesbury

Stonehenge, Amesbury

tall central tower is the only structure to survive from the pre-Norman monastery. A mile to the north of Amesbury, the A345 passes along the eastern side of **Woodhenge**, a ceremonial monument even older than Stonehenge. It was the first major prehistoric site to be discovered by aerial photography, its six concentric rings of post holes having been spotted as crop marks by Squadron Leader Insall in 1925. Like Stonehenge, it seems to have been used as an astronomical calendar. When major excavation was carried out in the 1920s, a number of neolithic tools and other artefacts were found, along with the skeleton of a three-year-old child whose fractured skull suggested some kind of ritual sacrifice.

Two miles west of Amesbury at the junction of the A303 and A344/A360 stands **Stonehenge** itself, perhaps the greatest mystery of the prehistoric world, one of the wonders of the world, and a monument of unique importance. The World Heritage Site is surrounded by the remains of ceremonial and domestic structures, many of them accessible by road or public footpath. The great stone blocks of the main ring are truly massive, and it seems certain that the stones in the outer rings – rare bluestones from the Preseli Hills of west Wales – had to be transported over 200 miles. Stonehenge's orientation on the rising and setting sun has always been one of its most remarkable features, leading to theories that the builders were from a sun-worshipping culture or that the whole structure is part of a huge astronomical calendar, or both. The mystery remains, and will probably remain for ever.

STRATFORD-SUB-CASTLE

2 miles NE of Salisbury off the A343

Figbury Rings

Old Sarum is not the only impressive mound hereabouts, as three miles to the east is the Iron Age hill fort of **Figbury Rings**. Above it, the bleak expanse of Porton Down is a largely undisturbed conservation area where the great bustard has been making a comeback. This large, long-legged bird was once a common sight on Salisbury Plain and is incorporated into Wiltshire's coat of arms.

CHOLDERTON

9 miles NE of Salisbury on the A338

Cholderton Charlie's Farm

Close to this pleasant village is **Cholderton Charlie's Farm**, which includes Cholderton Rare Breeds Farm Park and Rabbit World. A former dairy farm, it is set in beautiful countryside and has become a major family attraction since opening to the public in 1987. The 42-acre park is home to many rare breeds of rabbits and poultry, as well as other rare breeds saving them from extinction. At peak

THE OLD INN

Tidworth Road, Allington, Salisbury, Wiltshire SP4 OBN
Tel: 01980 619045
e-mail: dtandnasimpson@yahoo.co.uk
website: www.oldinnallington.com

The Old Inn is the heart and soul of Allington. It has been run for the past two years by David and Nicola Simpson who employ a cosy atmosphere at the inn. Traditional in both values and décor, the inn sports open log fires, warm tones and farmhouse furniture to create a laid back environment for dinner or drinks.

David, who runs the kitchen, and Nicola, who runs the front of house are both from a catering and hospitality background. A range of bar meals, lunch snacks and a la carte dishes are available, cooked fresh to order from quality locally sourced produce. Dishes are stylish and creative, adding restaurant quality presentation and attention to detail to all the old pub favourites including The Old Inn burger, herb crusted rack of lamb and lemon sole. Although elegantly presented, food is for all the family and the inn is popular with such. Traditional roasts are always available on a Sunday lunch time all year round, along with the daily specials board.

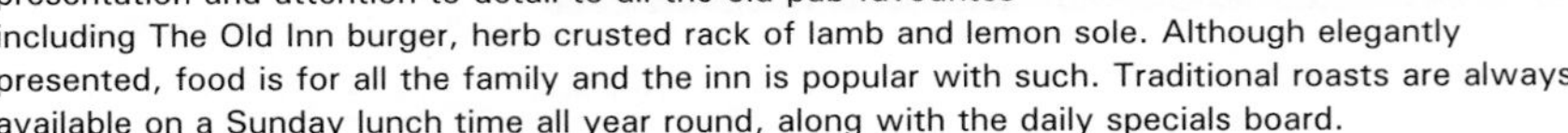

The bar is paid equal attention and is always well stocked with a handsome selection of real ales, beers, soft drinks and a carefully selected wine list to be enjoyed as it is or with a meal. In the summer months the inn's gardens can be enjoyed when popular barbeques are held for all. Themed food evenings and quiz evenings are also held each month, allowing guests the time and space to get together with friends, old and new.

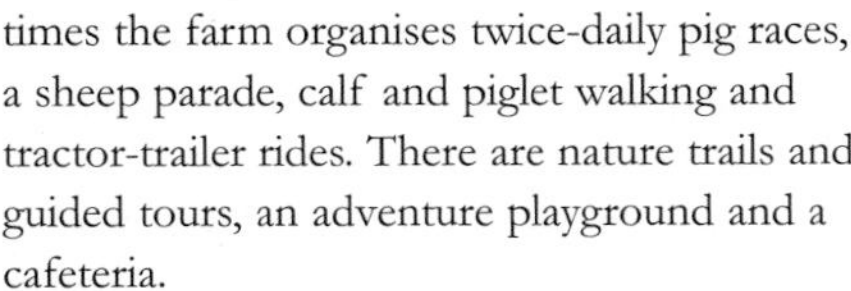

times the farm organises twice-daily pig races, a sheep parade, calf and piglet walking and tractor-trailer rides. There are nature trails and guided tours, an adventure playground and a cafeteria.

Marlborough

Marlborough College

Famous for its public school and its wide high street where markets are held every Wednesday and Saturday, Marlborough is situated in the rural eastern part of Wiltshire in the upland valley of the Kennet, which flows through the town. It was once an important staging post on the coaching run from London to Bath and Bristol, and the presence of the A4 means that it still has easy links both east and west. Its main street, one of the finest in the country, is dignified by many Tudor houses and handsome Georgian colonnaded shops, behind which are back alleys waiting to be explored. St Mary's Church, austere behind a 15th-century frontage, stands in Patten Alley, so named because pedestrians had to wear pattens (an overshoe with a metal sole) to negotiate the mud on rainy days. The porch of the church has a ledge where churchgoers would leave their pattens before entering. Other buildings of interest include those clustered round The Green (originally a Saxon village, and the working-class quarter in the 18th and 19th centuries); the turn-of-the-century Town Hall looking down the broad High Street; and the ornate 17th-century Merchant's House, now restored as a museum.

Marlborough College was founded in 1843 primarily for sons of the clergy. The

LEATHERCRAFT OF MARLBOROUGH

Old Hughenden Yard, High Street, Marlborough, Wiltshire SN8 1LT
Tel: 01672 512065 Fax: 01672 861656

If what you're looking for is made of leather, look no further than **Leathercraft of Marlborough**, a leading specialty retailer of fine quality handbags, , briefcases, belts, gloves, wallets and much more. Jean and Roger Upton run the country shop and their taste is evergreen, these items are fashion classics – some, if not most, you'd keep forever. Leather is one of nature's most versatile and sensual materials. It offers comfort and durability in a variety of beautiful finishes, textures and colours. Their son Mark is a well known Sporting Artist, his Racing, Equestrian and other scenes are displayed around the shop and are for sale.

Seymour family built a mansion near the site of the Norman castle, which was replaced in the early 18th century by a building that became the Castle Inn and is now C House, the oldest part of the College. A mound in the private grounds of the school is linked with King Arthur's personal magician, Merlin. It was said that he was buried under this mound and gave the town its name, Merle Barrow, or Merlin's Tomb. Among the many notable former pupils of the college were William Morris and John Betjeman.

Around Marlborough

SAVERNAKE FOREST

2 miles E of Marlborough off the A346

Savernake Forest

The ancient woodland of **Savernake Forest** is a magnificent 4500-acre expanse of unbroken woodland, open glades and bridle paths. King Henry VIII hunted wild deer here and the family home of his third wife, Jane Seymour, was nearby. Designated a Site of Special Scientific Interest, the forest is home to abundant wildlife, including a small herd of deer and 25 species of butterfly. One day each winter the forest is closed to prevent rights of way being established.

GREAT BEDWYN

6 miles SE of Marlborough off the A4

Bedwyn Stone Museum

In the chancel of the 11th-century Church of St Mary the Virgin is the tomb of Sir John Seymour, the father of Henry VIII's third wife Jane. Nearby is **Bedwyn Stone Museum**, a monument to the skills of the English stonemason. Great Bedwyn was the base of the Lloyd family of stonemasons who have been working in stone for some 200 years, the museum is based on their mason's yard. Among the items on display are an assortment

Savernake Forest

of tombstones and a stone aeroplane with an 11 foot wingspan.

To the east of Great Bedwyn, and four miles south of Hungerford off the A338 at Rivar Hill Airfield, is the home of Shalbourne Soaring Society. It is a popular gliding club, which offers affordable flying. Why not take a trial flight and share the thrill of flying over one of England's most beautiful Downland sites.

CROFTON

6 miles SE of Marlborough off the A338

Crofton Beam Engines

The eastern end of the Vale of Pewsey carries the London-Penzance railway and the Kennet and Avon Canal, which reaches its highest point near Crofton. The site is marked by a handsome Georgian pumping station, which houses the renowned **Crofton Beam Engines**. These engines – the 1812 Boulton & Watt and the 1845 Harvey of Hayle – have been superbly restored under the guidance of the Canal trust. The 1812 engine is the oldest working beam engine in the world, still in its original building and still doing its original job of pumping water to the summit level of the canal. Both engines are steamed from a hand-stoked, coal-fired Lancashire boiler. The brick chimney has also been restored to its original height of 82 feet.

WILTON

8 miles SE of Marlborough off the A338

Windmill

A footpath of about a mile links the Crofton Beam Engines with Wilton. This is the smaller of the two Wiltshire Wiltons and is the site of the **Wilton Windmill**. This traditional working mill, the only one operating in the

THE SWAN INN

Wilton, Marlborough, Wiltshire SN8 3SS
Tel: 01672 870274
e-mail: info@theswanwilton.co.uk
website: www.theswanwilton.co.uk

Nestled in the heart of the picturesque village of Wilton, **The Swan Inn** is a pub you will not regret visiting. Wilton is a traditional farming village and is home to the county's only working windmill. It is very popular with visitors to Wiltshire and the locals who frequent The Swan Inn offer a warm welcome.

The inn is close to the Kennet & Avon Canal and inside the décor is unfussy, with wooden floors, dried hops around the walls, and farmhouse style furniture. It is an ideal place to relax and enjoy a hearty meal and with a strong focus on home cooked food it isn't hard to see why people return here. The experienced chef produces a well-balanced menu, with a mix of haute cuisine and popular traditional pub meals. The ingredients are sourced locally wherever possible, with fresh fish delivered daily from Looe, Cornwall. The daily changing menus feature delights such as handmade terrines, pies and chutneys; and on Sundays a fine roast dinner heads the menu.

Owner Bill Clemence has a great knowledge of fine wines, which perhaps explains why the pub is renowned for its extensive selection of outstanding wines to complement any meal.

Wilton Windmill

county, was built in 1821 after the Canal Company had taken the water out of the River Bedwyn for their canal, thereby depriving the water mills of the power to drive their mills. The mill worked until 1920, when the availability of steam power and electricity literally took the wind out its sails. After standing derelict for 50 years the mill was restored at a cost of £25,000 and is now looked after by the Wilton Windmill Society. This superb old mill is floodlit from dusk until 10pm, making a wonderful sight on a chalk ridge 550 feet above sea level.

CLENCH COMMON

2 miles S of Marlborough on the A345

This is a lovely part of the world for walking or cycling. The Forestry Commission's West Woods, particularly notable for bluebells in May, has a picnic site; nearby is Martinsell Hill topped by an ancient fort.

WOOTTON RIVERS

4 miles S of Marlborough off the A345

An attractive village with a real curiosity in its highly unusual church clock. The Jack Sprat Clock was built by a local man from an assortment of scrap metal, including old bicycles, prams and farm tools, to mark the coronation of King George V in 1911. It has 24 different chimes and its face has letters instead of numbers.

PEWSEY

7 miles S of Marlborough on the A345

Heritage Centre   White Horse

In the heart of the beautiful valley that bears its name, this is a charming village of half-timbered houses and thatched cottages. It was once the personal property of Alfred the Great, and a statue of the king stands at the crossroads in the centre. The parish church, built on a foundation of sarsen stones, has an unusual altar rail made from timbers taken from the *San Josef*, a ship captured by Nelson in 1797.

Attractions for the visitor include the old wharf area and the **Heritage Centre**, housed in an 1870 foundry building. It contains an interesting collection of old and unusual machine tools and farm machinery.

The original **Pewsey White Horse**, south of the village on Pewsey Down, was cut in 1785, apparently including a rider, but was redesigned by a Mr George Marples and cut by the Pewsey Fire Brigade to celebrate the coronation of King George VI. Pewsey Carnival takes place each September, and the annual Devizes to Westminster canoe race passes through Pewsey Wharf.

A minor road runs past the White Horse across Pewsey Down to the isolated village of

THE BARGE INN

Honeystreet, Pewsey, Wiltshire SN9 5PS
Tel: 01672 851705

The community spirit at the Barge Inn is clear to see, with both locals and visitors welcomed with open arms. A long lease to the inn was acquired by a group of locals in a community project, and once again the inn has a rapidly growing reputation for the friendly service it offers, regular entertainment, a range of unusual real ales and ciders, and an excellent restaurant that won't break the bank!

The inn was one of six winners of a £400,000 BIG Lottery grant in a national competition, and will be featured in the BBC Village SOS series to be shown on BBC1 in 2011. With the grant funding awarded, plans to refurbish both the inn itself and its camp site are underway.

The Barge Inn has many delightful quirks that one would expect from a 200 year old watering hole. Built on the banks of the Kennet & Avon canal in the hamlet of Honeystreet, some 4 miles west of Pewsey, it lies in the heart of Wiltshire's internationally famed Crop Circle area. In the summer, and on warmer days, drinks and meals can be enjoyed in the Beer Garden right by the side of the canal.

The camp site is situated right next to the inn, and has at least 30 pitches, with additional space for some caravans. It also boasts brand new toilet, laundry and shower facilities, and a small shop. For full details, please phone 01672 851705, or see our website 'www.bargeinncommunityproject.com.

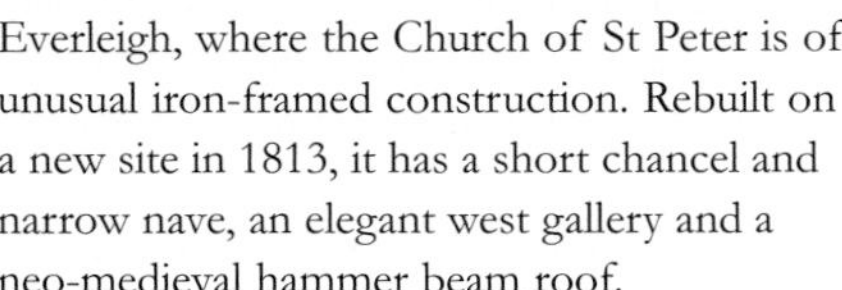

Everleigh, where the Church of St Peter is of unusual iron-framed construction. Rebuilt on a new site in 1813, it has a short chancel and narrow nave, an elegant west gallery and a neo-medieval hammer beam roof.

ALTON BARNES AND ALTON PRIORS

6 miles SW of Marlborough off the A345

White Horse

The largest **White Horse** in Wiltshire can be seen on the hillside above Alton Barnes; cut in 1812, it is 160 feet high and 155 feet long and is visible from Old Sarum, 20 miles away. According to the local story, the original contractor ran off with the £20 advance payment and the work was carried out by one Robert Pile, who owned the land. The runaway contractor was later arrested and hanged for a string of offences. Other notable Wiltshire White Horses in the locality are at Hackpen, just north of Marlborough (cut to commemorate Queen Victoria's coronation) and at Pewsey.

AVEBURY

6 miles W of Marlborough on the A4361

Stone Circles | Avebury Manor

Alexander Keiller Museum

An internationally renowned 28-acre World Heritage Site is the centre of the **Avebury Stone Circles** (see panel opposite), the most remarkable ritual megalithic monuments in Europe. A massive bank and ditch enclose an outer circle and two inner circles of stones. The outer circle has almost 100 sarsen stones (made of sand and silica); the two inner rings have 40 stones still standing. Some of the individual stones weigh 40 tons and had to be dragged here from Marlborough Downs. They

Avebury Manor House

are in two basic shapes, which have been equated with male and female, supporting the theory that the site was used in fertility rites. Archaeologists have also found the remains of a long-vanished avenue of stones leading south towards Beckhampton, a discovery that vindicated the theory of the 18th-century antiquary, William Stukeley, who made drawings of the stone circles with this avenue marked.

Many of the archaeological finds from the site are displayed in Avebury's **Alexander Keiller Museum**, which also describes the restoration of the site by Keiller in the 1930s.

Keiller's home is the 16th-century **Avebury Manor**, which stands on the site of a 12th-century priory. The house and its four-acre walled garden, which features a wishing well, topiary, a rose garden and an Italian walk, are owned by the National Trust.

Avebury Stone Circle

Avebury, nr Marlborough, Wiltshire SN8 1RF
Telephone: 01672 539250
website: www.nationaltrust.org.uk

This internationally renowned stone circle, a World Heritage Site, partly encompasses the pretty village of Avebury. Many of the stones were re-erected in the 1930s by the archaeologist Alexander Keiller, who uncovered the true wonder of one of the most important megalithic monuments in Europe. You can walk right up to the stones and touch them, then watch an exciting interactive audio-visual display which brings their story, and that of the people who strove to uncover their past, alive.

The Barn Gallery and the Stables Gallery house the museum, exhibiting many of the fascinating finds from all the local excavations. Another layer of history is provided by the buildings themselves: the dovecote is 16th-century, while the thatched threshing barn and stables are 17th-century. Nearby, the gentle rise of Windmill Hill, once the site of an important Neolithic settlement, has several well-preserved Bronze Age burial mounds and boasts commanding views. West of Avebury, the Iron Age earthwork of Oldbury Castle crowns Cherhill Down, along with the conspicuous Lansdowne Monument. With the spectacular folds of Calstone Coombes, this area of open downland provides wonderful walking.

WEST OVERTON

3 miles W of Marlborough off the A4

Overton Hill · Fyfield Down · Devil's Den

The area between Marlborough and Avebury sees the biggest concentration of prehistoric remains in the country. The scattered community of West Overton stands at the foot of **Overton Hill**, the site of an early Bronze Age monument called The Sanctuary. Concrete markers have now replaced the giant standing stones at the southeastern end of West Kennet Avenue, an ancient pathway that once connected them to the main megalithic circles at Avebury. Overton Hill is also the start point of the Ridgeway long-distance path, which runs for 80 miles to the Chilterns. Just off this path is **Fyfield Down**, now a nature reserve, where quarries once provided many of the great stones that are such a feature of the area. **Devil's Den** long barrow lies within the reserve. The local legend that Satan sometimes appears here at midnight attempting to pull down the stones with a team of white oxen, has not been corroborated in recent times.

EAST AND WEST KENNET

4 miles W of Marlborough on the A4

Long Barrow

West Kennet Long Barrow, one of Britain's largest neolithic burial tombs, is situated a gentle stroll away from the twin villages. The tomb is of impressive proportions – 330 feet long, 80 feet wide and 10 feet high – and is reached by squeezing past some massive stones in the semi-circular forecourt.

SILBURY HILL

5 miles W of Marlborough on the A4

The largest man-made prehistoric mound in Europe, built around 2800BC, standing 130 feet high and covering five acres. Excavation in the late 1960s revealed some details of how it was constructed but shed little light on its purpose. Theories include a burial place for King Sil and his horse, and a hiding place for a large gold statue built by the Devil on his way to Devizes. Scholarship generally favours the first.

Devizes

Wiltshire Heritage Museum · Canal Museum

Visitor Centre · Market Cross

Devizes Locks Trail

The central market town of Wiltshire, Devizes boasts no fewer than 500 listed buildings within a quarter of a square mile. Many of the town's finest buildings are situated in and around the old market place, including the Town Hall and the Corn Exchange. Also here is an unusual **Market Cross** inscribed with the story of Ruth Pierce, a market stall-holder who stood accused, on January 25th 1753, of short-changing a customer. When an ugly crowd gathered round her, she stood and pleaded her innocence, adding, "May I be struck dead if I am lying". A rash move, as she fell to the ground and died forthwith. The missing money (three pence – 1.4p) was found clutched in her hand.

Devizes was founded in 1080 by Bishop Osmund, nephew of William the Conqueror. The Bishop was responsible for building a timber castle between the lands of two powerful manors, and this act brought about the town's name, which is derived from the Latin *ad divisas*, or 'at the boundaries'. After the wooden structure burnt down, Roger, Bishop of Sarum, built a stone castle in 1138 that survived until the end of the Civil War, when it was demolished. Bishop Roger also built two

URBAN RUSTICS

1 Old Swan Yard, High Street,
Devizes, Wiltshire SN10 1AT
Tel: 01380 725593
e-mail: shop@urbanrustics.co.uk
website: www.urbanrustics.co.uk

With a fine range of niche products, including a generous handful from London-based home ware designers, **Urban Rustics** is a delightfully different shop. This fresh and charming establishment can be found in a period building in the unspoilt market town of Devizes and is run by brother and sister team Christopher and Kate.

Many locals and visitors think of Urban Rustics as the kind of independent shop you would find in London. There are some lovely collections on sale here from leading suppliers across the world. The fact that it is located in the middle of Wiltshire in a former pub, which dates back to the 17th century, makes it all that more interesting.

Christopher and Kate offer a personal one-to-one service tailored to each individual's needs. They are both extremely professional in their approach and are happy to offer any advice should you require it. If you are looking for the London style shopping environment and service outside of the M25 then Urban Rustics is definitely worth a look.

fine churches in Devizes. Long Street is lined with elegant Georgian houses and contains the **Wiltshire Heritage Museum**, which has a splendid collection of artefacts from the area, and an art gallery with a John Piper window and regularly changing exhibitions. Here, amongst other local industries, you can learn about the Wadworth Brewery, founded in 1875 and still a family business. The brewery continues to use Shire horses for local deliveries and they have become a familiar and much-loved part of the local scene. Their stables can be visited by prior arrangement.

Devizes Visitor Centre offers a unique insight into the town. The centre is based on a 12th-century castle and takes visitors back to medieval times, when Devizes boasted the finest castle in Europe. Other exhibits chronicle the scenes of anarchy and unrest during the struggle for power between Empress Matilda and King Stephen. An interactive exhibition shows how Devizes thrived as a medieval town, and came to be at the centre of the 12th-century civil war.

Devizes stands at a key point on the Kennet & Avon Canal, and the **Kennet and Avon Canal Museum** tells the complete story of the canal in fascinating detail. Many visitors combine a trip to the museum with a walk along the towpath, which is a public footpath. The route of the canal involved overcoming the rise of 237 feet from the Avon Valley to Devizes. The engineer John Rennie devised the solution, which was to build one vast flight of locks, 29 in all, of which 16 were set very close together down Caen Hill. The **Devizes Locks Discovery Trail** descends from Devizes Wharf, through the town and to the bottom of the flight at Lower Foxhangers, returning by way of open countryside and the village of Rowde. Each July the Canalfest, a weekend of family fun designed to raise funds for the upkeep of the canal, is held at the Wharf, which is also the start point of the annual

WILTSHIRE YEOMAN

9 Andover Road, Chirton, Devizes, Wiltshire SN10 3QN
Tel: 01380 840665
e-mail: thewiltshireyeoman@btconnect.com

If you are looking for a traditional country pub serving delicious wholesome food then look no further than the **Wiltshire Yeoman**. It was recently taken over at the end of summer 2010 by Jutta Hahn and Robert Coombes, who both have plenty of experience when it comes to running a public house.

The Wiltshire Yeoman is very attractive from the outside and the impressive establishment draws plenty of people through its doors. Everyone is welcomed here and inside you will often find a good mix of locals and visitors, including families, walkers and cyclists. The low ceiling gives the pub a cosy feel in the colder months and on warmer days there is a fantastic garden where customers can eat or drink.

The menu here is extensive and because of Jutta's nationality there are plans to introduce some German dishes to the menu. Sunday roasts are very popular at the Wiltshire Yeoman and there is a varied selection of dishes on offer throughout the week including pork shoulder confit, monk fish tail wrapped in pancetta and mushroom, leek and chestnut pie. If you have a lighter appetite a freshly filled baguette might be just what you need to fill the gap.

HORSE COUNTRY

The Barn, Manor Farm, Lydeway, Devizes,
Wiltshire SN10 3PU
Tel: 01380 840123
e-mail: horsecountryshop@aol.com

Horse Country is a shop that was opened out of need and it has proved to be extremely popular. When proprietor Rosie Cunningham's horse broke its lead rope she had to take a 25 mile round trip to get a new one and so decided on a new venture.

Horse Country opened in 2002 and specialises in equestrian and pet supplies. Rosie is well known among the horse community because she owns her own horse and also attends local shows. She offers a friendly service and it is why many people come to her for assistance. She has a strong passion for horses, is well respected locally and knows what she is talking about when it comes to equestrian matters.

Horse Country has plenty of stock including a wide range of riding wear, horse and pet food, bedding and gas bottles. Services such as riding hat and body protector fitting are offered as well as rug wash and repair, clipper servicing and blade sharpening. Rosettes are available to order for all occasions. Ring for details.

Devizes-Westminster canoe race held every year on Good Friday. This gruelling marathon takes in 75 locks on its 125-mile course.

Around Devizes

BISHOP'S CANNINGS

4 miles NE of Devizes on the A361

Parish Church of St Mary

The bishops of Salisbury once owned a manor here and built the very grand **Parish Church of St Mary** before they started work on the Cathedral. This church, dedicated to St Mary, has often been likened to the Cathedral and does indeed bear some resemblance, notably in its tall, tapering spire. This is Moonraker country and, according to legend, a group of 17th-century smugglers from Bishops Canning fooled excisemen when caught recovering dumped brandy kegs from a pond known as the Crammer. The smugglers pretended to be mad and claimed that the moon's reflection on the pond was actually a cheese, which they were trying to rake in. The ruse worked, so who were the real fools? A hollow in the downs west of the village was the scene of a bloody Civil War battle in 1643 when the Royalist forces under Prince Rupert's brother, Maurice, defeated the Parliamentarian forces at Roundway Down. According to a local legend the cries of the dead can be heard coming from a burial ditch on the anniversary of the battle (13 July).

MARKET LAVINGTON

5 miles S of Devizes on the B3098

Museum

The Village under the Plain is home to a little

museum in the former schoolmaster's cottage of 1846, located behind the old village school.

Displays at **Market Lavington Museum** include a Victorian kitchen and archive photographs – the village has had professional photographers since 1880 and their efforts record every aspect of farms, malting, brick making, transport and gardening, as well as highlights of village life.

Swindon

STEAM | National Monuments Record Centre | Museum & Art Gallery

Think Swindon, think the Great Western Railway. Think GWR, think Isambard Kingdom Brunel. The largest town in Wiltshire, lying in the northeast corner between the Cotswolds and the Marlborough Downs, Swindon was an insignificant agricultural community before the railway line between London and Bristol was completed in 1835. Swindon Station opened in that year, but it was some time later, in 1843, that Brunel, the GWR's principal engineer, decided that Swindon was the place to build his locomotive works. Within a few years it had grown to be one of the largest in the world, with as many as 12,000 people on a 320-acre site that incorporated the Railway Village; this was a model development of 300 workmen's houses built of limestone extracted from the construction of Box Tunnel. This unique example of early-Victorian town planning is open to the public as the Railway Village Museum, with a restored Victorian railway worker's cottage. Lit by gas, the cottage, open only by appointment, contains many original fittings such as the range and copper in the kitchen.

STEAM, the Museum of the Great Western Railway, provides both a great family day out and a tribute to one of the great railways of the world. Among the stars in its fascinating collection of locomotives are 4073 *Caerphilly Castle* and one of the distinctive Great Western diesel railcars, built in 1934 . As well as displaying railway memorabilia, such as engine nameplates, signalling equipment, and an exhibition of the life and achievements of Brunel, the centre also focuses on the human aspects of the industry, telling the story of the men and women who built and repaired the locomotives and carriages of the GWR (God's Wonderful Railway) for seven generations. The last locomotive to be built at the works, and now on display, was 92220 *Evening Star*, a powerful 2-10-0 freight engine of a type that proved surprisingly versatile but was destined to have all too short a working life. Engineering work continued on the site until 1986, when the works finally closed. STEAM has a shop with an impressive range of GWR and other railway gifts, books, souvenirs and pocket-money toys. It's family-friendly, and all areas are fully accessible to wheelchairs. The site now also contains the **National Monuments Record Centre** – the public archive of the Royal Commission on the

Swindon and Crickdale Railway

Historical Monuments of England, with seven million photographs, documents and texts.

Railway devotees are offered an additional treat in Swindon. To the northeast of the town, the **Swindon & Cricklade Railway** is Wiltshire's only Heritage Railway. The line uses part of the track bed of the former Midland & South Western Junction Railway and the trains run at weekends and on special days with either steam or diesel locomotives.

There's lots more to Swindon than the legacy of the GWR: it's a bustling and successful commercial town with excellent shopping and leisure facilities and plenty of open spaces. In an elegant early 19th-century house on the Bath Road, **Swindon Museum and Art Gallery** contains a variety of displays on the history, archaeology and geology of the town and the surrounding area, and also houses a fine collection of 20th-century British art.

The town offers a generous quantity of retail therapy at the Swindon Designer Outlet, which is housed in the beautifully renovated Grade II listed buildings of the former GWR works. One of the largest covered designer outlets in Europe, the centre has almost 90 top name stores, as well as a range of eateries.

Around Swindon

CRICKLADE

6 miles N of Swindon off the A419

Museum   North Meadow

The only Wiltshire town on the Thames was an important post on the Roman Ermine Street and had its own mint in Saxon times. There are many buildings of interest, notably the Church of St Sampson, with its cathedral-like four-spired tower, where a festival of music takes place each September; the famous school founded by the London goldsmith Robert Jenner in 1651; and the fancy Victorian clock tower. **Cricklade Museum**, in a Baptist chapel dating from 1852, contains displays on social history, Roman occupation, Rotten Borough elections and an archive of 2000 photographs. Nearby **North Meadow** is a National Nature Reserve where the rare snake's head fritillary grows.

HIGHWORTH

5 miles NE of Swindon on the A361

Highworth Hill

The name is appropriate, as the village stands at the top of a 400 foot incline, and the view from **Highworth Hill** takes in the counties of Wiltshire, Gloucestershire and Oxfordshire. There are some very fine 17th and 18th-century buildings round the old square, and the parish church is of interest – built in the 15th century, it was fortified during the Civil War and was attacked soon after by Parliamentarian forces under Fairfax. One of the cannonballs that struck it is on display outside. The church contains a memorial to Lieutenant Warneford, who was awarded the VC for destroying the first enemy Zeppelin in 1915.

WROUGHTON

3 miles S of Swindon on the A4361

Butterfly World   Clouts Wood Nature Reserve

Barbury Castle   Craft Village

Wroughton Airfield, with its historic Second World War hangars, now serves as a Science Museum, Swindon's storage facility for larger objects. It is only open for pre-booked tours and special events.

A popular attraction in Wroughton is **Butterfly World** at Studley Grange Garden &

Leisure Park. Visitors can get close to some of the largest and most spectacular insects on the planet. They fly freely against a backdrop of tropical plants, skimming over fish-filled pools. The mini-beasts house is home to a fascinating display of spiders, scorpions, mantis and other creepy -crawlies. More recent arrivals include otters and two playful meerkats, Thelma and Louise. Also within the Park is a **Craft Village** where craftspeople make and sell their work, which ranges from stained glass to silk flowers, from ceramics to crystals and jewellery.

Nearby, **Clouts Wood Nature Reserve** is a lovely place for a ramble, and a short drive south, by the Ridgeway, is the site of **Barbury Castle**, one of the most spectacular Iron Age forts in southern England. The open hillside was the scene of a bloody battle between the Britons and the Saxons in the 6th century; the Britons lost and the Saxon kingdom of Wessex was established under King Cealwin. The area around the castle is a country park.

BROAD HINTON

5 miles S of Swindon off the A4361

In the church at Broad Hinton is a memorial to local bigwig Sir Thomas Wroughton, who returned home from hunting to find his wife reading the Bible instead of making his tea. He seized the Bible and flung it into the fire; his wife retrieved it but in doing so severely burnt her hands. As punishment for his blasphemy Sir Thomas's hands and those of his four children withered away (very hard on the children, surely). The monument shows the whole handless family and a Bible with a corner burnt off.

LYDIARD TREGOZE

2 miles W of Swindon off the A3102

Lydiard Park

On the western outskirts of Swindon, **Lydiard Park** is the ancestral home of the Viscounts Bolingbroke. The park is a delightful place to explore, and the house, one of Wiltshire's smaller stately homes, is a real gem, described by Sir Hugh Casson as "a gentle Georgian house, sunning itself as serenely as an old grey cat". Chief attractions inside include the little blue Dressing Room devoted to the 18th-century society artist Lady Diana Spencer, who became the 2nd Viscountess Bolingbroke. She shared a common ancestry and a remarkable physical resemblance to the late Diana, Princess of Wales. Lydiard Park's grounds contain a recently restored walled garden, originally built in the 1740s, an excellent children's play area, and a café.

St Mary's Church, next to the house, contains many monuments to the St John family, who have lived here from Elizabethan times. The most striking is the Golden Cavalier, a life-size gilded effigy of Edward St John in full battledress (he was killed at the second Battle of Newbury in 1645).

Lydiard Lake

WOOTTON BASSETT

3 miles W of Swindon off the A3102

A small town with a big history, its records go back to the 7th century. In 1219, Henry III granted Wootton Bassett a market charter (the market is still held every Wednesday). The town boasts some fine Georgian buildings, a good range of family-run businesses – including a butcher, baker, greengrocer and ironmonger – and some good eating places. You can eat al fresco across from the striking Old Town Hall, which stands on a series of stone pillars, leaving an open-sided ground-floor area that once served as a covered market. The museum above, open on Saturday mornings, contains a rare ducking stool, silver maces and a mayoral sword of office.

A section of the Wilts & Berks Canal has been restored at Templars Fir. Opened in May 1998, about 50 boats of all kinds were launched on the canal and a day of festivities was enjoyed by all. The railway station, alas, has not been revived after falling to the Beeching axe in 1966.

Chippenham

Museum & Heritage Centre

Maud Heath's Causeway

Set on the banks of the Avon, Chippenham was founded around AD600 by the Saxon king Cyppa. It became an important administrative centre in King Alfred's time and later gained further prominence from the wool trade. It was a major stop on the London-Bristol coaching run and is served by the railway between the same two cities. Buildings of note include the Church of St Andrew (mainly 15th century) and the half-timbered Yelde Hall, once used by the burgesses and bailiffs of the Chippenham Hundred. This Grade I building now houses the tourist information office.

Maud Heath's Causeway, Chippenham

Chippenham Museum and Heritage Centre, in an 18th-century building in the Market Place, tells the story of the town from the Jurassic period onwards, and the displays focus on Saxon Chippenham, Alfred the Great, Brunel's railway, the celebrated cheese market, Victorian living conditions and Chippenham curiosities.

At Hardenhuish Hall on the edge of town, John Wood the Younger of Bath fame built the Church of St Nicholas; completed in 1779, it is notable for its domed steeple and elegant Venetian windows. Wealth from the wool trade built many fine houses using local stone and Bath stone, which led to Chippenham being called little Bath.

In the flood plain to the east of Chippenham, stands the four-and-a-half mile footpath known as **Maud Heath's Causeway**. This remarkable and ingenious walkway consisting of 64 brick and stone arches was built at the end of the 15th century at the bequest of Maud Heath, who spent most of her life as a market trader trudging her often muddy way between her village of Bremhill and Chippenham. She died a relatively wealthy woman, and the land and

ALLINGTON FARM SHOP

Allington Bar Farm, Allington,
Chippenham, Wiltshire SN14 6LJ
Tel: 01249 658112
website: www.allingtonfarmshop.co.uk

A visit to this family run farm shop, just on the outskirts of Chippenham, is a must.

Established for nearly 30 years, the shop is run by the Reynolds Family, in parallel with their 400 acre farm and specialises in quality, home produced and locally sourced food.

Throughout all the seasons of the year there is always a fantastic selection of salads, vegetables and fruit. Seasonal fruit & vegetables are home grown & sourced locally. Open daily, the in house butchery offers a range of home reared & locally reared meat; Pork including homemade sausages in a range of over 20 flavours, Lamb, Beef is hung for a minimum of 21 days to achieve optimum flavour & tenderness, local free range poultry, local seasonal game, dry cured bacon & gammon joints and homemade faggots & burgers. The Delicatessen has an array of local, artisan & continental cheeses, charcuterie, home cooked meats, olives & insalatas, pates, handmade scotch eggs, locally smoked fish & meats and locally made pies.

There is a huge range of both essential and speciality grocery items sourced from the local area and from further afield. Sample local freshly baked bread, home made cakes & pies, locally made biscuits, local eggs, local honey, preserves, chutneys & pickles, local organic jersey milk, cream, butter, yoghurt & cheesecakes, extensive range of local ice cream & frozen desserts, Prue's meringues from nearby Marshfield, loose frozen fruit, vegetables & pastries, local apple juice, freshly squeezed orange juice and much more!

Allington Farm Shop is open 7 days a week 9am – 6pm Mon – Sat (incl. Bank Holidays) and 10am – 5pm on Sundays.

The shop also stocks a range of convenience items & Calor Gas handy if you are self catering or camping in the area.

ALLINGTON CAFÉ AT ALLINGTON FARM SHOP

Allington Bar Farm, Allington, Chippenham, SN14 6LJ
T: 01249 463326 website: www.allingtoncafe.co.uk

Enjoy morning coffee, lunch or afternoon tea in cosy & relaxing surroundings. Choose from a selection of pastries, homemade soups & pies, mouth watering salads, paninis, baguettes & sandwiches, homemade pies, puddings and freshly baked scones & cakes. All food is freshly prepared & cooked on site using quality, fresh ingredients many of which are supplied by and sold within the farm shop. The Café is open 7 days a week

Monday - Friday 9am - 4.30pm, 9am – 5pm on Saturdays & Sunday 10am - 4pm.

DUTCH COTTAGE TEA ROOMS

56 St Mary Street, Chippenham, Wiltshire SN15 3JW
Tel: 01249 465993
e-mail: tearooms@dutch-cottage.co.uk
website: www.dutch-cottage.co.uk

Situated on the oldest street in Chippenham near to the Market Place is **Dutch Cottage Tea Rooms**. This beautiful property has listed status, maintained proudly by owners Robert and Elizabeth Perks who have been awarded the Civic Society Award for their sympathetic conversion to the tea room. Traditional to the core, visitors to the tea room can expect delicate china, log burning stoves to keep them warm, low oak beams and doorways benefitting from its original status as a local wool merchant's cottage in the 15th century.

Naturally, guests can expect to find a charming selection of fair trade accredited speciality teas and coffees to enjoy at Dutch Cottage, however it is probably best known for its food. The menu here is one hundred percent home cooked by Robert and Elizabeth who take great pride in providing their customers with wholesome, home cooked food. A range of breakfasts, lunches, cakes and cream teas are available, including a full two course roast with all the trimmings that is served each Wednesday and Friday, for which booking is essential. They also sell some of their own produce including homemade preserves. Private parties and business meetings can also be catered for and held at Dutch Cottage, adding a timeless feel to any event, private or corporate. Please call for details or visit the website.

property she left in her will provided sufficient funds for the upkeep of the causeway, which is best seen near the hamlet of Kellaways. A statue of Maud, basket in hand, stands overlooking the flood plain at Wick Hill.

Around Chippenham

CALNE

5 miles E of Chippenham on the A4

Bowood House | Atwell-Wilson Motor Museum

A former weaving centre in the valley of the River Marden; the prominent wool church reflects the prosperity of earlier times. One of the memorials in the church is to Dr Ingenhousz, who is widely credited with creating a smallpox vaccination before Jenner. Another remembers a King of the Gypsies who died of smallpox in 1774.

A short distance from Calne, to the west, stands **Bowood House**, built in 1625 and now a treasury of Shelborne family heirlooms, paintings, books and furniture. In the Bowood Laboratory, Dr Joseph Priestley, tutor to the 1st Marquess of Lansdowne's son, conducted experiments that resulted in the identification of oxygen. The house is set in lovely Capability Brown grounds with a lake and terraced garden, and the largest area of mown lawn in England. The mausoleum was commissioned in 1761 by the Dowager Countess of Shelborne as a memorial to her husband, and was Robert Adam's first work for them. A separate woodland garden of 60 acres, with azaleas and rhododendrons, is open from late April to early June. Also within the grounds are an adventure playground for

FOXHAM INN

Foxham, Chippenham, Wiltshire SN15 4NQ
Tel: 01249-740665
e-mail: thefoxhaminn@btconnect.com
website: www.thefoxhaminn.co.uk

The award-winning **Foxham Inn** is everything a good pub should be, and more. For a start it is an independently-owned freehouse, with chef Neil Cooper taking charge of the kitchen and his wife Sarah looking after the bar. Neil was born and raised in the West Country and learned his skills in many acclaimed country house hotels. In 2006 he and Sarah bought the historic Foxham Inn – up to 450 years old in places – and turned it into a roaring success.

Neil believes in using fresh local food, and it comes no better than here at the Foxham Inn. He grows his own fruit, vegetables and herbs, and even buys his own meat from farmers and local game shooters and does his own butchering. The result is a range of fantastic dishes like belly of free-range pork served with celeriac purée, or loin of Home Farm lamb served with liquorice and butternut squash purée. If you want something simpler there's a large bar snacks menu, and special diets can be catered for as well. There's even a special Vegetarian Tasting Menu. Add to this the immaculately-kept real ales, and you see why the Foxham Inn is indeed very special.

under-12s, a Soft Play Palace, a coffee shop and restaurant.

The **Atwell-Wilson Motor Museum**, on the A4 east of Calne, has a collection of more than 125 vintage and classic cars and motorcycles from the years 1924 to the late 1980s. Most of them are still in running order. Although the majority of the exhibits are cars, the museum also houses an impressive collection of lorries, mopeds and push bikes, as well as a large selection of vehicle manuals and other archive material, and an extensive collection of motor memorabilia. Richard and Hasell Atwell started the collection with a 1937 Buick Albermarle, and American cars are well represented. Other notable vehicles include a 1934 Alvis Speed 20, a 1954 Rolls-Royce Silver Wraith and a 1953 Allard Palm Beach. Sadly, Richard died in April 2010.

LACKHAM

3 miles S of Chippenham on the A350

Museum of Agricultural and Rural Life

The **Lackham Museum of Agriculture and Rural Life** offers a variety of displays set within a wonderful complex of historic Wiltshire farm buildings. With 18th-century Lackham House (private) as a backdrop, the extensive themed gardens contain a walled garden, a large ornamental pond, bog garden, sensory garden, wartime kitchen garden and Lackham's famous giant lemons. For children, there's a willow house, a maze and Rupert the Bear's House. Souvenirs and Lackham-grown produce are on sale in the walled garden shop.

LACOCK

4 miles S of Chippenham on the A350

Abbey Fox Talbot Museum

The National Trust village of Lacock is one

of the country's real treasures. The quadrangle of streets – East, High, West and Church – holds a delightful assortment of mellow stone buildings, and the period look (no intrusive power cables or other modern-day eyesores) keeps it in great demand as a film location, most recently in BBC-TV's *Cranford Chronicles*. Every building is a well-restored, well-preserved gem, and overlooking everything is **Lacock Abbey**, founded in 1232 by Ela, Countess of Salisbury, in memory of her husband William Longsword, stepbrother to Richard the Lionheart. In common with all monastic houses, Lacock was dissolved by Henry VIII, but the original cloisters, chapter houses, sacristy and kitchens survive.

Much of the remainder of what we see today dates from the mid 16th century, when the abbey was acquired by Sir William Sharington. He added an impressive country house and the elegant octagonal tower that overlooks the Avon. The estate next passed into the hands of the Talbot family, who held it for 370 years before ceding it to the National Trust in 1944.

The most distinguished member of the Talbot family was the pioneering photographer William Henry Fox Talbot, who carried out his experiments in the 1830s, mainly at the Abbey. The **Fox Talbot Museum** commemorates the life and achievements of a man who was not just a photographer, but also a mathematician, physicist, classicist, philologist and transcriber of Syrian and Chaldean cuneiform. In 1839, Fox Talbot presented to the Royal Society "an account of the art of photogenic drawing or the process by which natural objects may be made to delineate themselves without the aid of the artist's pencil" – photography, in short. Louis Daguerre was at the same time demonstrating a similar technique in France, and it is not certain which of the two pioneers should be called the father of photography. But it was indisputably true that Fox Talbot invented the positive/negative process that permitted multiple copies. The museum is located in an old barn at the entrance to the abbey and contains Fox Talbot memorabilia and a collection of early cameras. Fox Talbot also remodelled the south elevation of the abbey and added three new oriel windows. One of the world's earliest photographs shows a detail of a latticed oriel window of the abbey; the size of a postage stamp, it is the earliest known example of a photographic negative.

MELKSHAM

7 miles S of Chippenham on the A350

Once an important weaving centre, Melksham was also very briefly in vogue as a spa town. It didn't make much of a splash, being overshadowed by its near neighbour Bath, so it turned to manufacturing and was given a boost when the Wilts & Berks Canal was opened. The canal, built between 1795 and 1810, linked the Kennet & Avon Canal with Abingdon, on the Thames. The Wilts & Berks was abandoned in 1914, but much of its path still exists in the form of lock and bridge remains, towpaths and embankments.

TROWBRIDGE

13 miles S of Chippenham on the A350

Museum

The county town of Wiltshire, and another major weaving centre in its day. A large number of industrial buildings still stand, and the Town Council and Civic Society have devised an interesting walk that takes in many of them. The **Trowbridge Museum**, located in one of the town's last working woollen mills, has a variety of interesting displays, including a reconstructed medieval castle and tableaux of a weaver's cottage and Taylor's drapery shop. It also features some working textile looms.

The chancel of the parish church of St James, crowned by one of the finest spires in the county, contains the tomb of the poet and former rector George Crabbe, who wrote the work on which Benjamin Britten based his opera *Peter Grimes*. Trowbridge's most famous son was Isaac Pitman, the shorthand man, who was born in Nash Yard in 1813.

CORSHAM

3 miles SW of Chippenham off the A4

Corsham Court

A town made prosperous by wool and the quarrying of local Bath stone. Pevsner was very much taken with Corsham, asserting that it had no match in Wiltshire "for wealth of good houses". The composer Sir Michael Tippett spent the 10 years between 1960 and 1970 living at Parkside on the High Street – he was attracted here by the peace of the town and its easy access to the countryside.

Corsham Court, based on an Elizabethan house of 1582, was bought by Paul Methuen in 1745 and later housed his inherited collection of paintings. The present house and grounds are chiefly the work of John Nash, Capability Brown, Thomas Bellamy and Humphry Repton, a top-pedigree setting for the treasures within, which include paintings by Caravaggio, Fra Filippo Lippi, Reynolds, Rubens and Van Dyck, and furniture by

GREEN GINGER

34 High Street, Corsham, Wiltshire SN13 OHB
Tel: 01249 716631
e-mail: info@greengingerhealth.com
website: www.greengingerhealth.com

Green Ginger is a successful independent health food shop founded in 2001 by Nina Hammett and Stuart Hodgson who have a real passion for the industry.Through dedicating their time and energy to Green Ginger, they have been able to provide the inhabitants of Corsham an alternative and healthy way to enjoy food.

The Shop relocated in 2006 to a beautiful listed building on Corsham's High street.The ground floor is dedicated to health foods, specialising in ethical organic foods, self service bulk food and special dietary foods such as gluten free, dairy free, wheat free and sugar free. Nina and Stuart believe variety is the spice of life and ensure that there is always something new in stock to entice.

On the first floor customers will find various supplements,natural chemical free body care and household cleaning products.This leads through to Green Ginger's tranquil therapy room where customers can enjoy a range of natural therapies. Therapists and practitioners are all highly qualified as are the shop floor staff who are friendly and knowledgeable about the products and remedies in store. Nina and Stuart place great emphasis on providing good old fashioned customer service, ensuring any visit here is a pleasant one.

Chippendale. The house has been used as the location for several films, including *Northanger Abbey* and *Remains of the Day*. Among other important buildings in Corsham are the magnificent almshouses erected by Dame Margaret Hungerford in 1668 and still in use, the old market house (town hall) and a row of 16th-century Flemish weavers' cottages. Mansion House, now a youth centre, was the home of Robert Neale, a leading clothier and sometime MP for Wootton Bassett. His firm produced the red coats worn by the Duke of Wellington's troops. The parish church, St Bartholomew's, contains tombs and memorials to some of Corsham's eminent clothiers, and also the famous flat-stone grave of Sarah Jarvis, who died in 1753 at the age of 107 having grown a third set of teeth!

Corsham Tourist Information Centre has an ongoing exhibition about the wool trade and the mining of Bath stone. It includes items used in the old stone mine, which also served as an ammunition depot during the Second World War, and relates the story of Bath stone from rock face to architectural heritage.

BOX

6 miles SW of Chippenham on the A4

Box Tunnel

Bath stone is still quarried at this delightful spot, which is best known for one of the most remarkable engineering feats of its time, **Box Tunnel**. The 1 3/4 mile railway tunnel on a steady 1:100 gradient took five years to excavate, and when completed in 1841, was the longest railway tunnel in the world (Sapperton Tunnel, built in 1789 on the Thames & Severn Canal, was 500 metres longer). According to local legend the sun shines through its entire length on only one occasion each year – sunrise on 9th April, the

SALTBOX FARM

Drewetts Mill, Box, Corsham, Wiltshire SN13 8PT
Tel: 01225 742608
e-mail: bbsaltboxfarm@yahoo.co.uk
website: www.saltboxfarm.co.uk

Nestled in a beautiful location just below the Cotswolds, **Saltbox Farm** offers a high standard of B&B accommodation in an area of outstanding natural beauty.

The family-run dairy farm borders the Bybrook creating a natural sanctuary for wildlife which can be observed from the scenic footpaths meandering alongside the brook and through the meadows. It is definitely an ideal place to stay for those wanting to get away from the hustle and bustle of everyday life and soak up the tranquillity of a peaceful get-away.

Owned by Mary and Tony Gregory, Saltbox Farm, which dates back to the 18th century, is close to Corsham, Lacock, Bradford on Avon, and Bath. Inside it is full of character with a local stone fire place and beamed ceilings. It has two guest rooms, one of which has en-suite facilities and the other a private bathroom. The B&B is popular with walkers and birdwatchers and its rural location lends itself well to those who like being out in the fresh air.

The Gregory's have lived at Saltbox Farm for 50 years and have a milking herd of 130. All of the food they serve is sourced locally and the breakfasts are of the highest quality.

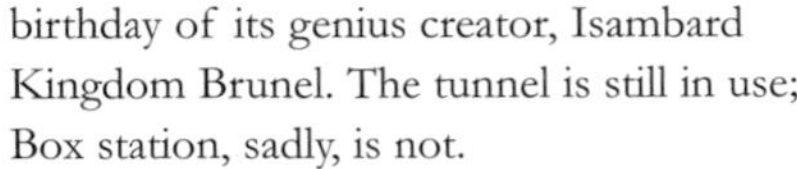

birthday of its genius creator, Isambard Kingdom Brunel. The tunnel is still in use; Box station, sadly, is not.

HOLT

9 miles SW of Chippenham on the B3107

The Courts

The village was once a small spa, and the old mineral well can still be seen in a factory here. Right at the heart of the village is **The Courts** (National Trust), an English country garden of mystery, with beautiful herbaceous borders divided by yew hedges and enriched by unusual topiary, ponds, water gardens and an arboretum. The garden is mainly the work of Sir George Hastings, and was created in the reign of Edward VII. The house is not open to the public.

GREAT CHALFIELD

9 miles SW of Chippenham off the B3107/3109

Great Chalfield Manor

Great Chalfield Manor (National Trust), completed in 1480, is a delightful moated manor house with an impressive great hall and a tiny parish church within its grounds.

Great Chalfield Manor

BRADFORD-ON-AVON

13 miles SW of Chippenham on the A363

Church of St Lawrence · Tithe Barn

Peto Garden · Westwood Manor

Barton Farm Country Park · Abbey Mill

A historic market town at a bridging point on the Avon, which it spans with a superb nine-arched bridge with a lock-up at one end. The town's oldest building is the **Church of St Lawrence**, believed to have been founded by St Aldhelm around AD700. It 'disappeared' for over 1000 years, when it was used variously as a school, a charnel house for storing the bones of the dead, and a residential dwelling. It was re-discovered by a keen-eyed clergyman who looked down from a hill and noticed the cruciform shape of a church. The surrounding buildings were gradually removed to reveal the little masterpiece we see today. Bradford's Norman church, restored in the 19th century, has an interesting memorial to Lieutenant-General Henry Shrapnel, the army officer who, in 1785, invented and gave his name to the shrapnel shell. Another of the town's outstanding buildings is the mighty **Tithe Barn**, once used to store the grain from local farms for Shaftesbury Abbey, now housing a collection of antique farm implements and agricultural machinery. The centrepiece of the museum in Bridge Street is a pharmacy, which had stood in the town for 120 years before being removed lock, stock and medicine bottles to its new site.

Another impressive building is **Abbey Mill**, which was built in 1875 as a cloth mill at a time when the industry was in steep decline. It managed to stay in production until 1902, became a barracks during the World War, and then, was taken over by Avon Rubber who

DOWNSIDE NURSERIES

143 Upper Westwood, Bradford-on-Avon, Wiltshire BA15 2DE
Tel: 01225 862392
e-mail: enquiries@downsidenurseries.co.uk
website: www.downsidenurseries.co.uk

Mother and son team Lorraine and Richard Younge are the hardworking owners of the coveted **Downside Nurseries**. Their beautiful gardens are found on the outskirts of the rural village of Bradford-on-Avon, within easy reach of Iford Manor, Westwood Manor and the glorious Iford Valley. The pair originally started off by supplying local markets with vegetables but over the years they have expanded to meet demand and now supply a variety of local garden centres, garden designers, landscapers and individuals. They specialised in herbaceous perennials, with a huge choice of evergreen and deciduous shrubs, ornamental and fruit trees, climbers, roses, vegetables and bedding plants. A hanging basket creation service is also available for either winter or summer displays, which has won awards for the past few years, also supplying various pubs throughout the UK. Last year Lorraine and Richard won two gold medals for their efforts at the Frome show, holding an enviable reputation amongst their competitors.

New visitors to the centre can enjoy wandering through acres of traditional glass houses, modern poly tunnels, and lush meadows overlooking the valley which is often full of chickens, sheep and lambs depending on the season. A team of friendly and knowledgeable staff are on hand to assist with advice, selection and maintenance.

used it as a factory until the early 1990s. It is now retirement apartments.

Off the A363, **Barton Farm Country Park** offers delightful walks in lovely countryside by the River Avon and the Kennet and Avon Canal. It was once a medieval farm serving Shaftesbury Abbey. Barton Bridge is the original packhorse bridge built to assist the transportation of grain from the farm to the tithe barn.

Iford Manor, Bradford-on-Avon

Half a mile south of town by the River Frome is the Italian-style **Peto Garden** at Iford Manor. Famous for its romantic, tranquil beauty, its steps and terraces, statues, colonnades and ponds, the garden was laid out by the architect and landscape gardener Harold Ainsworth Peto between 1899 and 1933. He was inspired by the works of Lutyens and Jekyll to turn a difficult hillside site into "a haunt of ancient peace".

Outside Bradford, off the A366, the charming 15th- century **Westwood Manor** (altered in the 17th- century) has many interesting features, including Jacobean and Gothic windows, ornate plasterwork, 17th and 18th century tapestries and needlework, a notable collection of stringed instruments and a modern topiary garden.

Malmesbury

Abbey · Abbey House Gardens · Athelstan Museum

Abbey Gardens, Malmesbury

"The Queen of Hilltop Towns" is England's oldest borough and one of its most attractive. The town is dominated by the impressive remains of the **Benedictine Malmesbury Abbey**, founded in the 7th century by St Aldhelm. In the 10th century, King Athelstan, Alfred's grandson and the first Saxon king to unite England, granted 500 acres of land to the townspeople in gratitude for their help in resisting a Norse invasion. Those acres are still known as King's Heath and are owned by 200 residents who are descended from those far-off heroes. Athelstan made Malmesbury his capital and is buried in the abbey, where several centuries later a monument was put up in his honour.

Within the precincts of the abbey are **Abbey House Gardens**, an enchanting place

PATTINI

5 High Street, Malmesbury, Wiltshire SN16 9AA
Tel: 01666 822102
e-mail: pattlinimalmesbury@yahoo.co.uk
website: www.pattinimalmesbury.co.uk

The hill top town of Malmesbury, built with beautiful Cotswold stone is known for its history and idyllic charm. It's most visited for its Abbey which provides its visitors with restful place for quiet contemplation regardless of faith. The Abbey is just a short walk from **Pattini** which is the area's best Italian shoe and accessory shop.

Pattini was opened in 2007 by Rukshi Watson and Trina Masters who fell in love with the four hundred year old building within which the shop is housed. They combined this with their love of Italian shoes and forged a successful business thereafter.

Rukshi and Trina sell a whole variety of men and women's shoes including Barkers and John Spencer brands. Along with this they stock an interesting collection of jewellery, bags, belts, gloves, Indian shawls and gifts. A small hand selected range of ladies clothing is also available to browse, including ranges from Unisa, Lisa Kay and Cabootswood Outdoors. The ladies offer a 'made to order' fascinator service for customers wanting to add their own stamp to their clothes or bag. Many other accessories are available and Rukshi and Trina's keen eye for fashion means that they are well placed to help their clients choose the right look to make a statement.

with an abundance of flowers, around 2000 medicinal herbs, woodland and laburnum walks, fish ponds and a waterfall.

The abbey tower was the scene of an early attempt at human-powered flight when, in the early part of the 11th century, Brother Elmer strapped a pair of wings to his arms, flew for about 200 yards and crashed to earth, breaking both legs, becoming a cripple for the rest of his long life. The flight of this intrepid cleric, who reputedly forecast the Norman invasion following a sighting of Halley's Comet, is commemorated in a stained glass window. Another window, by Burne-Jones, portrays Faith, Courage and Devotion.

The octagonal Market Cross in the town square is one of many interesting buildings that also include the Old Stone House with its colonnade and gargoyles, and the arched Tolsey Gate, whose two cells once served as the town jail.

In the **Malmesbury Athelstan Museum** in the Town Hall, are displays of lace-making, costume, rural life, coins, early bicycles and tricycles, a manually-operated fire pump, photographs and maps. Here, too, are the ceremonial wheelbarrow and spade used to cut the first sod of the Wiltshire & Gloucestershire Railway in 1865. Among the local notables featured in the Museum are Thomas Hobbes, author of *Leviathan* and tutor to Charles II, and Walter Powell, MP for Malmesbury from 1868 to 1881. In December of 1881, the unfortunate Powell was carried out to sea in a War Office balloon and was never seen again.

Around Malmesbury

CASTLE COMBE

8 miles SW of Malmesbury on the B4039

The loveliest village in the region, and for some the loveliest in the country, Castle Combe was once a centre of the prosperous wool trade, famed for its red and white cloth. Many of the present-day buildings date from the 15th and 16th centuries, including the Perpendicular Church of St Andrew, the covered market cross and the manor house, which was built with stones from the Norman castle that gave the village its name. One of the Lords of the Manor in the 14th century was Sir John Fastolf, who was reputedly the inspiration for Shakespeare's Falstaff. A small museum dealing with the village's history is open on summer Sunday afternoons.

EASTON GREY

3 miles W of Malmesbury on the B4040

Here the southern branch of the River Avon is spanned by a handsome 16th-century bridge with five stone arches. A manor house has overlooked the village since the 13th century; the present house, with a classical facade and an elegant covered portico, dates from the 18th century. It was used as a summer retreat by Herbert Asquith, British Prime Minister from 1908 to 1916, and in 1923 the then Prince of Wales was in residence during the Duke of Beaufort's hunting season at Badminton.

TOURIST INFORMATION CENTRES

Bedfordshire

BEDFORD

Town Hall, St Paul's Square, Bedford MK40 1SJ
e-mail: TouristInfo@bedford.gov.uk
Tel: 01234 221712

LUTON

Luton Central Library, St George's Square, Luton, Bedfordshire, LU1 2NG
e-mail: tourist.information@luton.gov.uk
Tel: 01582 401579

SANDY

Rear of 10 Cambridge Road, Sandy, Bedfordshire, SG19 1JE
e-mail: tourism@sandytowncouncil.gov.uk
Tel: 01767 682 728

Berkshire

BRACKNELL

The Look Out, Discovery Centre, Nine Mile Ride, Bracknell, Berkshire, RG12 7QW
e-mail: TheLookOut@bracknell-forest.gov.uk
Tel: 01344 354409

MAIDENHEAD

Maidenhead Library, St Ives Road, Maidenhead, Berkshire, SL6 1QU
e-mail: maidenhead.tic@rbwm.gov.uk
Tel: 01628 796502

NEWBURY

The Wharf, Newbury, Berkshire, RG14 5AS
e-mail: tourism@westberks.gov.uk
Tel: 01635 30267

WINDSOR

Royal Windsor Shopping Centre, Royal Windsor Central Station, Windsor, Berkshire, SL4 1PJ
e-mail: windsor.tic@rbwm.gov.uk
Tel: 01753 743900

Buckinghamshire

AYLESBURY

The Kings Head, Market Square, Aylesbury, Buckinghamshire, HP20 2RW
e-mail: tic@aylesburyvaledc.gov.uk
Tel: 01296 330559

BUCKINGHAM

The Old Gaol Museum, Market Hill, Buckingham, Buckinghamshire, MK18 1JX
e-mail: buckingham.t.i.c@btconnect.com
Tel: 01280 823020

HIGH WYCOMBE

High Wycombe Library, 5 Eden Place, High Wycombe, Buckinghamshire, HP11 2DH
e-mail: tourism_enquiries@wycombe.gov.uk
Tel: 01494 421892

MARLOW

31 High Street, Marlow, Buckinghamshire, SL7 1AU
e-mail: tourism_enquiries@wycombe.gov.uk
Tel: 01628 483597

PRINCES RISBOROUGH

Tower Court, Horns Lane, Princes Risborough, Buckinghamshire, HP27 0AJ
e-mail: risborough_office@wycombe.gov.uk
Tel: 01844 274795

Gloucestershire

BOURTON-ON-THE-WATER

Victoria Street, Bourton-on-the-Water, Gloucestershire, GL54 2BU
e-mail: bourtonvic@btconnect.com
Tel: 01451 820211

CHELTENHAM

Municipal Offices, 77 Promenade, Cheltenham, Gloucestershire, GL50 1PJ
e-mail: tic@cheltenham.gov.uk
Tel: 01242 522878

CHIPPING CAMPDEN

The Old Police Station, High Street, Chipping Campden, Gloucestershire, GL55 6HB
e-mail: information@visitchippingcampden.com
Tel: 01386 841206

CIRENCESTER

Corinium Museum, Park Street, Cirencester, Gloucestershire, GL7 2BX
e-mail: cirencestervic@cotswold.gov.uk
Tel: 01285 654180

GLOUCESTER

28 Southgate Street, Gloucester, Gloucestershire, GL1 2DP
e-mail: tourism@gloucester.gov.uk
Tel: 01452 396572

MORETON-IN-MARSH

High Street, Moreton-in-Marsh, Gloucestershire, GL56 0AZ
e-mail: moreton@cotswold.gov.uk
Tel: 01608 650881

STROUD

Subscription Rooms, George Street, Stroud, Gloucestershire, GL5 1AE
e-mail: tic@stroud.gov.uk
Tel: 01453 760960

TEWKESBURY

100 Church Street, Tewkesbury GL20 5AB
Tel: 01684 855040

WINCHCOMBE

Town Hall, High Street, Winchcombe, Gloucestershire, GL54 5LJ
e-mail: winchcombetic@tewkesbury.gov.uk
Tel: 01242 602925

Hampshire

ALDERSHOT

Prince's Hall, Prince's Way, Aldershot, Hampshire, GU11 1NX
e-mail: aldershotVIC@rushmoor.gov.uk
Tel: 01252 320968

ANDOVER

Andover Museum, 6 Church Close, Andover, Hampshire, SP10 1DP
e-mail: andovertic@testvalley.gov.uk
Tel: 01264 324320

FAREHAM

Westbury Manor, 84 West Street, Fareham, Hampshire, PO16 0JJ
e-mail: touristinfo@fareham.gov.uk
Tel: 01329 221342

FORDINGBRIDGE

Kings Yard, Salisbury Street, Fordingbridge, Hampshire, SP6 1AB
e-mail: fordingbridgetic@tourismse.com
Tel: 01425 654560

GOSPORT

Bus Station Complex, South Street, Gosport, Hampshire, PO12 1EP
e-mail: tourism@gosport.gov.uk
Tel: 023 9252 2944

HAYLING ISLAND

Central Beachlands, Seafront, Hayling Island, Hampshire, PO11 0AG
e-mail: tourism@havant.gov.uk
Tel: 023 9246 7111

LYMINGTON

St Barbe Museum & Visitor Centre, New Street, Lymington, Hampshire, SO41 9BH
e-mail: information@nfdc.gov.uk
Tel: 01590 689000

TOURIST INFORMATION CENTRES

LYNDHURST & NEW FOREST

New Forest Museum & Visitor Centre, Main Car Park, Lyndhurst, Hampshire, SO43 7NY
e-mail: information@nfdc.gov.uk
Tel: 023 8028 2269

PETERSFIELD

County Library, 27 The Square, Petersfield, Hampshire, GU32 3HH
e-mail: petersfieldinfo@btconnect.com
Tel: 01730 268829

PORTSMOUTH (THE HARD)

The Hard, Portsmouth, Hampshire, PO1 3QJ
e-mail: vis@portsmouthcc.gov.uk
Tel: 023 9282 6722

PORTSMOUTH CLARENCE ESPLANADE

Clarence Esplanade, Southsea, Portsmouth, Hampshire, PO5 3PB
e-mail: vis@portsmouthcc.gov.uk
Tel: 023 9282 6722

RINGWOOD

The Furlong, Ringwood, Hampshire, BH24 1AT
e-mail: information@nfdc.gov.uk
Tel: 01425 470896

ROMSEY

Heritage & Visitor Centre, 13 Church Street, Romsey, Hampshire, SO51 8BT
e-mail: romseytic@testvalley.gov.uk
Tel: 01794 512987

SOUTHAMPTON

9 Civic Centre Road, Southampton, Hampshire, SO14 7FJ
e-mail: tourist.information@southampton.gov.uk
Tel: 023 80 833 333

WINCHESTER

Winchester Guildhall, High Street, Winchester, Hampshire, SO23 9GH
e-mail: tourism@winchester.gov.uk
Tel: 01962 840500

Herefordshire

BROMYARD

The Bromyard Centre, Cruxwell Street, Bromyard, Herefordshire, HR7 4EB
e-mail: tic-bromyard@herefordshire.gov.uk
Tel: 01432 260280

HEREFORD

1 King Street, Hereford, Herefordshire, HR4 9BW
e-mail: tic-hereford@herefordshire.gov.uk
Tel: 01432 268430

LEDBURY

The Master's House, St Katherine's, Ledbury, Herefordshire, HR8 1EA
e-mail: tic-ledbury@herefordshire.gov.uk
Tel: 01531 636147

LEOMINSTER

1 Corn Square, Leominster, Herefordshire, HR6 8LR
Tel: 01568 616460

QUEENSWOOD

Queenswood Country Park, Dinmore Hill, Leominster, Herefordshire, HR6 0PY
Tel: 01568 797842

ROSS-ON-WYE

Swan House, Edde Cross Street, Ross-on-Wye, Herefordshire, HR9 7BZ
e-mail: tic-ross@herefordshire.gov.uk
Tel: 01989 562768

Isle of Wight

COWES

9 The Arcade, Cowes, Isle of Wight, PO31 7AR
e-mail: info@islandbreaks.co.uk
Tel: 01983 813818

NEWPORT

*The Guildhall, High Street, Newport,
Isle of Wight, PO30 1TY
e-mail: info@islandbreaks.co.uk
Tel: 01983 813818*

RYDE

*81-83 Union Street, Ryde, Isle of Wight, PO33 2LW
e-mail: info@islandbreaks.co.uk
Tel: 01983 813818*

SANDOWN

*8 High Street, Sandown, Isle of Wight, PO36 8DG
info@islandbreaks.co.uk
Tel: 01983 813818*

SHANKLIN

*67 High Street, Shanklin, Isle of Wight, PO37 6JJ
e-mail: info@islandbreaks.co.uk
Tel: 01983 813818*

YARMOUTH

*The Quay, Yarmouth, Isle of Wight, PO41 4PQ
e-mail: info@islandbreaks.co.uk
Tel: 01983 813818*

Oxfordshire

BANBURY

*Within Castle Quay Shopping Centre,
Spiceball Park Road, Banbury, Oxon, OX16 2PQ
e-mail: banbury.tic@cherwell-dc.gov.uk
Tel: 01295 753752*

BICESTER

*Bicester Visitor Centre, Unit 86a, Bicester Village,
Pingle Drive, Bicester, Oxfordshire, OX26 6WD
e-mail: bicestervisitorcentre@valueretail.com
Tel: 01869 369055*

BURFORD

*The Brewery, Sheep Street, Burford,
Oxfordshire, OX18 4LP
e-mail: burford.vic@westoxon.gov.uk
Tel: 01993 823558*

DIDCOT

*118 Broadway, Didcot, Oxfordshire, OX11 8AB
e-mail: didcottic@tourismse.com
Tel: 01235 813243*

FARINGDON

*The Corn Exchage, Cornmarket, Faringdon,
Oxfordshire, SN7 7JA
e-mail: tourism@faringdontowncouncil.org.uk
Tel: 01367 242191*

HENLEY-ON-THAMES

*Henley Town Hall, Henley on Thames,
Oxfordshire RG9 2AQ
e-mail: vic@henleytowncouncil.gov.uk
Tel: 01491 578034*

OXFORD

*Oxford Information Centre, 15/16 Broad Street, Oxford,
Oxfordshire, OX1 3AS
e-mail: tic@oxford.gov.uk
Tel: 01865 252200*

THAME

*Town Hall, Thame Town Canal, High Street, Thame,
Oxfordshire, OX9 3DP
e-mail: thame.tic@btconnect.com
Tel: 01844 212834*

WITNEY

*26A Market Square, Witney, Oxfordshire, OX28 6BB
e-mail: witney.vic@westoxon.gov.uk
Tel: 01993 775802*

WOODSTOCK

*Oxfordshire Museum, Park Street, Woodstock,
Oxfordshire, OX20 1SN
e-mail: woodstock.vic@westoxon.gov.uk
Tel: 01993 813276*

TOURIST INFORMATION CENTRES

Wiltshire

AMESBURY

Amesbury Library, Smithfield Street, Amesbury, Wiltshire, SP4 7AL
e-mail: amesburytic@salisbury.gov.uk
Tel: 01980 622833

AVEBURY

Avebury Chapel Centre, Green Street, Avebury, Wiltshire, SN8 1RE
e-mail: all.tics@wiltshire.gov.uk
Tel: 01672 539179

BRADFORD ON AVON

The Greenhouse, 50 St. Margaret's Street, Bradford on Avon, Wiltshire, BA15 1DE
e-mail: tic@bradfordonavon.co.uk
Tel: 01225 865797

CHIPPENHAM

Yelde Hall, Market Place, Chippenham, Wiltshire, SN15 3HL
e-mail: tourism@chippenham.gov.uk
Tel: 01249 665970

CORSHAM

Arnold House, 31 High Street, Corsham, Wiltshire, SN13 0EZ
e-mail: enquiries@corshamheritage.org.uk
Tel: 01249 714660

DEVIZES

Cromwell House, The Market Place, Devizes, Wiltshire, SN10 1JG
e-mail: all.tic's@wiltshire.gov.uk
Tel:01380 734669

MALMESBURY

Town Hall, Cross Hayes, Malmesbury, Wiltshire, SN16 9BZ
e-mail: tic@malmesbury.gov.uk
Tel: 0166 682 3748

MARLBOROUGH

The Library, High Street, Marlborough, Wiltshire, SN8 1HD
e-mail: all.tic's@kennet.gov.uk
Tel: 01380 734669

MELKSHAM

Church Street, Melksham, Wiltshire, SN12 6LS
e-mail: visitmelksham@tiscali.co.uk
Tel: 01225 707424

MERE

The Library, Barton Lane (between Castle St. & Church St.), Mere, Warminster, Wiltshire, BA12 6JA
e-mail: MereTIC@Salisbury.gov.uk
Tel: 01747 861211

SALISBURY

Fish Row, Salisbury, Wiltshire, SP1 1EJ
e-mail: visitorinfo@salisbury.gov.uk
Tel: 01722 334956

SWINDON

37 Regent Street, Swindon, Wiltshire, SN1 1JL
e-mail: infocentre@swindon.gov.uk
Tel:01793 530328

TROWBRIDGE

St Stephen's Place, Trowbridge, Wiltshire, BA14 8AH
e-mail: visittrowbridge@westwiltshire.gov.uk
Tel: 01225 777054

WARMINSTER

Central Car Park, Station Rd, Warminster, Wiltshire, BA12 9BT
e-mail: visitwarminster@westwiltshire.gov.uk
Tel: 01985 218548

INDEX OF ADVERTISERS

ACCOMMODATION, FOOD AND DRINK

ACTIVITIES

INDEX OF ADVERTISERS

ANTIQUES AND RESTORATION

ARTS AND CRAFTS

FASHIONS

GIFTWARE

INDEX OF ADVERTISERS

HOME AND GARDEN

JEWELLERY

INDEX OF ADVERTISERS

PLACES OF INTEREST

SPECIALIST FOOD AND DRINK SHOPS

IMAGE COPYRIGHT HOLDERS

COPYRIGHT HOLDERS ARE AS FOLLOWS:

Luton Hoo, Luton © Dave Skinner pg 5
Dunstable Downs, Dunstable © Martin Addison pg 6
Leighton Buzzard Railway, Leighton Buzzard © Nigel Cox pg 7
Amphill Park House, Amphill © Paul Dixon pg 9
Sandy Lodge, Sandy © Cameraman pg 13
Swiss Cottage, Old Warden © Mick Lobb pg 15
Houghton House, Houghton Conquest © Dennis Jackson pg 16
Priory Country Park, Bedford © M J Richardson pg 18
St Mary's Church, Cardington © David Savell pg 19
Bromham Church, Bromham © Oliver White pg 20
Harrold Odell Country Park, Harold © Nigel Homer pg 21
Dun Mill Lock, Hungerford © Paul Gillett pg 23
St Michael's Church, Lambourn © Pam Brophy pg 24
Kennet & Avon Canal, Newbury © Sebastian Ballard pg 25
Donnington Castle, Donnington © Chris Talbot pg 26
Trip Barge, Hungerford © Jonathan Billinger pg 29
Swallowfield Park, Reading © Andrew Smith pg 35
The Wharf, Aldermaston © Steve F pg 36
Basildon House, Basildon © Pam Brophy pg 37
Windsor Castle, Windsor © Peter Trimming pg 38
Frogmore House, Windsor © Gill Hicks pg 39
Ascot Racecourse, Ascot © Nigel Fox pg 40
Maidenhead Clock Tower, Maidenhead © Nigel Cox pg 43
Alexandra Gardens, Eton © Richard Slessor pg 45
Milton's House, Chalfont St Giles © David Squire pg 48
Stoke Park, Stoke Poges © Stephen Daglish pg 49
Bekonscot Model Village, Bekonscot © Peter Roberts pg 50
Cliveden, Taplow © Roger pg 51
Chenies Manor House, Chenies © Nigel Cox pg 52
Shambles, High Wycombe © Colin Smith pg 53
West Wycombe Park, West Wycombe © David Ellis pg 54
Bradenham Woods, Hughenden © Shaun Ferguson pg 57
Manor House, Princes Risborough © Nigel Cox pg 59
Mentmore Towers, Mentmore © Rob Farrow pg 61
Pitstone Windmill, Pitstone © Cameraman pg 62
Boarstall Tower, Boarstall © Shaun Ferguson pg 63
Old Gaol , Buckingham © Colin Smith pg 65
Ascott House, Wing © Rob Farrow pg 66
The Lake, Bletchley park © Paul Buckingham pg 69
William Cowper's Garden , Olney © Robin Drayton pg 69
Cowper and Newton Museum, Olney © Robin Drayton pg 70
Great Linford Manor, Great Linford © Mick Finn pg 73
The Old Market House, Newent © Eirian Evans pg 76
St Mary's Church, Upleadon © David Stowell pg 77
Ruardean Hill, Ruardean © Philip Halling pg 82
Hopewell Colliery, Cannop © Graham Horn pg 85
Ventilation Shaft , Clearwell © Penny Mayes pg 86
St Briavels Castle, St Briavels © Bob Tinley pg 87
Frampton Court, Frampton © Roger May pg 88
Berkeley Castle, Berkeley © Philip Halling pg 89
Thornbury Castle, Thornbury © Charles Drown pg 91
Dyram House, Dyram © David Gearing pg 92
Badminton Park, Badminton © George Evans pg 93
Gloucester Cathedral, Gloucester © Philip Halling pg 95
Tewkesbury Abbey, Tewkesbury © Philip Halling pg 99
Chavenage House, Tetbury © Philip Halling pg 101
Cam Long Down, Dursley © Colin Travis pg 102
Winchcombe Church, Winchcombe © Philip Halling pg 115
Stanway House, Stanway © Philip Halling pg 117
Chipping Campden Church, Chipping Campden © Stephen Mckay pg 121
Cotswold Water Park, Shorncote © David Griffiths pg 129
The Vyne, Basingstoke © Michael Robinson pg 133
Odiham Castle, Odiham © Andrew Mathewson pg 136
Aldershot Park, Aldershot © Brian Evans pg 138
Lavendar Fields, Alton © Peter Trimming pg 140
Jane Austins House, Chawton © Tony Grant pg 142
Petersfield Physic Garden, Petersfield © Bashed Eyre pg 146
Buster Ancient Farm , Chalton © Shazz pg 148

IMAGE COPYRIGHT HOLDERS

East Meon, Village © *Barry Shimmon* *pg 149*
Highclere Castle, Faccombe © *Mike Searle* *pg 151*
St Andrew's Church, Nether Wallop © *Chris Talbot* *pg 154*
Danbury Ring, Middle Wallop © *Chris Talbot* *pg 155*
Winchester Cathedral, Winchester © *Peter Trimming* *pg 158*
The Great Hall, Winchester © *Graham Horn* *pg 160*
Romsey Abbey, Romsey © *Andrew Mcdonald* *pg 163*
Mottisfont Abbey, Mottisfont © *Michael Ford* *pg 166*
Bursledon Windmill, Bursledon © *Rob Candlish* *pg 170*
Portchester Castle, Portchester © *Geoff Barker* *pg 178*
Rufus Stone, Minstead © *Jim Champion* *pg 184*
Eling Tide Mill, Totton © *Colin Babb* *pg 185*
Abbey Cloisters, Beaulieu © *Jim Champion* *pg 185*
Exbury Gardens, Exbury © *Chris Downer* *pg 187*
Hurst Castle, Milford-on-Sea © *Lewis Clarke* *pg 192*
New Forest, Burley © *Jim Champion* *pg 195*
Breamore House, Breamore © *Mike Searle* *pg 197*
New River, Great Amwell © *Melvyn Cousins* *pg 199*
River Stort, Bishop's Stortford © *Thomas Nugent* *pg 201*
Knebworth House, Knebworth © *Tony Osler* *pg 202*
Cromer Windmill, Cromer © *Ellie May* *pg 203*
Town Hall, Letchworth Garden City © *Keith Evans* *pg 204*
Swallow Fledglings, Hitchin © *Dylan Mills* *pg 205*
Hertford Castle, Herford © *Melvyn Cousins* *pg 206*
Ware Gazebos, Ware © *Mike Ryan* *pg 210*
Northaw Great Wood, Brookmans park © *Peter Walker* *pg 212*
Clock Tower, St Albans © *Chris Downer* *pg 216*
Aldenham Park, Aldenham © *ROW17* *pg 218*
Charter Tower & Walled Garden, Hemel Hempstead © *Geoff Harris* *pg 219*
Tring Church, Tring © *Paul Buckingham* *pg 222*
The Stocks & Pond, Aldbury © *Cameraman* *pg 223*
The Needles, Isle of Wight © *Christina Burford* *pg 227*
Calbourne Mill, Calbourne © *Chris Allen* *pg 231*
Cowes, Cowes © *Anthony Eden* *pg 232*
Quarr Abbey, Fishbourne © *Lambert* *pg 234*
Bembridge Windmill, Bembridge © *Roger Pagram* *pg 237*
Blackgang Chine, St Lawrence © *Steve Daniels* *pg 246*
Appuldurcombe House, Wroxhall © *Chris Cole* *pg 247*
Yarmouth Castle, Yarmouth © *Christine Matthews* *pg 250*
Beach next to Fort Victoria Park, Yarmouth © *Steve Daniels* *pg 251*
Hart Street, Henley on Thames © *Colin Smith* *pg 254*
Mapledurham House, Mapledurham © *Pam Brophy* *pg 256*
Watlington Hill, Watlington © *Steve Daniels* *pg 257*
Abingdon Museum, Abingdon © *Nigel Cox* *pg 259*
Village Centre, Dorchester © *Colin Smith* *pg 260*
Church of St Peter & St Paul, Wantage © *John Salmon* *pg 265*
Blowing Stone, Kingston Lisle © *Steve Daniels* *pg 268*
Radcot Bridge, Radcot © *Nigel James* *pg 273*
Balliol College, Oxford © *Peter Trimming* *pg 276*
Bodleian Library, Oxford © *Steve Daniels* *pg 277*
Nuneham House, Nuneham Courtenay © *Andrew Smith* *pg 282*
Blenheim Palace, Woodstock © *Richard Law* *pg 284*
Secret Garden at Blenheim Palace, Woodstock © *David Hawgood* *pg 284*
Cornbury Park, Charlbury © *Pauline Eccles* *pg 285*
Tooley's Boatyard, Banbury © *Bill Nicholls* *pg 290*
Abbey, Wroxton © *David Stowell* *pg 292*
Chastleton House, Chastleton © *Roger May* *pg 295*
Minster Lovell Hall, Minster Lovell © *Chris Gunns* *pg 296*
Whispering Knights, Little Rollright © *Chris Gunns* *pg 299*
Larmer Tree Gardens, Tollard Royal © *Chris Gunns* *pg 307*
Salisbury Cathedral, Salisbury © *Chris Talbot* *pg 309*
The Pepperbox, Lover © *Mike Searle* *pg 311*
Fovant Badges, Fovant © *Trish Steel* *pg 313*
Woodhenge, Amesbury © *Trish Steel* *pg 314*
Stonehenge, Amesbury © *Pam Brophy* *pg 315*
Savernake Forest, Savernake Forest © *Brian Robert Marshall* *pg 317*
Wilton Windmill, Wilton © *Chris Talbot* *pg 319*
Avebury Manor House, Avebury © *Stuart Buchan* *pg 321*
Swindon and Crickdale Railway, Swindon © *Brian Robert Marshall* *pg 326*
Lydiard Tregoze, Lydiard © *Rick Crowley* *pg 328*
Maud Heath's Causeway, Chippenham © *Chris Downer* *pg 329*
Ilford Manor, Bradford-on-Avon © *David Anstiss* *pg 338*

ORDER FORM

To order any of our publications just fill in the payment details below and complete the order form. For orders of less than 4 copies please add £1 per book for postage and packing. Orders over 4 copies are P & P free.

Please Complete Either:

I enclose a cheque for £ [ ] *made payable to Travel Publishing Ltd*

Or:

CARD NO: [ ] EXPIRY DATE: [ ]

SIGNATURE: [ ]

NAME: [ ]

ADDRESS: [ ]

TEL NO: [ ]

Please either send, telephone, fax or e-mail your order to:

Travel Publishing Ltd, Airport Business Centre, 10 Thornbury Road, Estover, Plymouth PL6 7PP
Tel: 01752 697280 Fax: 01752 697299 e-mail: info@travelpublishing.co.uk

	Price	Quantity
Hidden Places Regional Titles		
Cornwall	£8.99	....
Devon	£8.99	....
Dorset, Hants & Isle of Wight	£8.99	....
East Anglia	£8.99	....
Lake District & Cumbria	£8.99	....
Lancashire & Cheshire	£8.99	....
Northumberland & Durham	£8.99	....
Peak District and Derbyshire	£8.99	....
Yorkshire	£8.99	....
Hidden Places National Titles		
England	£11.99	....
Ireland	£11.99	....
Scotland	£11.99	....
Wales	£11.99	....
Other Titles		
Off The Motorway	£11.99	....
Garden Centres and Nurseries of Britain	£11.99	....

	Price	Quantity
Country Living Rural Guides		
East Anglia	£10.99	....
Heart of England	£10.99	....
Ireland	£11.99	....
North East of England	£10.99	....
North West of England	£10.99	....
Scotland	£11.99	....
South of England	£10.99	....
South East of England	£10.99	....
Wales	£11.99	....
West Country	£10.99	....

TOTAL QUANTITY [ ]

TOTAL VALUE [ ]

READER REACTION FORM

The **Travel Publishing** *research team would like to receive readers' comments on any visitor attractions or places reviewed in the book and also recommendations for suitable entries to be included in the next edition. This will help ensure that the* **Country Living series of Rural Guides** *continues to provide its readers with useful information on the more interesting, unusual or unique features of each attraction or place ensuring that their visit to the local area is an enjoyable and stimulating experience. To provide your comments or recommendations would you please complete the forms below and overleaf as indicated and send to:*

The Research Department, Travel Publishing Ltd, Airport Business Centre, 10 Thornbury Road, Estover, Plymouth PL6 7PP

YOUR NAME:

YOUR ADDRESS:

YOUR TEL NO:

Please tick as appropriate: COMMENTS ☐ RECOMMENDATION ☐

ESTABLISHMENT:

ADDRESS:

TEL NO:

CONTACT NAME:

PLEASE COMPLETE FORM OVERLEAF

READER REACTION FORM

COMMENT OR REASON FOR RECOMMENDATION:

....

....

....

....

....

....

....

....

....

....

....

....

READER REACTION FORM

The **Travel Publishing** *research team would like to receive readers' comments on any visitor attractions or places reviewed in the book and also recommendations for suitable entries to be included in the next edition. This will help ensure that the* **Country Living series of Rural Guides** *continues to provide its readers with useful information on the more interesting, unusual or unique features of each attraction or place ensuring that their visit to the local area is an enjoyable and stimulating experience. To provide your comments or recommendations would you please complete the forms below and overleaf as indicated and send to:*

The Research Department, Travel Publishing Ltd, Airport Business Centre, 10 Thornbury Road, Estover, Plymouth PL6 7PP

YOUR NAME:

YOUR ADDRESS:

YOUR TEL NO:

Please tick as appropriate: COMMENTS ☐ RECOMMENDATION ☐

ESTABLISHMENT:

ADDRESS:

TEL NO:

CONTACT NAME:

PLEASE COMPLETE FORM OVERLEAF

READER REACTION FORM

COMMENT OR REASON FOR RECOMMENDATION:

....

....

....

....

....

....

....

....

....

....

....

....

READER REACTION FORM

The **Travel Publishing** *research team would like to receive readers' comments on any visitor attractions or places reviewed in the book and also recommendations for suitable entries to be included in the next edition. This will help ensure that the* **Country Living series of Rural Guides** *continues to provide its readers with useful information on the more interesting, unusual or unique features of each attraction or place ensuring that their visit to the local area is an enjoyable and stimulating experience. To provide your comments or recommendations would you please complete the forms below and overleaf as indicated and send to:*

The Research Department, Travel Publishing Ltd, Airport Business Centre, 10 Thornbury Road, Estover, Plymouth PL6 7PP

YOUR NAME:

YOUR ADDRESS:

YOUR TEL NO:

Please tick as appropriate: COMMENTS ☐ RECOMMENDATION ☐

ESTABLISHMENT:

ADDRESS:

TEL NO:

CONTACT NAME:

PLEASE COMPLETE FORM OVERLEAF

READER REACTION FORM

COMMENT OR REASON FOR RECOMMENDATION:

TOWNS, VILLAGES AND PLACES OF INTEREST

A

TOWNS, VILLAGES AND PLACES OF INTEREST

B

TOWNS, VILLAGES AND PLACES OF INTEREST

TOWNS, VILLAGES AND PLACES OF INTEREST

D

TOWNS, VILLAGES AND PLACES OF INTEREST

E

F

TOWNS, VILLAGES AND PLACES OF INTEREST

G

H

TOWNS, VILLAGES AND PLACES OF INTEREST

TOWNS, VILLAGES AND PLACES OF INTEREST

L

TOWNS, VILLAGES AND PLACES OF INTEREST

TOWNS, VILLAGES AND PLACES OF INTEREST

N

O

TOWNS, VILLAGES AND PLACES OF INTEREST

P

Q

R

S

TOWNS, VILLAGES AND PLACES OF INTEREST

TOWNS, VILLAGES AND PLACES OF INTEREST

TOWNS, VILLAGES AND PLACES OF INTEREST

TOWNS, VILLAGES AND PLACES OF INTEREST

Y